CEYA

SHONEN JUMP

THE WORLD'S MO...

**STORY AND ART BY
TITE KUBO**

**STORY AND ART BY
EIICHIRO ODA**

**STORY AND ART BY
HIROYUKI ASADA**

JUMP INTO THE ACTION BY TELLING US WHAT YOU LOVE (AND WHAT YOU DON'T)

LET YOUR VOICE BE HEARD!

SHONENJUMP.VIZ.COM/MANGASURVEY

HELP US MAKE MORE OF THE WORLD'S MOST POPULAR MANGA!

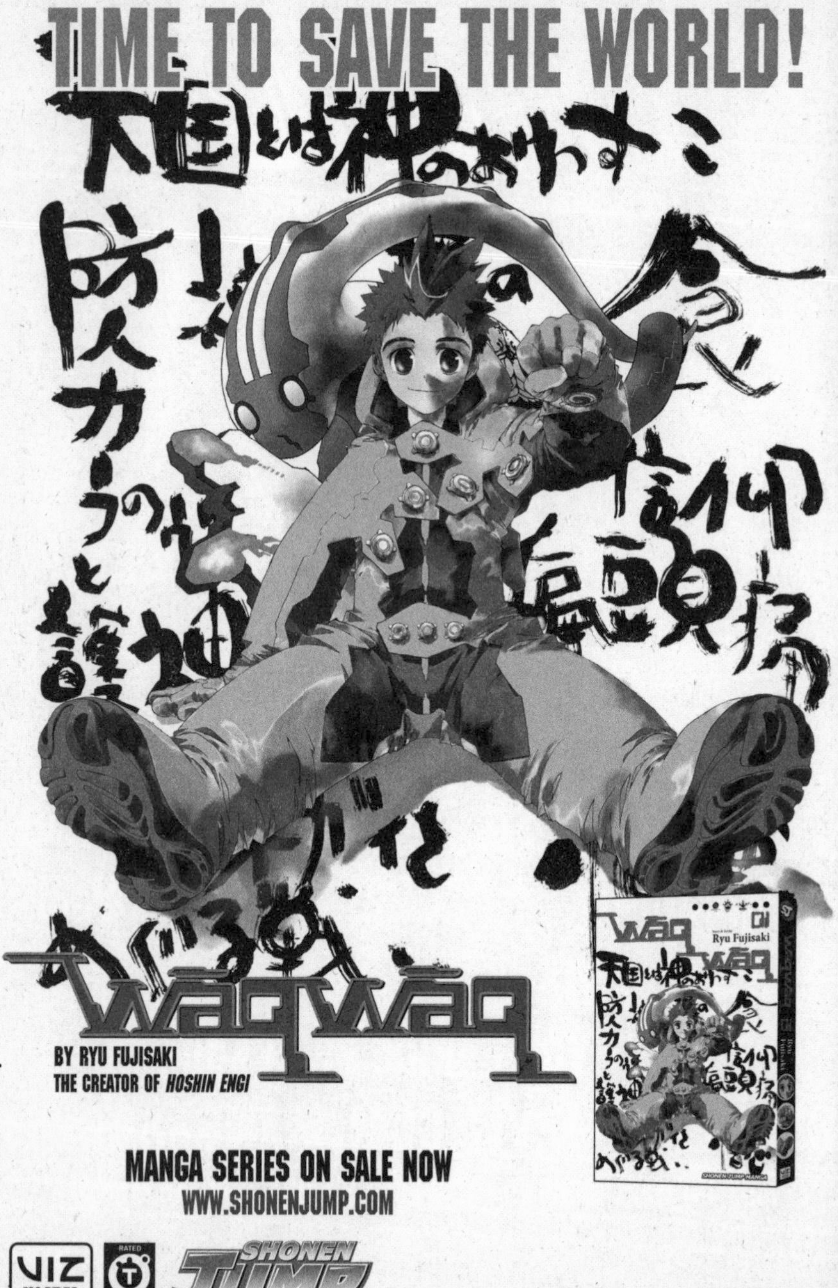
TIME TO SAVE THE WORLD!
Wāqwāq
BY RYU FUJISAKI
THE CREATOR OF HOSHIN ENGI
Ryu Fujisaki
SHONEN JUMP MANGA
MANGA SERIES ON SALE NOW
WWW.SHONENJUMP.COM
VIZ media
www.viz.com
RATED T FOR TEEN
ratings.viz.com
SHONEN JUMP
THE WORLD'S MOST POPULAR MANGA
Wāqwāq © 2004 by Ryu Fujisaki/SHUEISHA Inc.

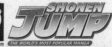

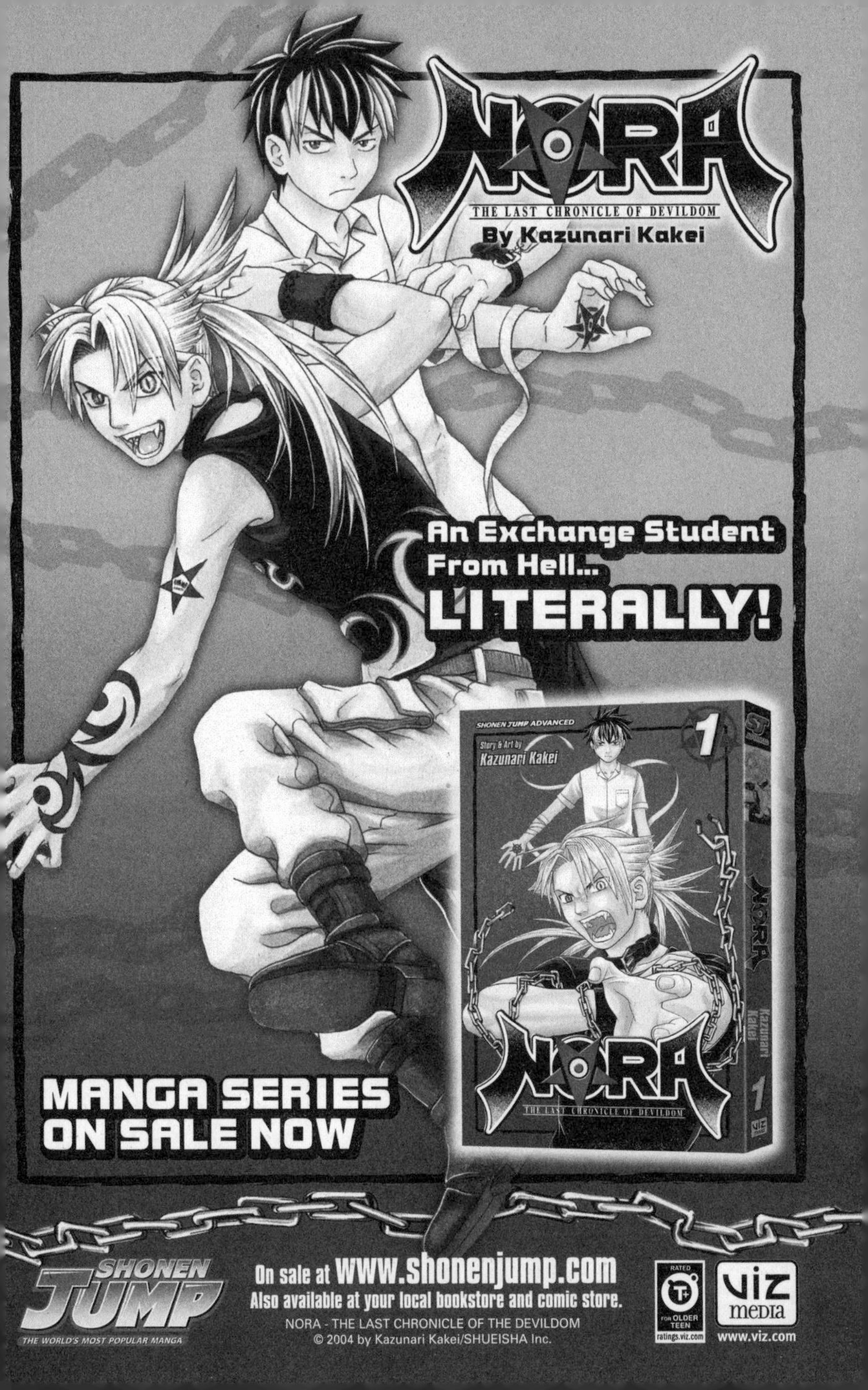
NORA
THE LAST CHRONICLE OF DEVILDOM
By Kazunari Kakei
An Exchange Student From Hell...
LITERALLY!
SHONEN JUMP ADVANCED
1
Story & Art by
Kazunari Kakei
NORA
THE LAST CHRONICLE OF DEVILDOM
MANGA SERIES
ON SALE NOW
SHONEN JUMP
THE WORLD'S MOST POPULAR MANGA
On sale at www.shonenjump.com
Also available at your local bookstore and comic store.
NORA - THE LAST CHRONICLE OF THE DEVILDOM
© 2004 by Kazunari Kakei/SHUEISHA Inc.
RATED
T+
FOR OLDER TEEN
ratings.viz.com
viz media
www.viz.com

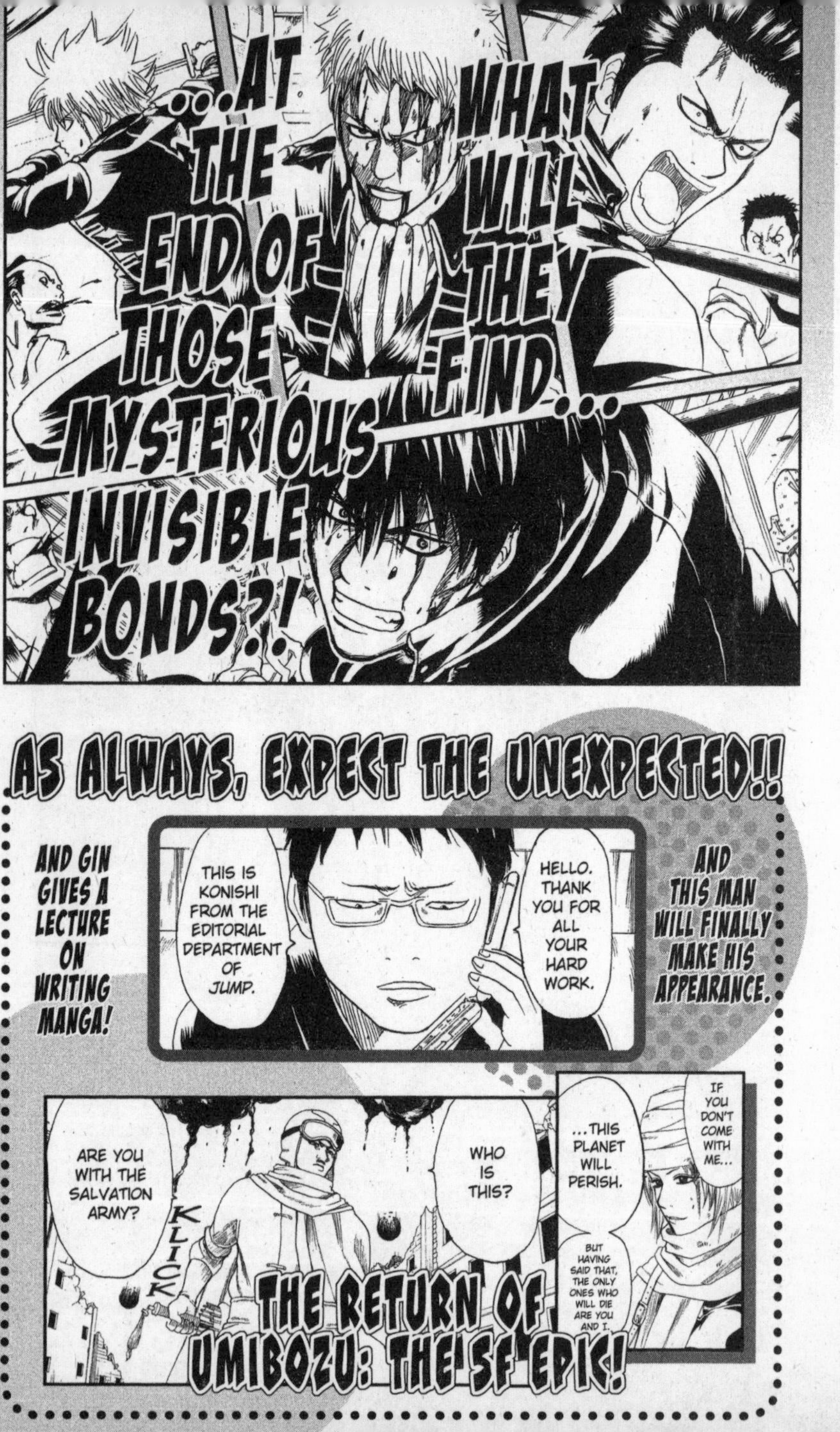
WHAT WILL THEY FIND...
...AT THE END OF THOSE MYSTERIOUS INVISIBLE BONDS?!
AS ALWAYS, EXPECT THE UNEXPECTED!!
AND THIS MAN WILL FINALLY MAKE HIS APPEARANCE.
HELLO. THANK YOU FOR ALL YOUR HARD WORK.
THIS IS KONISHI FROM THE EDITORIAL DEPARTMENT OF JUMP.
AND GIN GIVES A LECTURE ON WRITING MANGA!
IF YOU DON'T COME WITH ME...
...THIS PLANET WILL PERISH.
BUT HAVING SAID THAT, THE ONLY ONES WHO WILL DIE ARE YOU AND I.
WHO IS THIS?
ARE YOU WITH THE SALVATION ARMY?
KLICK
THE RETURN OF UMIBOZU: THE SF EPIC!

GIN TAMA

STORY & ART BY
HIDEAKI
SORACHI

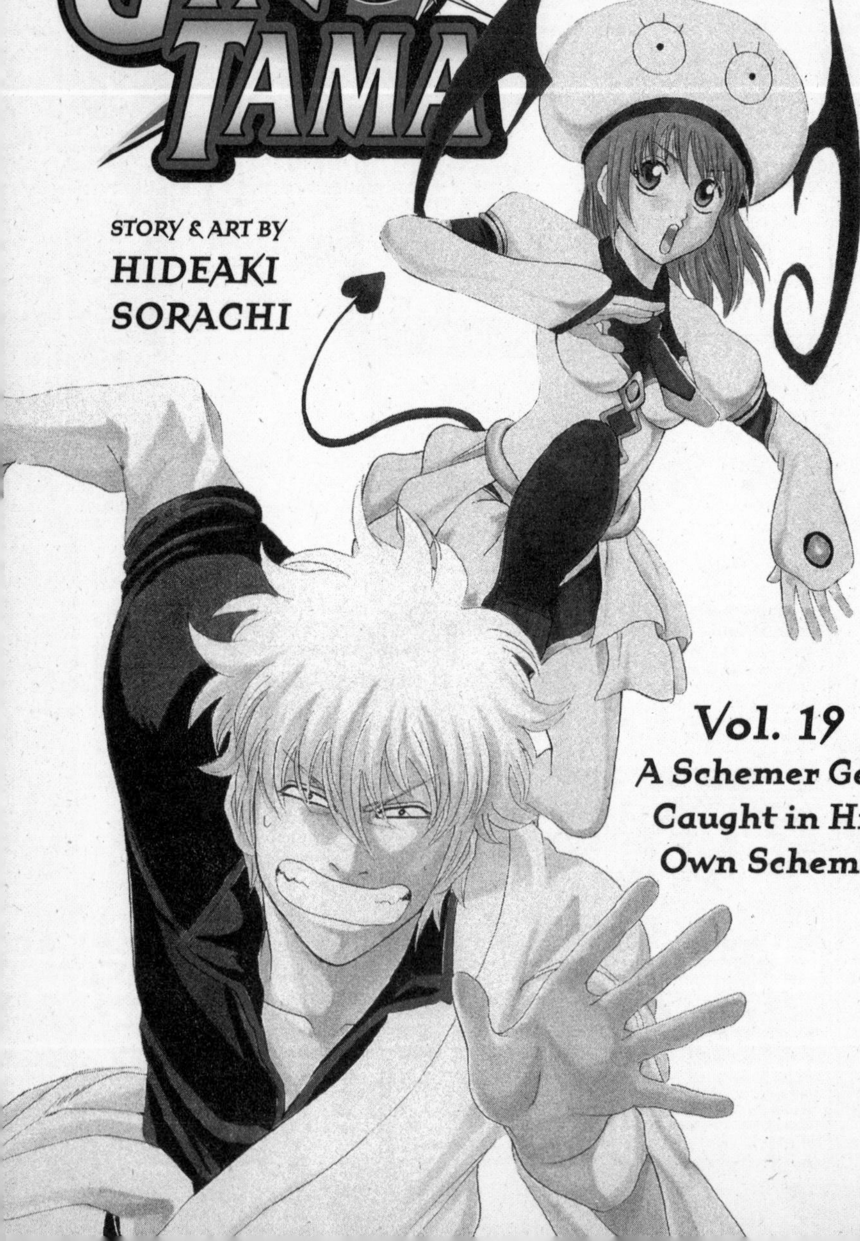

Vol. 19
A Schemer Gets Caught in His Own Scheme

Yorozuya Members

Shinpachi Shimura

Works under Gintoki in an attempt to learn about the samurai spirit but has often come to regret his decision recently. President of the Tsu Terakado Fan Club.

Gintoki Sakata

The hero of our story. If he doesn't eat something sweet periodically he gets cranky—really cranky. He boasts a powerful sword arm, but he's one step away from diabetes. A former member of the exclusionist faction that seeks to expel the space aliens and protect the nation.

Kagura

A member of the Yato Clan, the most powerful warrior race in the universe. Her voracious appetite and alien worldview lead frequently to laughter…and sometimes contusions.

Sadaharu

A giant space creature turned office pet. Likes to bite people (especially Gin).

Shinsengumi Members

Okita

The Shinsengumi's most formidable swordsman. Behind a facade of amiability, he tirelessly schemes to eliminate Hijikata and usurp his position.

Hijikata

Vice chief of the Shinsengumi, Edo's elite counter-terrorist police unit. His air of detached cool transforms into hot rage the instant he draws his sword…or when someone disparages mayonnaise.

Kondo

The trusted chief of the Shinsengumi (and the remorseless stalker of Shinpachi's older sister Otae).

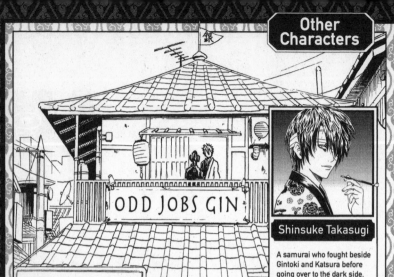

Other Characters

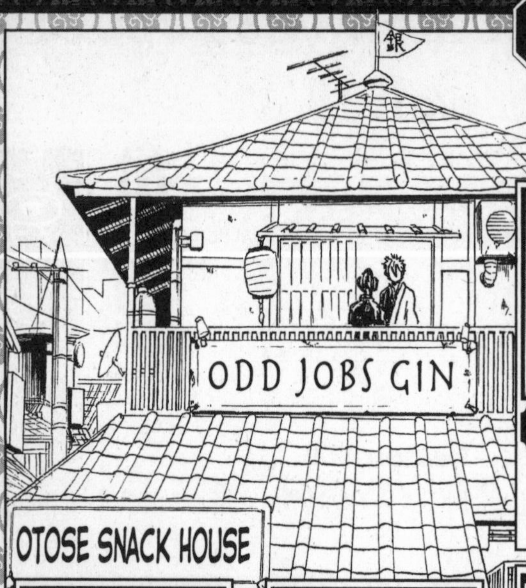
ODD JOBS GIN
OTOSE SNACK HOUSE

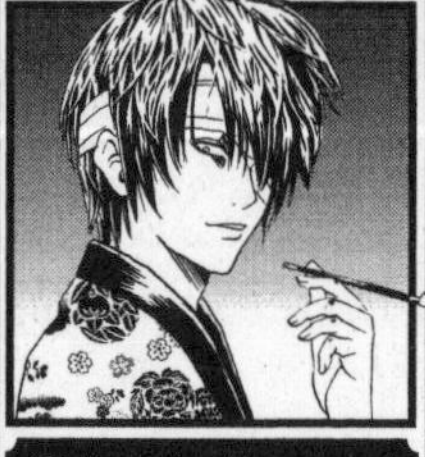

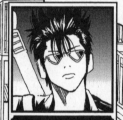

Shinsuke Takasugi

A samurai who fought beside Gintoki and Katsura before going over to the dark side.

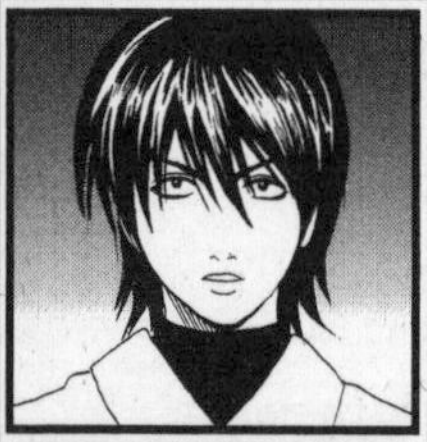

Sagaru Yamazaki

A member of the Shinsengumi who works as an observer (spy). His favorite pastime is badminton.

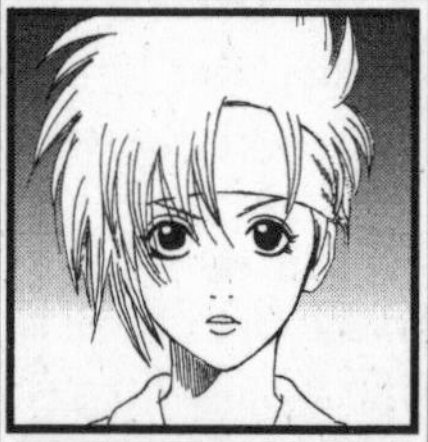

Tetsuko Murata

The daughter of swordsmith Jintetsu Tamura. Her goal is to make a sword that protects people.

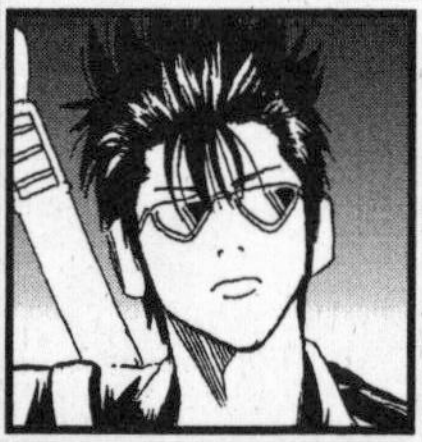

Bansai Kawakami

A Kiheitai swordsman whose nickname is "the Manslayer." He's a music producer on the side.

The story thus far

In an alternate-universe Edo (Tokyo), extraterrestrials land in Japan, and the new government issues an order outlawing swords. The samurai, who have reached the pinnacle of power and prosperity, fall into rapid decline.

Twenty years hence, only one samurai has managed to hold on to his fighting spirit: a somewhat eccentric fellow named Gintoki "Odd Jobs Gin" Sakata. A lover of sweets and near diabetic, our hero sets up shop as a *yorozuya*—an expert at managing trouble and handling the oddest of jobs.

Joining "Gin" in his business is Shinpachi Shimura, whose sister Gin saved from the clutches of nefarious debt collectors. After a series of unexpected circumstances, the trio meets a powerful alien named Kagura, who becomes—after some arm-twisting—a part-time team member.

The Yorozuya trio and the Shinsengumi face off in a video game challenge; the Lake Toya sage gets less than he bargained for when he offers Gin a deadly new technique; Gin has a close encounter with a meticulous assassin...without realizing it; Gin defends Hasegawa in court for what seems to be a case of serious misconduct; and the women do battle with their weight and each other at a fasting dojo. What's in store for Edo this time?!

WHAT THIS MANGA'S FULL OF
vol. 19

Lesson 158
Most New Things Have Too Many Functions
7

Lesson 159
Rules Are Meant to Be Broken
27

Lesson 160
Otaku Are Very Talkative
47

Lesson 161
True Fanatics Need Three Each
67

Lesson 162
There's a Fine Line Between One's Good Points and Bad Points
87

Lesson 163
A Uniform Makes You Look 20 Percent Better
107

Lesson 164
Don't Play on the Railroad Tracks
127

Lesson 165
A Schemer Gets Caught in His Own Scheme
147

Lesson 166
Important Things Are Hard to See
167

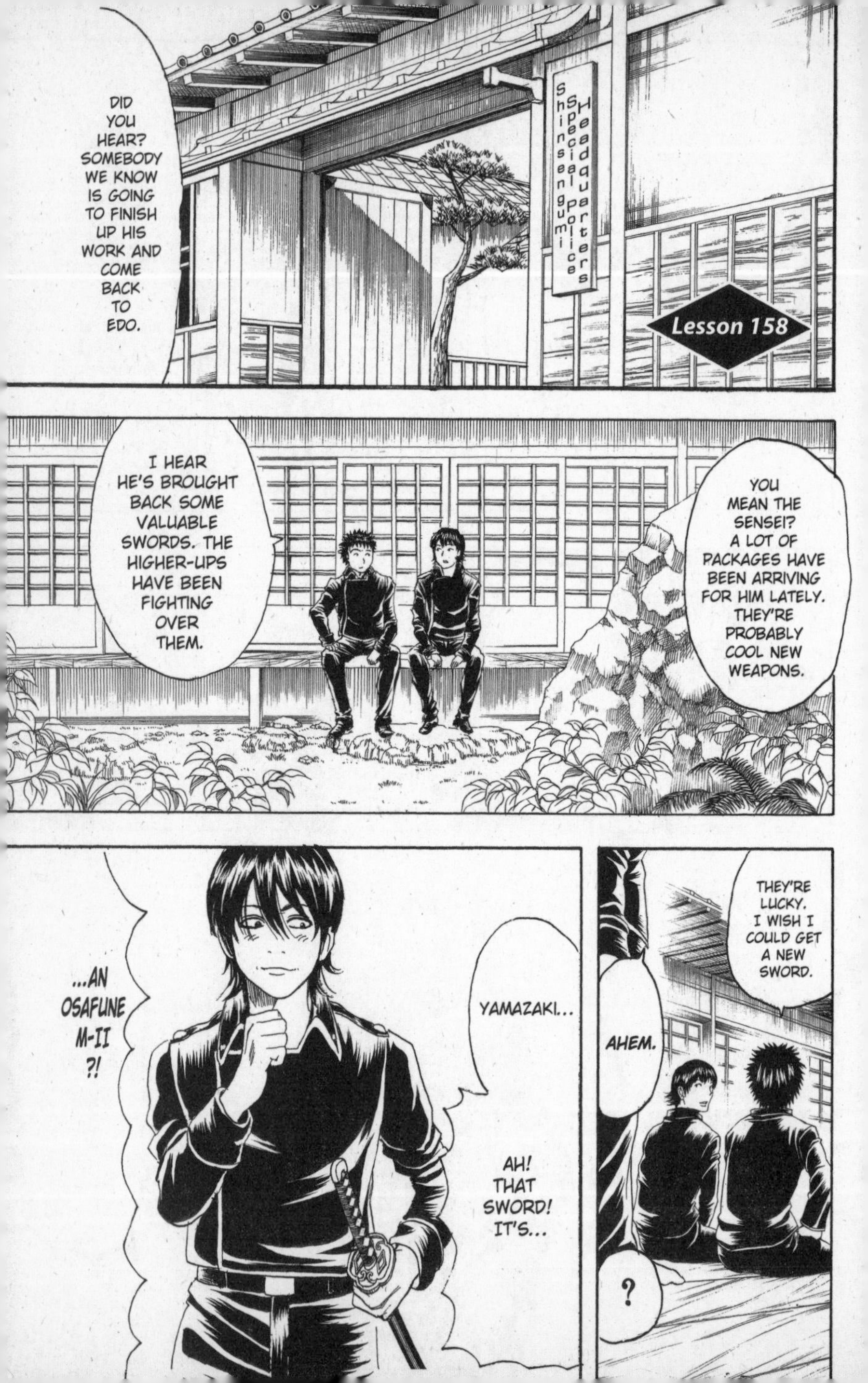
Shinsengumi Special Police Headquarters
Lesson 158
DID YOU HEAR? SOMEBODY WE KNOW IS GOING TO FINISH UP HIS WORK AND COME BACK TO EDO.
YOU MEAN THE SENSEI? A LOT OF PACKAGES HAVE BEEN ARRIVING FOR HIM LATELY. THEY'RE PROBABLY COOL NEW WEAPONS.
I HEAR HE'S BROUGHT BACK SOME VALUABLE SWORDS. THE HIGHER-UPS HAVE BEEN FIGHTING OVER THEM.
THEY'RE LUCKY. I WISH I COULD GET A NEW SWORD.
AHEM.
?
YAMAZAKI...
AH! THAT SWORD! IT'S...
...AN OSAFUNE M-II ?!

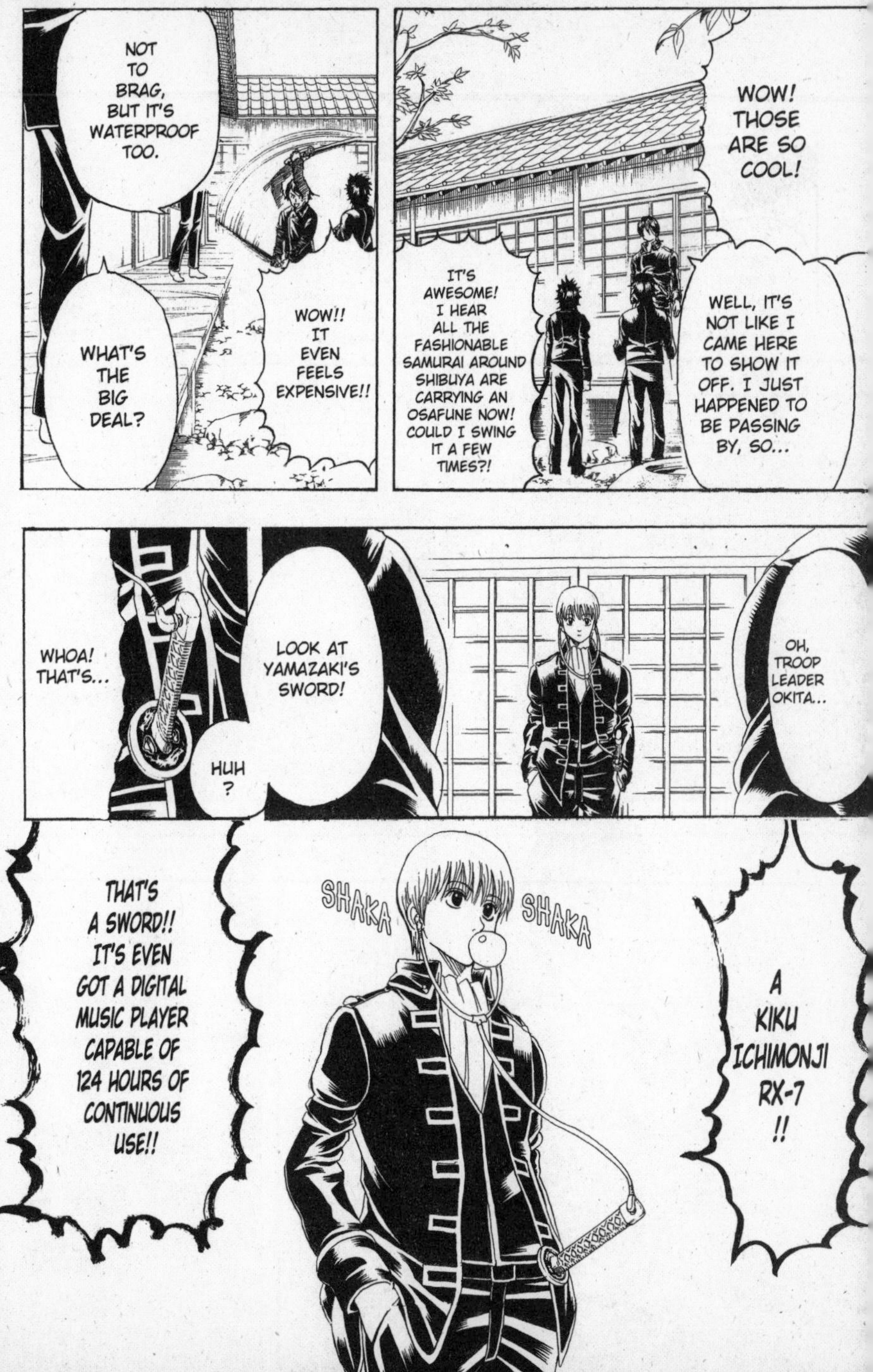
WOW! THOSE ARE SO COOL!
WELL, IT'S NOT LIKE I CAME HERE TO SHOW IT OFF. I JUST HAPPENED TO BE PASSING BY, SO...
IT'S AWESOME! I HEAR ALL THE FASHIONABLE SAMURAI AROUND SHIBUYA ARE CARRYING AN OSAFUNE NOW! COULD I SWING IT A FEW TIMES?!
NOT TO BRAG, BUT IT'S WATERPROOF TOO.
WOW!! IT EVEN FEELS EXPENSIVE!!
WHAT'S THE BIG DEAL?
OH, TROOP LEADER OKITA...
LOOK AT YAMAZAKI'S SWORD!
HUH?
WHOA! THAT'S...
A KIKU ICHIMONJI RX-7!!
SHAKA
SHAKA
THAT'S A SWORD!! IT'S EVEN GOT A DIGITAL MUSIC PLAYER CAPABLE OF 124 HOURS OF CONTINUOUS USE!!

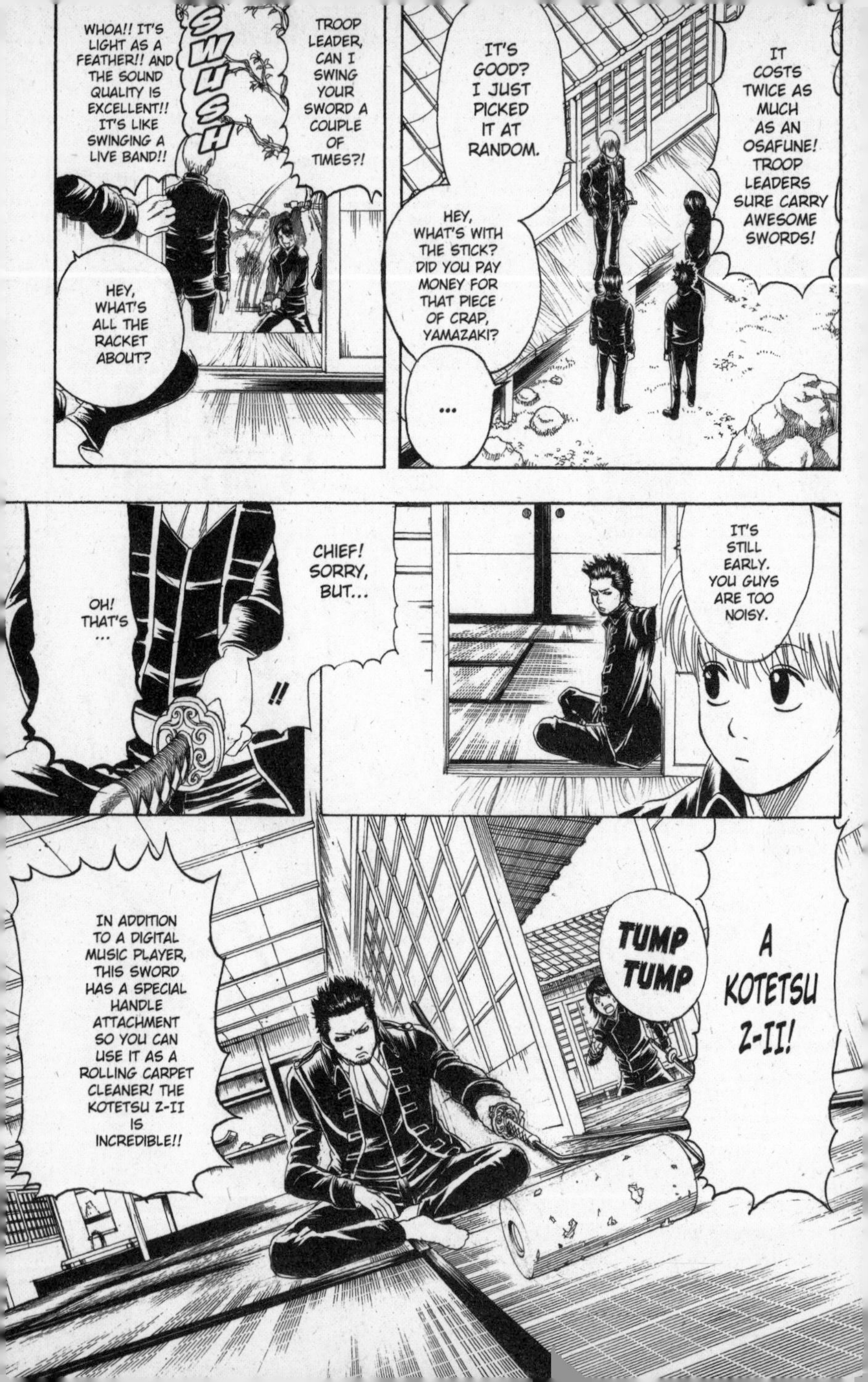
IT COSTS TWICE AS MUCH AS AN OSAFUNE! TROOP LEADERS SURE CARRY AWESOME SWORDS!
IT'S GOOD? I JUST PICKED IT AT RANDOM.
HEY, WHAT'S WITH THE STICK? DID YOU PAY MONEY FOR THAT PIECE OF CRAP, YAMAZAKI?
...
TROOP LEADER, CAN I SWING YOUR SWORD A COUPLE OF TIMES?!
SWUSH
WHOA!! IT'S LIGHT AS A FEATHER!! AND THE SOUND QUALITY IS EXCELLENT!! IT'S LIKE SWINGING A LIVE BAND!!
HEY, WHAT'S ALL THE RACKET ABOUT?
IT'S STILL EARLY. YOU GUYS ARE TOO NOISY.
CHIEF! SORRY, BUT...
!!
OH! THAT'S ...
A KOTETSU Z-II!
TUMP TUMP
IN ADDITION TO A DIGITAL MUSIC PLAYER, THIS SWORD HAS A SPECIAL HANDLE ATTACHMENT SO YOU CAN USE IT AS A ROLLING CARPET CLEANER! THE KOTETSU Z-II IS INCREDIBLE!!

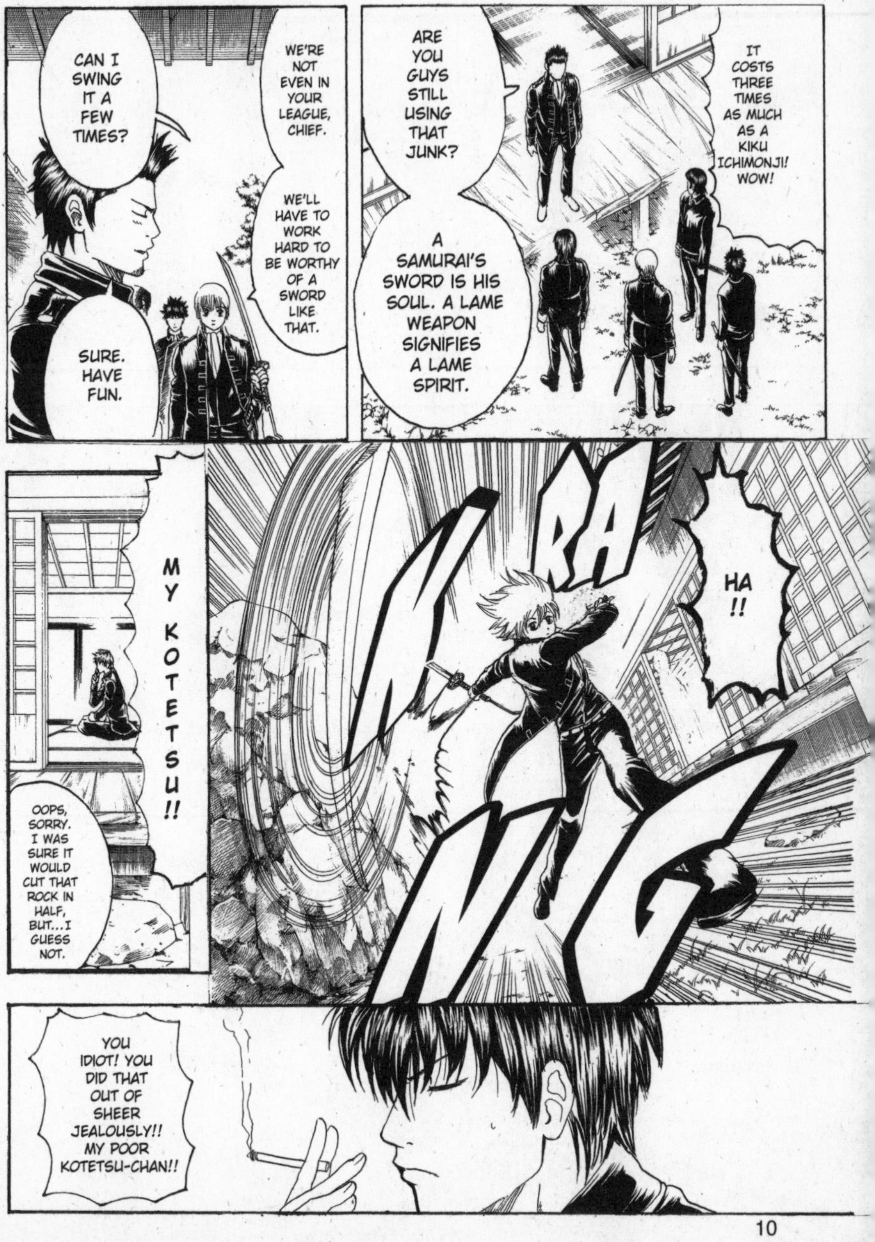
IT COSTS THREE TIMES AS MUCH AS A KIKU ICHIMONJI! WOW!
ARE YOU GUYS STILL USING THAT JUNK?
A SAMURAI'S SWORD IS HIS SOUL. A LAME WEAPON SIGNIFIES A LAME SPIRIT.
WE'RE NOT EVEN IN YOUR LEAGUE, CHIEF.
WE'LL HAVE TO WORK HARD TO BE WORTHY OF A SWORD LIKE THAT.
CAN I SWING IT A FEW TIMES?
SURE. HAVE FUN.
HA!!
RA
NG
MY KOTETSU!!
OOPS, SORRY. I WAS SURE IT WOULD CUT THAT ROCK IN HALF, BUT...I GUESS NOT.
YOU IDIOT! YOU DID THAT OUT OF SHEER JEALOUSLY!! MY POOR KOTETSU-CHAN!!

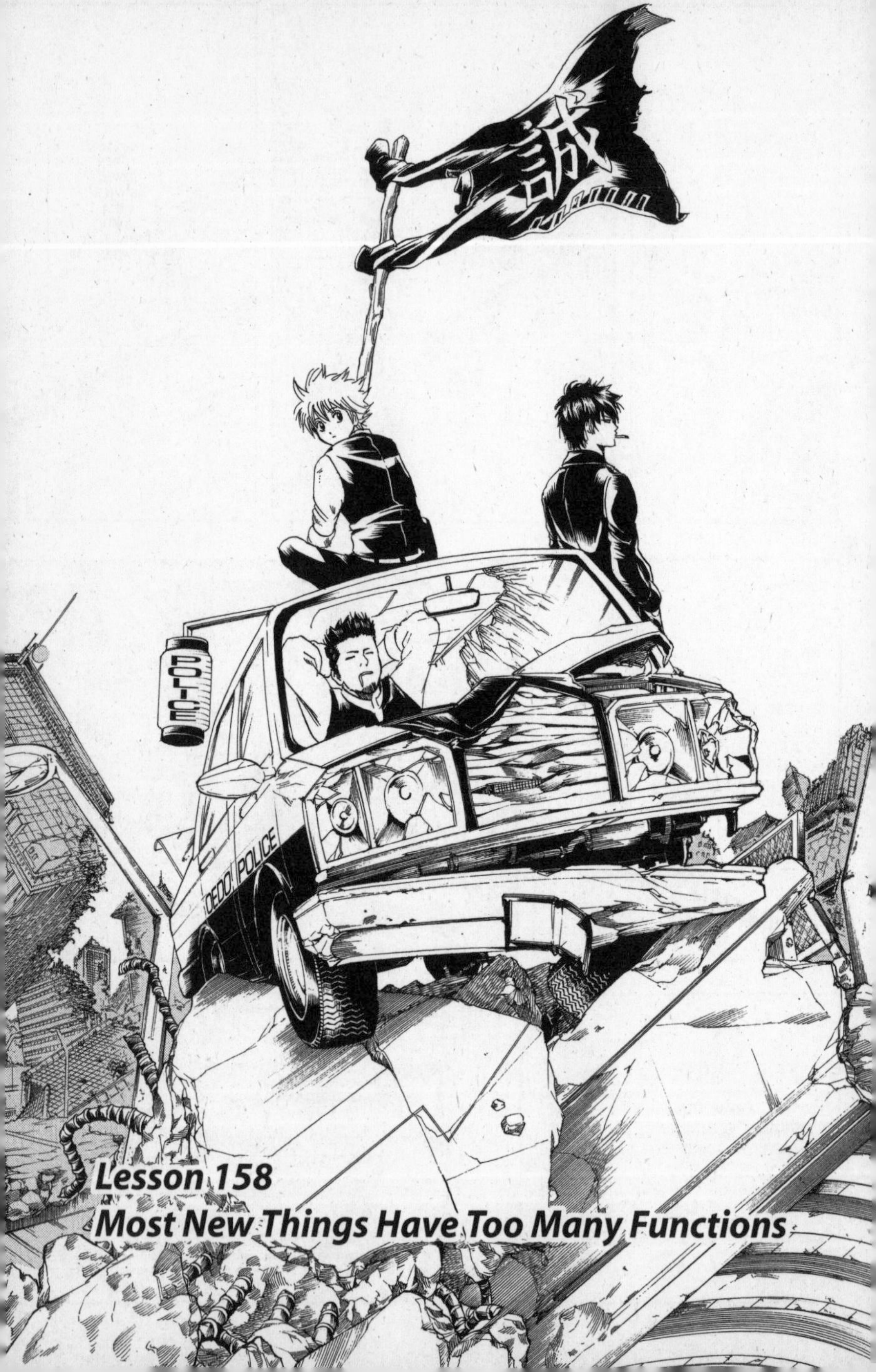
誠
POLICE
OEDO POLICE
Lesson 158
Most New Things Have Too Many Functions

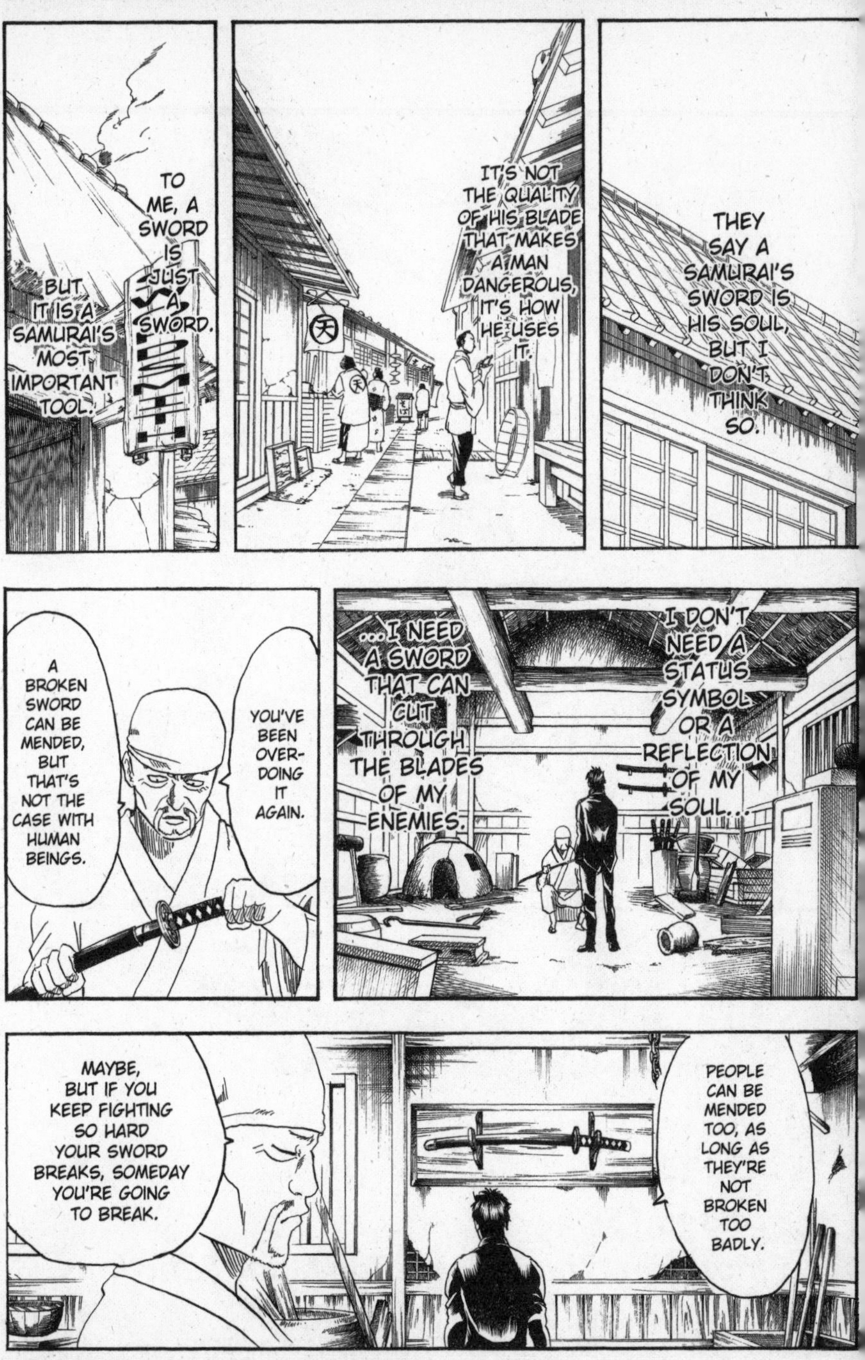
THEY SAY A SAMURAI'S SWORD IS HIS SOUL, BUT I DON'T THINK SO.
IT'S NOT THE QUALITY OF HIS BLADE THAT MAKES A MAN DANGEROUS, IT'S HOW HE USES IT.
TO ME, A SWORD IS JUST A SWORD.
BUT IT IS A SAMURAI'S MOST IMPORTANT TOOL.
I DON'T NEED A STATUS SYMBOL OR A REFLECTION OF MY SOUL...
...I NEED A SWORD THAT CAN CUT THROUGH THE BLADES OF MY ENEMIES.
YOU'VE BEEN OVER-DOING IT AGAIN.
A BROKEN SWORD CAN BE MENDED, BUT THAT'S NOT THE CASE WITH HUMAN BEINGS.
PEOPLE CAN BE MENDED TOO, AS LONG AS THEY'RE NOT BROKEN TOO BADLY.
MAYBE, BUT IF YOU KEEP FIGHTING SO HARD YOUR SWORD BREAKS, SOMEDAY YOU'RE GOING TO BREAK.

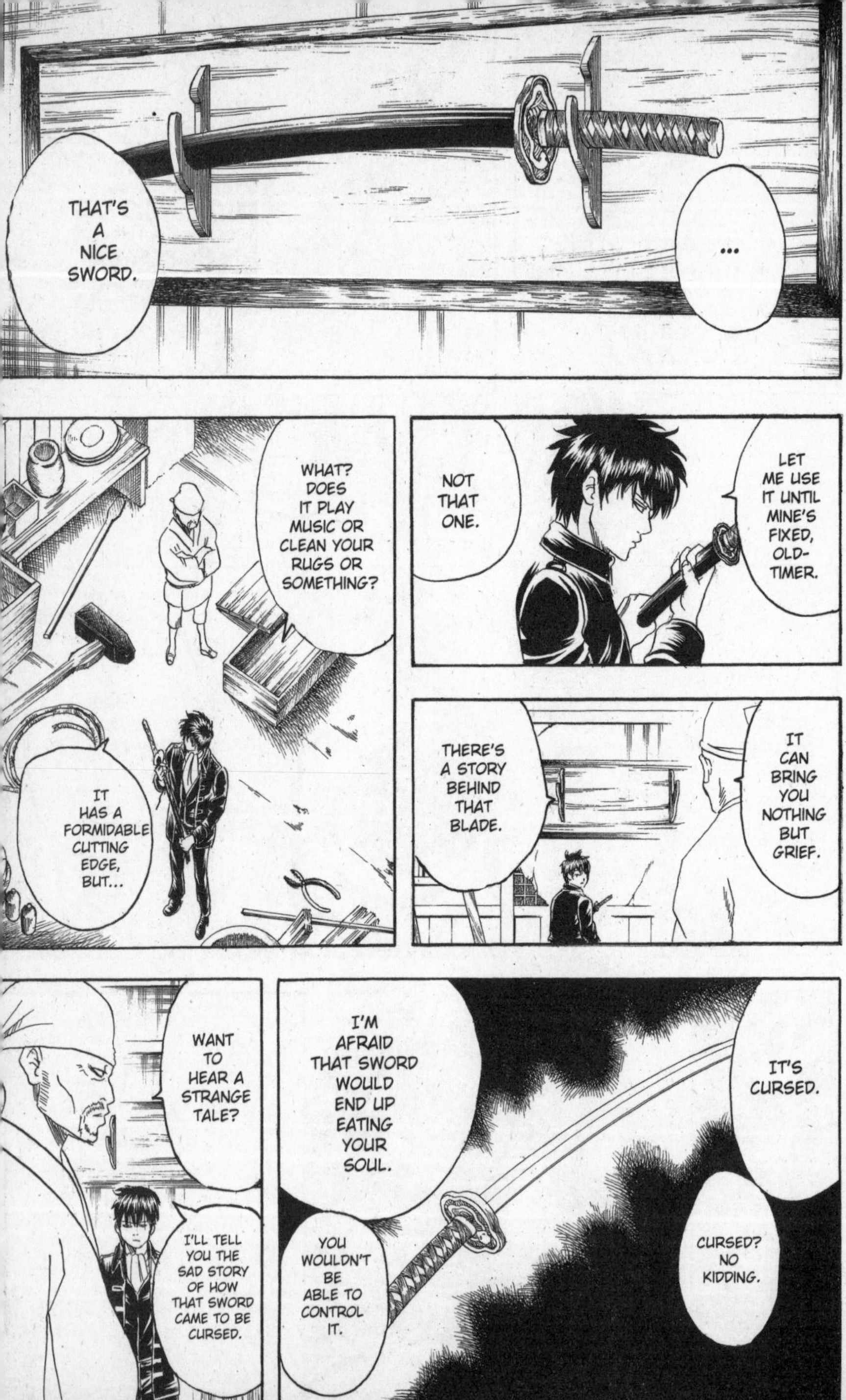
...
THAT'S A NICE SWORD.
LET ME USE IT UNTIL MINE'S FIXED, OLD-TIMER.
NOT THAT ONE.
IT CAN BRING YOU NOTHING BUT GRIEF.
THERE'S A STORY BEHIND THAT BLADE.
WHAT? DOES IT PLAY MUSIC OR CLEAN YOUR RUGS OR SOMETHING?
IT HAS A FORMIDABLE CUTTING EDGE, BUT...
IT'S CURSED.
I'M AFRAID THAT SWORD WOULD END UP EATING YOUR SOUL.
CURSED? NO KIDDING.
YOU WOULDN'T BE ABLE TO CONTROL IT.
WANT TO HEAR A STRANGE TALE?
I'LL TELL YOU THE SAD STORY OF HOW THAT SWORD CAME TO BE CURSED.

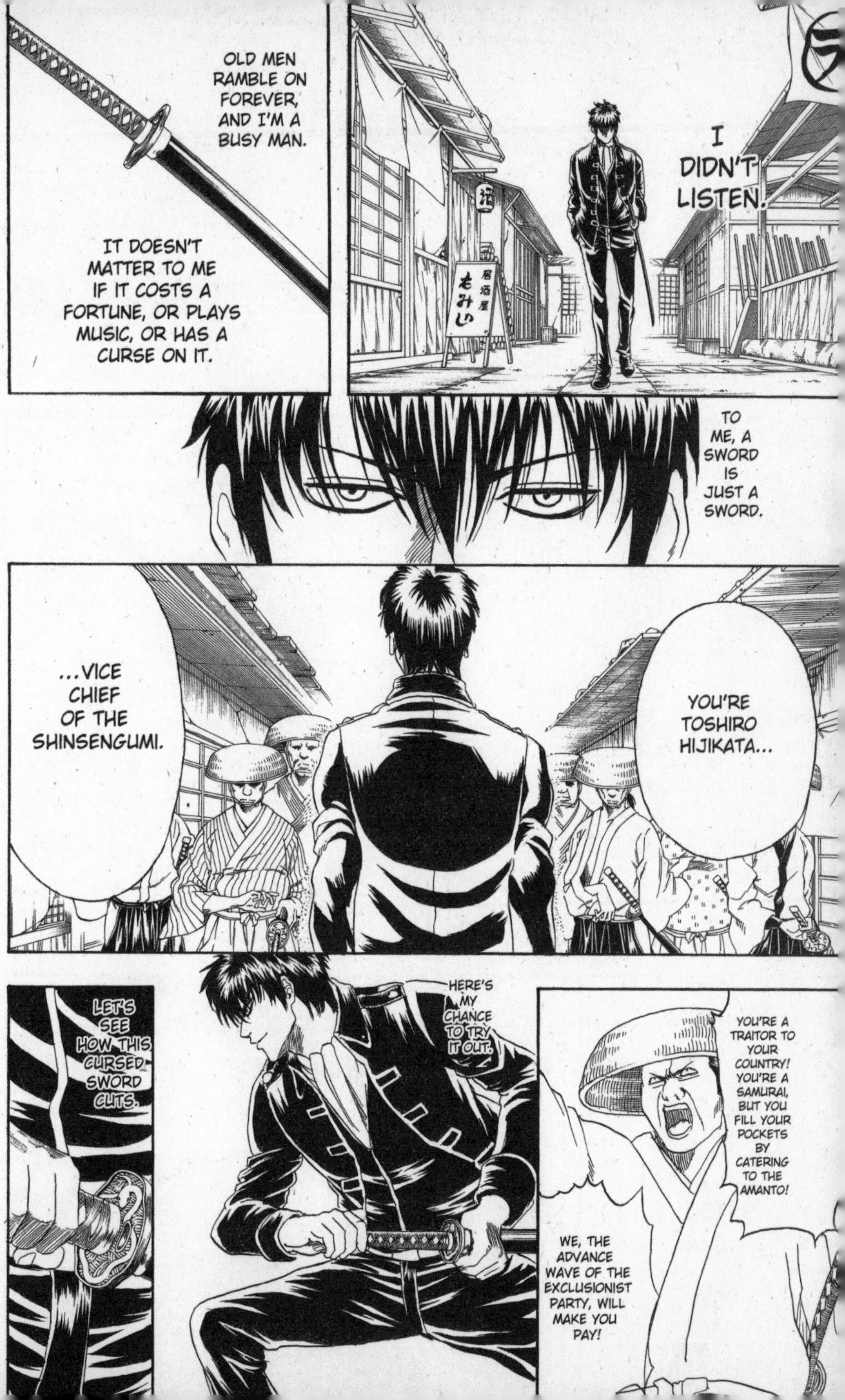
I DIDN'T LISTEN.
居酒屋 もみじ
OLD MEN RAMBLE ON FOREVER, AND I'M A BUSY MAN.
IT DOESN'T MATTER TO ME IF IT COSTS A FORTUNE, OR PLAYS MUSIC, OR HAS A CURSE ON IT.
TO ME, A SWORD IS JUST A SWORD.
YOU'RE TOSHIRO HIJIKATA...
...VICE CHIEF OF THE SHINSENGUMI.
YOU'RE A TRAITOR TO YOUR COUNTRY! YOU'RE A SAMURAI, BUT YOU FILL YOUR POCKETS BY CATERING TO THE AMANTO!
WE, THE ADVANCE WAVE OF THE EXCLUSIONIST PARTY, WILL MAKE YOU PAY!
HERE'S MY CHANCE TO TRY IT OUT.
LET'S SEE HOW THIS CURSED SWORD CUTS.

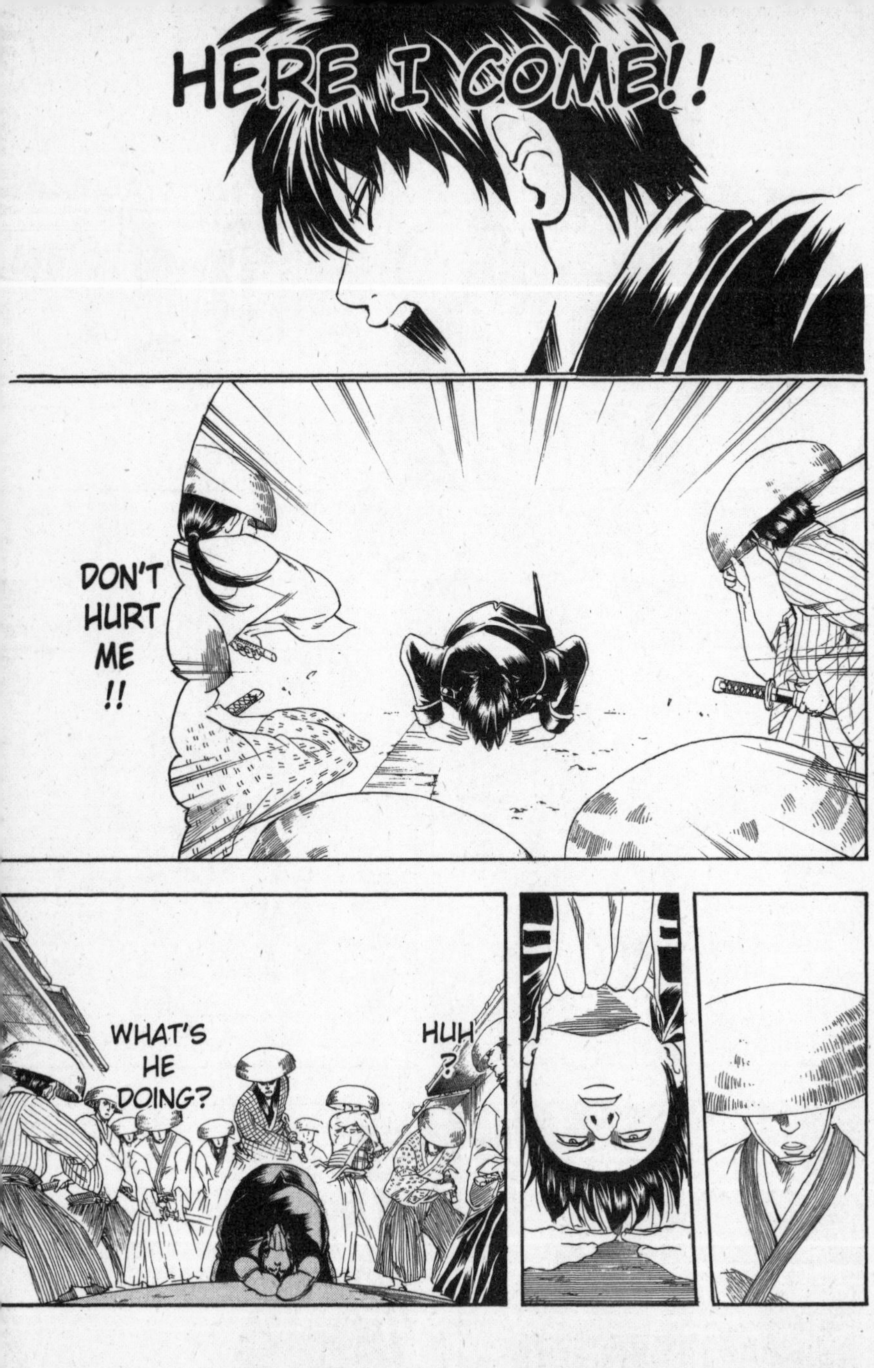
HERE I COME!!
DON'T HURT ME !!
HUH ?
WHAT'S HE DOING?

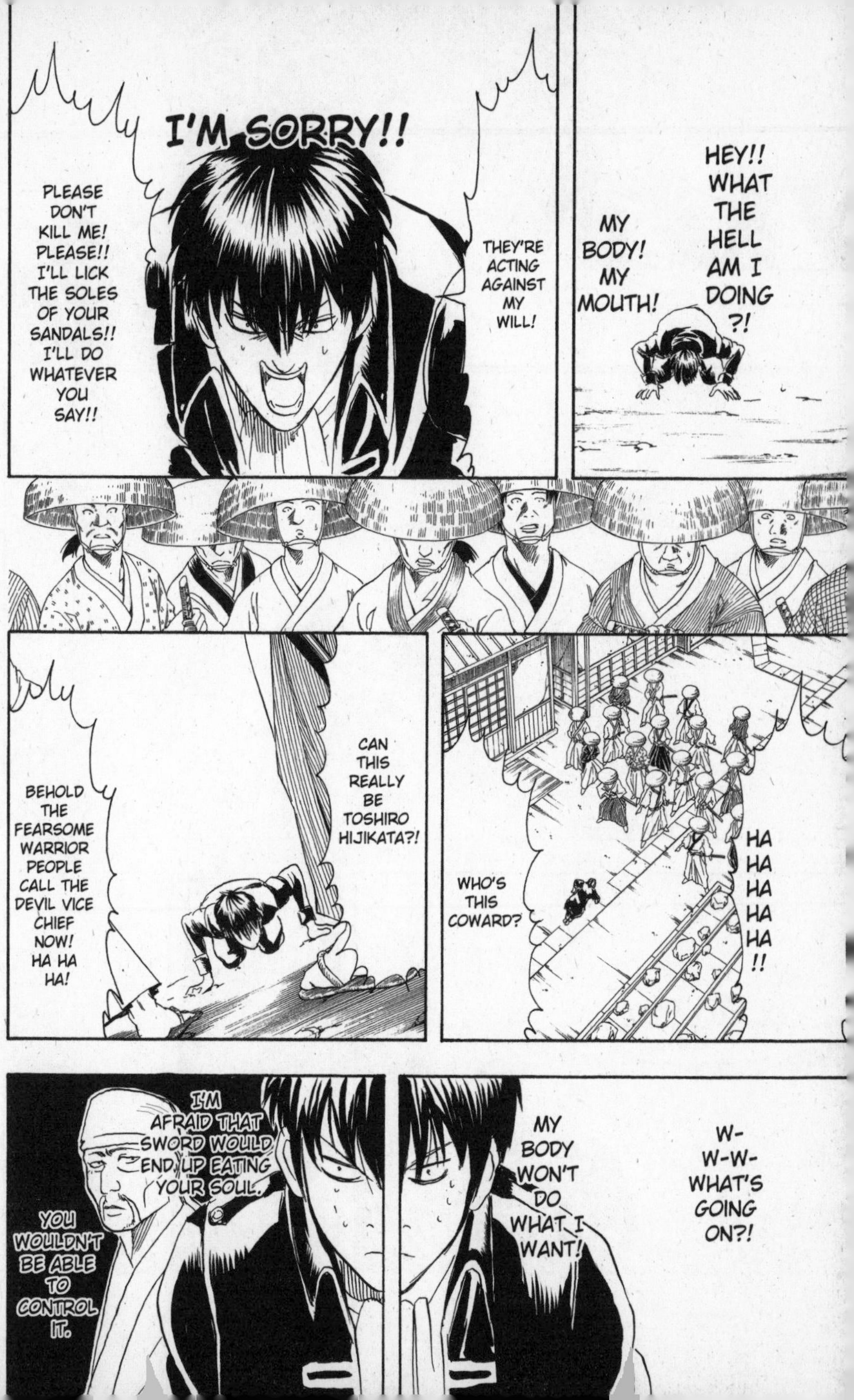
HEY!! WHAT THE HELL AM I DOING?!
MY BODY! MY MOUTH!
I'M SORRY!!
THEY'RE ACTING AGAINST MY WILL!
PLEASE DON'T KILL ME! PLEASE!! I'LL LICK THE SOLES OF YOUR SANDALS!! I'LL DO WHATEVER YOU SAY!!
HA HA HA HA HA!!
WHO'S THIS COWARD?
CAN THIS REALLY BE TOSHIRO HIJIKATA?!
BEHOLD THE FEARSOME WARRIOR PEOPLE CALL THE DEVIL VICE CHIEF NOW! HA HA HA!
W-W-W-WHAT'S GOING ON?!
MY BODY WON'T DO WHAT I WANT!
I'M AFRAID THAT SWORD WOULD END UP EATING YOUR SOUL.
YOU WOULDN'T BE ABLE TO CONTROL IT.

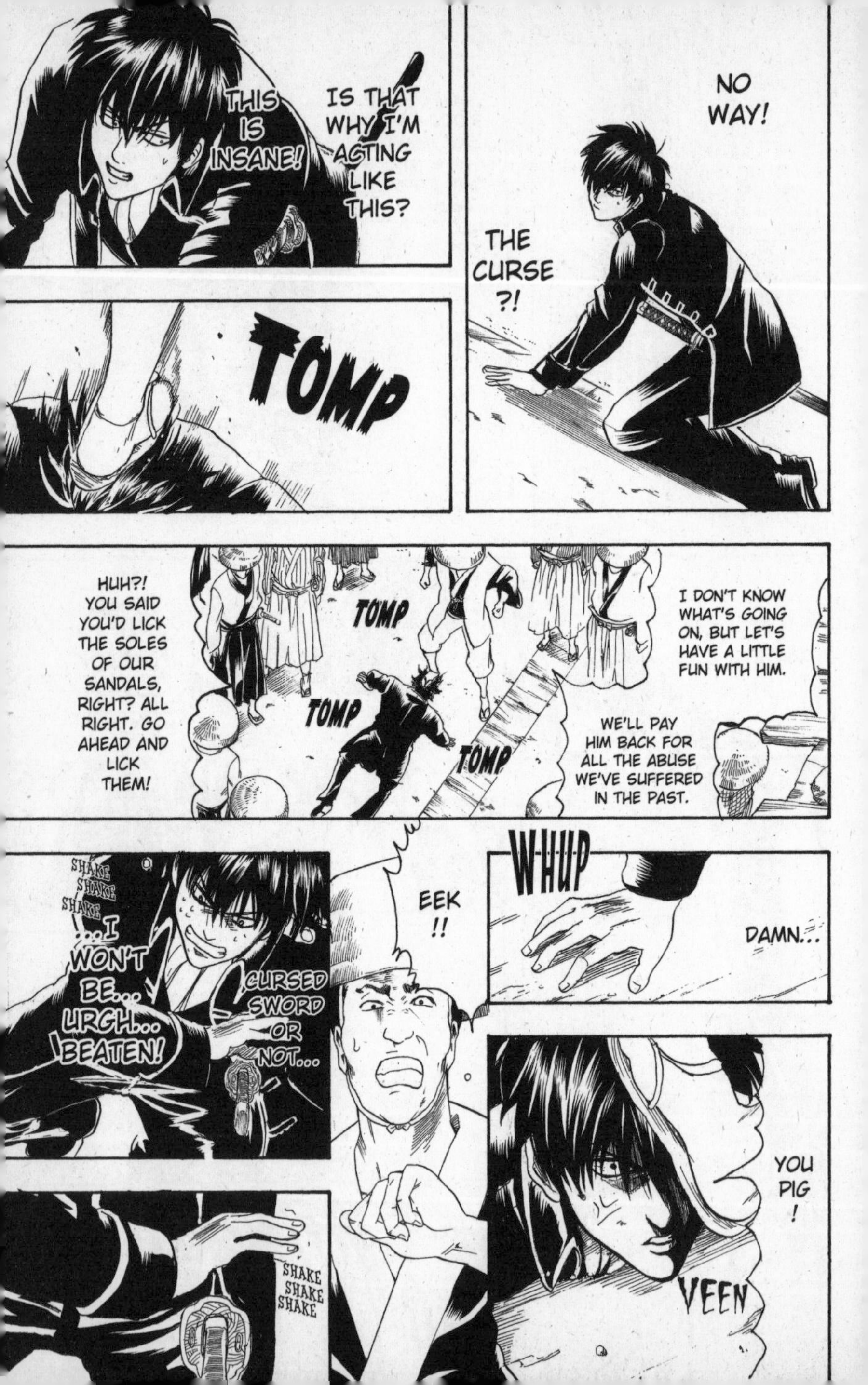
NO WAY!
THE CURSE ?!
IS THAT WHY I'M ACTING LIKE THIS?
THIS IS INSANE!
TOMP
I DON'T KNOW WHAT'S GOING ON, BUT LET'S HAVE A LITTLE FUN WITH HIM.
WE'LL PAY HIM BACK FOR ALL THE ABUSE WE'VE SUFFERED IN THE PAST.
TOMP
TOMP
TOMP
HUH?! YOU SAID YOU'D LICK THE SOLES OF OUR SANDALS, RIGHT? ALL RIGHT. GO AHEAD AND LICK THEM!
WHUP
DAMN...
YOU PIG!
VEEN
EEK !!
CURSED SWORD OR NOT...
...I WON'T BE... URGH... BEATEN!
SHAKE SHAKE SHAKE
SHAKE SHAKE SHAKE

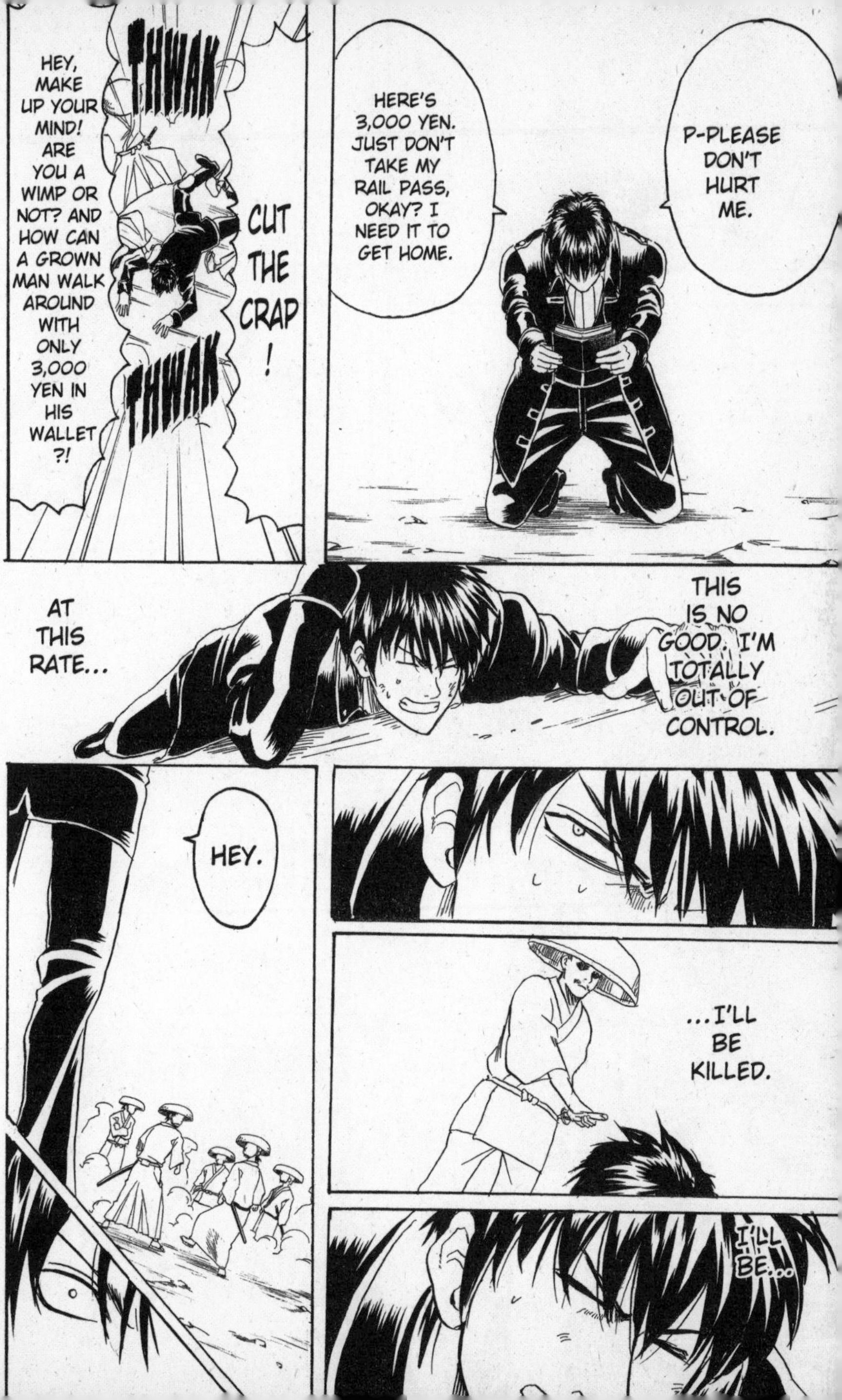
P-PLEASE DON'T HURT ME.
HERE'S 3,000 YEN. JUST DON'T TAKE MY RAIL PASS, OKAY? I NEED IT TO GET HOME.
CUT THE CRAP!
THWAK
THWAK
HEY, MAKE UP YOUR MIND! ARE YOU A WIMP OR NOT? AND HOW CAN A GROWN MAN WALK AROUND WITH ONLY 3,000 YEN IN HIS WALLET?!
THIS IS NO GOOD. I'M TOTALLY OUT OF CONTROL.
AT THIS RATE...
...I'LL BE KILLED.
I'LL BE...
HEY.

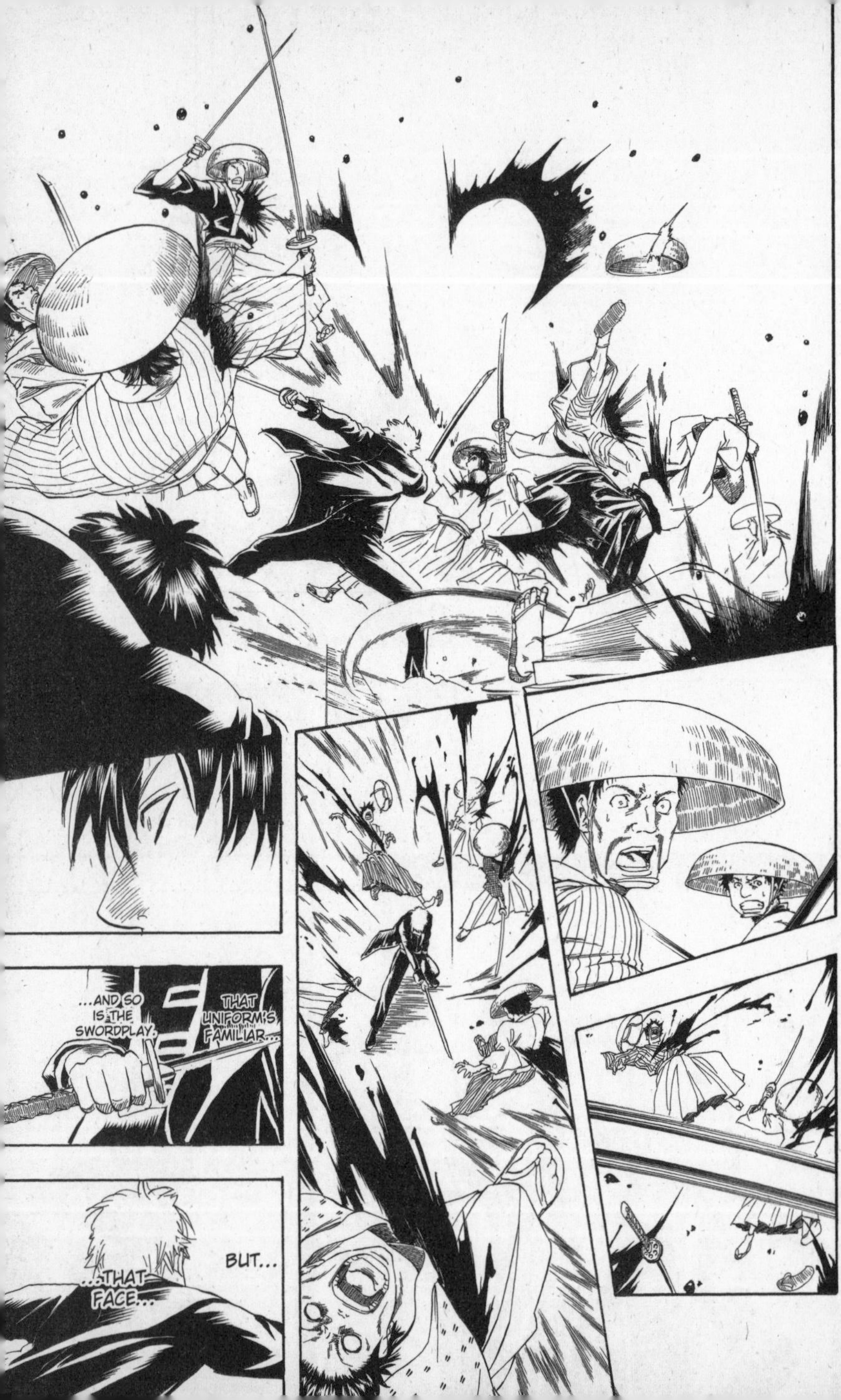
THAT UNIFORM'S FAMILIAR...
...AND SO IS THE SWORDPLAY.
BUT...
...THAT FACE...

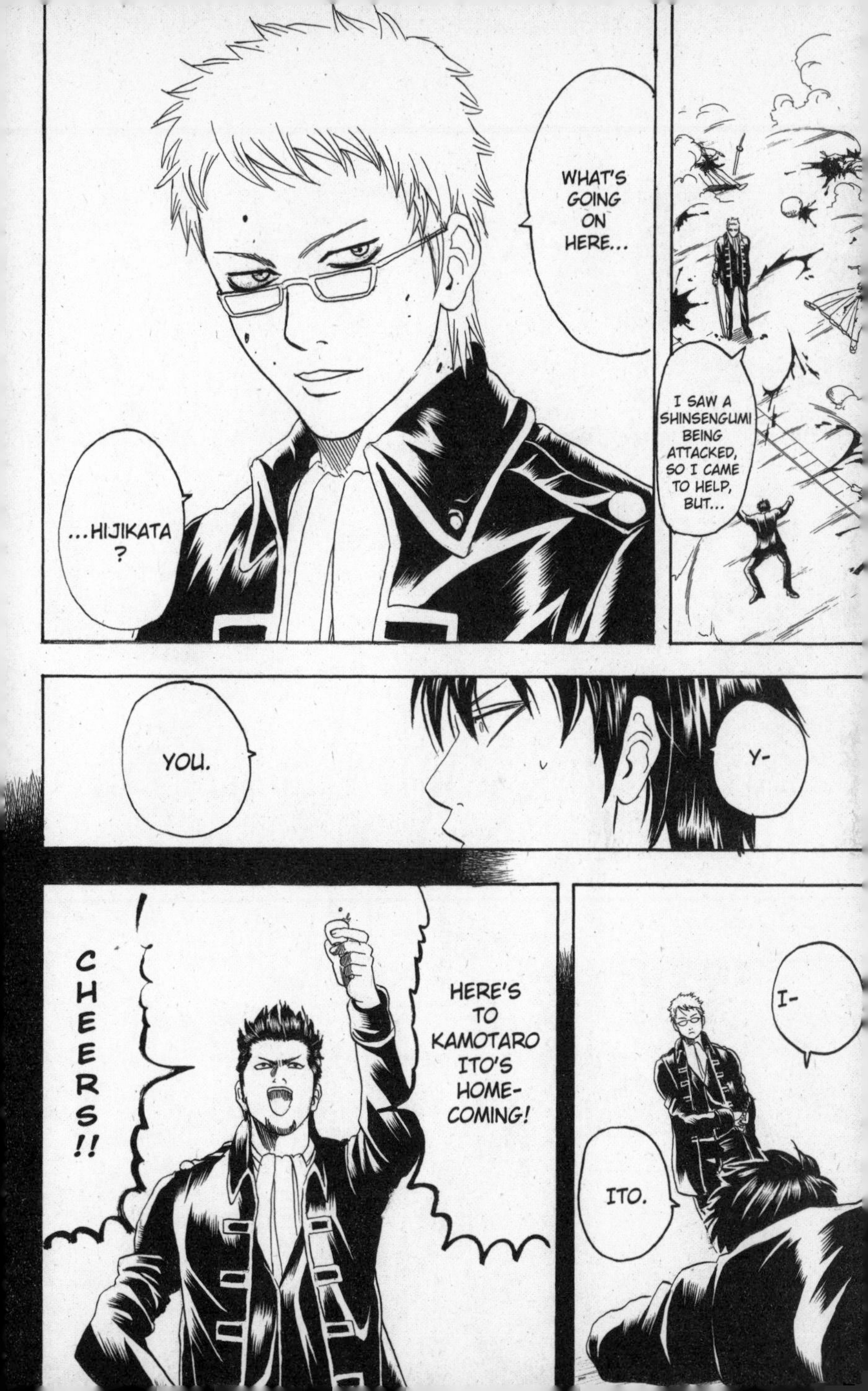
I SAW A SHINSENGUMI BEING ATTACKED, SO I CAME TO HELP, BUT...
WHAT'S GOING ON HERE...
...HIJIKATA?
Y-
YOU.
I-
ITO.
HERE'S TO KAMOTARO ITO'S HOME-COMING!
CHEERS!!

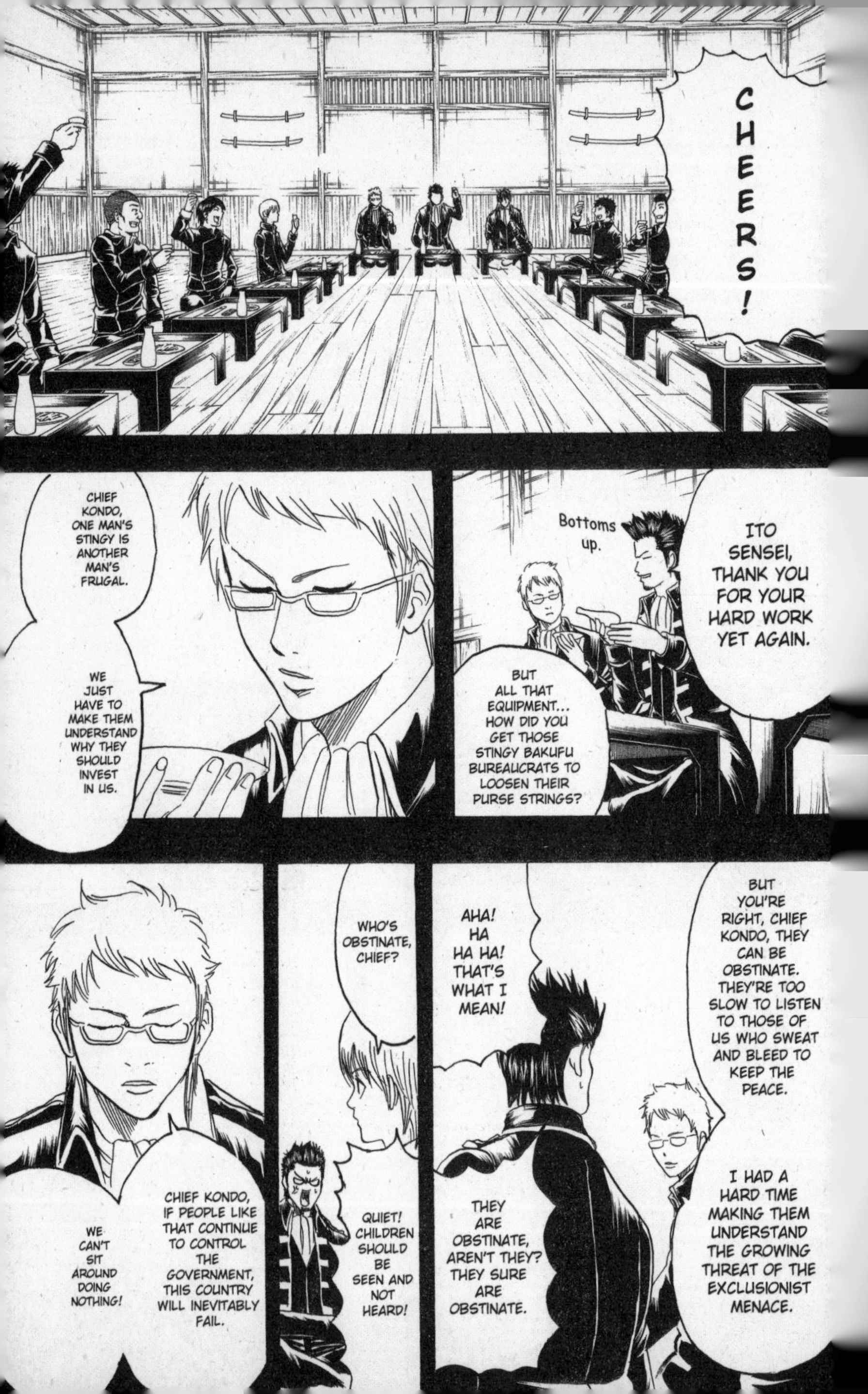
CHEERS!
ITO SENSEI, THANK YOU FOR YOUR HARD WORK YET AGAIN.
Bottoms up.
BUT ALL THAT EQUIPMENT... HOW DID YOU GET THOSE STINGY BAKUFU BUREAUCRATS TO LOOSEN THEIR PURSE STRINGS?
CHIEF KONDO, ONE MAN'S STINGY IS ANOTHER MAN'S FRUGAL.
WE JUST HAVE TO MAKE THEM UNDERSTAND WHY THEY SHOULD INVEST IN US.
BUT YOU'RE RIGHT, CHIEF KONDO, THEY CAN BE OBSTINATE. THEY'RE TOO SLOW TO LISTEN TO THOSE OF US WHO SWEAT AND BLEED TO KEEP THE PEACE.
AHA! HA HA HA! THAT'S WHAT I MEAN!
I HAD A HARD TIME MAKING THEM UNDERSTAND THE GROWING THREAT OF THE EXCLUSIONIST MENACE.
THEY ARE OBSTINATE, AREN'T THEY? THEY SURE ARE OBSTINATE.
WHO'S OBSTINATE, CHIEF?
QUIET! CHILDREN SHOULD BE SEEN AND NOT HEARD!
CHIEF KONDO, IF PEOPLE LIKE THAT CONTINUE TO CONTROL THE GOVERNMENT, THIS COUNTRY WILL INEVITABLY FAIL.
WE CAN'T SIT AROUND DOING NOTHING!

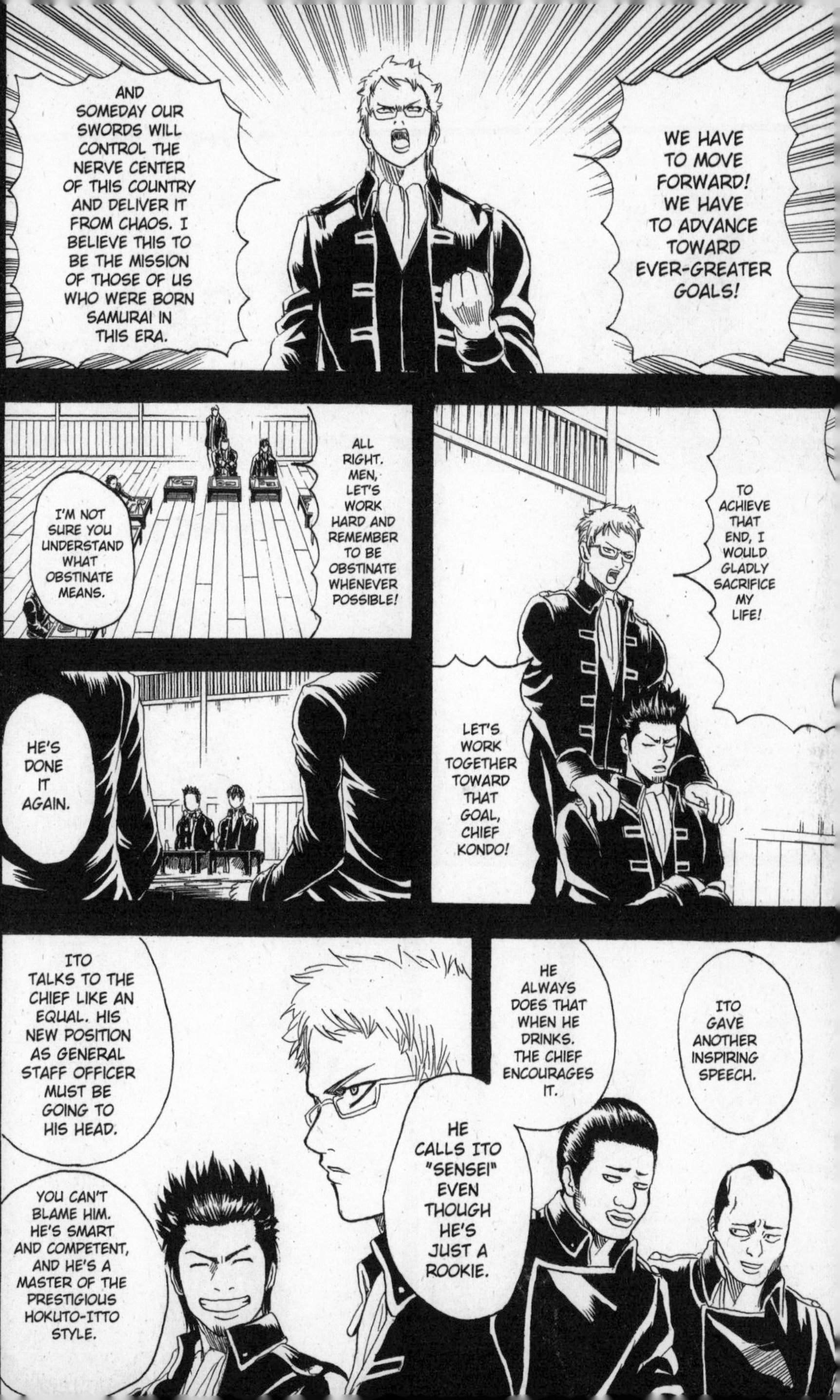
WE HAVE TO MOVE FORWARD! WE HAVE TO ADVANCE TOWARD EVER-GREATER GOALS!
AND SOMEDAY OUR SWORDS WILL CONTROL THE NERVE CENTER OF THIS COUNTRY AND DELIVER IT FROM CHAOS. I BELIEVE THIS TO BE THE MISSION OF THOSE OF US WHO WERE BORN SAMURAI IN THIS ERA.
TO ACHIEVE THAT END, I WOULD GLADLY SACRIFICE MY LIFE!
LET'S WORK TOGETHER TOWARD THAT GOAL, CHIEF KONDO!
ALL RIGHT. MEN, LET'S WORK HARD AND REMEMBER TO BE OBSTINATE WHENEVER POSSIBLE!
I'M NOT SURE YOU UNDERSTAND WHAT OBSTINATE MEANS.
HE'S DONE IT AGAIN.
ITO GAVE ANOTHER INSPIRING SPEECH.
HE ALWAYS DOES THAT WHEN HE DRINKS. THE CHIEF ENCOURAGES IT.
HE CALLS ITO "SENSEI" EVEN THOUGH HE'S JUST A ROOKIE.
ITO TALKS TO THE CHIEF LIKE AN EQUAL. HIS NEW POSITION AS GENERAL STAFF OFFICER MUST BE GOING TO HIS HEAD.
YOU CAN'T BLAME HIM. HE'S SMART AND COMPETENT, AND HE'S A MASTER OF THE PRESTIGIOUS HOKUTO-ITTO STYLE.

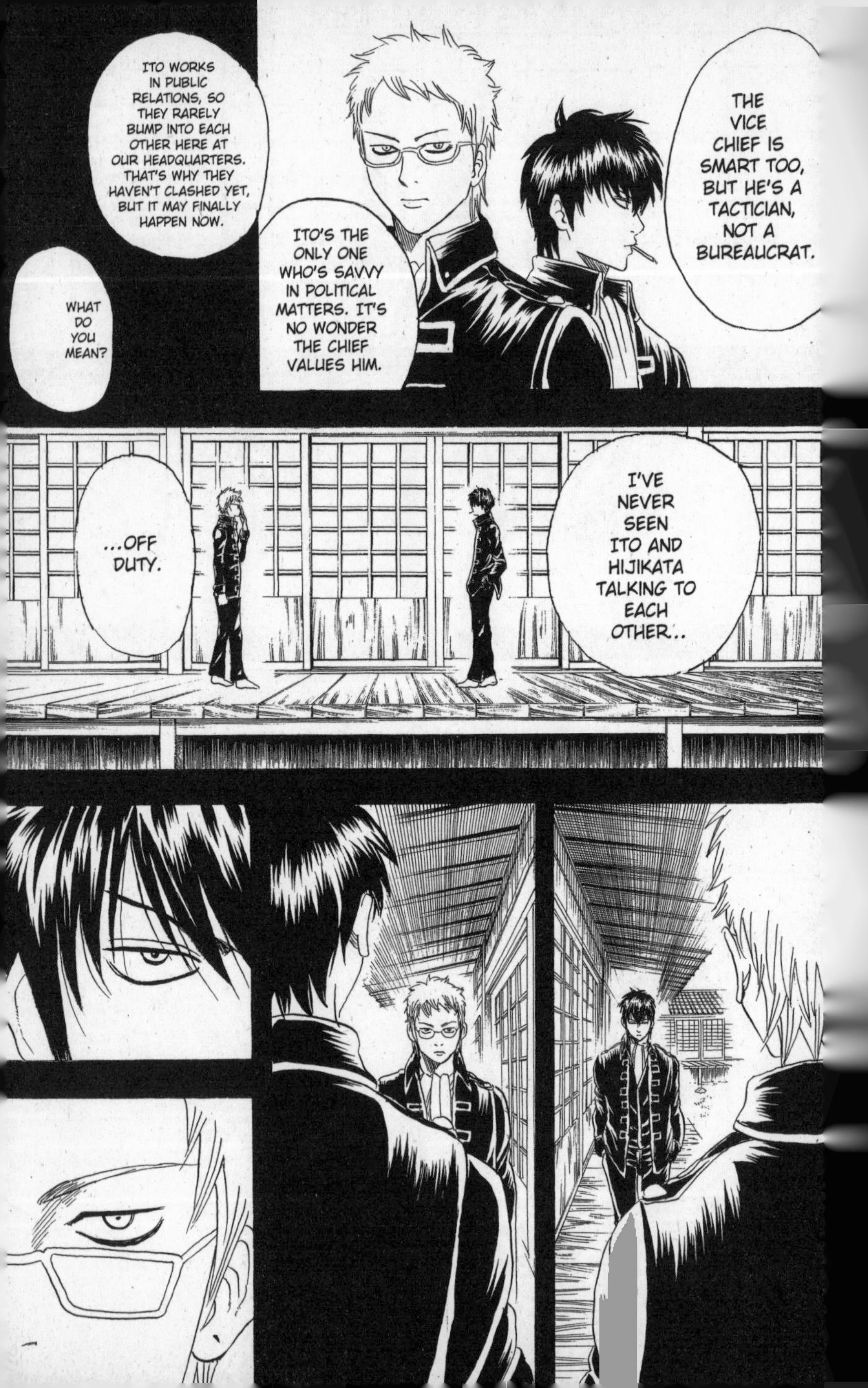
THE VICE CHIEF IS SMART TOO, BUT HE'S A TACTICIAN, NOT A BUREAUCRAT.
ITO'S THE ONLY ONE WHO'S SAVVY IN POLITICAL MATTERS. IT'S NO WONDER THE CHIEF VALUES HIM.
ITO WORKS IN PUBLIC RELATIONS, SO THEY RARELY BUMP INTO EACH OTHER HERE AT OUR HEADQUARTERS. THAT'S WHY THEY HAVEN'T CLASHED YET, BUT IT MAY FINALLY HAPPEN NOW.
WHAT DO YOU MEAN?
I'VE NEVER SEEN ITO AND HIJIKATA TALKING TO EACH OTHER..
...OFF DUTY.

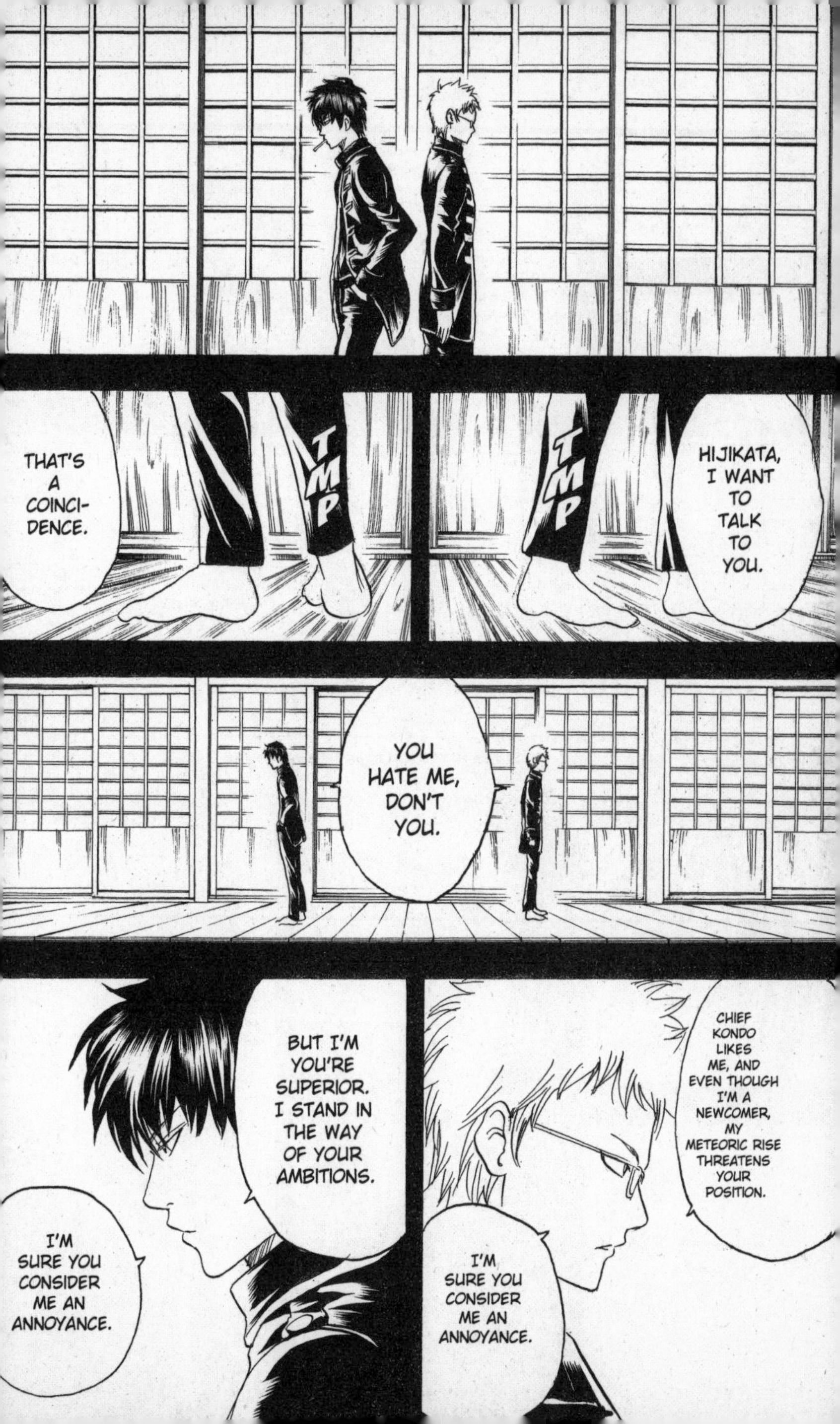
TMP
HIJIKATA, I WANT TO TALK TO YOU.
TMP
THAT'S A COINCI-DENCE.
YOU HATE ME, DON'T YOU.
CHIEF KONDO LIKES ME, AND EVEN THOUGH I'M A NEWCOMER, MY METEORIC RISE THREATENS YOUR POSITION.
I'M SURE YOU CONSIDER ME AN ANNOYANCE.
BUT I'M YOU'RE SUPERIOR. I STAND IN THE WAY OF YOUR AMBITIONS.
I'M SURE YOU CONSIDER ME AN ANNOYANCE.

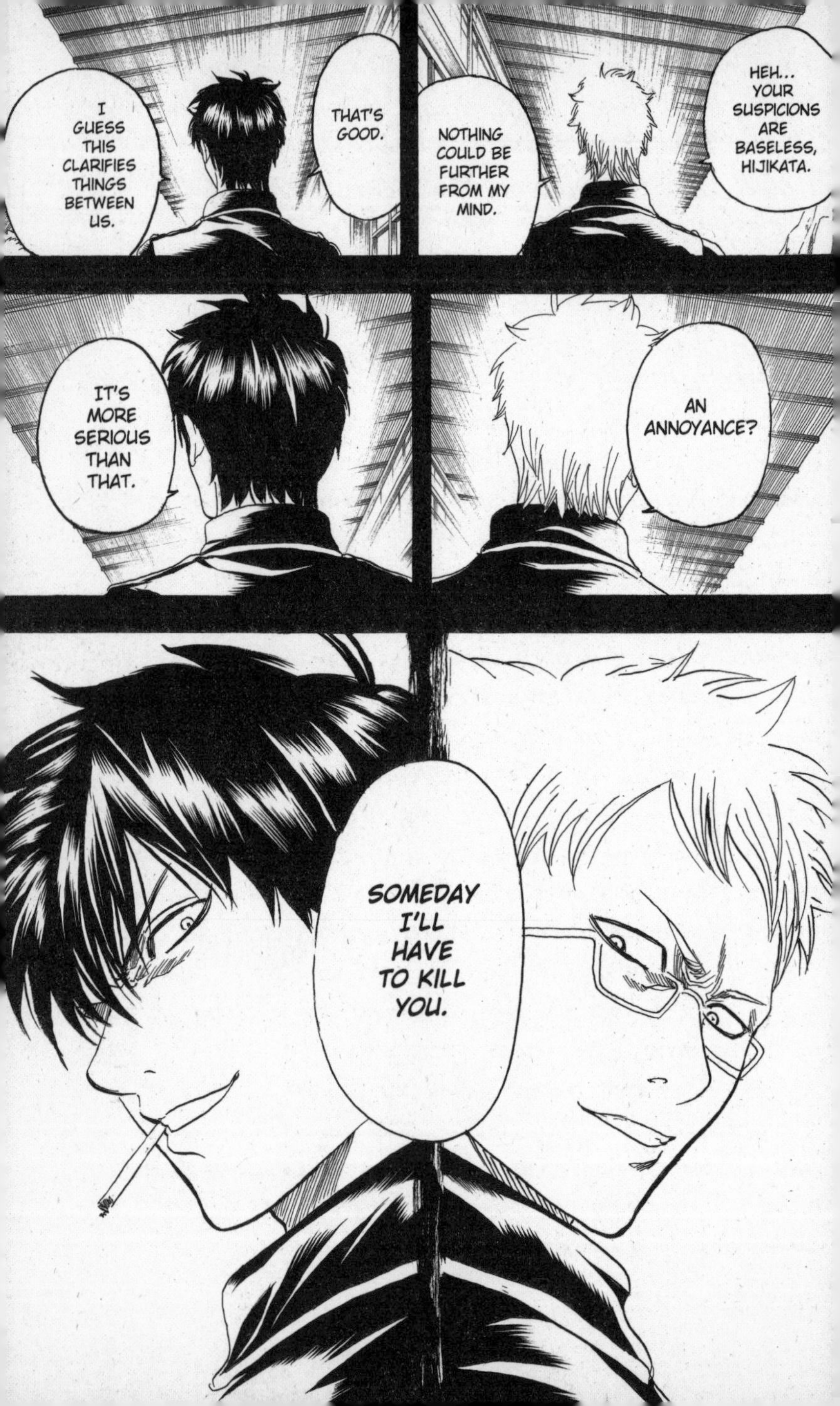
HEH... YOUR SUSPICIONS ARE BASELESS, HIJIKATA.
NOTHING COULD BE FURTHER FROM MY MIND.
THAT'S GOOD.
I GUESS THIS CLARIFIES THINGS BETWEEN US.
AN ANNOYANCE?
IT'S MORE SERIOUS THAN THAT.
SOMEDAY I'LL HAVE TO KILL YOU.

Thank you for purchasing **Gin Tama**, volume 19. For a long time, I avoided it because I thought it would distract me from my work, but I finally started playing **Monster Hunter** (the second version for PSP). People warned me that I'd get so into it that I'd never come back to the real world, but I told them, "I'm a work-oriented person. There's no way I'd get caught up in a silly video game where all you do is kill monsters. It doesn't even have a dramatic storyline! The character's father wasn't killed or enslaved, and the son isn't secretly a legendary warrior, right? There's no way I'll get addicted to it." So I decided to test my courage and play the game. A few weeks later, I'd grown into a capable hunter. I'd take my PSP over to Yodobashi Camera like all the kids just to download the special-event quests. Now my life revolves around two activities: writing manga and hunting. This week I finished one episode of manga and made one helmet in the video game. I have to live in a fantasy world when writing manga, so the only time I spend in the real world is when I'm going to the bathroom, bathing and eating. This is becoming a serious problem.

Lately I'm not sure whether I am a hunter or a manga writer. My editor has begun to look like Yian Kut Ku, one of the monsters in the game. I've been tempted to plunge my Great Sword into him many times...

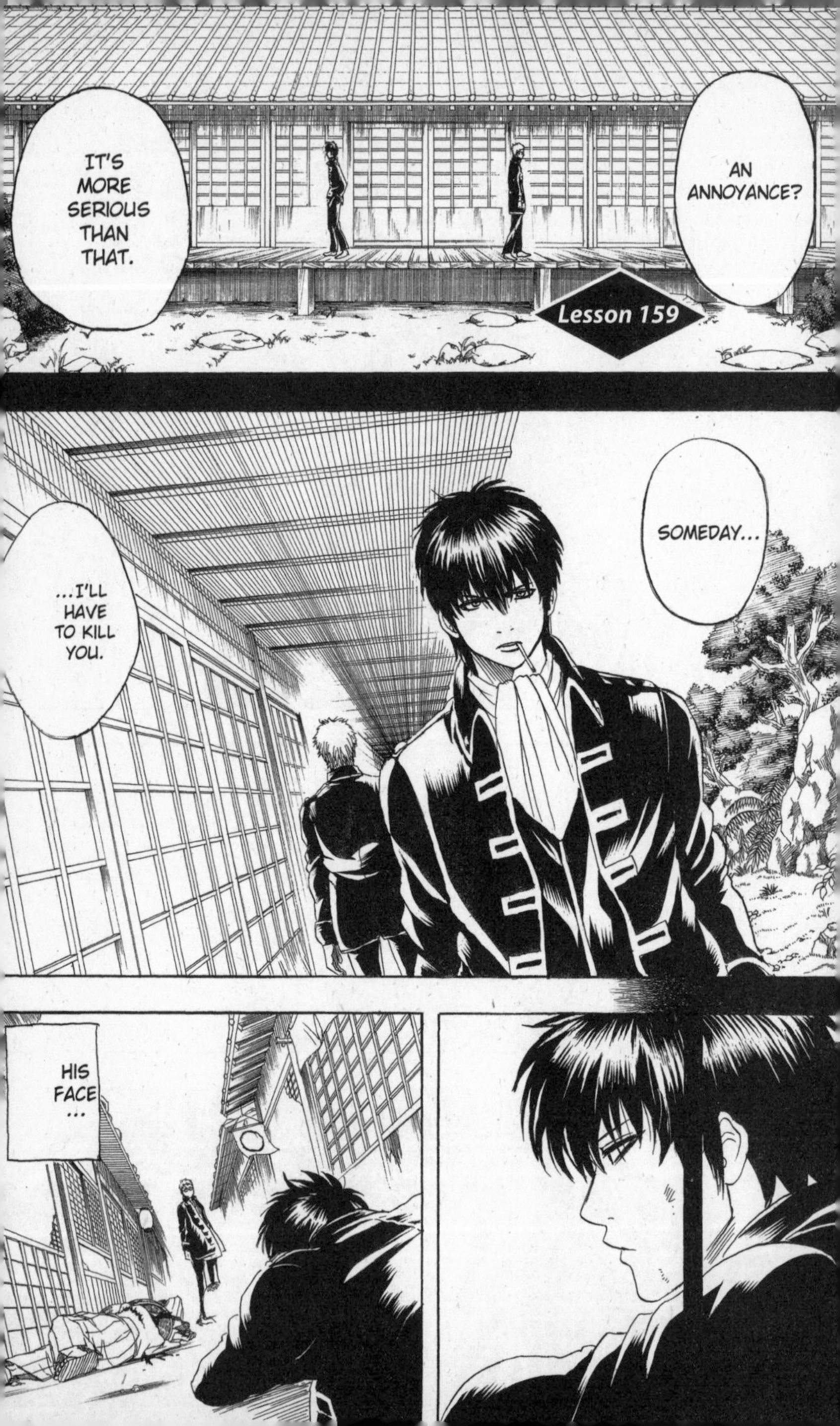
AN ANNOYANCE?
IT'S MORE SERIOUS THAN THAT.
Lesson 159
SOMEDAY...
...I'LL HAVE TO KILL YOU.
HIS FACE ...

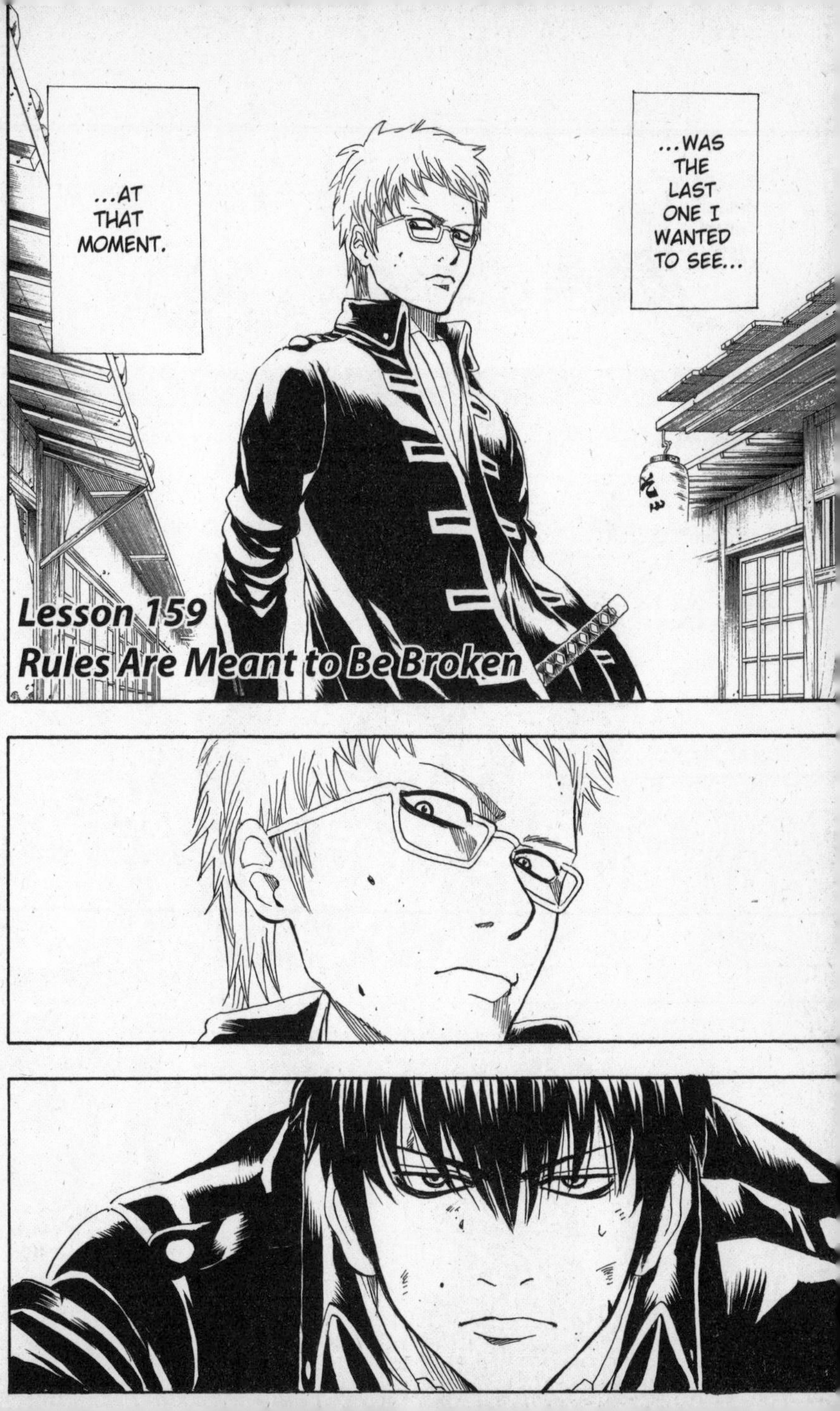
...WAS THE LAST ONE I WANTED TO SEE...
...AT THAT MOMENT.
Lesson 159
Rules Are Meant to Be Broken

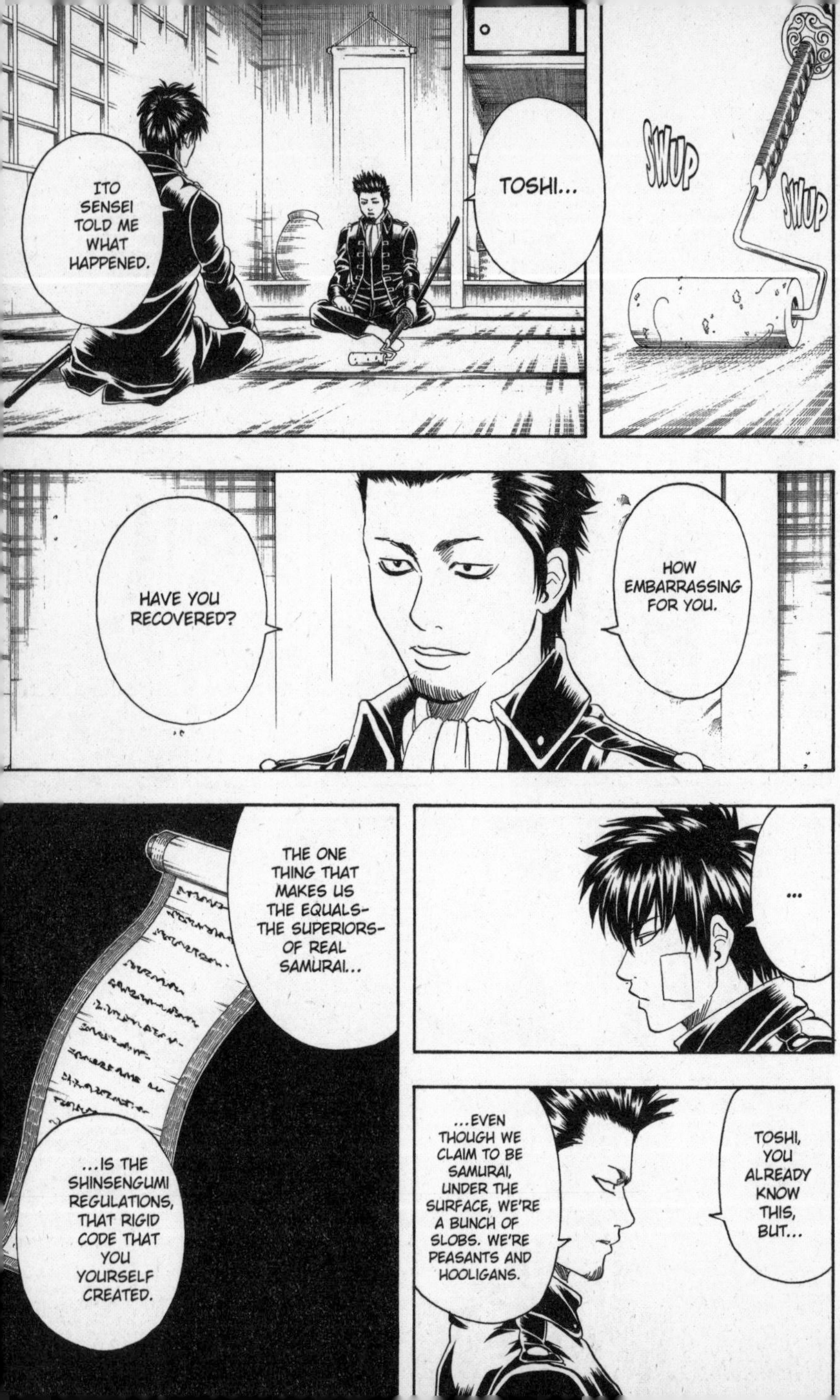
SWUP
SWUP
TOSHI...
ITO SENSEI TOLD ME WHAT HAPPENED.
HOW EMBARRASSING FOR YOU.
HAVE YOU RECOVERED?
...
TOSHI, YOU ALREADY KNOW THIS, BUT...
...EVEN THOUGH WE CLAIM TO BE SAMURAI, UNDER THE SURFACE, WE'RE A BUNCH OF SLOBS. WE'RE PEASANTS AND HOOLIGANS.
THE ONE THING THAT MAKES US THE EQUALS- THE SUPERIORS- OF REAL SAMURAI...
...IS THE SHINSENGUMI REGULATIONS, THAT RIGID CODE THAT YOU YOURSELF CREATED.

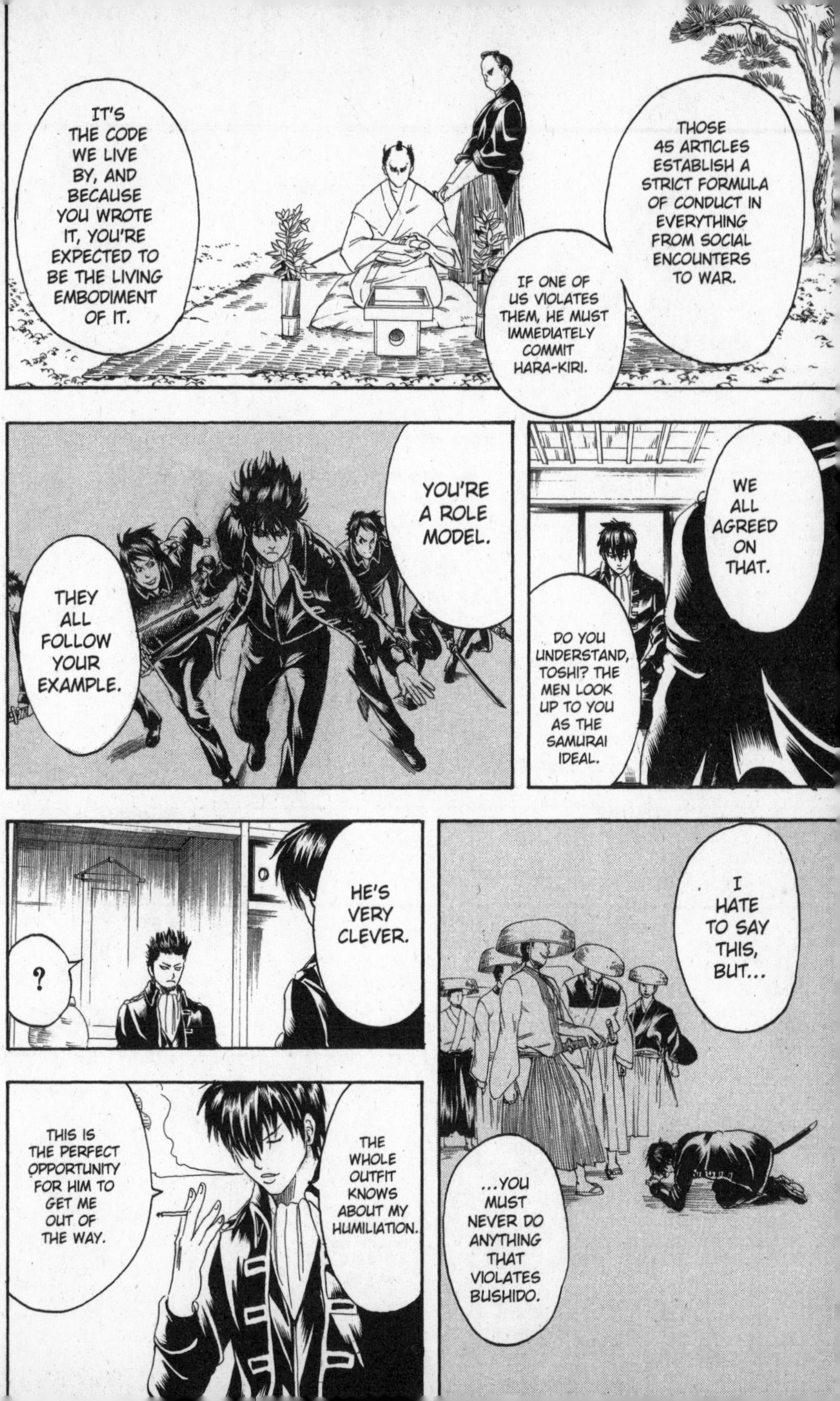
THOSE 45 ARTICLES ESTABLISH A STRICT FORMULA OF CONDUCT IN EVERYTHING FROM SOCIAL ENCOUNTERS TO WAR.
IF ONE OF US VIOLATES THEM, HE MUST IMMEDIATELY COMMIT HARA-KIRI.
IT'S THE CODE WE LIVE BY, AND BECAUSE YOU WROTE IT, YOU'RE EXPECTED TO BE THE LIVING EMBODIMENT OF IT.
WE ALL AGREED ON THAT.
DO YOU UNDERSTAND, TOSHI? THE MEN LOOK UP TO YOU AS THE SAMURAI IDEAL.
YOU'RE A ROLE MODEL.
THEY ALL FOLLOW YOUR EXAMPLE.
I HATE TO SAY THIS, BUT...
...YOU MUST NEVER DO ANYTHING THAT VIOLATES BUSHIDO.
HE'S VERY CLEVER.
?
THE WHOLE OUTFIT KNOWS ABOUT MY HUMILIATION.
THIS IS THE PERFECT OPPORTUNITY FOR HIM TO GET ME OUT OF THE WAY.

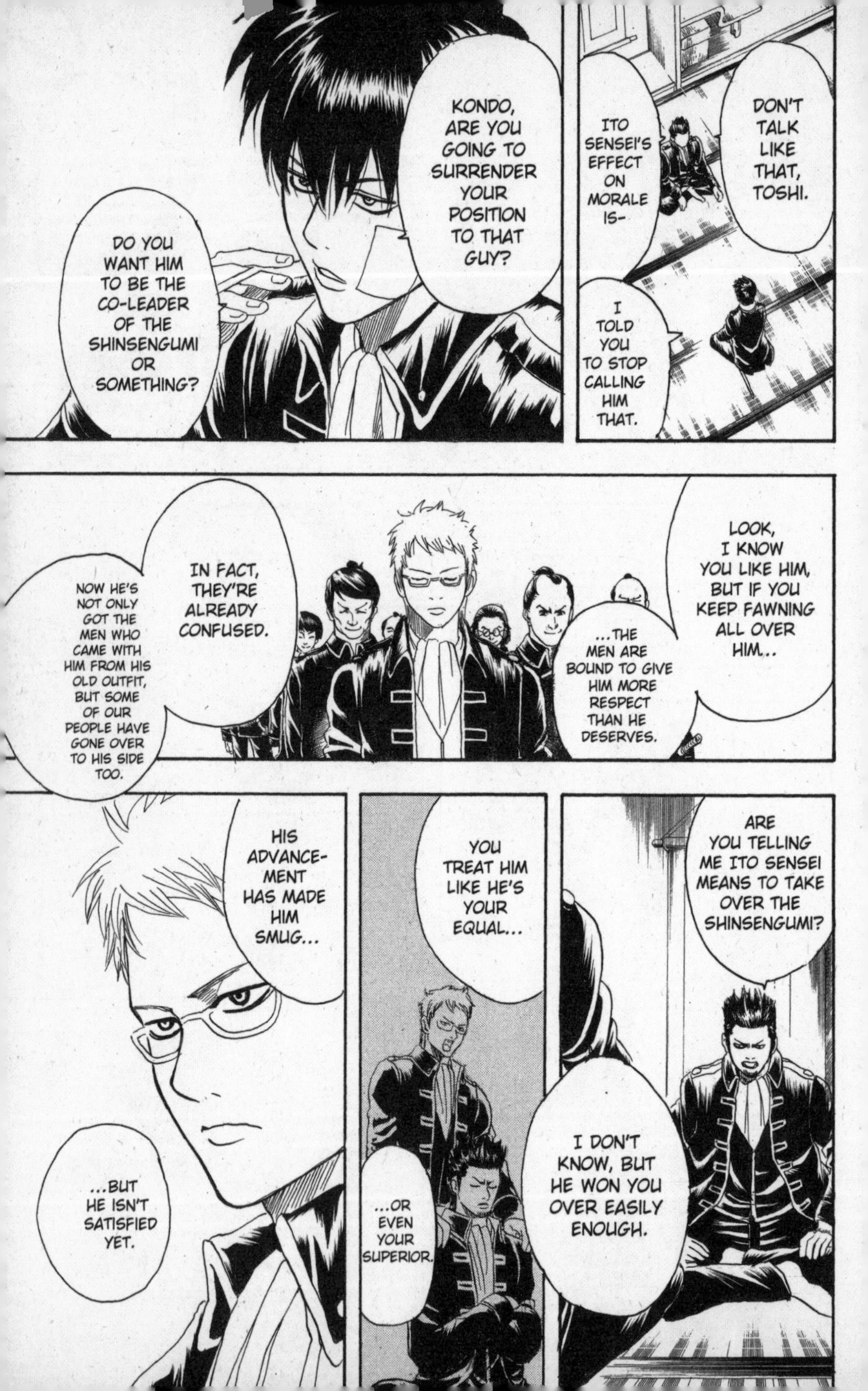
DON'T TALK LIKE THAT, TOSHI.
ITO SENSEI'S EFFECT ON MORALE IS-
I TOLD YOU TO STOP CALLING HIM THAT.
KONDO, ARE YOU GOING TO SURRENDER YOUR POSITION TO THAT GUY?
DO YOU WANT HIM TO BE THE CO-LEADER OF THE SHINSENGUMI OR SOMETHING?
LOOK, I KNOW YOU LIKE HIM, BUT IF YOU KEEP FAWNING ALL OVER HIM...
...THE MEN ARE BOUND TO GIVE HIM MORE RESPECT THAN HE DESERVES.
IN FACT, THEY'RE ALREADY CONFUSED.
NOW HE'S NOT ONLY GOT THE MEN WHO CAME WITH HIM FROM HIS OLD OUTFIT, BUT SOME OF OUR PEOPLE HAVE GONE OVER TO HIS SIDE TOO.
ARE YOU TELLING ME ITO SENSEI MEANS TO TAKE OVER THE SHINSENGUMI?
I DON'T KNOW, BUT HE WON YOU OVER EASILY ENOUGH.
YOU TREAT HIM LIKE HE'S YOUR EQUAL...
...OR EVEN YOUR SUPERIOR.
HIS ADVANCEMENT HAS MADE HIM SMUG...
...BUT HE ISN'T SATISFIED YET.

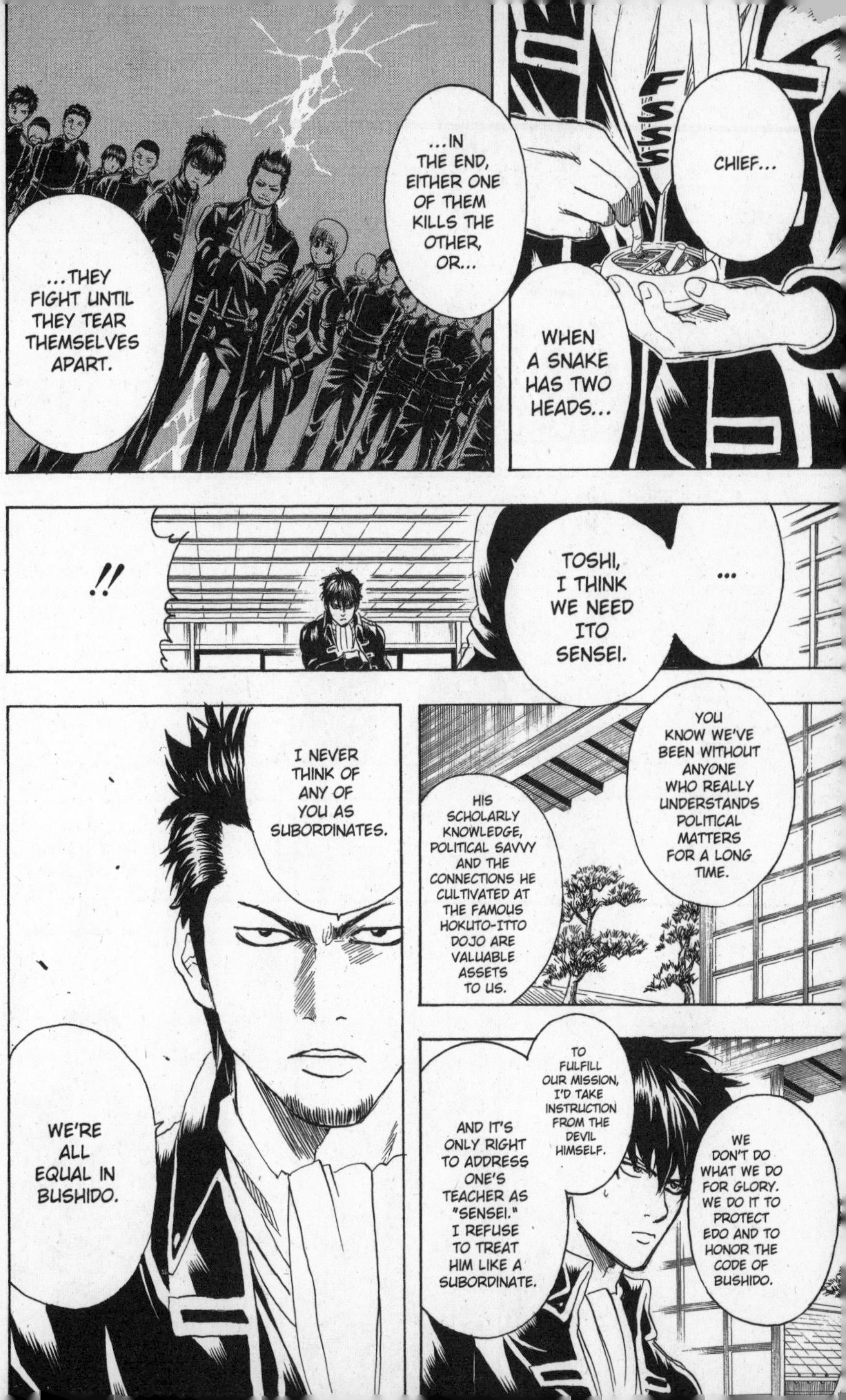
CHIEF...
FSSS
WHEN A SNAKE HAS TWO HEADS...
...IN THE END, EITHER ONE OF THEM KILLS THE OTHER, OR...
...THEY FIGHT UNTIL THEY TEAR THEMSELVES APART.
...
TOSHI, I THINK WE NEED ITO SENSEI.
!!
YOU KNOW WE'VE BEEN WITHOUT ANYONE WHO REALLY UNDERSTANDS POLITICAL MATTERS FOR A LONG TIME.
HIS SCHOLARLY KNOWLEDGE, POLITICAL SAVVY AND THE CONNECTIONS HE CULTIVATED AT THE FAMOUS HOKUTO-ITTO DOJO ARE VALUABLE ASSETS TO US.
WE DON'T DO WHAT WE DO FOR GLORY. WE DO IT TO PROTECT EDO AND TO HONOR THE CODE OF BUSHIDO.
TO FULFILL OUR MISSION, I'D TAKE INSTRUCTION FROM THE DEVIL HIMSELF.
AND IT'S ONLY RIGHT TO ADDRESS ONE'S TEACHER AS "SENSEI." I REFUSE TO TREAT HIM LIKE A SUBORDINATE.
I NEVER THINK OF ANY OF YOU AS SUBORDINATES.
WE'RE ALL EQUAL IN BUSHIDO.

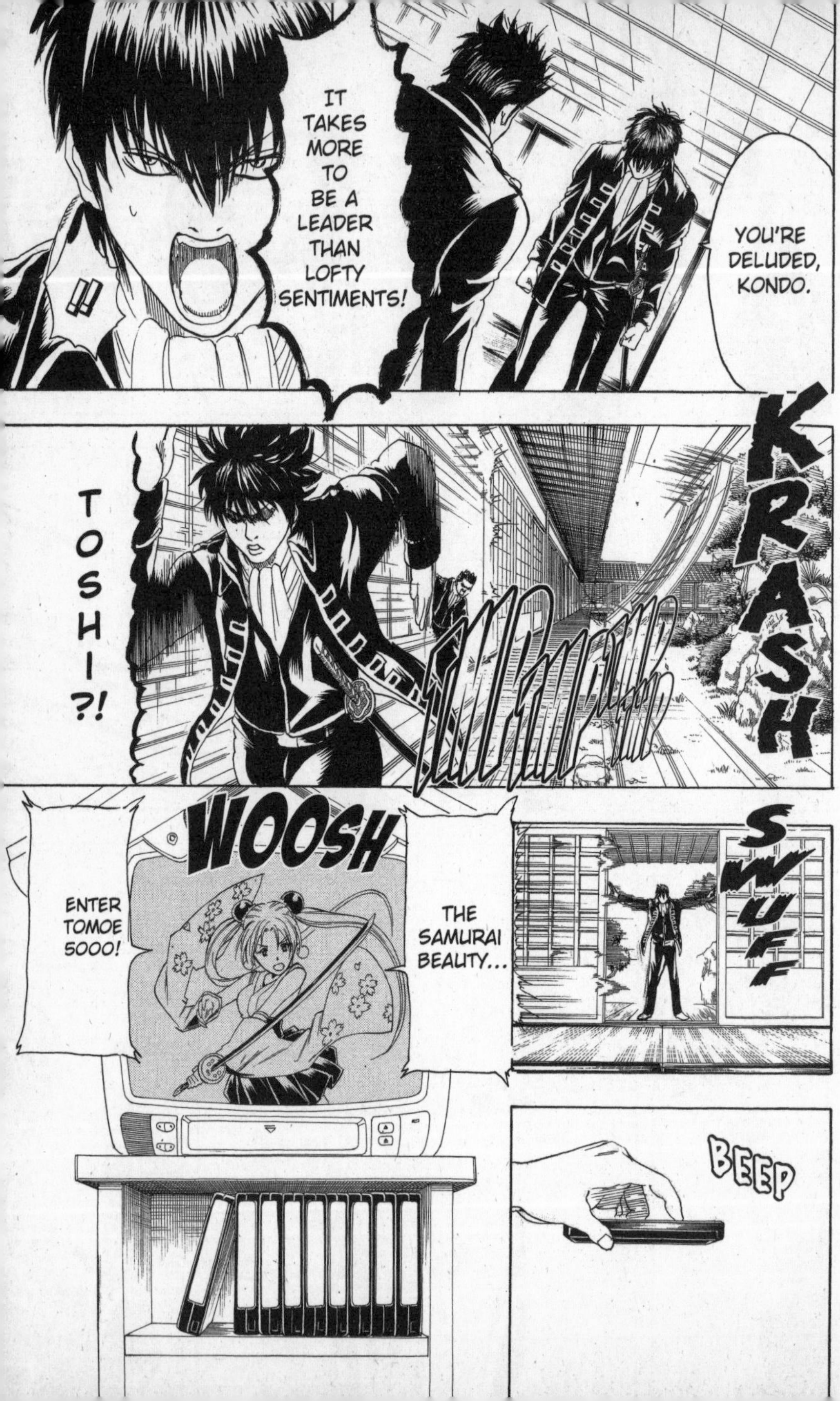
YOU'RE DELUDED, KONDO.
IT TAKES MORE TO BE A LEADER THAN LOFTY SENTIMENTS!
!!
KRASH
TOSHI?!
SWUFF
WOOSH
THE SAMURAI BEAUTY...
ENTER TOMOE 5000!
BEEP

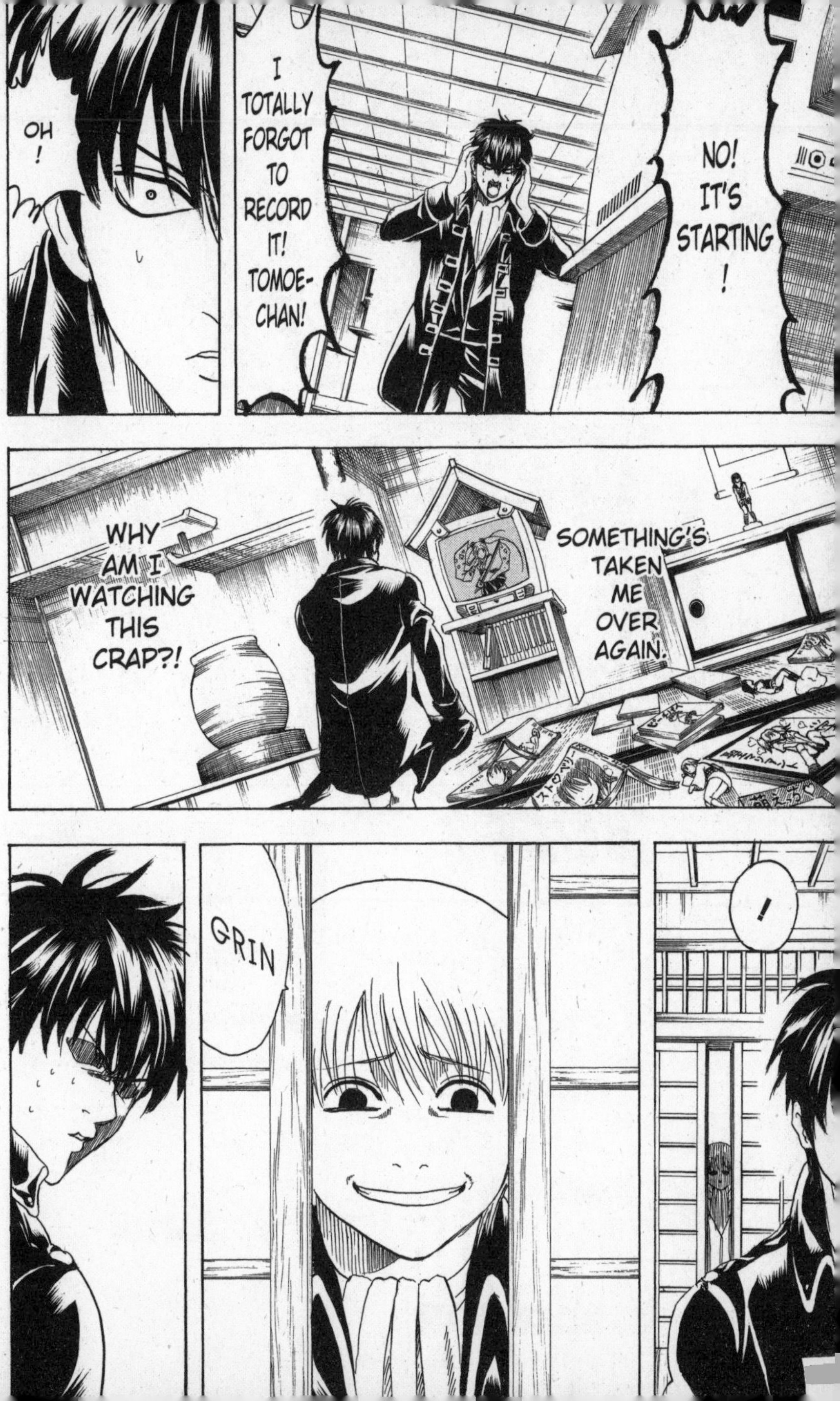
NO! IT'S STARTING!
I TOTALLY FORGOT TO RECORD IT! TOMOE-CHAN!
OH!
SOMETHING'S TAKEN ME OVER AGAIN.
WHY AM I WATCHING THIS CRAP?!
!
GRIN

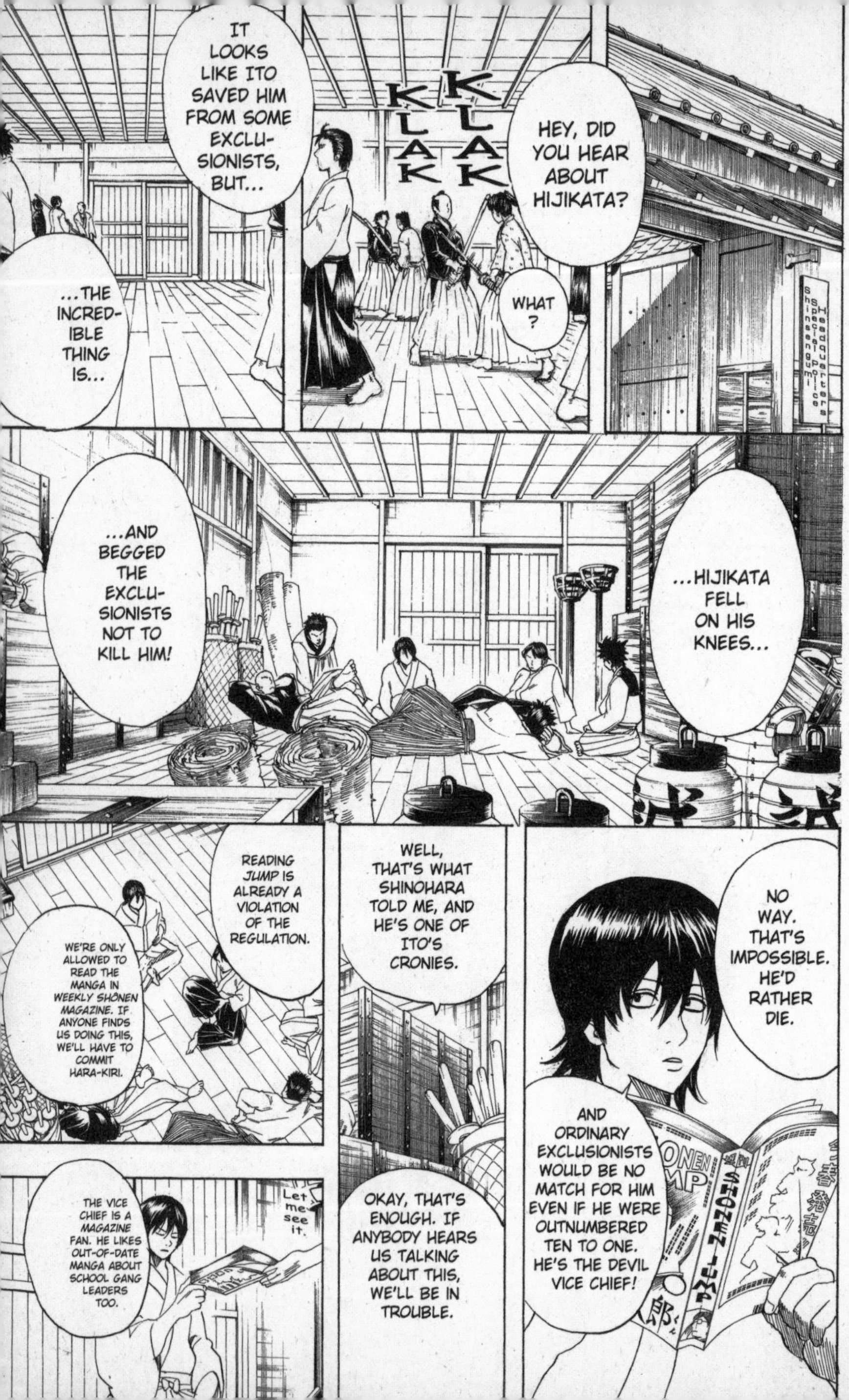
KLAK KLAK
HEY, DID YOU HEAR ABOUT HIJIKATA?
WHAT?
Shinsengumi Special Police Headquarters
IT LOOKS LIKE ITO SAVED HIM FROM SOME EXCLUSIONISTS, BUT...
...THE INCREDIBLE THING IS...
...HIJIKATA FELL ON HIS KNEES...
...AND BEGGED THE EXCLUSIONISTS NOT TO KILL HIM!
NO WAY. THAT'S IMPOSSIBLE. HE'D RATHER DIE.
AND ORDINARY EXCLUSIONISTS WOULD BE NO MATCH FOR HIM EVEN IF HE WERE OUTNUMBERED TEN TO ONE. HE'S THE DEVIL VICE CHIEF!
WELL, THAT'S WHAT SHINOHARA TOLD ME, AND HE'S ONE OF ITO'S CRONIES.
OKAY, THAT'S ENOUGH. IF ANYBODY HEARS US TALKING ABOUT THIS, WE'LL BE IN TROUBLE.
READING JUMP IS ALREADY A VIOLATION OF THE REGULATION.
WE'RE ONLY ALLOWED TO READ THE MANGA IN WEEKLY SHŌNEN MAGAZINE. IF ANYONE FINDS US DOING THIS, WE'LL HAVE TO COMMIT HARA-KIRI.
Let me see it.
THE VICE CHIEF IS A MAGAZINE FAN. HE LIKES OUT-OF-DATE MANGA ABOUT SCHOOL GANG LEADERS TOO.

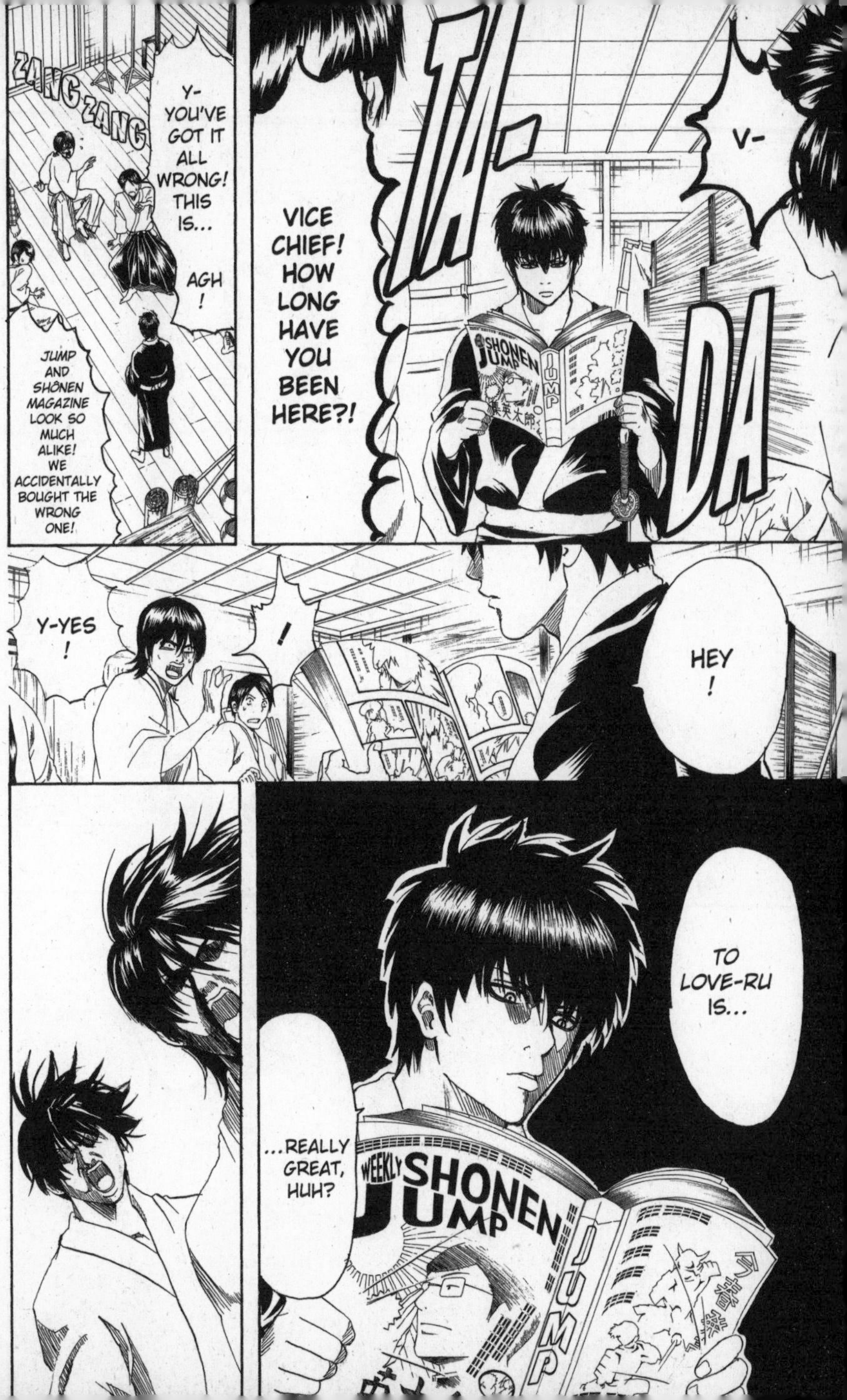
V-
TA-
DA
SHONEN JUMP
JUMP
VICE CHIEF! HOW LONG HAVE YOU BEEN HERE?!
ZANG ZANG
Y- YOU'VE GOT IT ALL WRONG! THIS IS...
AGH!
JUMP AND SHŌNEN MAGAZINE LOOK SO MUCH ALIKE! WE ACCIDENTALLY BOUGHT THE WRONG ONE!
HEY!
!
Y-YES!
TO LOVE-RU IS...
...REALLY GREAT, HUH?
WEEKLY SHONEN JUMP
JUMP

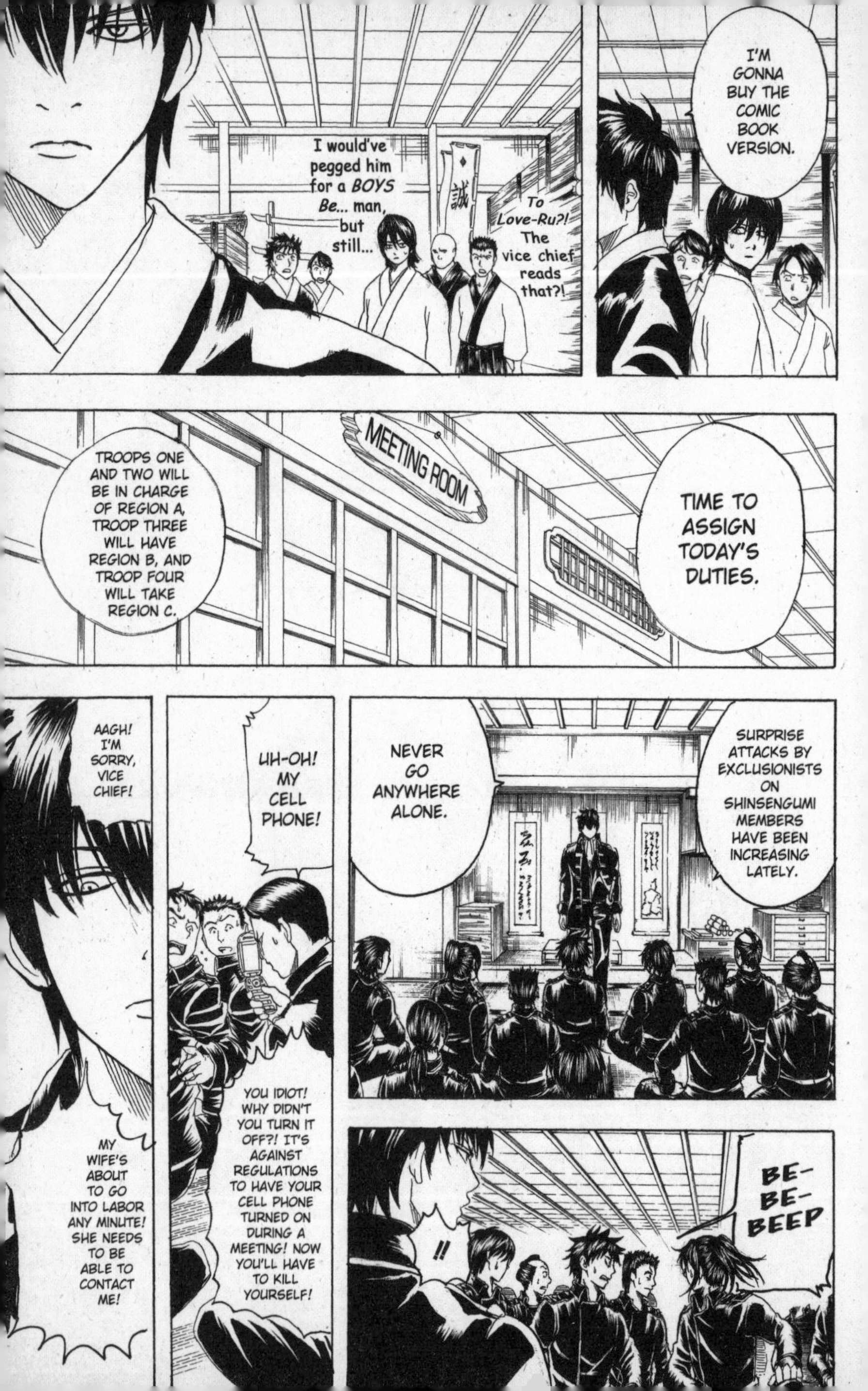
I'M GONNA BUY THE COMIC BOOK VERSION.
To Love-Ru?! The vice chief reads that?!
I would've pegged him for a *BOYS Be...* man, but still...
TIME TO ASSIGN TODAY'S DUTIES.
MEETING ROOM
TROOPS ONE AND TWO WILL BE IN CHARGE OF REGION A, TROOP THREE WILL HAVE REGION B, AND TROOP FOUR WILL TAKE REGION C.
SURPRISE ATTACKS BY EXCLUSIONISTS ON SHINSENGUMI MEMBERS HAVE BEEN INCREASING LATELY.
NEVER GO ANYWHERE ALONE.
BE-BE-BEEP
!!
UH-OH! MY CELL PHONE!
YOU IDIOT! WHY DIDN'T YOU TURN IT OFF?! IT'S AGAINST REGULATIONS TO HAVE YOUR CELL PHONE TURNED ON DURING A MEETING! NOW YOU'LL HAVE TO KILL YOURSELF!
AAGH! I'M SORRY, VICE CHIEF!
MY WIFE'S ABOUT TO GO INTO LABOR ANY MINUTE! SHE NEEDS TO BE ABLE TO CONTACT ME!

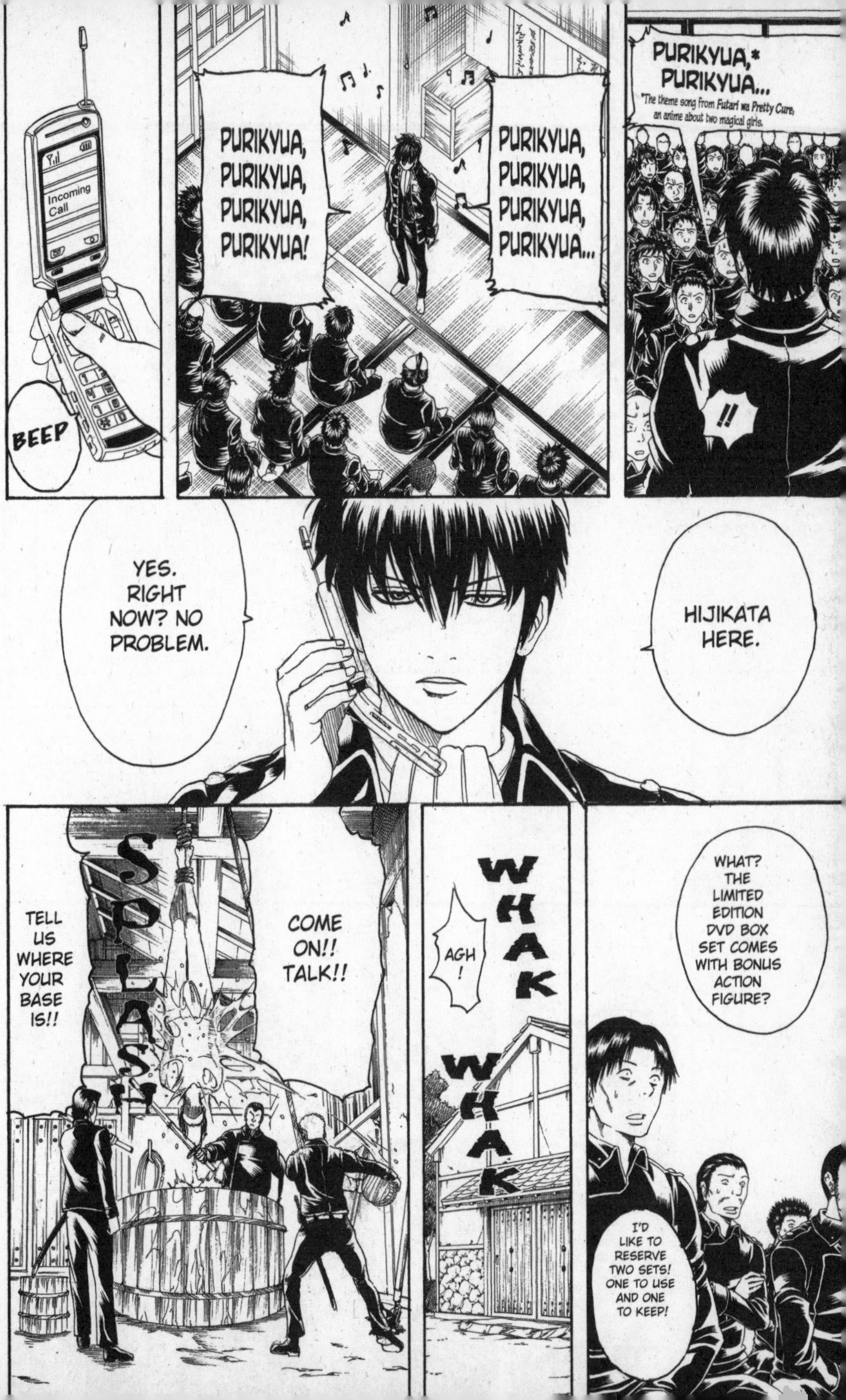
PURIKYUA,* PURIKYUA...
*The theme song from Futari wa Pretty Cure, an anime about two magical girls.
!!
PURIKYUA, PURIKYUA, PURIKYUA, PURIKYUA...
PURIKYUA, PURIKYUA, PURIKYUA, PURIKYUA!
Incoming Call
BEEP
HIJIKATA HERE.
YES. RIGHT NOW? NO PROBLEM.
WHAT? THE LIMITED EDITION DVD BOX SET COMES WITH BONUS ACTION FIGURE?
I'D LIKE TO RESERVE TWO SETS! ONE TO USE AND ONE TO KEEP!
WHAK
WHAK
AGH!
COME ON!! TALK!!
SPLASH
TELL US WHERE YOUR BASE IS!!

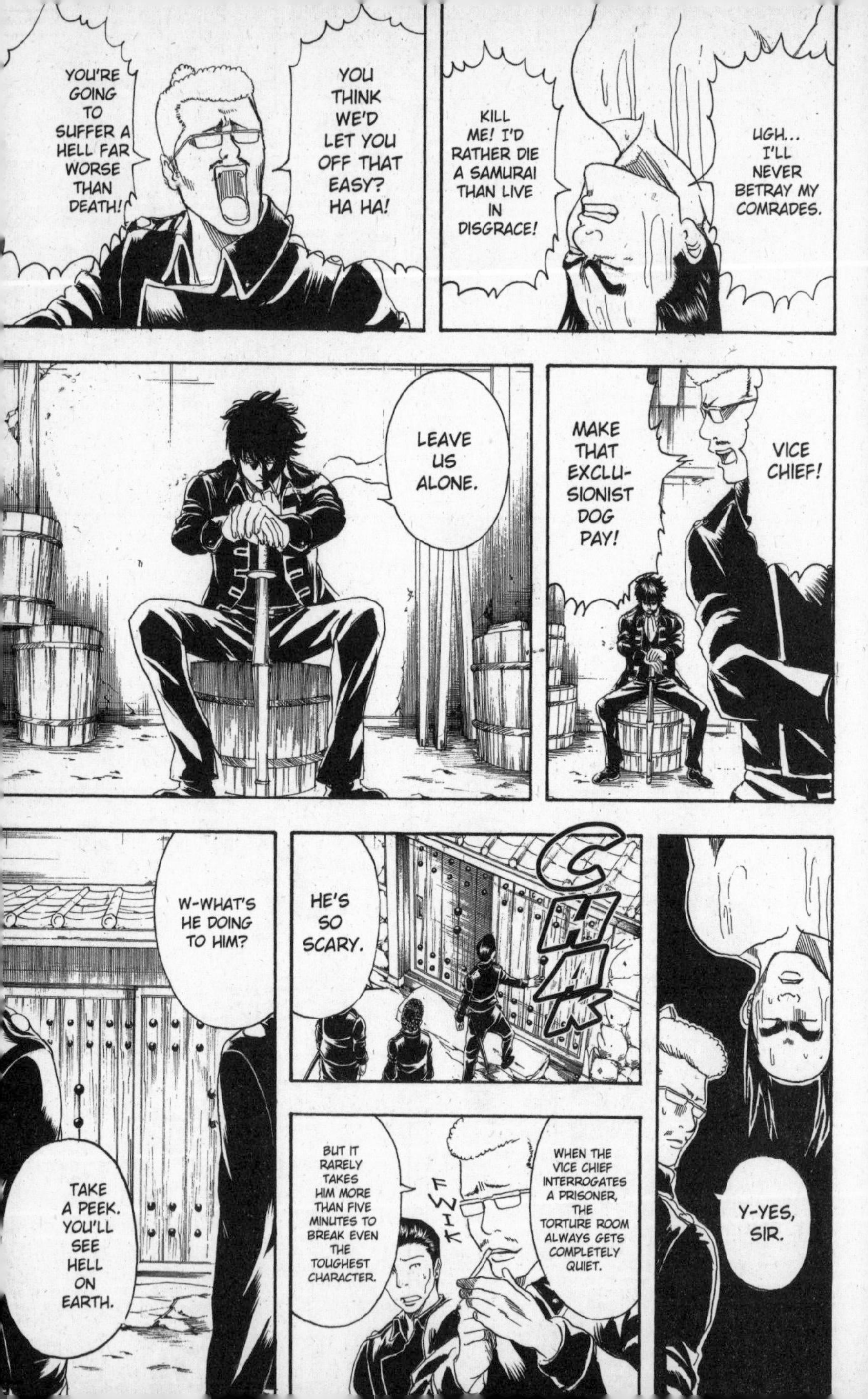
UGH... I'LL NEVER BETRAY MY COMRADES.
KILL ME! I'D RATHER DIE A SAMURAI THAN LIVE IN DISGRACE!
YOU THINK WE'D LET YOU OFF THAT EASY? HA HA!
YOU'RE GOING TO SUFFER A HELL FAR WORSE THAN DEATH!
VICE CHIEF!
MAKE THAT EXCLUSIONIST DOG PAY!
LEAVE US ALONE.
Y-YES, SIR.
CHAK
HE'S SO SCARY.
WHEN THE VICE CHIEF INTERROGATES A PRISONER, THE TORTURE ROOM ALWAYS GETS COMPLETELY QUIET.
FWIK
BUT IT RARELY TAKES HIM MORE THAN FIVE MINUTES TO BREAK EVEN THE TOUGHEST CHARACTER.
W-WHAT'S HE DOING TO HIM?
TAKE A PEEK. YOU'LL SEE HELL ON EARTH.

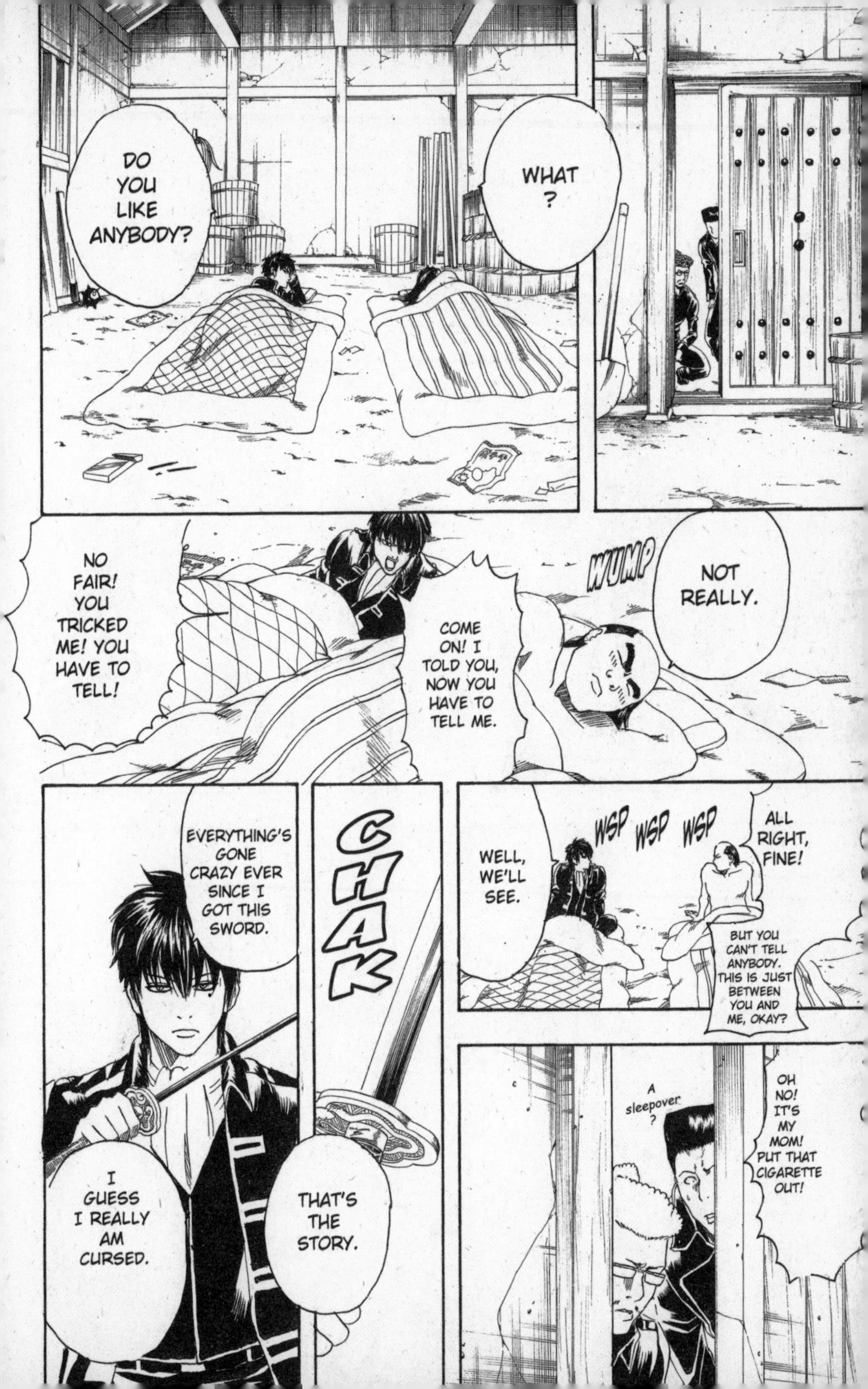
WHAT ?
DO YOU LIKE ANYBODY?
NOT REALLY.
WUMP
COME ON! I TOLD YOU, NOW YOU HAVE TO TELL ME.
NO FAIR! YOU TRICKED ME! YOU HAVE TO TELL!
ALL RIGHT, FINE!
WSP WSP WSP
WELL, WE'LL SEE.
BUT YOU CAN'T TELL ANYBODY. THIS IS JUST BETWEEN YOU AND ME, OKAY?
OH NO! IT'S MY MOM! PUT THAT CIGARETTE OUT!
A sleepover ?
CHAK
EVERYTHING'S GONE CRAZY EVER SINCE I GOT THIS SWORD.
THAT'S THE STORY.
I GUESS I REALLY AM CURSED.

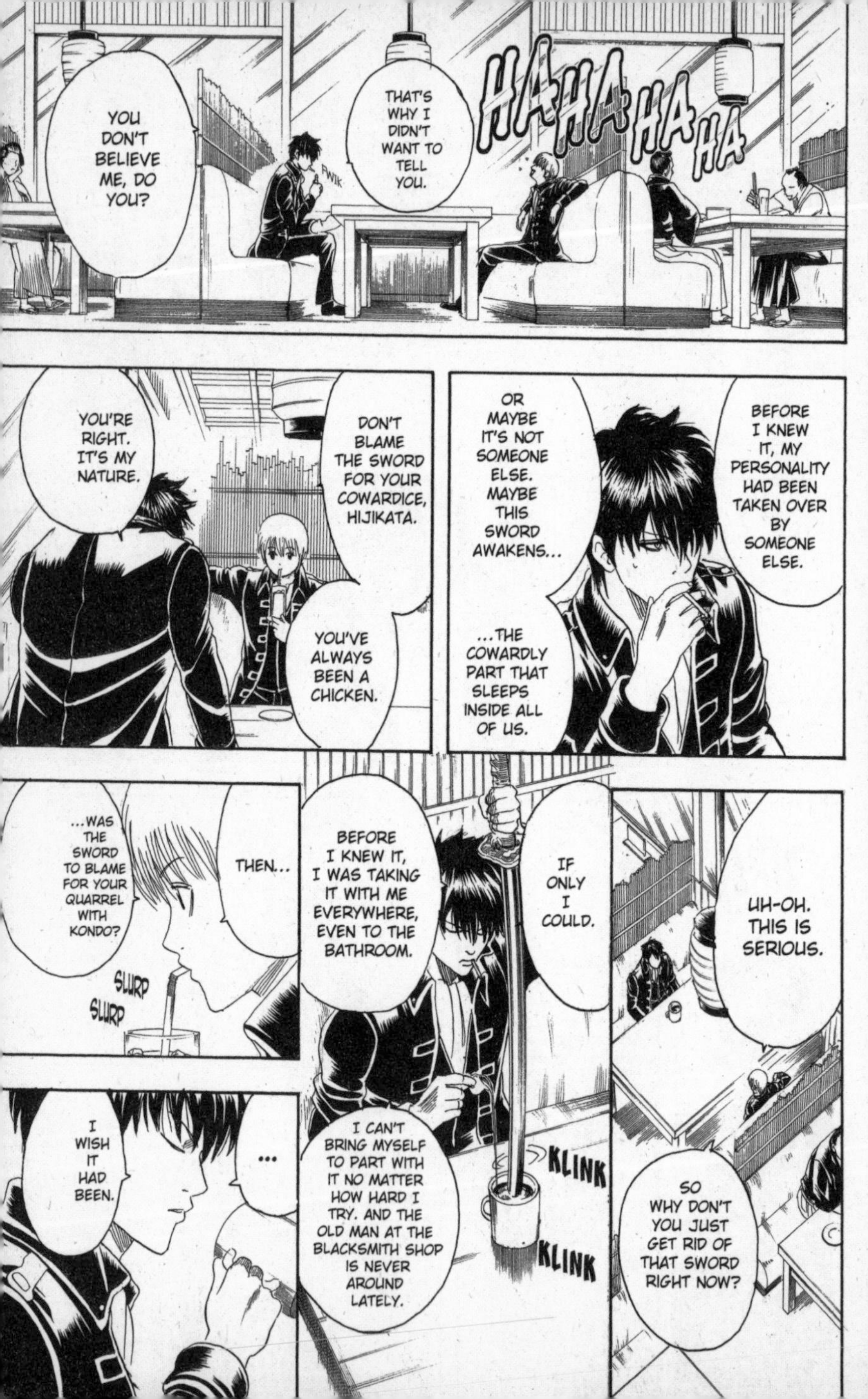
HAHAHAHA
THAT'S WHY I DIDN'T WANT TO TELL YOU.
FWIK
YOU DON'T BELIEVE ME, DO YOU?
BEFORE I KNEW IT, MY PERSONALITY HAD BEEN TAKEN OVER BY SOMEONE ELSE.
OR MAYBE IT'S NOT SOMEONE ELSE. MAYBE THIS SWORD AWAKENS...
...THE COWARDLY PART THAT SLEEPS INSIDE ALL OF US.
DON'T BLAME THE SWORD FOR YOUR COWARDICE, HIJIKATA.
YOU'VE ALWAYS BEEN A CHICKEN.
YOU'RE RIGHT. IT'S MY NATURE.
UH-OH. THIS IS SERIOUS.
SO WHY DON'T YOU JUST GET RID OF THAT SWORD RIGHT NOW?
IF ONLY I COULD.
BEFORE I KNEW IT, I WAS TAKING IT WITH ME EVERYWHERE, EVEN TO THE BATHROOM.
I CAN'T BRING MYSELF TO PART WITH IT NO MATTER HOW HARD I TRY. AND THE OLD MAN AT THE BLACKSMITH SHOP IS NEVER AROUND LATELY.
KLINK
KLINK
THEN...
...WAS THE SWORD TO BLAME FOR YOUR QUARREL WITH KONDO?
SLURP
SLURP
...
I WISH IT HAD BEEN.

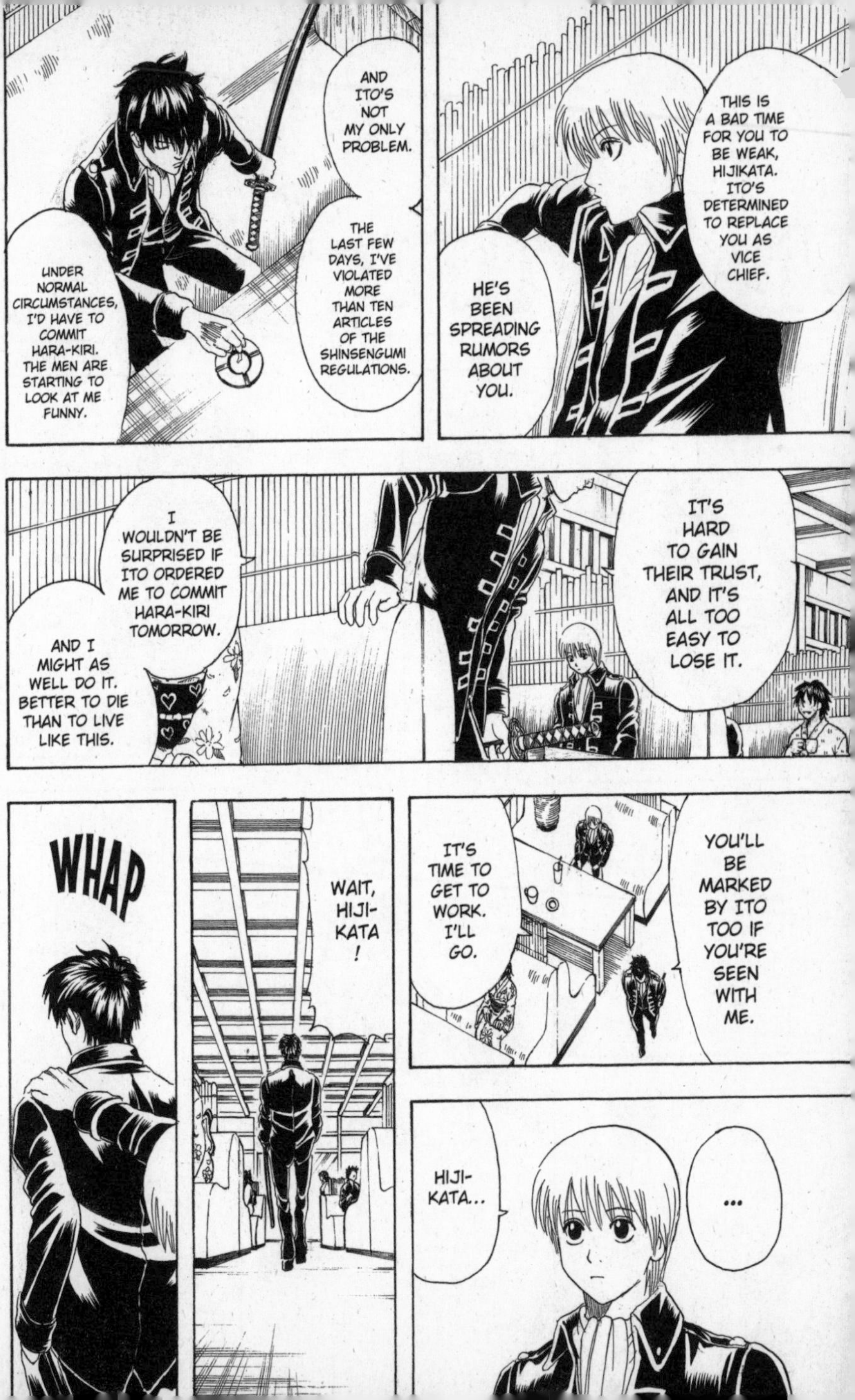
THIS IS A BAD TIME FOR YOU TO BE WEAK, HIJIKATA. ITO'S DETERMINED TO REPLACE YOU AS VICE CHIEF.
HE'S BEEN SPREADING RUMORS ABOUT YOU.
AND ITO'S NOT MY ONLY PROBLEM.
THE LAST FEW DAYS, I'VE VIOLATED MORE THAN TEN ARTICLES OF THE SHINSENGUMI REGULATIONS.
UNDER NORMAL CIRCUMSTANCES, I'D HAVE TO COMMIT HARA-KIRI. THE MEN ARE STARTING TO LOOK AT ME FUNNY.
IT'S HARD TO GAIN THEIR TRUST, AND IT'S ALL TOO EASY TO LOSE IT.
I WOULDN'T BE SURPRISED IF ITO ORDERED ME TO COMMIT HARA-KIRI TOMORROW.
AND I MIGHT AS WELL DO IT. BETTER TO DIE THAN TO LIVE LIKE THIS.
YOU'LL BE MARKED BY ITO TOO IF YOU'RE SEEN WITH ME.
IT'S TIME TO GET TO WORK. I'LL GO.
...
HIJI-KATA...
WAIT, HIJI-KATA!
WHAP

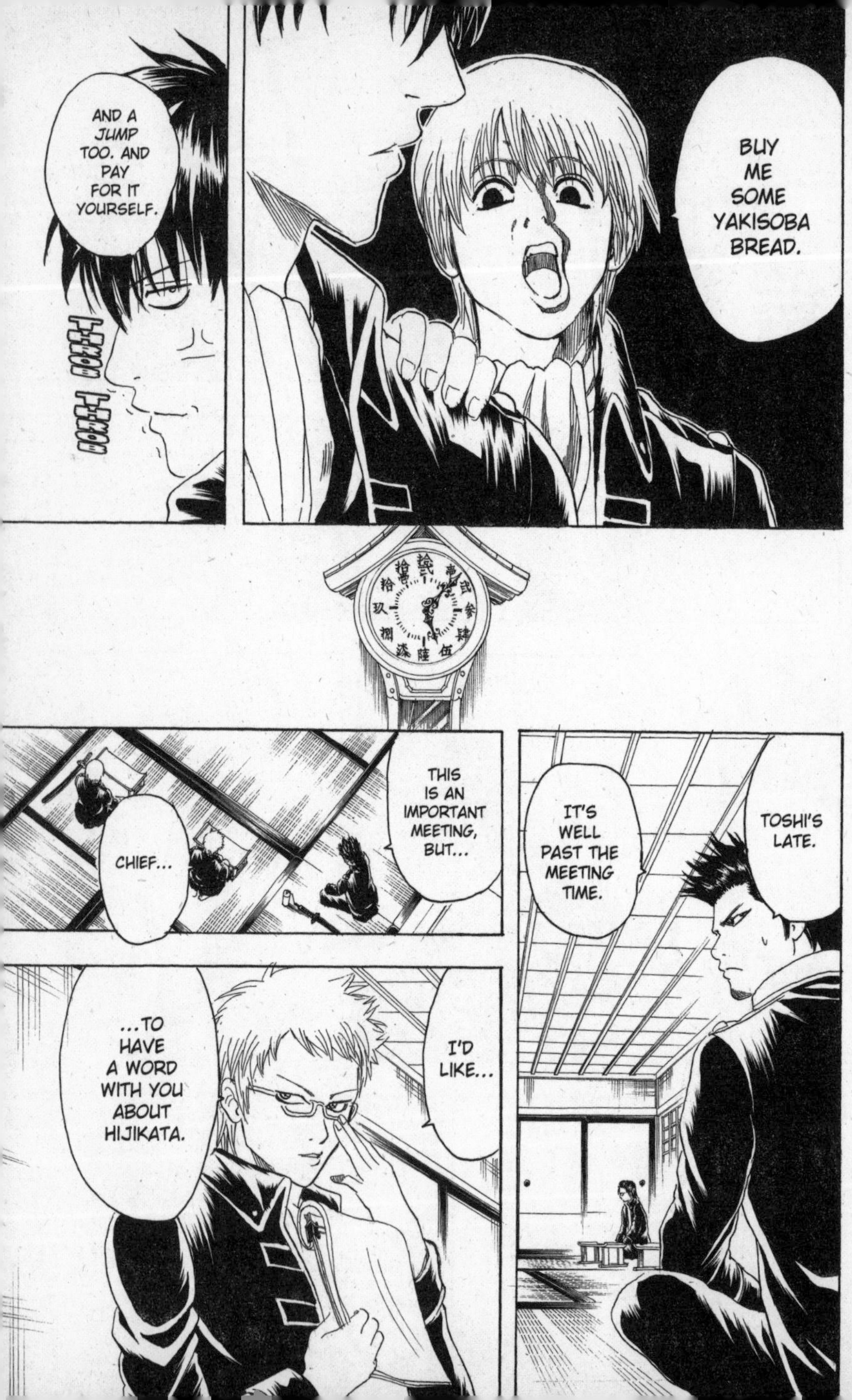
BUY ME SOME YAKISOBA BREAD.
AND A JUMP TOO. AND PAY FOR IT YOURSELF.
TOSHI'S LATE.
IT'S WELL PAST THE MEETING TIME.
THIS IS AN IMPORTANT MEETING, BUT...
CHIEF...
I'D LIKE...
...TO HAVE A WORD WITH YOU ABOUT HIJIKATA.

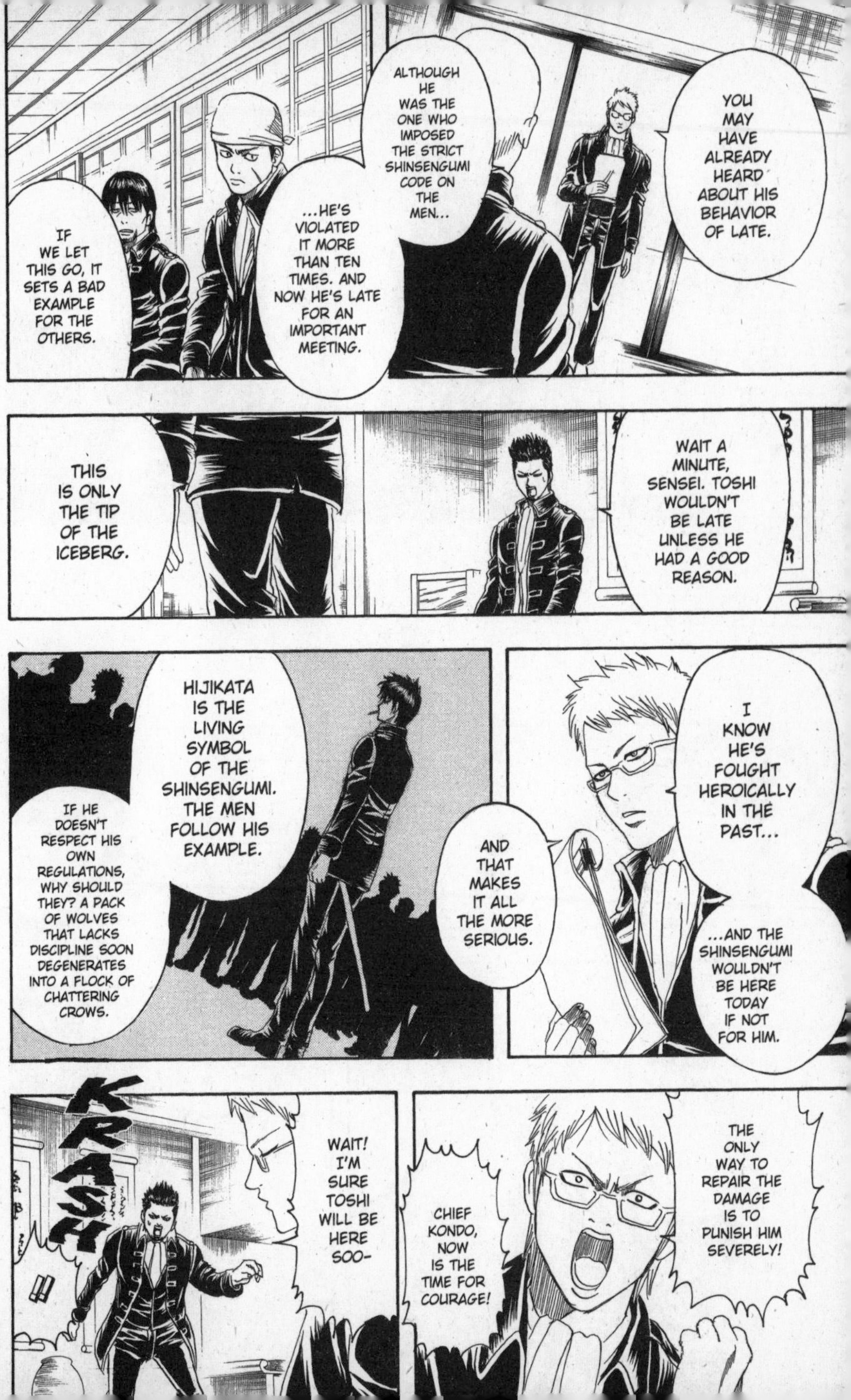
YOU MAY HAVE ALREADY HEARD ABOUT HIS BEHAVIOR OF LATE.
ALTHOUGH HE WAS THE ONE WHO IMPOSED THE STRICT SHINSENGUMI CODE ON THE MEN...
...HE'S VIOLATED IT MORE THAN TEN TIMES. AND NOW HE'S LATE FOR AN IMPORTANT MEETING.
IF WE LET THIS GO, IT SETS A BAD EXAMPLE FOR THE OTHERS.
WAIT A MINUTE, SENSEI. TOSHI WOULDN'T BE LATE UNLESS HE HAD A GOOD REASON.
THIS IS ONLY THE TIP OF THE ICEBERG.
I KNOW HE'S FOUGHT HEROICALLY IN THE PAST...
...AND THE SHINSENGUMI WOULDN'T BE HERE TODAY IF NOT FOR HIM.
AND THAT MAKES IT ALL THE MORE SERIOUS.
HIJIKATA IS THE LIVING SYMBOL OF THE SHINSENGUMI. THE MEN FOLLOW HIS EXAMPLE.
IF HE DOESN'T RESPECT HIS OWN REGULATIONS, WHY SHOULD THEY? A PACK OF WOLVES THAT LACKS DISCIPLINE SOON DEGENERATES INTO A FLOCK OF CHATTERING CROWS.
THE ONLY WAY TO REPAIR THE DAMAGE IS TO PUNISH HIM SEVERELY!
CHIEF KONDO, NOW IS THE TIME FOR COURAGE!
WAIT! I'M SURE TOSHI WILL BE HERE SOO-
KRASH

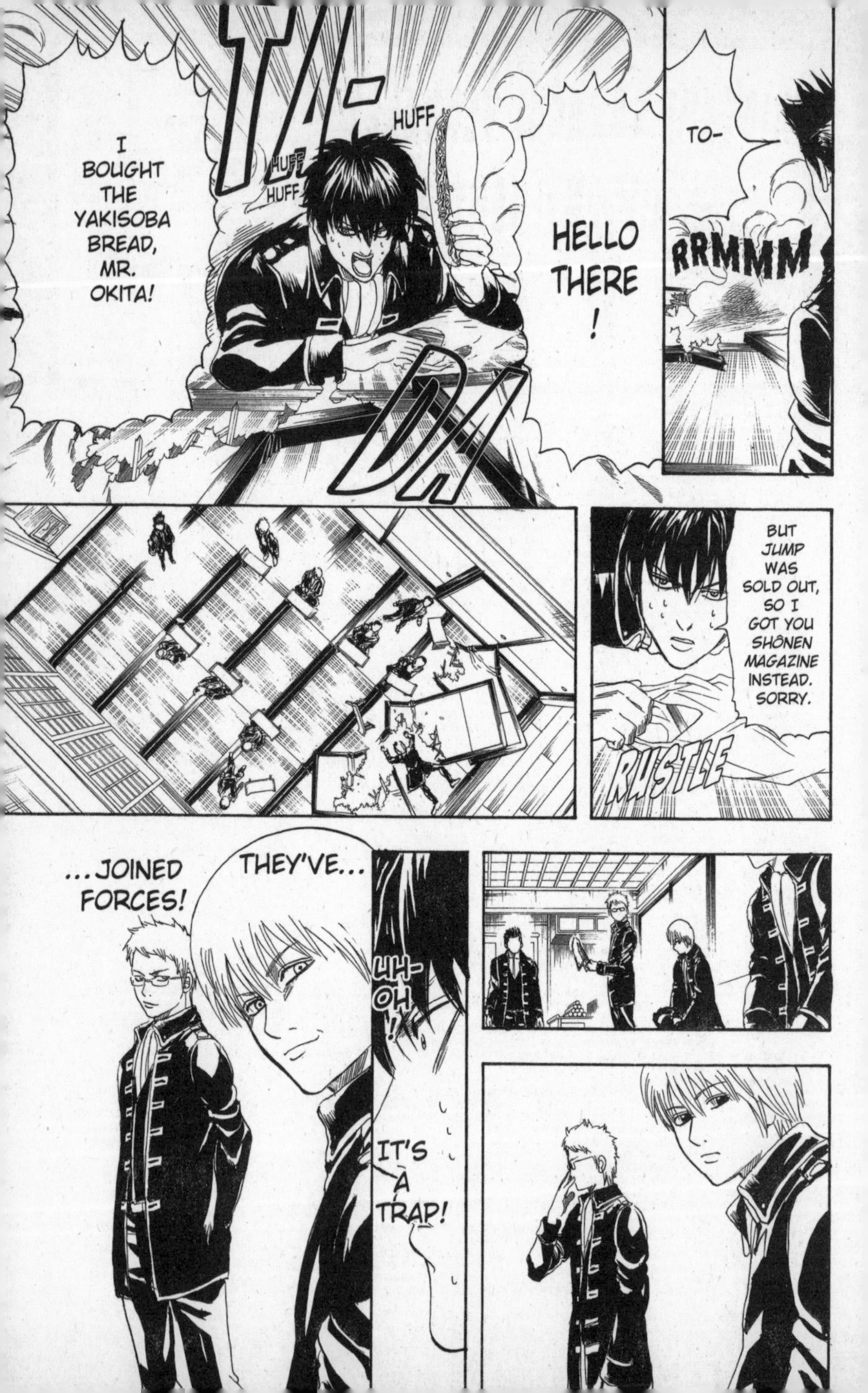
TO-
RRMMM
HELLO THERE!
TA-
HUFF
HUFF
HUFF
I BOUGHT THE YAKISOBA BREAD, MR. OKITA!
DA
BUT JUMP WAS SOLD OUT, SO I GOT YOU SHŌNEN MAGAZINE INSTEAD. SORRY.
RUSTLE
UH-OH!
IT'S A TRAP!
THEY'VE...
...JOINED FORCES!

HIDEAKI SORACHI VERBALLY INCONTINENT ROUGHLY

BECAUSE 30,000 CHARACTERS WASN'T ENOUGH

43,000 CHARACTER INTERVIEW

INTERVIEWEE: AUTHOR, HIDEAKI SORACHI

INTERVIEWER: MANAGING EDITOR, ONISHI

*THIS INTERVIEW IS TAKEN FROM THE EXTRA ISSUE OF *AKAMARU JUMP*, JUNE 15, 2007.

[HOW DO YOU SPEND YOUR HOLIDAYS?]

ONISHI: WHAT DO YOU DO ON YOUR DAYS OFF? DO YOU GO OUT DRINKING?
SORACHI: WHEN I FINISH MY MANUSCRIPT EARLY, I SOMETIMES GO OUT TO EAT WITH MY ASSISTANTS.
ONISHI: DO YOU HOLD YOUR ALCOHOL WELL?
SORACHI: I'M AVERAGE, I GUESS. I DON'T DRINK TOO MUCH.
ONISHI: SO YOU DON'T LIKE IT OR HATE IT?
SORACHI: I JUST LIKE THE FEELING I GET WHEN I'M DRUNK, NOT THE TASTE OF IT.
ONISHI: WHAT DO YOU DRINK?
SORACHI: I DON'T HAVE ANY SPECIFIC PREFERENCE IN PARTICULAR.
ONISHI: SO YOU DRINK SOMETHING DIFFERENT EACH TIME?
SORACHI: I START OFF WITH A BEER, AND THEN I TAKE OFF FROM THERE.
ONISHI: I GUESS THAT IS AVERAGE. (LAUGH)
SORACHI: WHAT DO YOU MEAN? (LAUGH) WHY ARE YOU SURPRISED?
ONISHI: YOU HAVEN'T PLAYED ANY VIDEO GAMES RECENTLY, RIGHT?
SORACHI: WELL, THERE'S NOTHING I REALLY LIKE RIGHT NOW.
ONISHI: DO YOU HAVE ANY GAMES THAT YOU'VE BEATEN THESE PAST FEW YEARS?
SORACHI: YOU'RE GOING TO PUT THAT IN PRINT?
ONISHI: I WILL IF I CAN. JUST TELL ME ANY GAME.
SORACHI: I DON'T WANT SOMETHING LIKE THAT IN PRINT.
ONISHI: COME ON.
SORACHI: LET'S NOT DO THE INTERVIEW LIKE THIS, MAN. (LAUGH)
ONISHI: NO.
SORACHI: HUH?
ONISHI: THAT'S NOT THE WAY IT'S GOING TO GO.
SORACHI: BUT YOU DON'T KNOW HOW PEOPLE WILL TAKE WHAT I SAY AFTER IT GOES INTO PRINT.
ONISHI: WE JUST NEED TO GO THROUGH TEXT FOR SOME EDITING BEFORE IT'S FINAL.
SORACHI: OH. WAIT, REALLY?
ONISHI: YES. NOW TELL ME WHAT GAME.
SORACHI: TO BE HONEST, I HAVEN'T REALLY GOTTEN INTO ANY PARTICULAR GAME SINCE THE SERIALIZATION STARTED.
ONISHI: SO WHAT GAME DID YOU BEAT?
SORACHI: *YAKUZA*, I GUESS? (NOTE: JAPANESE TITLE IS *RYU GA GOTOKU*)
ONISHI: I KNEW YOU WERE PLAYING SOMETHING.
SORACHI: THAT WAS ABOUT A YEAR AGO. ONE YEAR, MAN. IT WAS LIKE AROUND THE TIME I ATE A BUG. (DURING THE PRODUCTION OF THE *GIN CHANNEL!*)
ONISHI: SO YOU DON'T PLAY A LOT OF RPGS?
SORACHI: I DO. A LOT.
ONISHI: LIKE *DRAGON QUEST* AND *FINAL FANTASY?*
SORACHI: I PLAYED *DQ*, BUT I DON'T REMEMBER ANYTHING ABOUT IT.
ONISHI: WHAT ABOUT *FF?*
SORACHI: I DON'T PLAY *FF*.
ONISHI: SO YOU'RE A *DQ* ZEALOT?
SORACHI: I JUST DON'T LIKE HOW THE MAIN CHARACTERS START RAMBLING ON LIKE THEY DO IN *FF*.
ONISHI: SO IT'S HARD TO IMMERSE YOURSELF IN THAT WORLD?
SORACHI: I'M THE KIND OF PERSON THAT NAMES MY OWN HEROES IN THE GAME.

[THE REASON YOU WANTED TO BECOME A COMIC AUTHOR]

ONISHI: WAS YOUR BLOOD TYPE AB?
SORACHI: WELL, YOU CAN'T DRAW COMICS UNLESS YOU'RE SELF-CENTERED. (NOTE: PEOPLE OF CERTAIN BLOOD TYPES ARE STEREOTYPED TO HAVE CERTAIN PERSONALITY TRAITS.)
ONISHI: YEAH. IF YOU FOLLOWED WHAT PEOPLE TOLD YOU, YOU'D JUST END UP BEING GULLIBLE. I GUESS YOU CAN ONLY CREATE SOMETHING OF VALUE WHEN YOU LOOK AT THINGS FROM A DIFFERENT POINT OF VIEW. WERE YOU SERIOUS ABOUT ACADEMICS WHEN YOU WERE IN SCHOOL?
SORACHI: I WAS. I WENT TO HIGH SCHOOL AND STUDIED FOR MY COLLEGE ENTRANCE EXAMS TOO.
ONISHI: OH, YOU DID?
SORACHI: YOU THOUGHT I DIDN'T?
ONISHI: I MEANT, DIDN'T YOU READ OR DRAW COMICS THEN?
SORACHI: I DIDN'T DRAW COMICS BACK THEN. THERE WAS A TIME I DREW ONE WHEN I WAS IN ELEMENTARY SCHOOL. MY DAD PROMPTLY MADE FUN OF ME. HE SAID SOMETHING LIKE, "WHAT THE HELL IS THIS?" I WAS JUST SHOCKED WHEN I HEARD THAT.
ONISHI: LIKE HE MADE FUN OF YOUR CHARACTERS' NAMES?
SORACHI: SOMETHING LIKE THAT.
ONISHI: DID YOUR COMIC RESEMBLE *DRAGON BALL* OR SOMETHING?
SORACHI: IT WAS A FANTASY COMIC. I ONLY DREW FANTASY STUFF AT THE TIME.
ONISHI: AND YOU DREW IT WITH A PEN?
SORACHI: NO. I USED A PENCIL ON SOME NOTEBOOK PAPER. I KEPT IT HIDDEN, BUT HE FOUND IT...
ONISHI: HOW OLD WERE YOU THEN?
SORACHI: I THINK I WAS IN THE THIRD OR FOURTH GRADE AT THAT TIME. ACTUALLY, I KEPT DRAWING EVEN WHEN I WAS IN HIGH SCHOOL. I DOODLED IN MY NOTEBOOK.
ONISHI: AND YOU NEVER THOUGHT ABOUT GETTING THEM PUBLISHED?
SORACHI: I THOUGHT TO MYSELF THAT IT WAS TOO LATE FOR ME TO DRAW COMICS FOR A LIVING. WHEN I WAS SMALL, I TALKED TO MY FOLKS ABOUT BECOMING A COMIC AUTHOR. THEY TOLD ME THAT I COULDN'T BE ONE UNLESS I WAS SMART. YOU KNOW HOW PARENTS ALWAYS SAY THAT SO THEY CAN GET YOU TO STUDY?
ONISHI: SO YOU GAVE UP?
SORACHI: WELL, I STILL WANTED TO DRAW COMICS, BUT I COULDN'T TELL MY...

CONTINUED ON PAGE 66

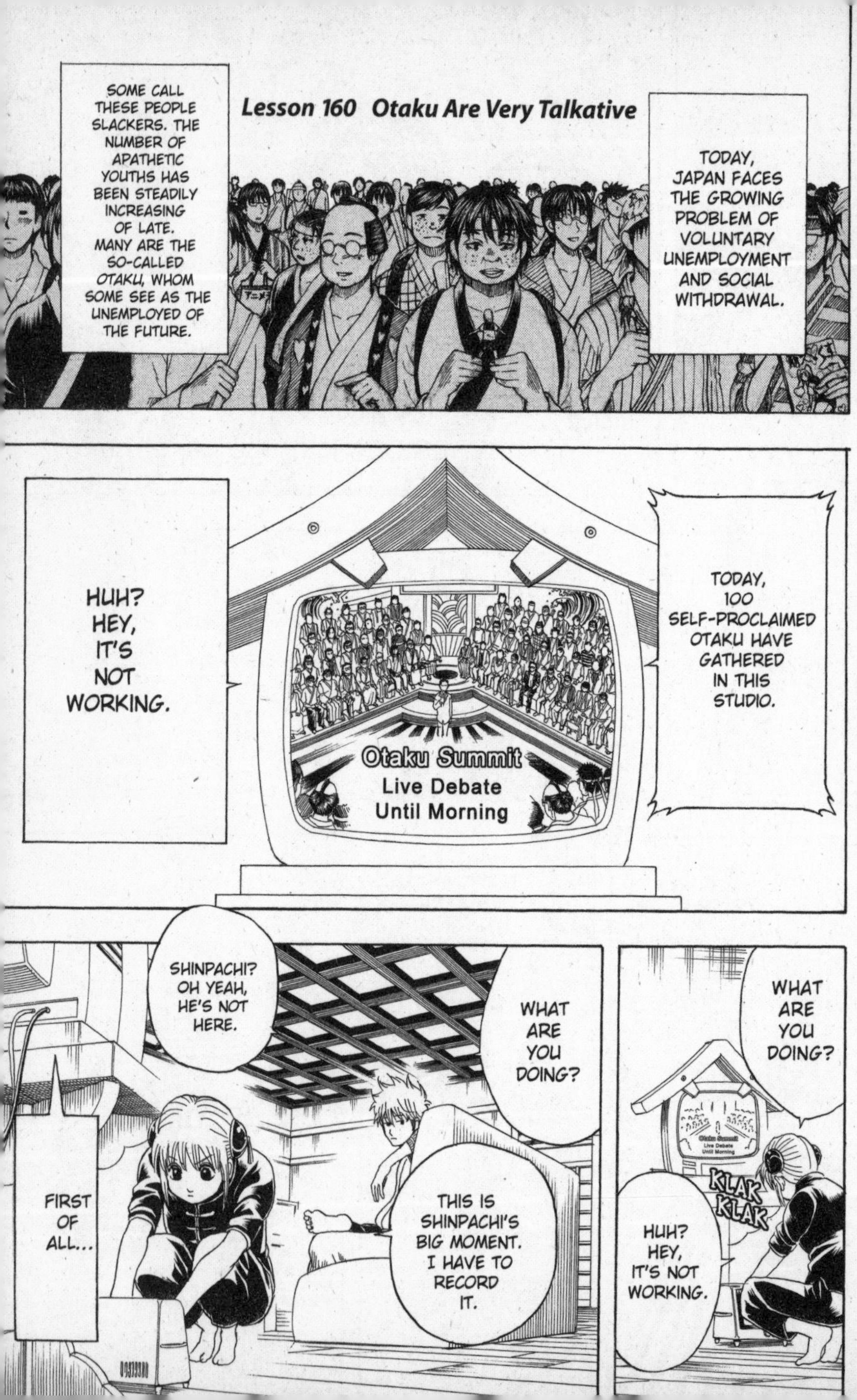
Lesson 160 Otaku Are Very Talkative
TODAY, JAPAN FACES THE GROWING PROBLEM OF VOLUNTARY UNEMPLOYMENT AND SOCIAL WITHDRAWAL.
SOME CALL THESE PEOPLE SLACKERS. THE NUMBER OF APATHETIC YOUTHS HAS BEEN STEADILY INCREASING OF LATE. MANY ARE THE SO-CALLED OTAKU, WHOM SOME SEE AS THE UNEMPLOYED OF THE FUTURE.
TODAY, 100 SELF-PROCLAIMED OTAKU HAVE GATHERED IN THIS STUDIO.
Otaku Summit
Live Debate Until Morning
HUH? HEY, IT'S NOT WORKING.
WHAT ARE YOU DOING?
KLAK KLAK
HUH? HEY, IT'S NOT WORKING.
WHAT ARE YOU DOING?
SHINPACHI? OH YEAH, HE'S NOT HERE.
THIS IS SHINPACHI'S BIG MOMENT. I HAVE TO RECORD IT.
FIRST OF ALL...

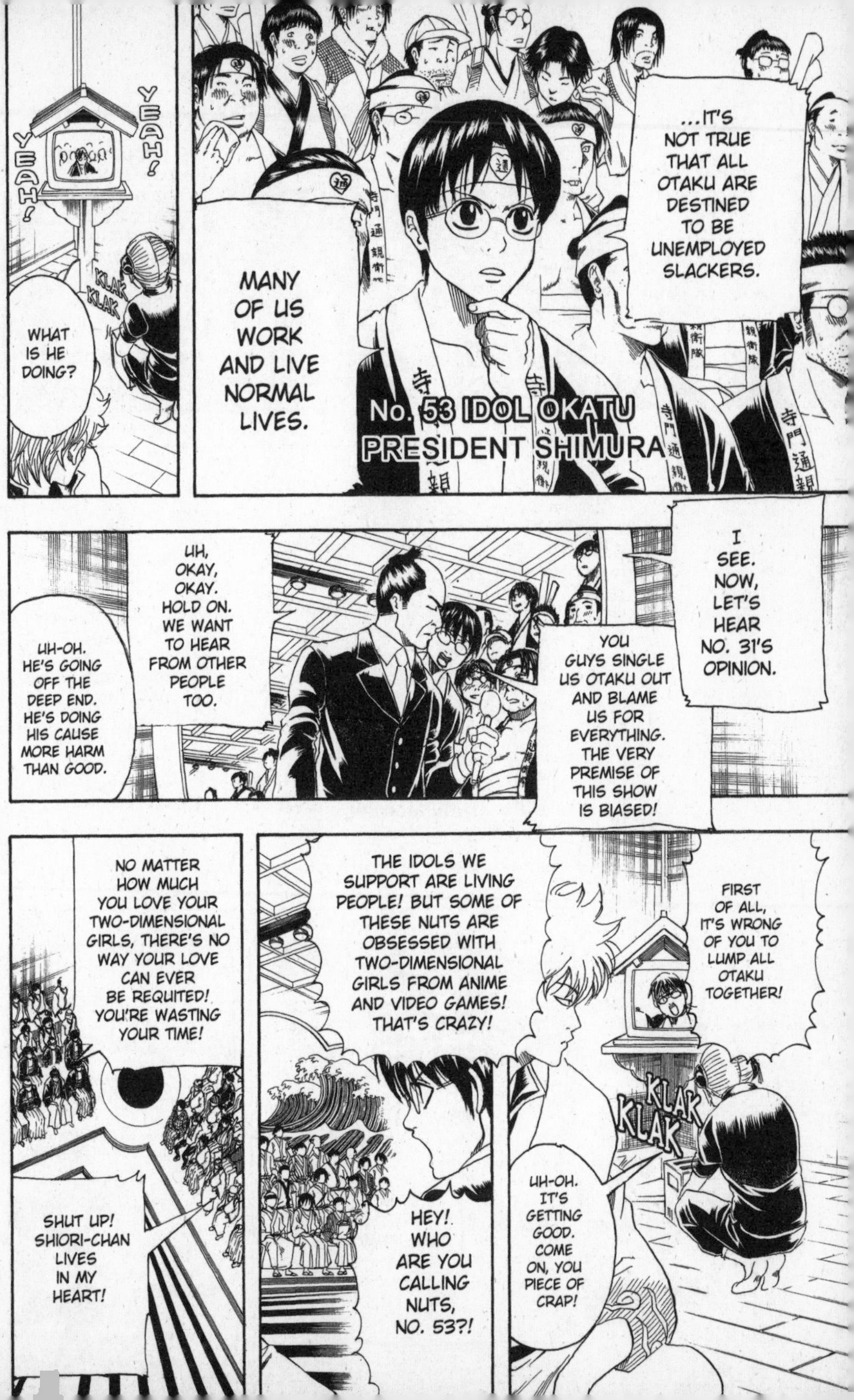
...IT'S NOT TRUE THAT ALL OTAKU ARE DESTINED TO BE UNEMPLOYED SLACKERS.
MANY OF US WORK AND LIVE NORMAL LIVES.
No. 53 IDOL OKATU PRESIDENT SHIMURA
YEAH!
YEAH!
KLAK KLAK
WHAT IS HE DOING?
I SEE. NOW, LET'S HEAR NO. 31'S OPINION.
YOU GUYS SINGLE US OTAKU OUT AND BLAME US FOR EVERYTHING. THE VERY PREMISE OF THIS SHOW IS BIASED!
UH, OKAY, OKAY. HOLD ON. WE WANT TO HEAR FROM OTHER PEOPLE TOO.
UH-OH. HE'S GOING OFF THE DEEP END. HE'S DOING HIS CAUSE MORE HARM THAN GOOD.
FIRST OF ALL, IT'S WRONG OF YOU TO LUMP ALL OTAKU TOGETHER!
KLAK KLAK
UH-OH. IT'S GETTING GOOD. COME ON, YOU PIECE OF CRAP!
THE IDOLS WE SUPPORT ARE LIVING PEOPLE! BUT SOME OF THESE NUTS ARE OBSESSED WITH TWO-DIMENSIONAL GIRLS FROM ANIME AND VIDEO GAMES! THAT'S CRAZY!
HEY! WHO ARE YOU CALLING NUTS, NO. 53?!
NO MATTER HOW MUCH YOU LOVE YOUR TWO-DIMENSIONAL GIRLS, THERE'S NO WAY YOUR LOVE CAN EVER BE REQUITED! YOU'RE WASTING YOUR TIME!
SHUT UP! SHIORI-CHAN LIVES IN MY HEART!

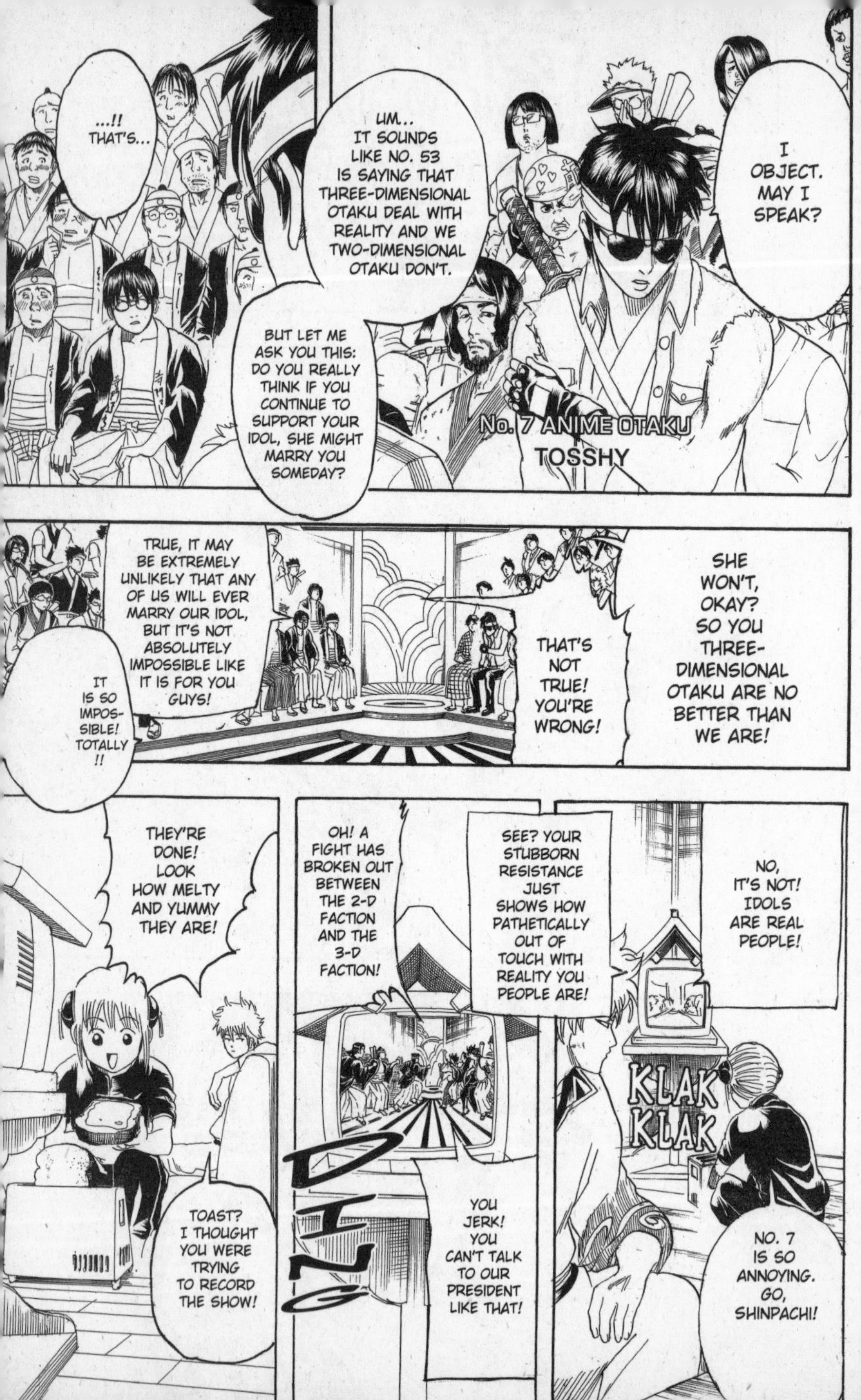
I OBJECT. MAY I SPEAK?
UM... IT SOUNDS LIKE NO. 53 IS SAYING THAT THREE-DIMENSIONAL OTAKU DEAL WITH REALITY AND WE TWO-DIMENSIONAL OTAKU DON'T.
BUT LET ME ASK YOU THIS: DO YOU REALLY THINK IF YOU CONTINUE TO SUPPORT YOUR IDOL, SHE MIGHT MARRY YOU SOMEDAY?
No. 7 ANIME OTAKU
TOSSHY
...!! THAT'S...
SHE WON'T, OKAY? SO YOU THREE-DIMENSIONAL OTAKU ARE NO BETTER THAN WE ARE!
THAT'S NOT TRUE! YOU'RE WRONG!
TRUE, IT MAY BE EXTREMELY UNLIKELY THAT ANY OF US WILL EVER MARRY OUR IDOL, BUT IT'S NOT ABSOLUTELY IMPOSSIBLE LIKE IT IS FOR YOU GUYS!
IT IS SO IMPOSSIBLE! TOTALLY !!
NO, IT'S NOT! IDOLS ARE REAL PEOPLE!
KLAK KLAK
NO. 7 IS SO ANNOYING. GO, SHINPACHI!
SEE? YOUR STUBBORN RESISTANCE JUST SHOWS HOW PATHETICALLY OUT OF TOUCH WITH REALITY YOU PEOPLE ARE!
OH! A FIGHT HAS BROKEN OUT BETWEEN THE 2-D FACTION AND THE 3-D FACTION!
YOU JERK! YOU CAN'T TALK TO OUR PRESIDENT LIKE THAT!
DING
THEY'RE DONE! LOOK HOW MELTY AND YUMMY THEY ARE!
TOAST? I THOUGHT YOU WERE TRYING TO RECORD THE SHOW!

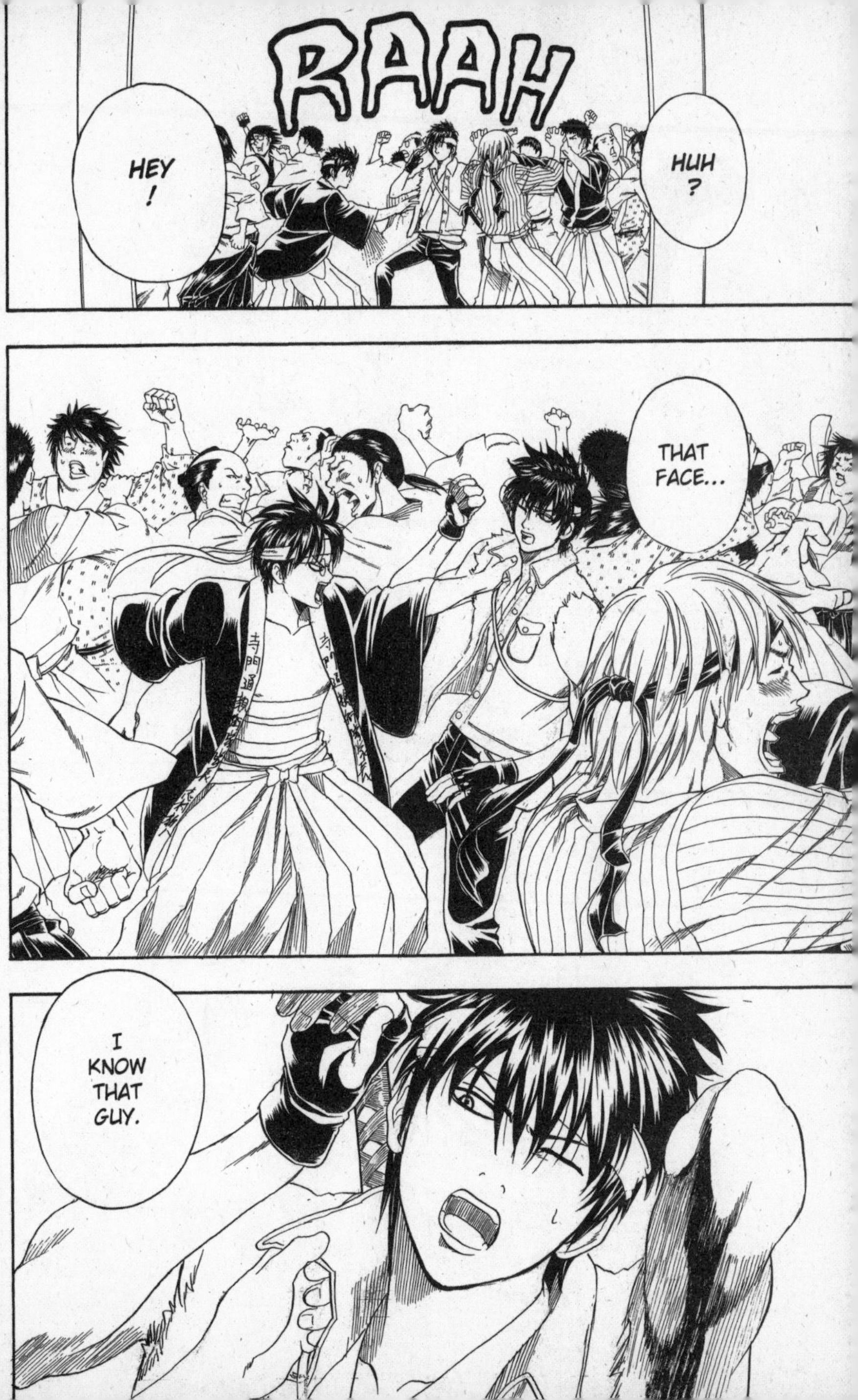
RAAH
HUH?
HEY!
THAT FACE...
I KNOW THAT GUY.

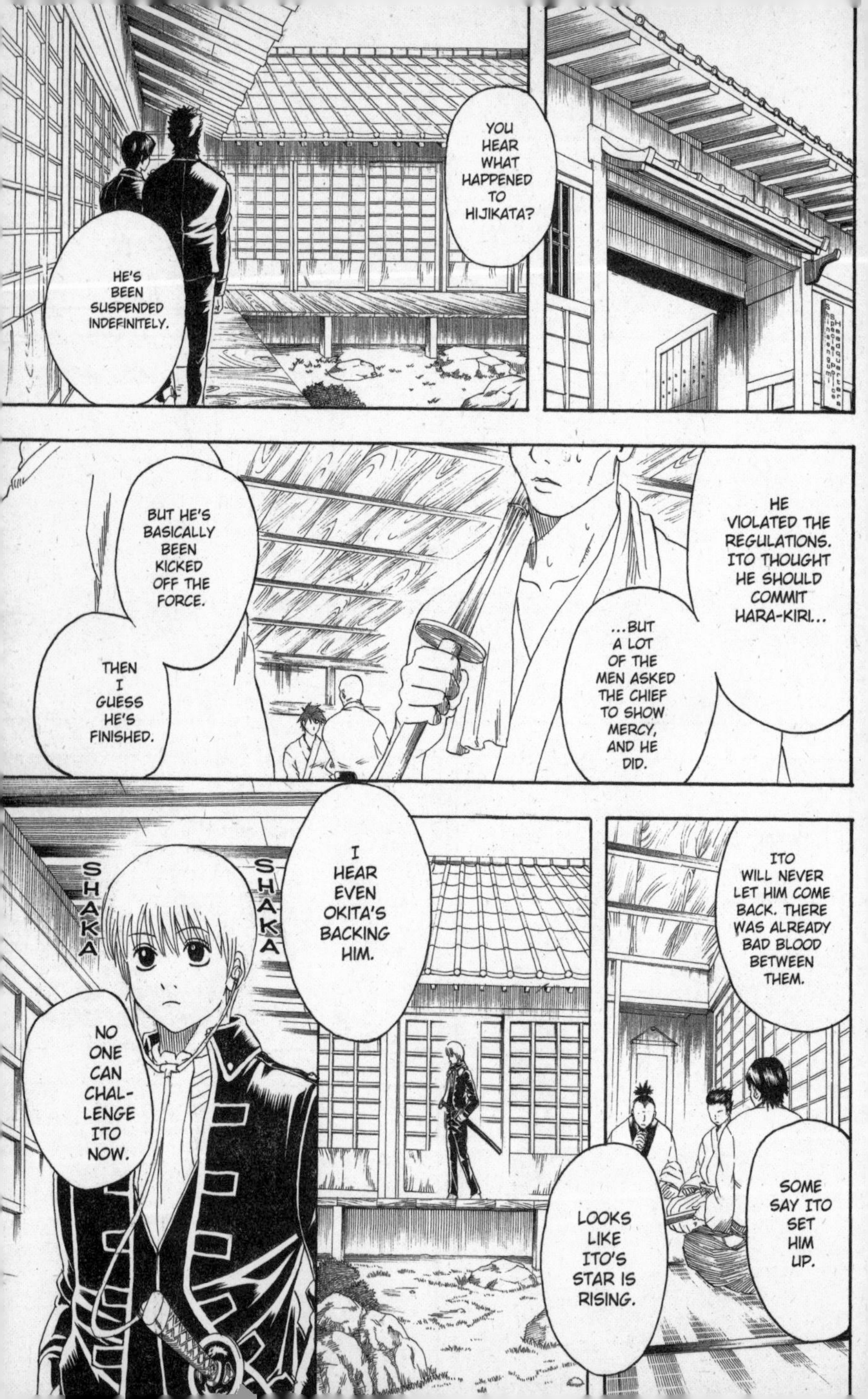
Headquarters Special Police Shinsengumi
YOU HEAR WHAT HAPPENED TO HIJIKATA?
HE'S BEEN SUSPENDED INDEFINITELY.
HE VIOLATED THE REGULATIONS. ITO THOUGHT HE SHOULD COMMIT HARA-KIRI...
...BUT A LOT OF THE MEN ASKED THE CHIEF TO SHOW MERCY, AND HE DID.
BUT HE'S BASICALLY BEEN KICKED OFF THE FORCE.
THEN I GUESS HE'S FINISHED.
ITO WILL NEVER LET HIM COME BACK. THERE WAS ALREADY BAD BLOOD BETWEEN THEM.
SOME SAY ITO SET HIM UP.
LOOKS LIKE ITO'S STAR IS RISING.
I HEAR EVEN OKITA'S BACKING HIM.
SHAKA
SHAKA
NO ONE CAN CHALLENGE ITO NOW.

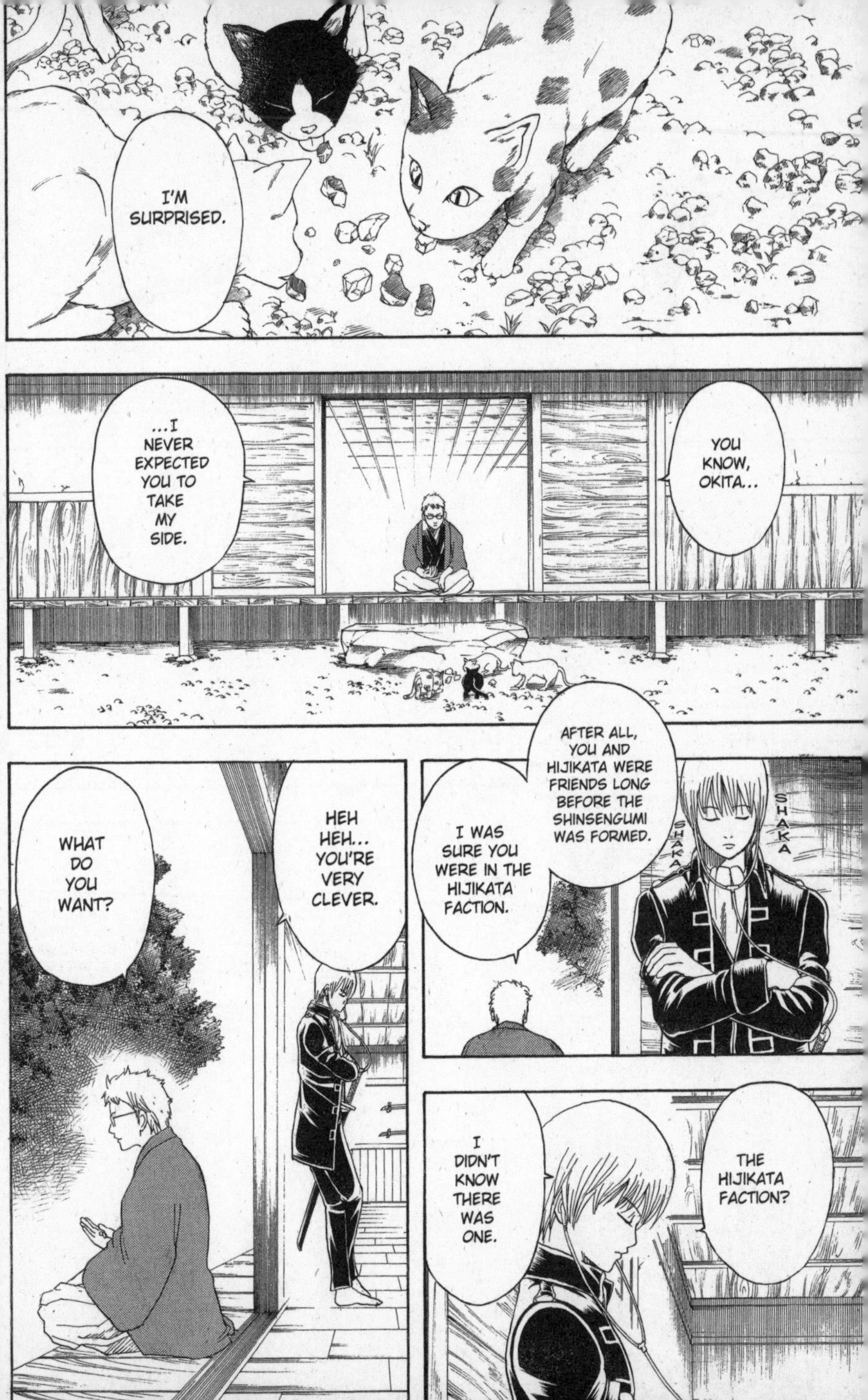
I'M SURPRISED.
YOU KNOW, OKITA...
...I NEVER EXPECTED YOU TO TAKE MY SIDE.
AFTER ALL, YOU AND HIJIKATA WERE FRIENDS LONG BEFORE THE SHINSENGUMI WAS FORMED.
SHAKA
SHAKA
I WAS SURE YOU WERE IN THE HIJIKATA FACTION.
THE HIJIKATA FACTION?
I DIDN'T KNOW THERE WAS ONE.
HEH HEH... YOU'RE VERY CLEVER.
WHAT DO YOU WANT?

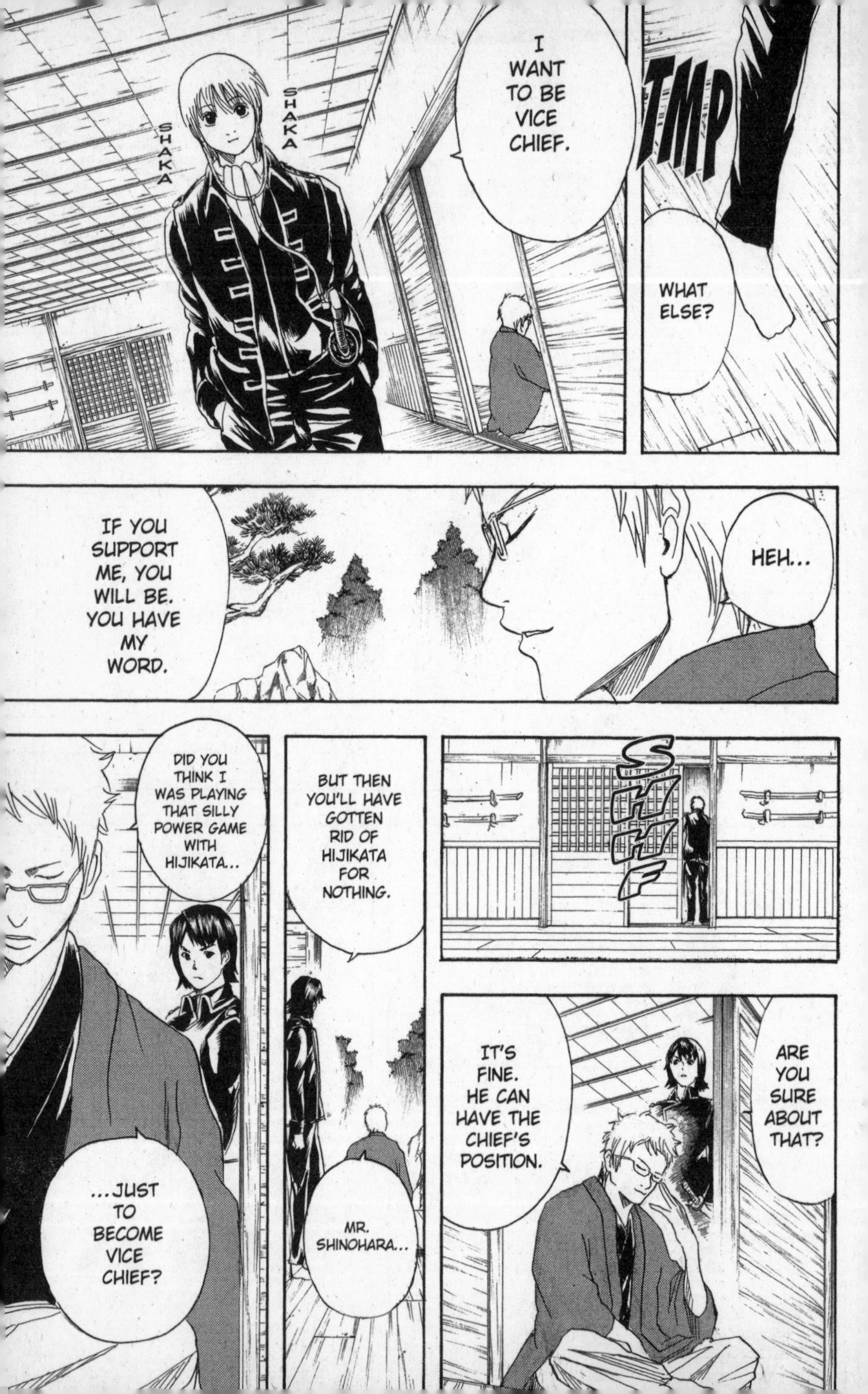
TMP
WHAT ELSE?
I WANT TO BE VICE CHIEF.
SHAKA
SHAKA
HEH...
IF YOU SUPPORT ME, YOU WILL BE. YOU HAVE MY WORD.
SHHF
ARE YOU SURE ABOUT THAT?
IT'S FINE. HE CAN HAVE THE CHIEF'S POSITION.
BUT THEN YOU'LL HAVE GOTTEN RID OF HIJIKATA FOR NOTHING.
MR. SHINOHARA...
DID YOU THINK I WAS PLAYING THAT SILLY POWER GAME WITH HIJIKATA...
...JUST TO BECOME VICE CHIEF?

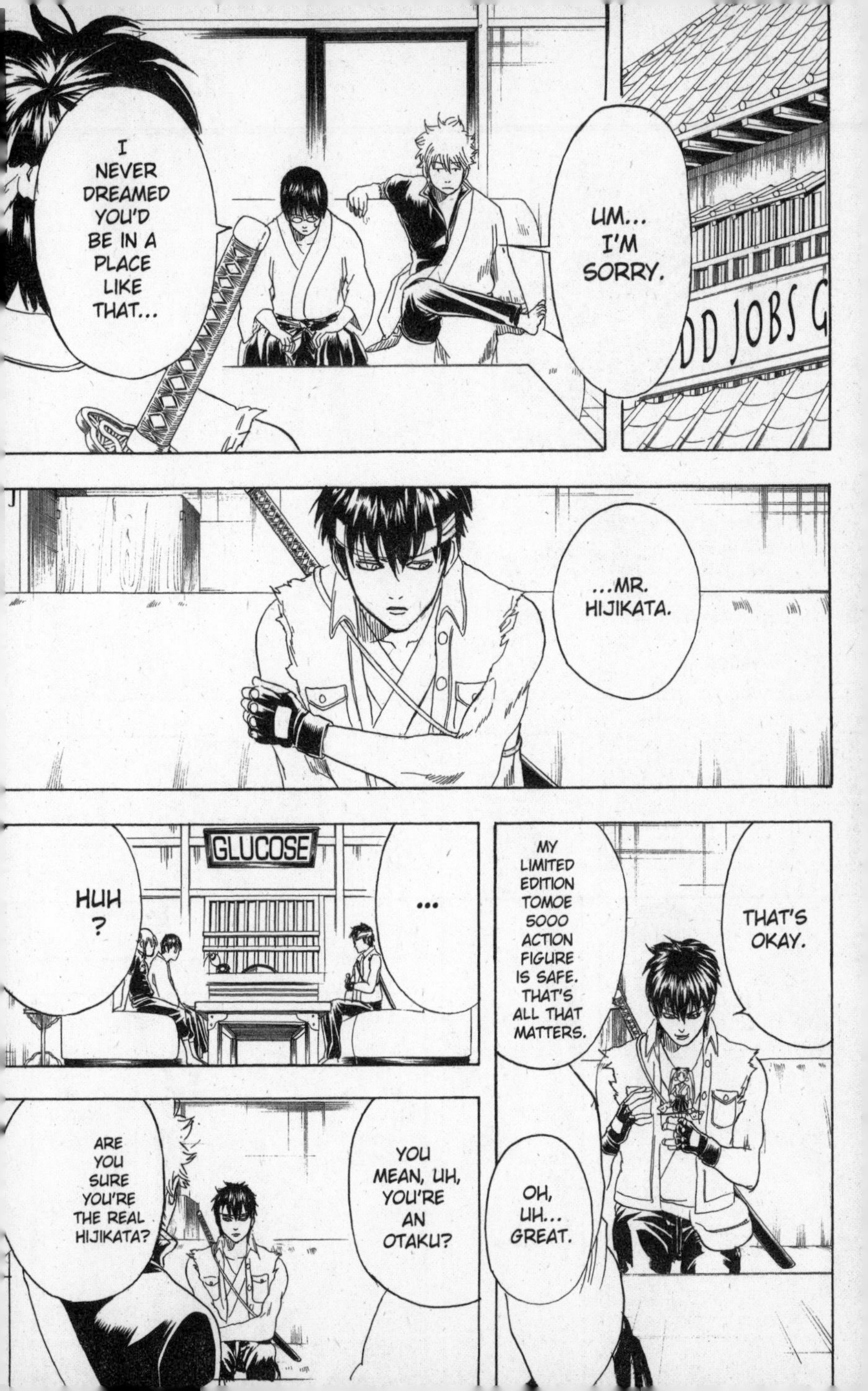
DD JOBS G
UM... I'M SORRY.
I NEVER DREAMED YOU'D BE IN A PLACE LIKE THAT...
...MR. HIJIKATA.
THAT'S OKAY.
MY LIMITED EDITION TOMOE 5000 ACTION FIGURE IS SAFE. THAT'S ALL THAT MATTERS.
OH, UH... GREAT.
GLUCOSE
...
HUH?
YOU MEAN, UH, YOU'RE AN OTAKU?
ARE YOU SURE YOU'RE THE REAL HIJIKATA?

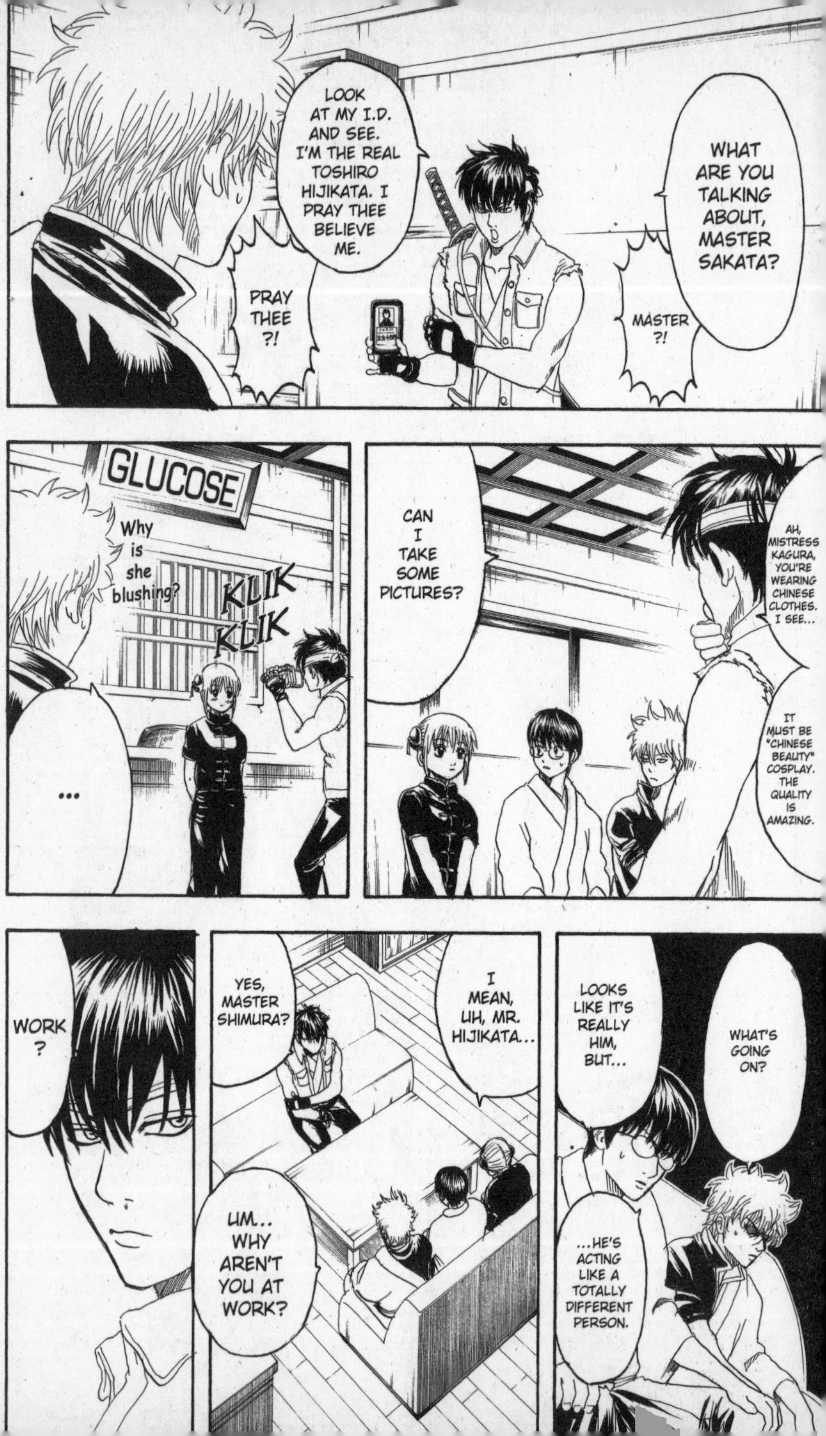

WHAT ARE YOU TALKING ABOUT, MASTER SAKATA?
MASTER ?!
LOOK AT MY I.D. AND SEE. I'M THE REAL TOSHIRO HIJIKATA. I PRAY THEE BELIEVE ME.
PRAY THEE ?!
AH, MISTRESS KAGURA, YOU'RE WEARING CHINESE CLOTHES. I SEE...
IT MUST BE "CHINESE BEAUTY" COSPLAY. THE QUALITY IS AMAZING.
CAN I TAKE SOME PICTURES?
GLUCOSE
KLIK KLIK
Why is she blushing?
...
WHAT'S GOING ON?
LOOKS LIKE IT'S REALLY HIM, BUT...
...HE'S ACTING LIKE A TOTALLY DIFFERENT PERSON.
I MEAN, UH, MR. HIJIKATA...
YES, MASTER SHIMURA?
UM... WHY AREN'T YOU AT WORK?
WORK ?

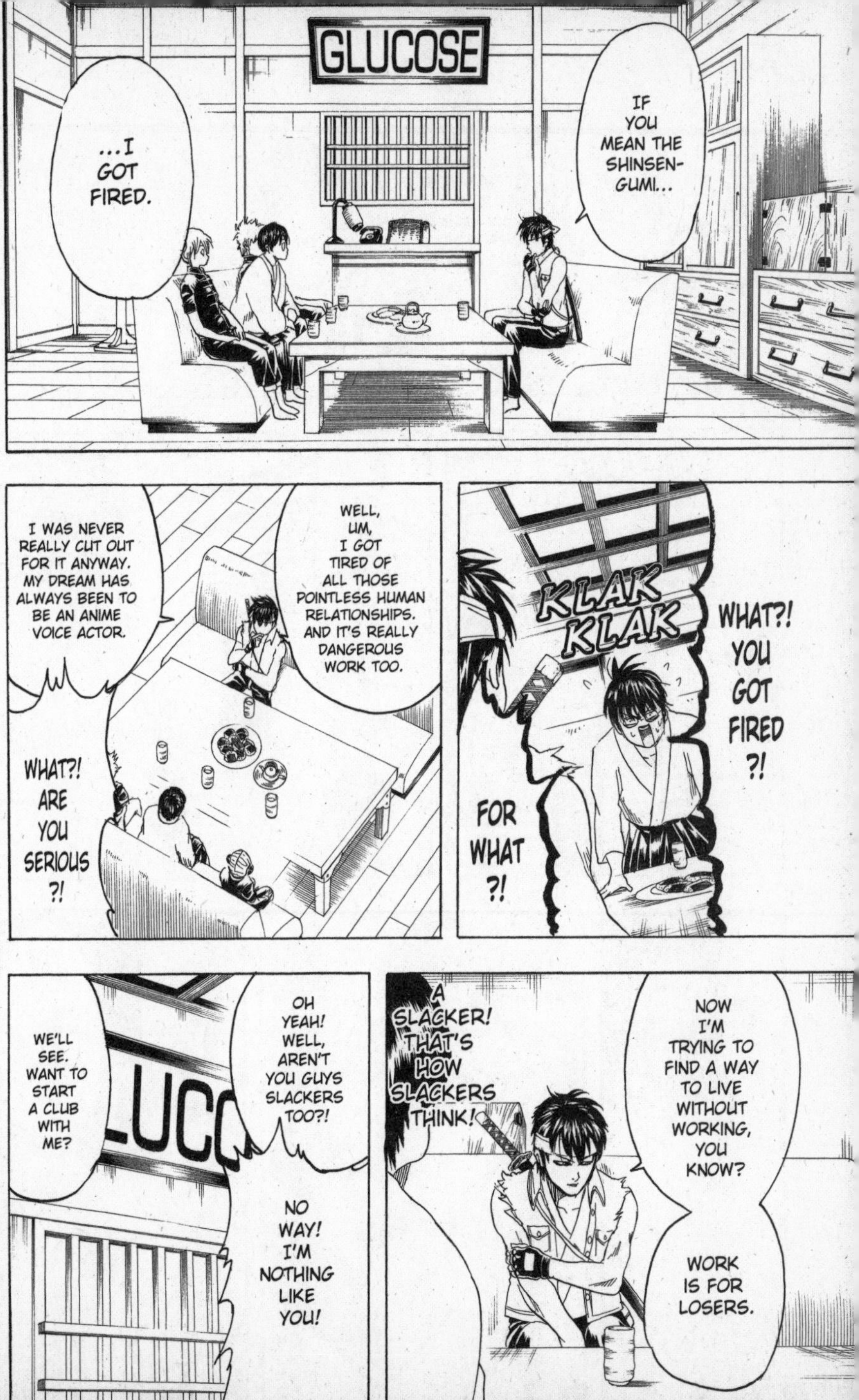
GLUCOSE
IF YOU MEAN THE SHINSEN-GUMI...
...I GOT FIRED.
KLAK KLAK
WHAT?! YOU GOT FIRED ?!
FOR WHAT ?!
WELL, UM, I GOT TIRED OF ALL THOSE POINTLESS HUMAN RELATIONSHIPS. AND IT'S REALLY DANGEROUS WORK TOO.
I WAS NEVER REALLY CUT OUT FOR IT ANYWAY. MY DREAM HAS ALWAYS BEEN TO BE AN ANIME VOICE ACTOR.
WHAT?! ARE YOU SERIOUS ?!
NOW I'M TRYING TO FIND A WAY TO LIVE WITHOUT WORKING, YOU KNOW?
A SLACKER! THAT'S HOW SLACKERS THINK!
WORK IS FOR LOSERS.
OH YEAH! WELL, AREN'T YOU GUYS SLACKERS TOO?!
WE'LL SEE. WANT TO START A CLUB WITH ME?
NO WAY! I'M NOTHING LIKE YOU!

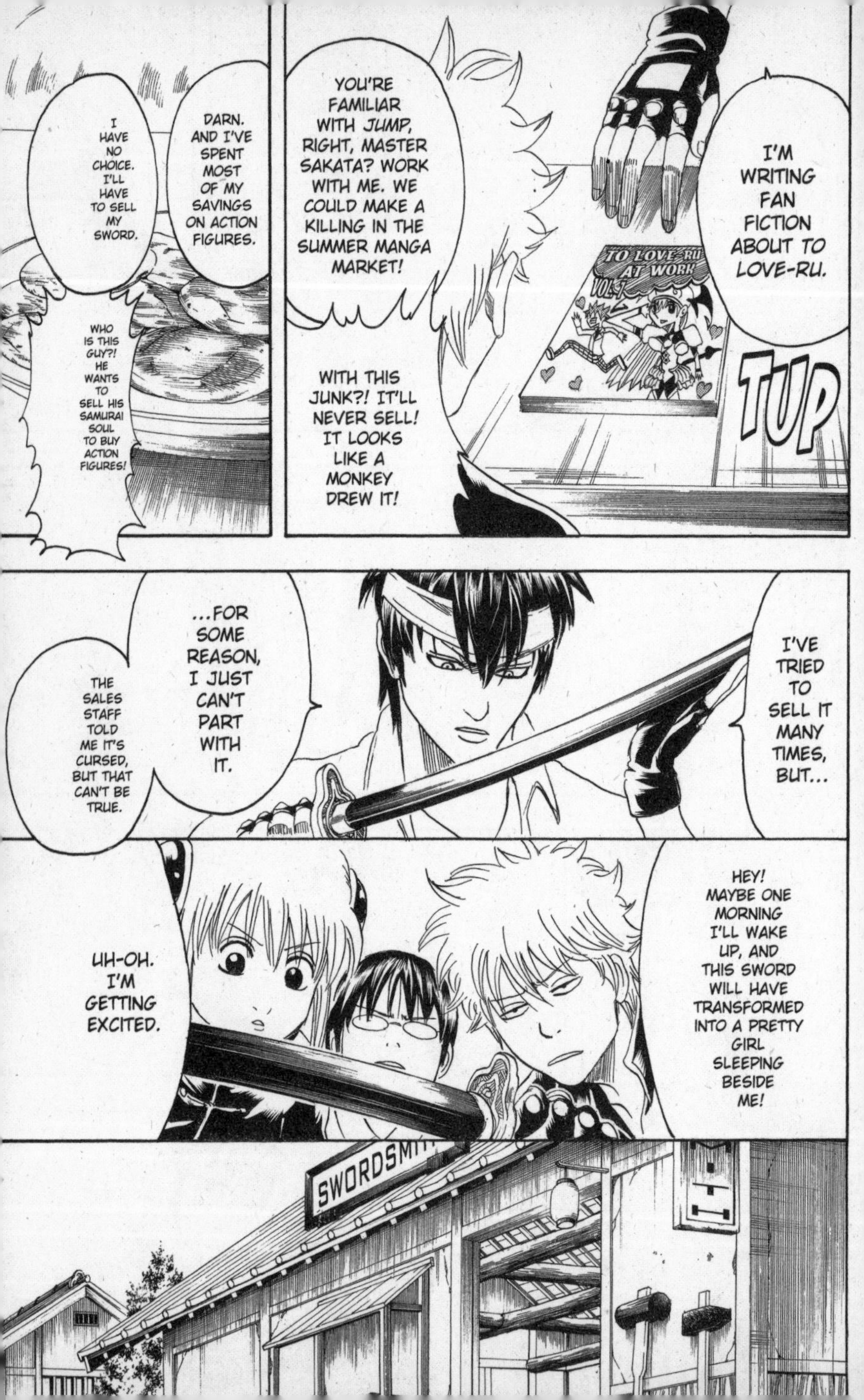
I'M WRITING FAN FICTION ABOUT TO LOVE-RU.
TO LOVE-RU AT WORK
TUP
YOU'RE FAMILIAR WITH JUMP, RIGHT, MASTER SAKATA? WORK WITH ME. WE COULD MAKE A KILLING IN THE SUMMER MANGA MARKET!
WITH THIS JUNK?! IT'LL NEVER SELL! IT LOOKS LIKE A MONKEY DREW IT!
DARN. AND I'VE SPENT MOST OF MY SAVINGS ON ACTION FIGURES.
I HAVE NO CHOICE. I'LL HAVE TO SELL MY SWORD.
WHO IS THIS GUY?! HE WANTS TO SELL HIS SAMURAI SOUL TO BUY ACTION FIGURES!
I'VE TRIED TO SELL IT MANY TIMES, BUT...
...FOR SOME REASON, I JUST CAN'T PART WITH IT.
THE SALES STAFF TOLD ME IT'S CURSED, BUT THAT CAN'T BE TRUE.
HEY! MAYBE ONE MORNING I'LL WAKE UP, AND THIS SWORD WILL HAVE TRANSFORMED INTO A PRETTY GIRL SLEEPING BESIDE ME!
UH-OH. I'M GETTING EXCITED.
SWORDSMI

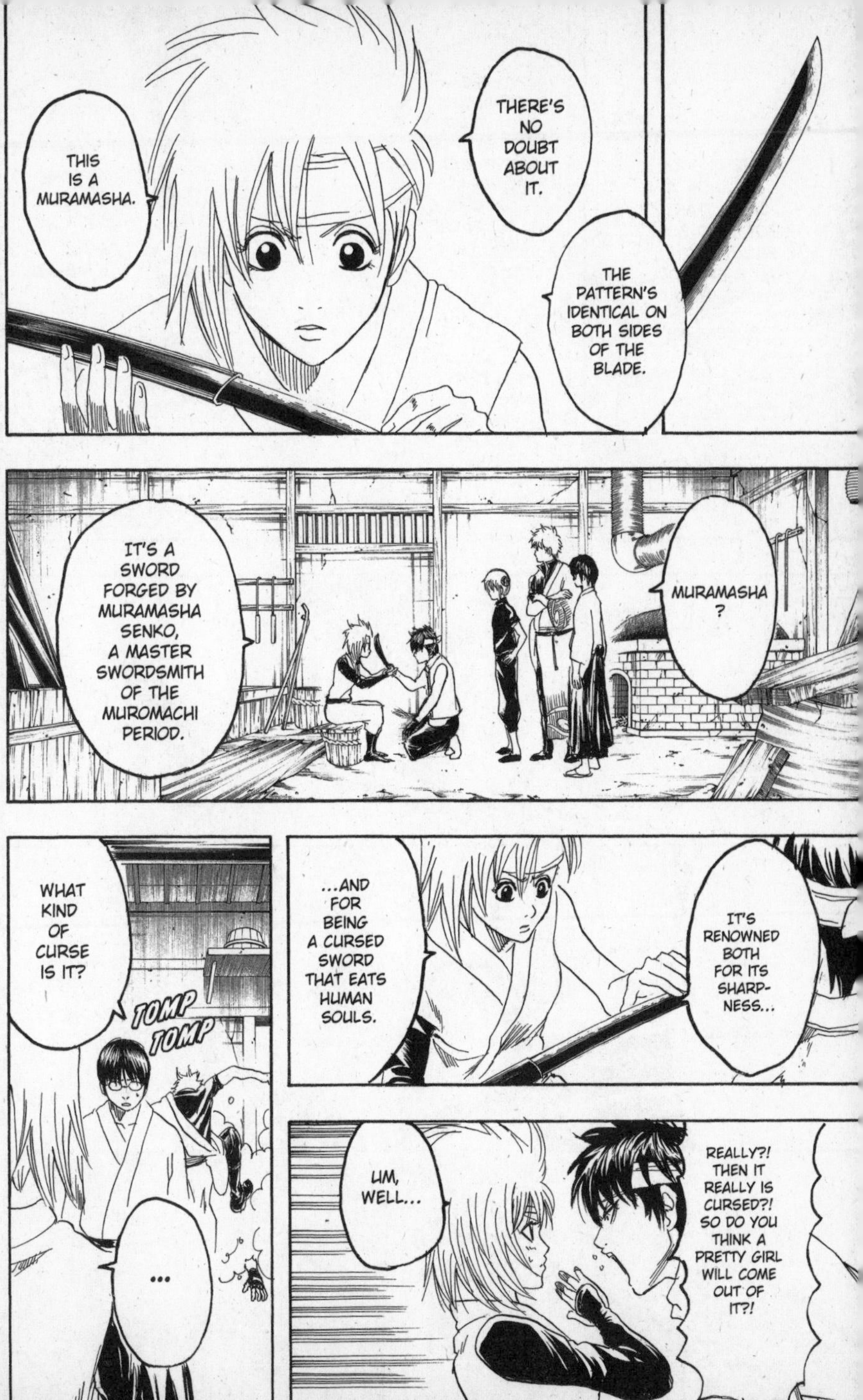
THERE'S NO DOUBT ABOUT IT.
THE PATTERN'S IDENTICAL ON BOTH SIDES OF THE BLADE.
THIS IS A MURAMASHA.
MURAMASHA?
IT'S A SWORD FORGED BY MURAMASHA SENKO, A MASTER SWORDSMITH OF THE MUROMACHI PERIOD.
IT'S RENOWNED BOTH FOR ITS SHARPNESS...
...AND FOR BEING A CURSED SWORD THAT EATS HUMAN SOULS.
REALLY?! THEN IT REALLY IS CURSED?! SO DO YOU THINK A PRETTY GIRL WILL COME OUT OF IT?!
UM, WELL...
WHAT KIND OF CURSE IS IT?
TOMP TOMP
...

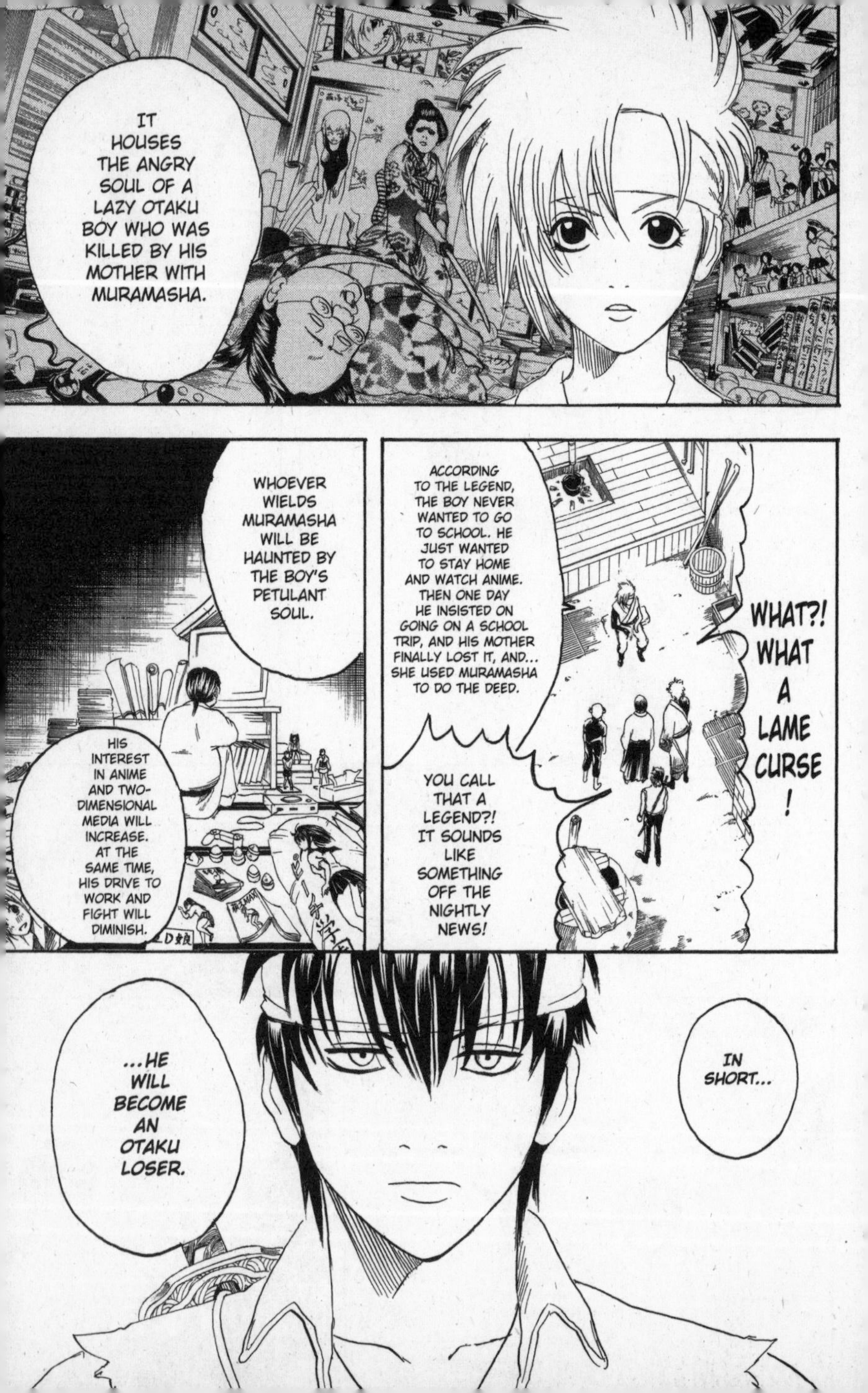
IT HOUSES THE ANGRY SOUL OF A LAZY OTAKU BOY WHO WAS KILLED BY HIS MOTHER WITH MURAMASHA.
ACCORDING TO THE LEGEND, THE BOY NEVER WANTED TO GO TO SCHOOL. HE JUST WANTED TO STAY HOME AND WATCH ANIME. THEN ONE DAY HE INSISTED ON GOING ON A SCHOOL TRIP, AND HIS MOTHER FINALLY LOST IT, AND... SHE USED MURAMASHA TO DO THE DEED.
WHAT?! WHAT A LAME CURSE!
YOU CALL THAT A LEGEND?! IT SOUNDS LIKE SOMETHING OFF THE NIGHTLY NEWS!
WHOEVER WIELDS MURAMASHA WILL BE HAUNTED BY THE BOY'S PETULANT SOUL.
HIS INTEREST IN ANIME AND TWO-DIMENSIONAL MEDIA WILL INCREASE. AT THE SAME TIME, HIS DRIVE TO WORK AND FIGHT WILL DIMINISH.
IN SHORT...
...HE WILL BECOME AN OTAKU LOSER.

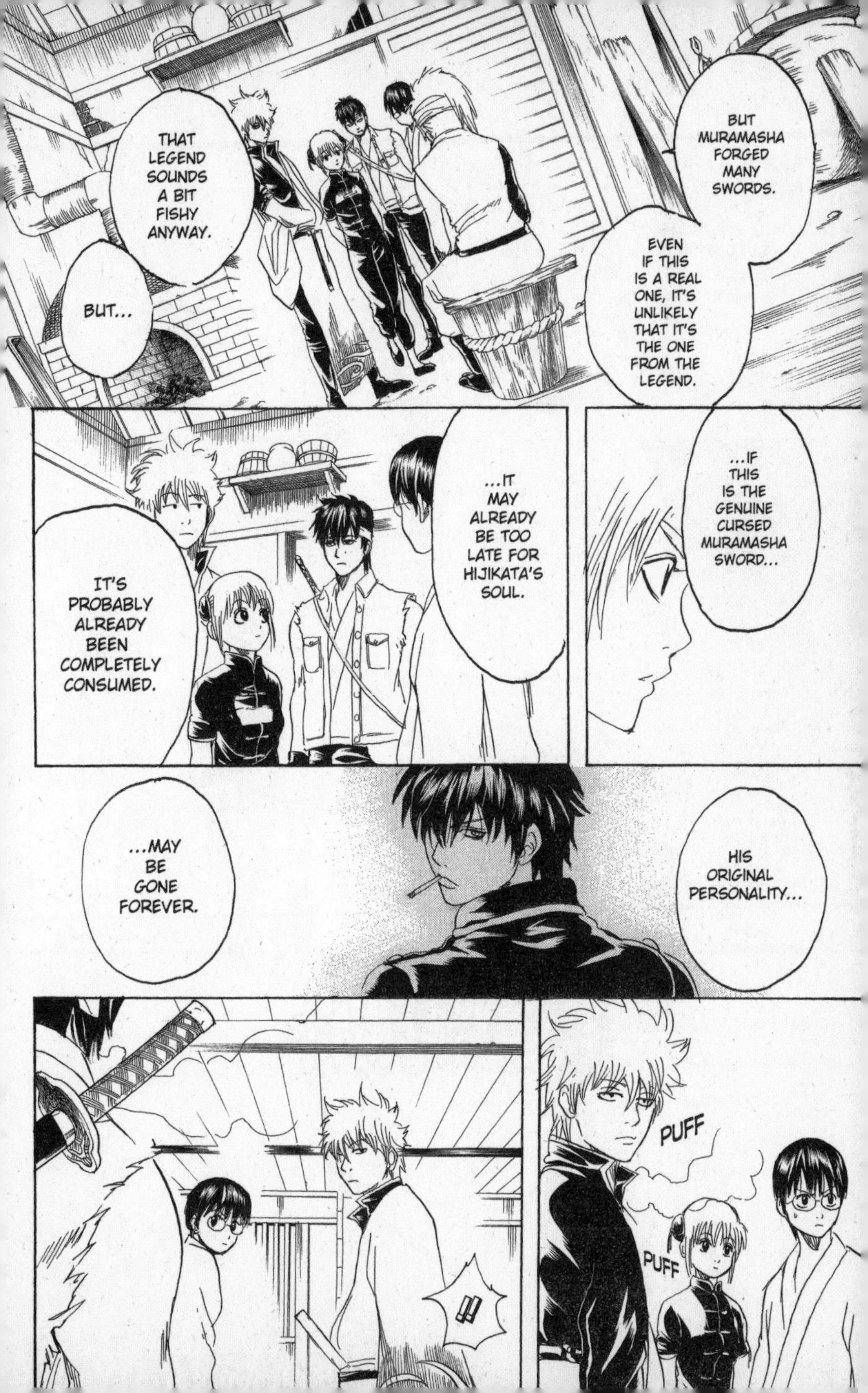
BUT MURAMASHA FORGED MANY SWORDS.
EVEN IF THIS IS A REAL ONE, IT'S UNLIKELY THAT IT'S THE ONE FROM THE LEGEND.
THAT LEGEND SOUNDS A BIT FISHY ANYWAY.
BUT...
...IF THIS IS THE GENUINE CURSED MURAMASHA SWORD...
...IT MAY ALREADY BE TOO LATE FOR HIJIKATA'S SOUL.
IT'S PROBABLY ALREADY BEEN COMPLETELY CONSUMED.
HIS ORIGINAL PERSONALITY...
...MAY BE GONE FOREVER.
PUFF
PUFF
!!

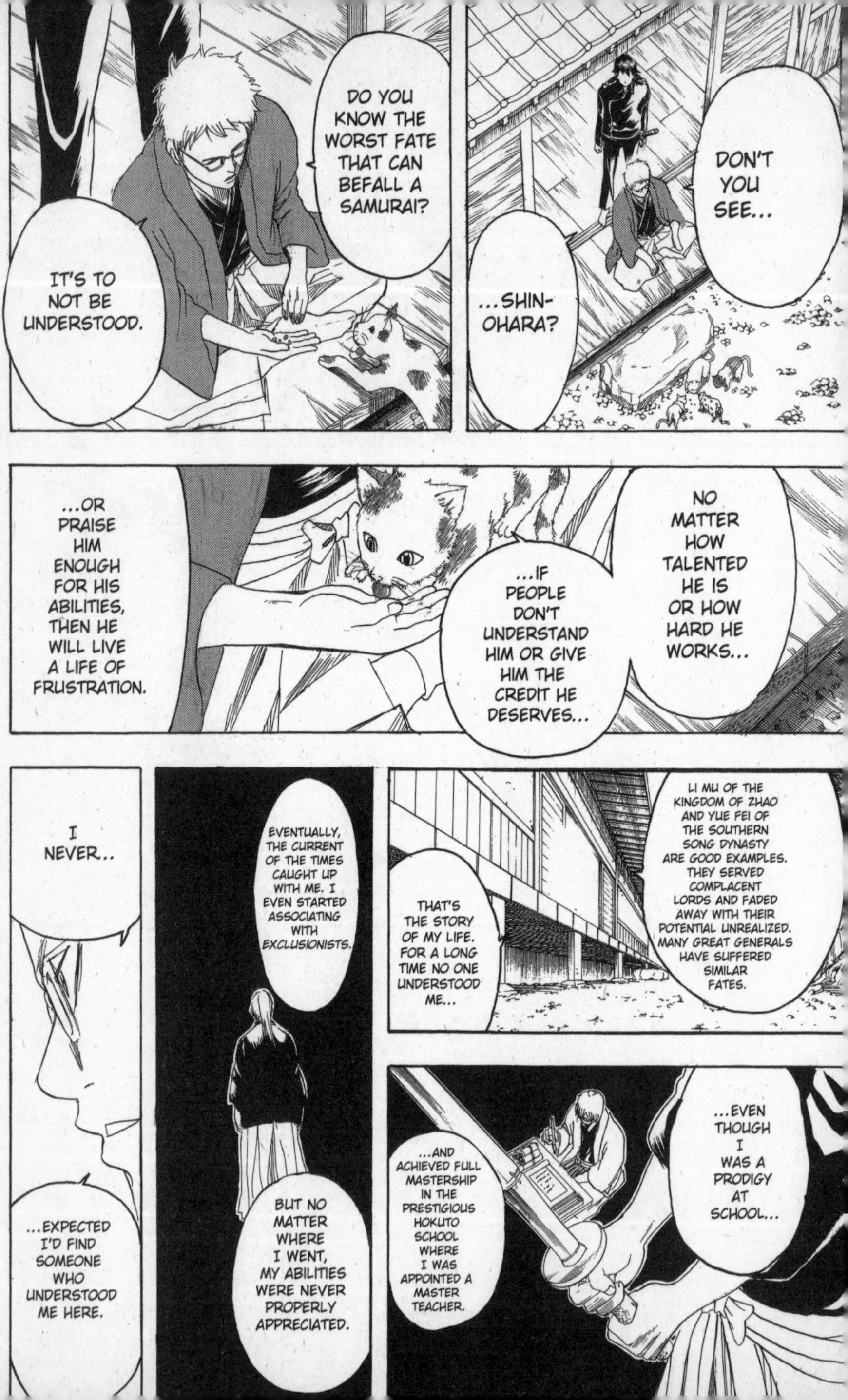
DON'T YOU SEE...
...SHIN-OHARA?
DO YOU KNOW THE WORST FATE THAT CAN BEFALL A SAMURAI?
IT'S TO NOT BE UNDERSTOOD.
NO MATTER HOW TALENTED HE IS OR HOW HARD HE WORKS...
...IF PEOPLE DON'T UNDERSTAND HIM OR GIVE HIM THE CREDIT HE DESERVES...
...OR PRAISE HIM ENOUGH FOR HIS ABILITIES, THEN HE WILL LIVE A LIFE OF FRUSTRATION.
LI MU OF THE KINGDOM OF ZHAO AND YUE FEI OF THE SOUTHERN SONG DYNASTY ARE GOOD EXAMPLES. THEY SERVED COMPLACENT LORDS AND FADED AWAY WITH THEIR POTENTIAL UNREALIZED. MANY GREAT GENERALS HAVE SUFFERED SIMILAR FATES.
THAT'S THE STORY OF MY LIFE. FOR A LONG TIME NO ONE UNDERSTOOD ME...
...EVEN THOUGH I WAS A PRODIGY AT SCHOOL...
...AND ACHIEVED FULL MASTERSHIP IN THE PRESTIGIOUS HOKUTO SCHOOL WHERE I WAS APPOINTED A MASTER TEACHER.
EVENTUALLY, THE CURRENT OF THE TIMES CAUGHT UP WITH ME. I EVEN STARTED ASSOCIATING WITH EXCLUSIONISTS.
BUT NO MATTER WHERE I WENT, MY ABILITIES WERE NEVER PROPERLY APPRECIATED.
I NEVER...
...EXPECTED I'D FIND SOMEONE WHO UNDERSTOOD ME HERE.

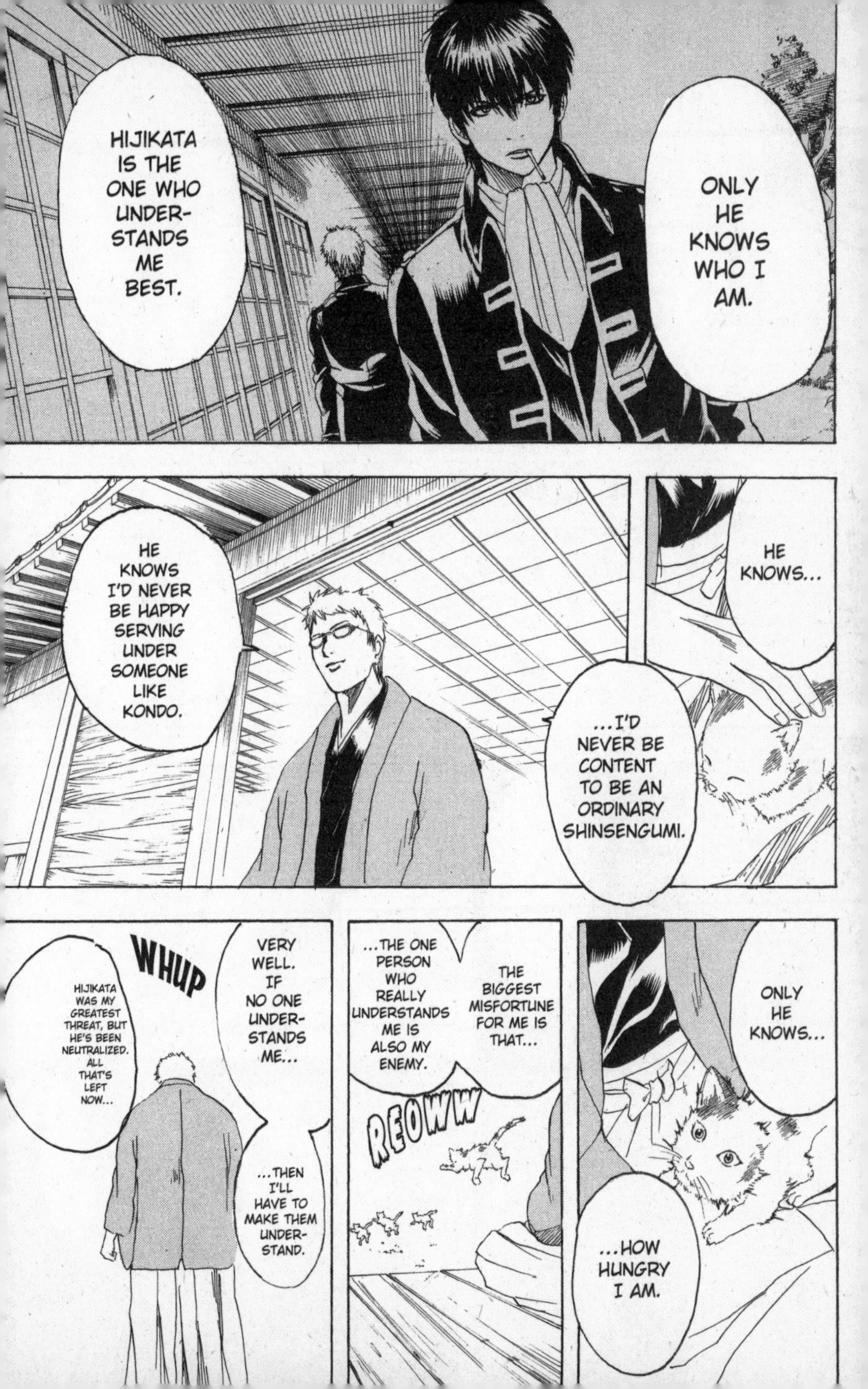
ONLY HE KNOWS WHO I AM.
HIJIKATA IS THE ONE WHO UNDER-STANDS ME BEST.
HE KNOWS...
...I'D NEVER BE CONTENT TO BE AN ORDINARY SHINSENGUMI.
HE KNOWS I'D NEVER BE HAPPY SERVING UNDER SOMEONE LIKE KONDO.
ONLY HE KNOWS...
...HOW HUNGRY I AM.
THE BIGGEST MISFORTUNE FOR ME IS THAT...
...THE ONE PERSON WHO REALLY UNDERSTANDS ME IS ALSO MY ENEMY.
REOWW
VERY WELL. IF NO ONE UNDER-STANDS ME...
WHUP
HIJIKATA WAS MY GREATEST THREAT, BUT HE'S BEEN NEUTRALIZED. ALL THAT'S LEFT NOW...
...THEN I'LL HAVE TO MAKE THEM UNDER-STAND.

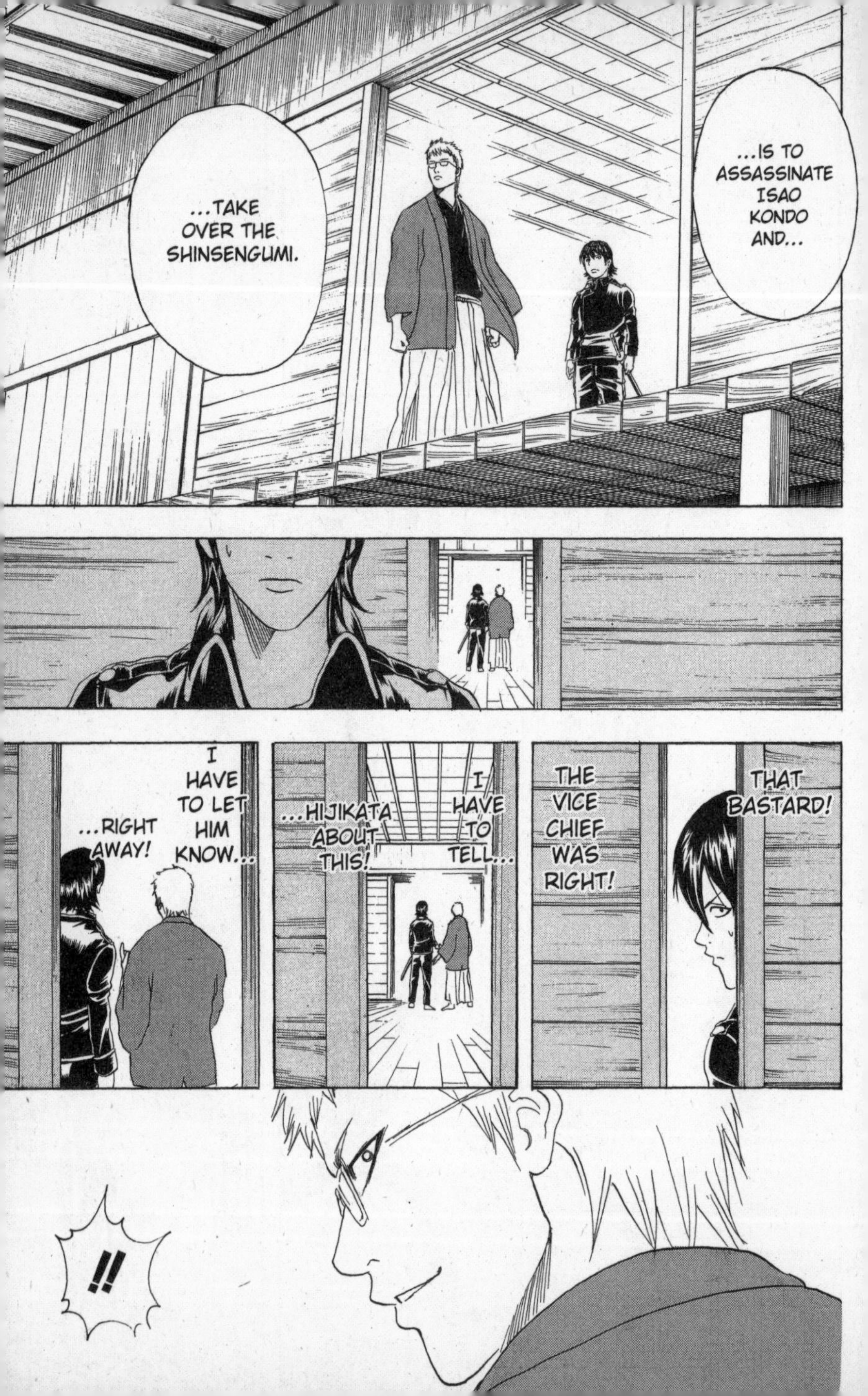
...IS TO ASSASSINATE ISAO KONDO AND...
...TAKE OVER THE SHINSENGUMI.
THAT BASTARD!
THE VICE CHIEF WAS RIGHT!
I HAVE TO TELL...
...HIJIKATA ABOUT THIS!
I HAVE TO LET HIM KNOW...
...RIGHT AWAY!
!!

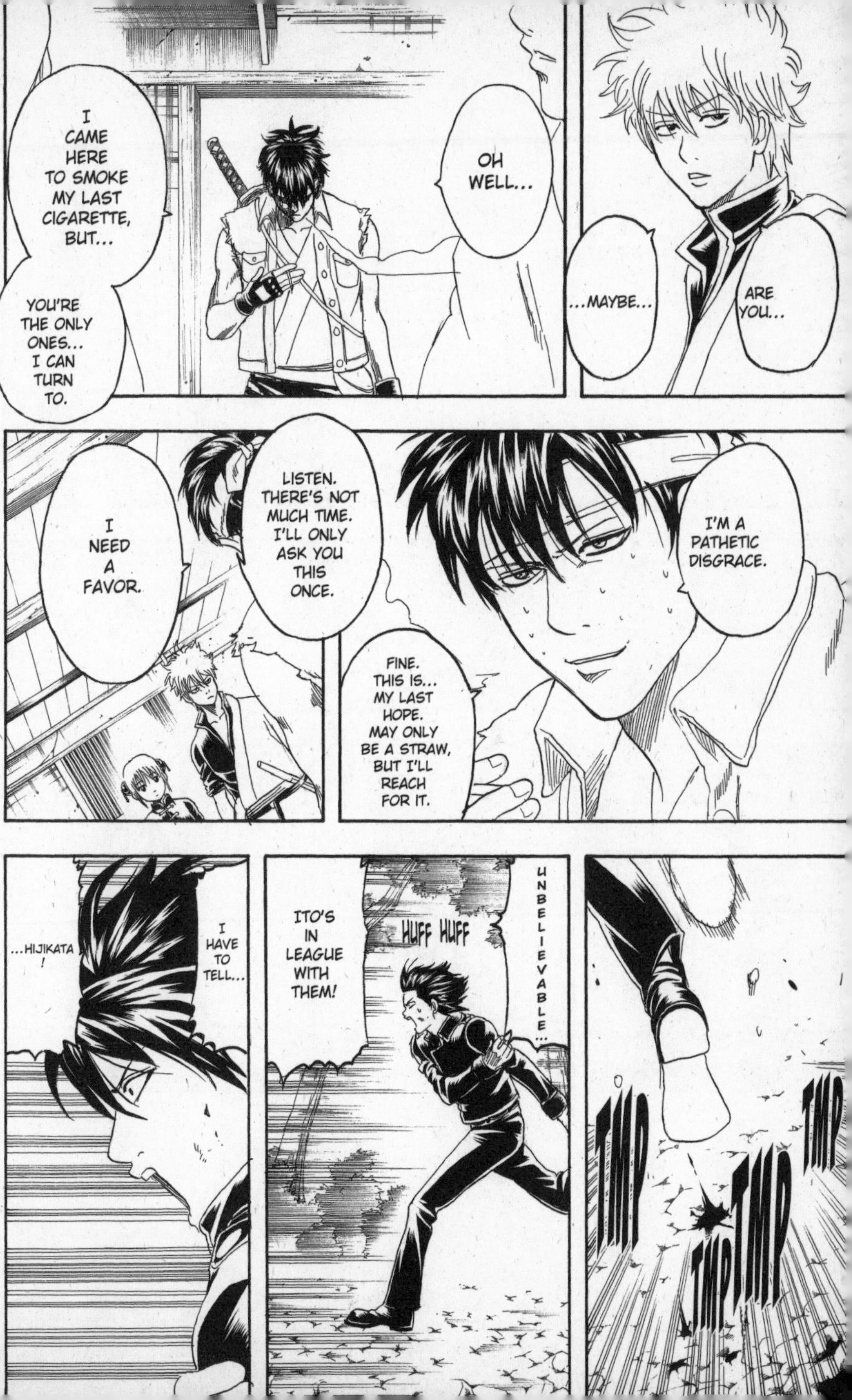
ARE YOU...
...MAYBE...
OH WELL...
I CAME HERE TO SMOKE MY LAST CIGARETTE, BUT...
YOU'RE THE ONLY ONES... I CAN TURN TO.
I'M A PATHETIC DISGRACE.
FINE. THIS IS... MY LAST HOPE. MAY ONLY BE A STRAW, BUT I'LL REACH FOR IT.
LISTEN. THERE'S NOT MUCH TIME. I'LL ONLY ASK YOU THIS ONCE.
I NEED A FAVOR.
THMP
THMP
THMP
THMP
UNBELIEVABLE...
HUFF HUFF
ITO'S IN LEAGUE WITH THEM!
I HAVE TO TELL...
...HIJIKATA!

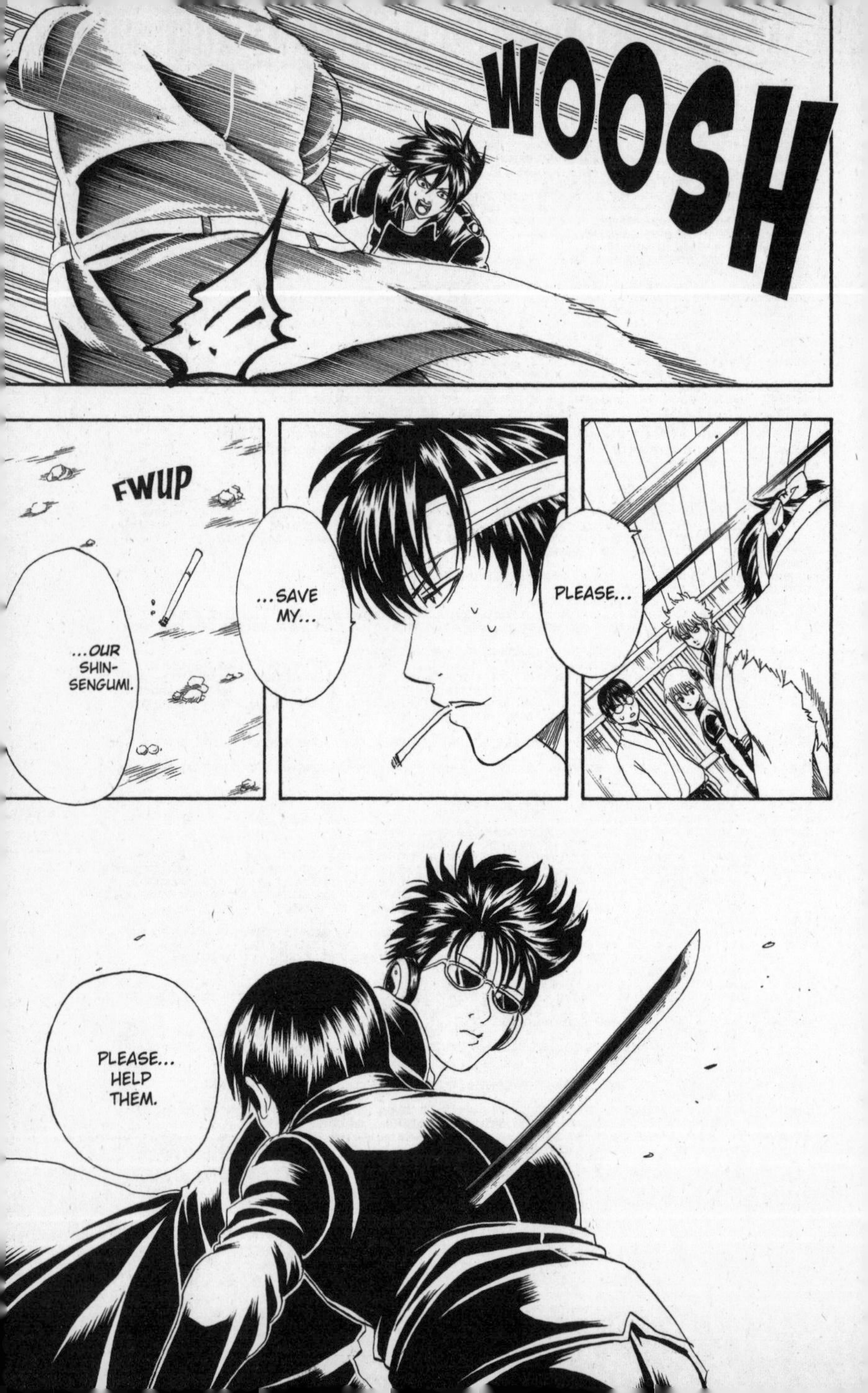
WOOSH
PLEASE...
...SAVE MY...
FWUP
...OUR SHIN-SENGUMI.
PLEASE... HELP THEM.

SORACHI: (CONTINUED) ...FRIENDS YOU KNOW, IT WAS TOO EMBARRASSING. THAT'S WHY I JUST TOLD THEM THAT I WANTED TO BE AN ARCHITECT.

ONISHI: I SEE.

SORACHI: "I'M GOING TO LEARN CG." THAT'S WHAT I WOULD SAY WHEN I WENT TO LEARN HOW TO DRAW.

ONISHI: WHAT DO YOU MEAN BY LEARNING TO DRAW?

SORACHI: IT HAD NOTHING TO DO WITH COLLEGE, BUT IT WAS A COLLEGE THAT SPECIALIZED IN ADVERTISEMENT.

ONISHI: SO YOU KEPT ON DRAWING AND...

SORACHI: BUT I WANTED TO TRY MY LUCK AT LEAST ONCE.

ONISHI: WHEN DID YOU SUBMIT YOUR WORK FOR THE FIRST TIME?

SORACHI: I WAS IN MY JUNIOR YEAR OF COLLEGE.

ONISHI: WAS IT THE NOODLE HOUSE THING?

SORACHI: IT WAS ABOUT MONSTERS.

ONISHI: IT WAS SOMETHING ABOUT A NOODLE HOUSE GUY DOING SOMETHING? LIKE FIGHTING MONSTERS?

SORACHI: YEAH.

ONISHI: SO YOU SUBMITTED THAT WHILE YOU WERE IN COLLEGE...

SORACHI: I WAS SO CONFIDENT THAT I WOULD GET A PRIZE FOR IT. AND IT WENT STRAIGHT INTO THE SHREDDER. I'VE NEVER SAID THIS IN PUBLIC. EVERYONE HAS ALWAYS THOUGHT THAT MY FIRST WORK GOT A PRIZE. NOT EVEN MY FOLKS KNOW ABOUT THIS. I ACTUALLY FAILED THE FIRST TIME AROUND.

ONISHI: WHY DO YOU KEEP IT A SECRET?

SORACHI: I ACTUALLY DON'T CARE IF PEOPLE KNOW ABOUT IT.

ONISHI: WHAT WAS THE SETTING FOR THAT ONE LIKE? IT MIGHT BE INTERESTING IF YOU TALKED ABOUT IT NOW. YOU COULD TALK ABOUT THINGS LIKE WHAT KIND OF CHARACTERS IT HAD.

SORACHI: BUT THE CHARACTERS WEREN'T VERY INTERESTING.

ONISHI: IT WAS ABOUT NOTHING BUT THE ESTABLISHED SETTINGS AND WORLDVIEW?

SORACHI: IT WAS JUST A SELF-SATISFYING COMIC WHERE I WAS TRYING TO SHOW OFF.

"I WAS SURE THAT (SORACHI) WAS LYING ABOUT HIS AGE." -ONISHI

ONISHI: WHAT DO YOU MEAN BY THAT? LIKE HOW YOU MADE UP WORDS WITH THE MONSTERS?

SORACHI: NOT EXACTLY. JUST SOMETHING LIKE THAT.

ONISHI: SO IT WAS JUST MEANT TO LOOK "COOL."

SORACHI: BUT THE MAIN CHARACTER WAS PRETTY MUCH THE SAME AS GIN-SAN EXCEPT FOR THE PART WHERE HE RAN A NOODLE HOUSE. THE STORY OF THAT COMIC WENT WITH HOW HE GOES TO SAVE A MONSTER CAT. SINCE THE COMIC WAS A ONE-SHOT THING, I HAD TO DRAW THE WHOLE THING BY MYSELF. IT WAS THE FIRST TIME I DREW THE BACKGROUND. I HAD TO USE RULERS EVERYWHERE, SO IT BECAME A HUGE PAIN. THAT'S WHEN I THOUGHT, "IT WOULD SUCK TO BE A COMIC AUTHOR" AND "I CAN'T DO THIS."

ONISHI: BUT YOU STILL FINISHED IT, RIGHT?

SORACHI: YES.

ONISHI: AND YOU THOUGHT YOU WOULD HAVE WON SOME KIND OF PRIZE?

SORACHI: I WAS TOTALLY CONFIDENT.

ONISHI: SO YOU WERE REALLY DISAPPOINTED?

SORACHI: SO SINCE I FAILED, I JUST CALLED IT QUITS. I STARTED LOOKING FOR WORK IN MY SENIOR YEAR IN COLLEGE, BUT I TRIED IT ONE MORE TIME, AND THIS TIME I ACTUALLY WON A PRIZE. BUT THAT ONE TOOK ME FOUR MONTHS.

ONISHI: YOU MEAN BETWEEN THE ROUGH DRAFT AND THE FINAL PRODUCT?

SORACHI: YEAH. JUST LIKE NOW, I ALWAYS TAKE MY TIME AND TURN IT IN RIGHT BEFORE THE DEADLINE. I WAS SUPPOSED TO TURN IT IN AT THE END OF THE MONTH. SO I TRIED TO MATCH THE DEADLINE AND ENDED UP NOT MAKING IT. SO SINCE I GOT ANOTHER MONTH, I LOOKED IT OVER AND FIXED WHATEVER PARTS I THOUGHT NEEDED IT. THEN I FOUND MORE SPOTS THAT NEEDED TO BE FIXED. AND THEN I MISSED THE DEADLINE AFTER THAT. THEN I FIXED MORE PARTS OF IT...

ONISHI: SO THAT'S HOW IT WENT.

SORACHI: BUT LOOKING BACK, I GUESS IT WAS BETTER THAT WAY SINCE I GOT TO EDIT MY OWN WORK. BUT I GUESS FOUR MONTHS IS WAY TOO LONG.

ONISHI: I WAS SURE THAT YOU WERE LYING ABOUT YOUR AGE. FROM YOUR DRAWINGS, I THOUGHT THAT YOU WERE AT LEAST 30 YEARS OLD.

SORACHI: YOU EVEN THOUGHT THAT I WAS A WOMAN.

ONISHI: I COULDN'T BELIEVE IT UNTIL I MET YOU IN PERSON.

SORACHI: THAT I WAS LYING?

ONISHI: I WOULDN'T BE SURPRISED IF YOU WERE A 40-YEAR-OLD MAN.

SORACHI: YOU THOUGHT I CARED ABOUT MY IMAGE SO I LIED ABOUT MY AGE?

ONISHI: "DANDELION" WAS ALSO DIFFERENT FROM WHAT YOU FIRST SUBMITTED. WHAT HAPPENS TO THAT OLD LADY?

SORACHI: TORN TO PIECES. THERE WAS NOTHING HEARTWARMING ABOUT THAT STORY. I GOT A LOT OF FAN LETTERS TALKING ABOUT HOW THEY WERE TOUCHED AT SEEING THE OLD MAN AND OLD LADY REUNITING. ORIGINALLY, THAT SCENE DIDN'T EXIST. THE OLD LADY GETS RUN OVER BY A CAR AND GETS DISMEMBERED. I WAS JUST TOLD, "WE'RE GOING TO PUBLISH THIS IN JUMP, SO REDO THE WHOLE THING."

ONISHI: INCLUDING THE ART.

SORACHI: I WAS TOLD THAT IT WOULD ACTUALLY GET IN THE ISSUE... AND THEY SAID, "AT THE VERY LEAST, FIX THE PART WITH THE OLD LADY BECAUSE WE CAN'T PUBLISH IT AS IS." SO AT FIRST, I HAD NO INTENTION OF LETTING THE OLD MAN AND OLD LADY REUNITE. WE ENDED UP ARGUING ABOUT IT. RIGHT IN THE BEGINNING, I GOT INTO AN ARGUMENT. (LAUGH)

ONISHI: AND AFTER THAT, YOU HAD "SAMURAIDER" AND THEN "SHIROKURO (WHITE & BLACK)." "SAMURAIDER" WAS THE ONE WITH THE OLD DUDE IN THE SWEAT SUIT RIGHT? THE ONE WHERE THE CHARACTERS DID NOTHING BUT TALK.

SORACHI: THAT WASN'T A SWEAT SUIT. IT WAS SUPPOSED TO BE A PRISON JUMPSUIT.

ONISHI: BUT THE LAST BOSS WAS SOME BALDING DUDE.

SORACHI: YEAH. BUT THAT'S ACTUALLY THE PROTOTYPE FOR GIN TAMA. I USED THE SAME SETTING OF THE "ALIENS FROM OUTER SPACE COME TO EARTH DURING THE EDO PERIOD." IN THAT SENSE, "SAMURAIDER" WASN'T A TOTAL WASTE OF TIME.

ONISHI: I GUESS.

SORACHI: I THOUGHT IT WAS REALLY INTERESTING WHEN I DREW IT. IT GOT CANNED, AND I FELT REALLY DISAPPOINTED IN YOU.

ONISHI: AFTER THAT, YOU WEREN'T ABLE TO BRING IN A LOT OF IDEAS, SO I MADE YOU PROMISE ME TO FAX AT LEAST SIX PAGES OF YOUR ROUGH GROUNDWORK SKETCHES PER DAY.

SORACHI: BUT I COULDN'T EVEN DO THOSE SIX PAGES. I WAS WORKING AT THE PACE OF ONE LINE OF SPEECH PER DAY. OF COURSE, I WOULD GET A CALL ABOUT IT FROM YOU, ONISHI. YOU'D ASK ME, "HOW MANY PAGES DID YOU GET DONE?" I WOULD SAY THAT I FINISHED, BUT I WAS LYING OF COURSE. (LAUGH) THAT'S WHY I QUICKLY DREW UP THREE PAGES ON THE SPOT AND SENT IT OUT. (LAUGH) BUT YOU KNOW...

CONTINUED ON PAGE 86

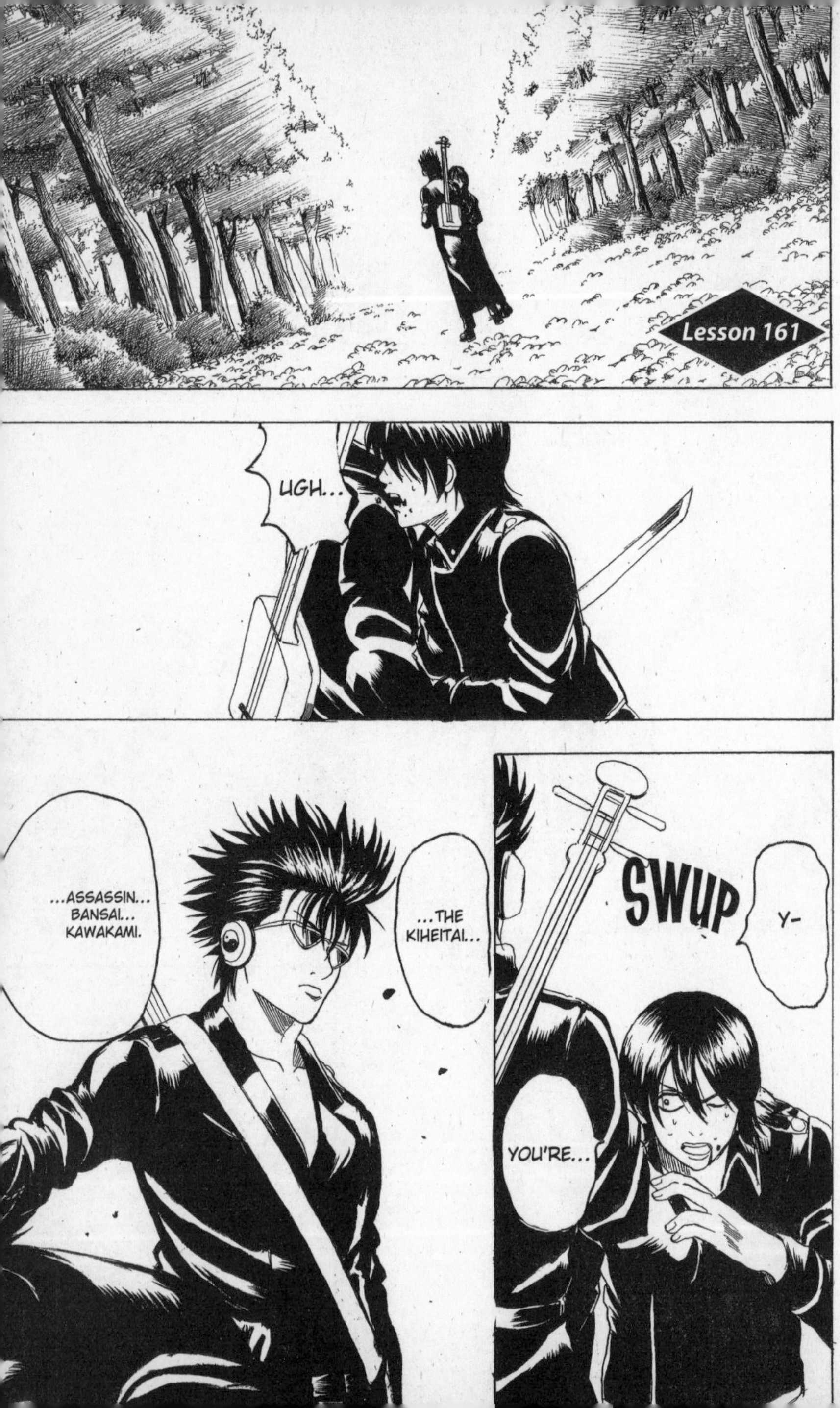
Lesson 161
UGH...
Y-
SWUP
YOU'RE...
...THE KIHEITAI...
...ASSASSIN... BANSAI... KAWAKAMI.

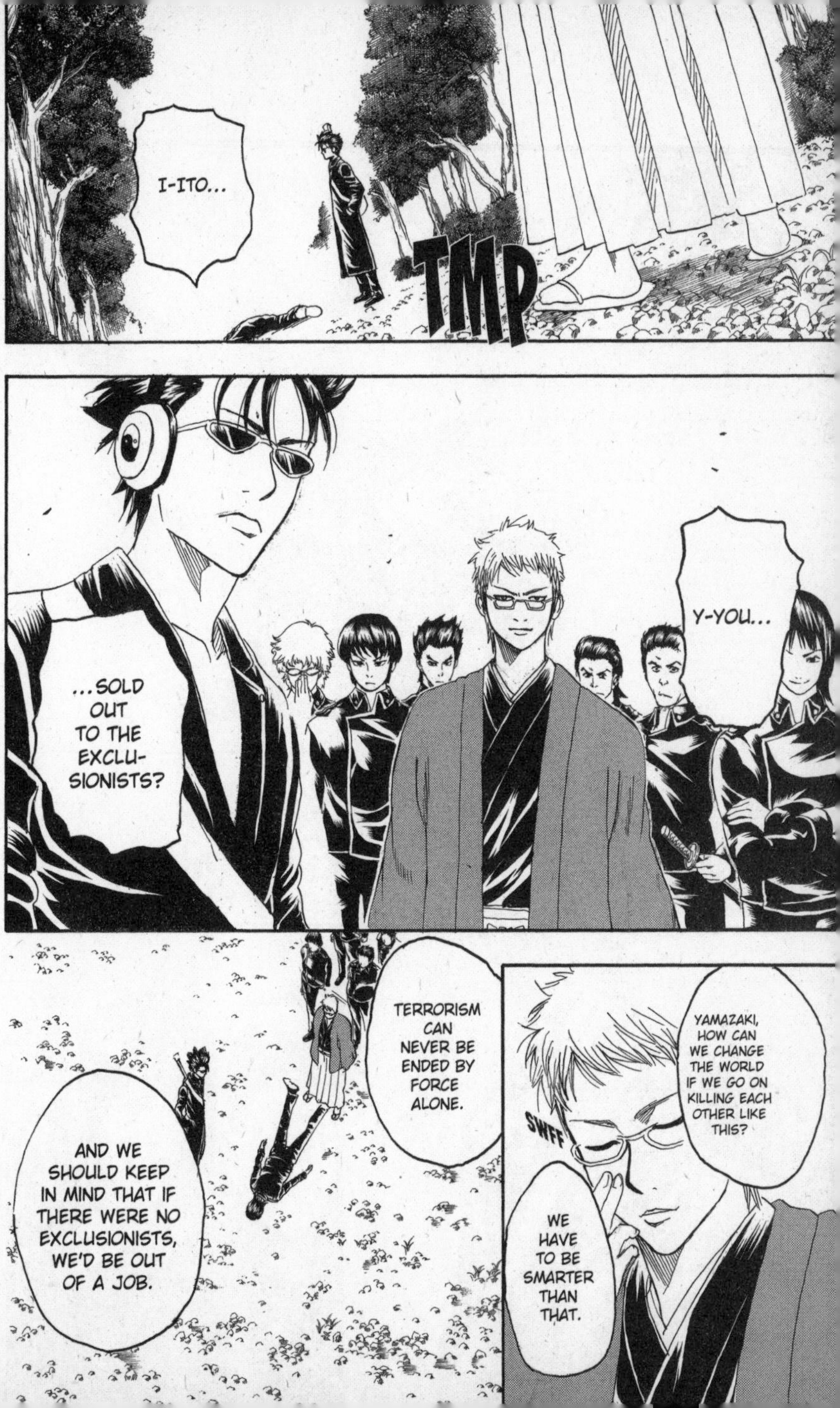
TMP
I-ITO...
Y-YOU...
...SOLD OUT TO THE EXCLUSIONISTS?
YAMAZAKI, HOW CAN WE CHANGE THE WORLD IF WE GO ON KILLING EACH OTHER LIKE THIS?
SWFF
WE HAVE TO BE SMARTER THAN THAT.
TERRORISM CAN NEVER BE ENDED BY FORCE ALONE.
AND WE SHOULD KEEP IN MIND THAT IF THERE WERE NO EXCLUSIONISTS, WE'D BE OUT OF A JOB.

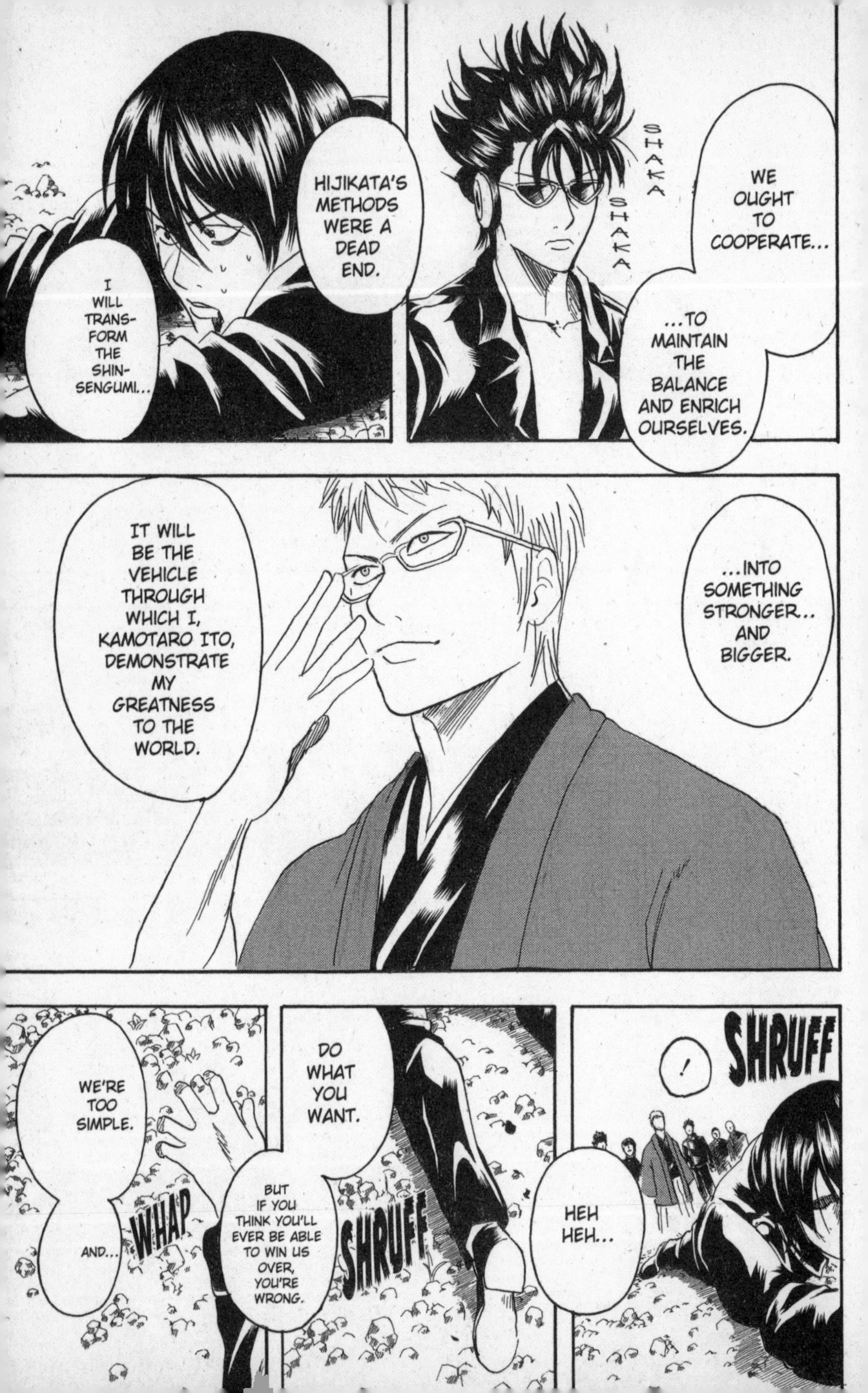
WE OUGHT TO COOPERATE...
...TO MAINTAIN THE BALANCE AND ENRICH OURSELVES.
SHAKA SHAKA
HIJIKATA'S METHODS WERE A DEAD END.
I WILL TRANSFORM THE SHINSENGUMI...
...INTO SOMETHING STRONGER... AND BIGGER.
IT WILL BE THE VEHICLE THROUGH WHICH I, KAMOTARO ITO, DEMONSTRATE MY GREATNESS TO THE WORLD.
SHRUFF
!
HEH HEH...
DO WHAT YOU WANT.
SHRUFF
BUT IF YOU THINK YOU'LL EVER BE ABLE TO WIN US OVER, YOU'RE WRONG.
WE'RE TOO SIMPLE.
WHAP
AND...

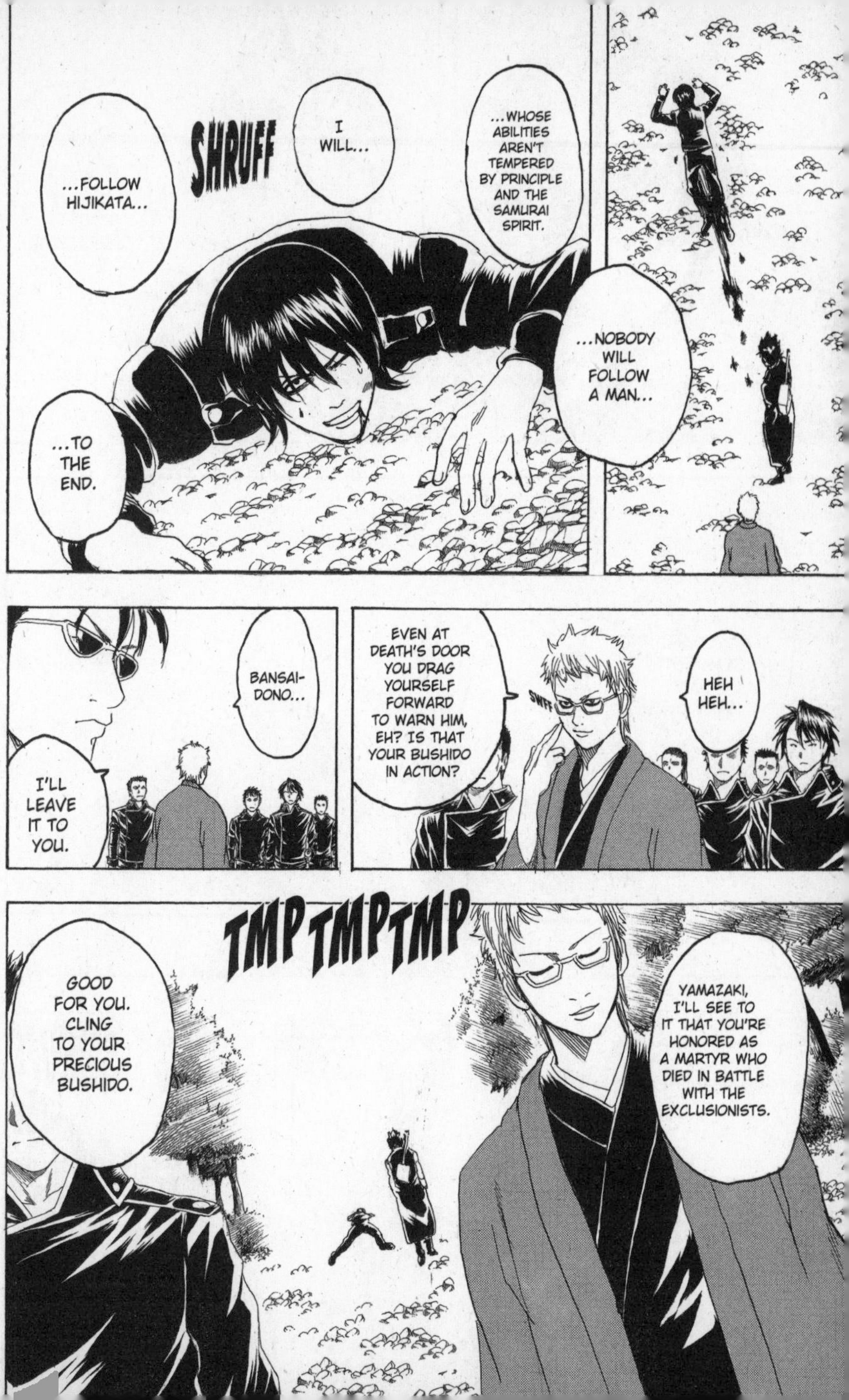
...NOBODY WILL FOLLOW A MAN...
...WHOSE ABILITIES AREN'T TEMPERED BY PRINCIPLE AND THE SAMURAI SPIRIT.
I WILL...
SHRUFF
...FOLLOW HIJIKATA...
...TO THE END.
HEH HEH...
SWFF
EVEN AT DEATH'S DOOR YOU DRAG YOURSELF FORWARD TO WARN HIM, EH? IS THAT YOUR BUSHIDO IN ACTION?
BANSAI-DONO...
I'LL LEAVE IT TO YOU.
YAMAZAKI, I'LL SEE TO IT THAT YOU'RE HONORED AS A MARTYR WHO DIED IN BATTLE WITH THE EXCLUSIONISTS.
TMP TMP TMP
GOOD FOR YOU. CLING TO YOUR PRECIOUS BUSHIDO.

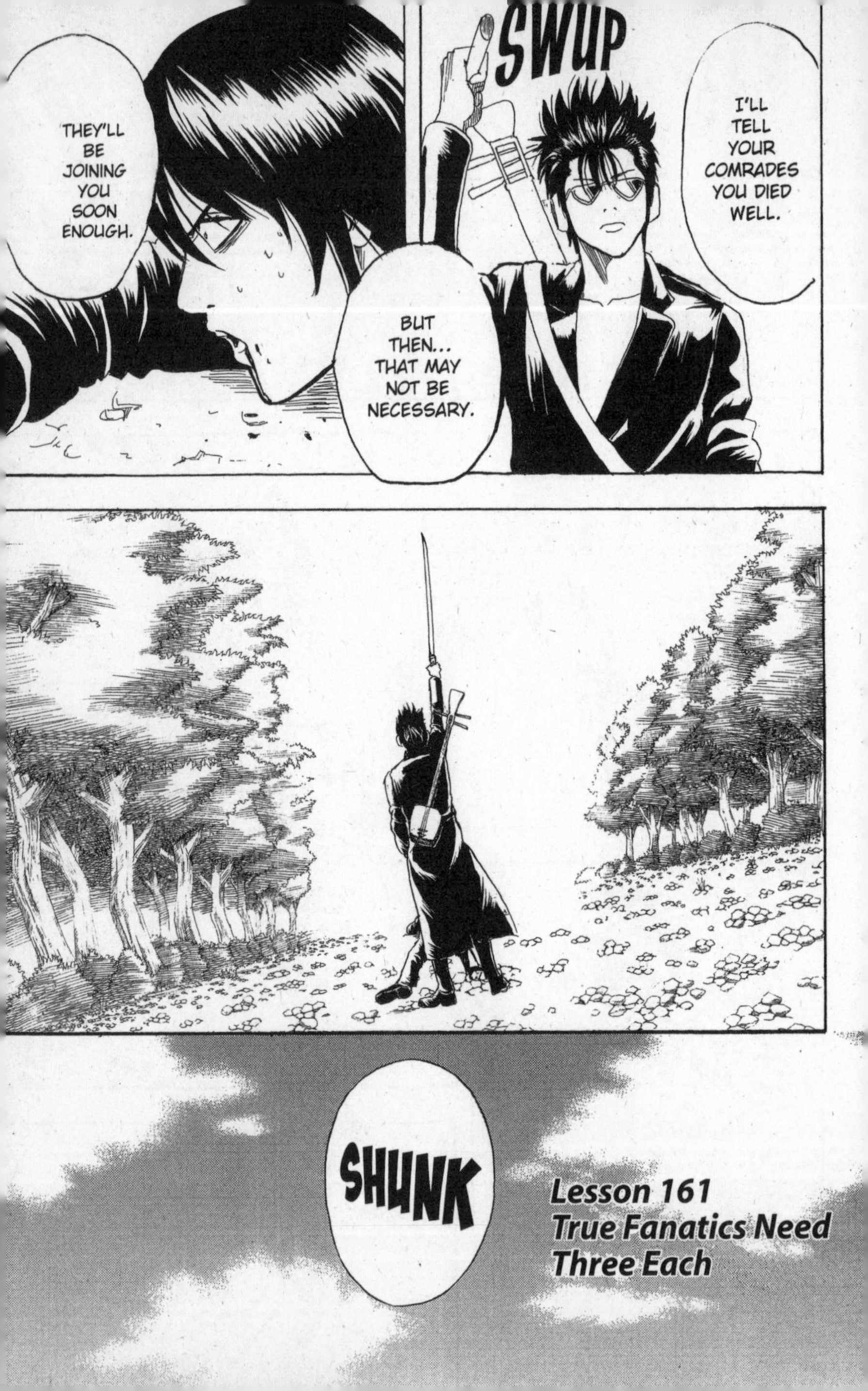
SWUP
I'LL TELL YOUR COMRADES YOU DIED WELL.
BUT THEN... THAT MAY NOT BE NECESSARY.
THEY'LL BE JOINING YOU SOON ENOUGH.
SHUNK
Lesson 161
True Fanatics Need Three Each

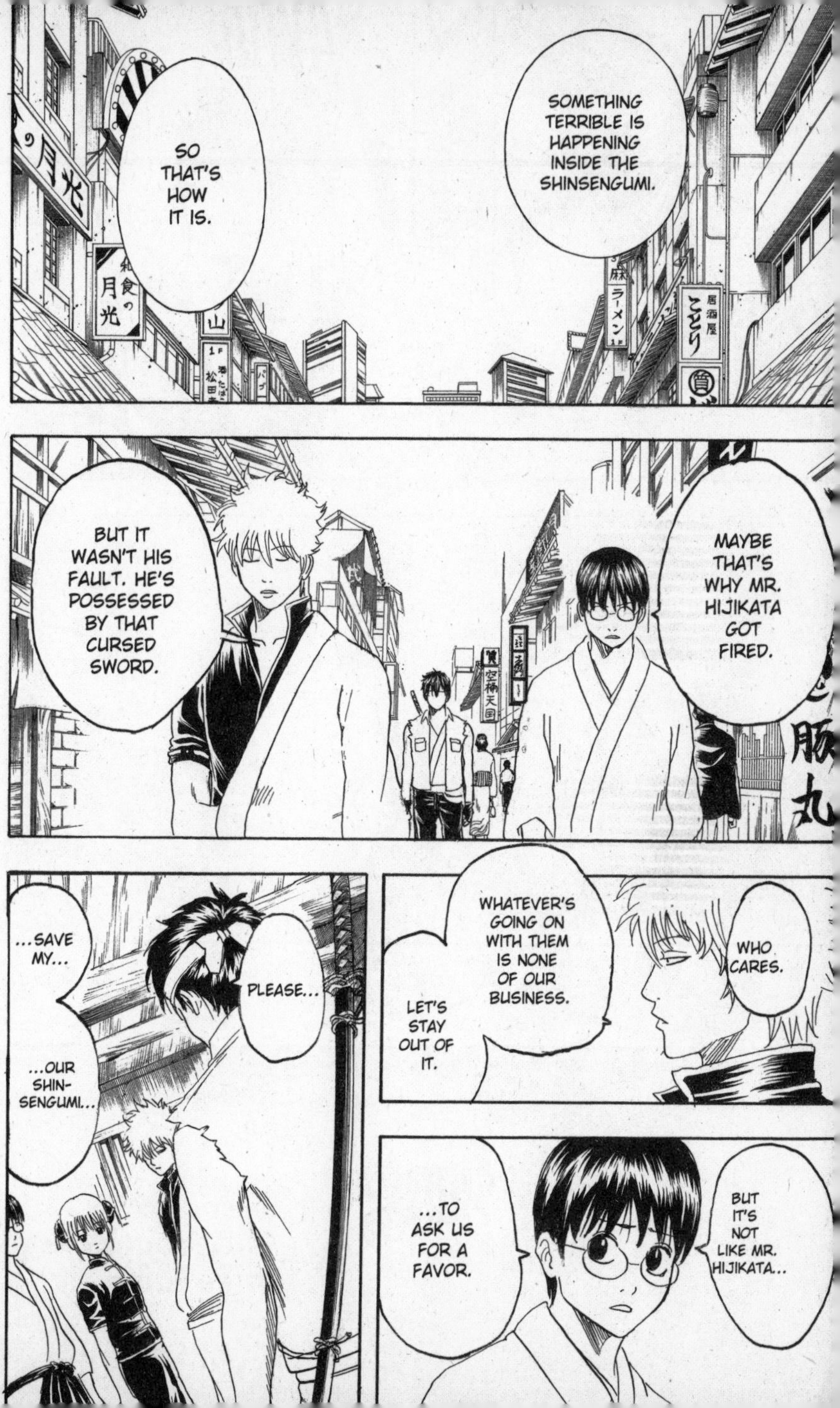
SOMETHING TERRIBLE IS HAPPENING INSIDE THE SHINSENGUMI.
SO THAT'S HOW IT IS.
MAYBE THAT'S WHY MR. HIJIKATA GOT FIRED.
BUT IT WASN'T HIS FAULT. HE'S POSSESSED BY THAT CURSED SWORD.
WHO CARES.
WHATEVER'S GOING ON WITH THEM IS NONE OF OUR BUSINESS.
LET'S STAY OUT OF IT.
BUT IT'S NOT LIKE MR. HIJIKATA...
...TO ASK US FOR A FAVOR.
PLEASE...
...SAVE MY...
...OUR SHIN-SENGUMI...

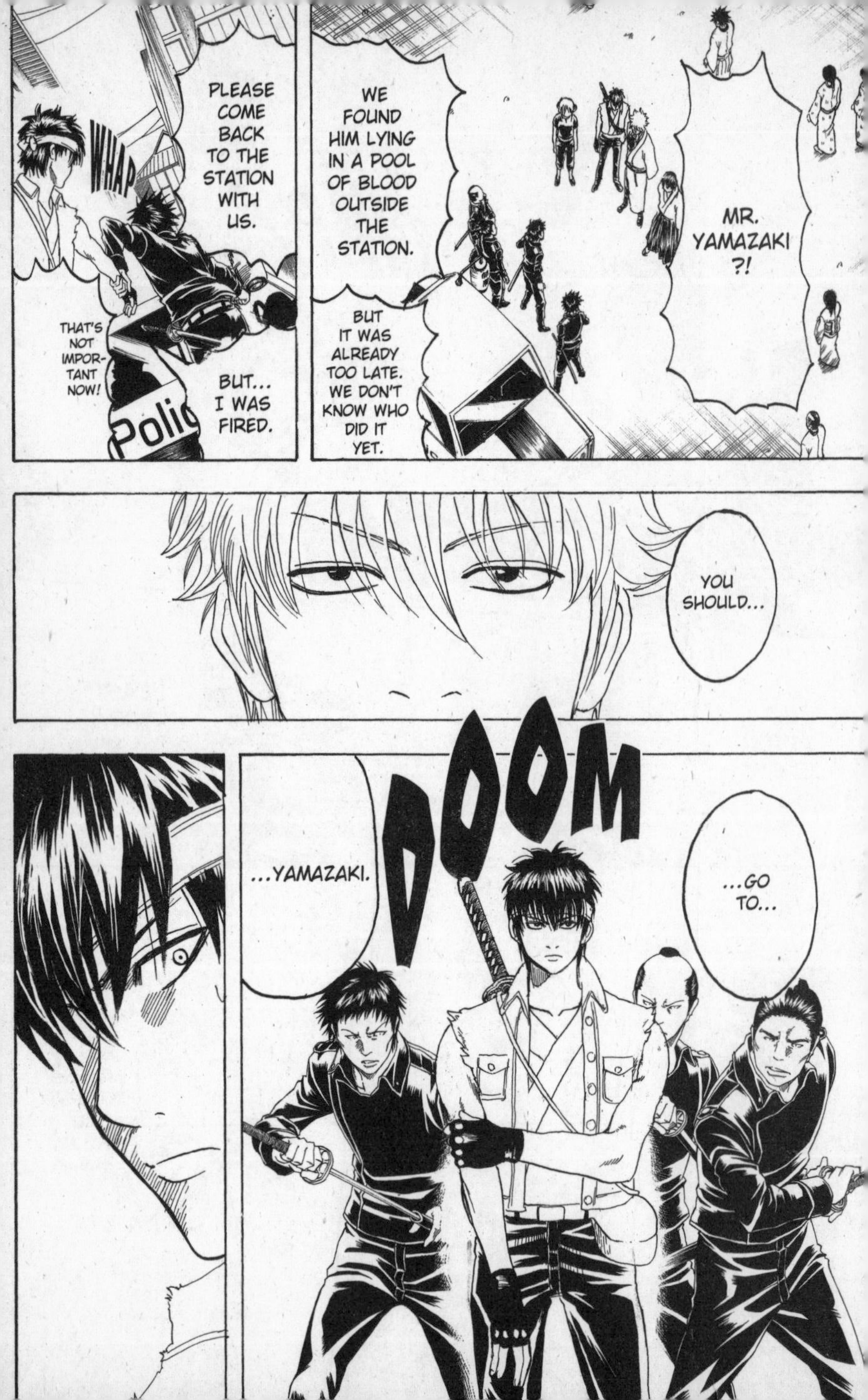
MR. YAMAZAKI ?!
WE FOUND HIM LYING IN A POOL OF BLOOD OUTSIDE THE STATION.
BUT IT WAS ALREADY TOO LATE. WE DON'T KNOW WHO DID IT YET.
PLEASE COME BACK TO THE STATION WITH US.
WHAP
BUT... I WAS FIRED.
THAT'S NOT IMPORTANT NOW!
Polic
YOU SHOULD...
...GO TO...
DOOM
...YAMAZAKI.

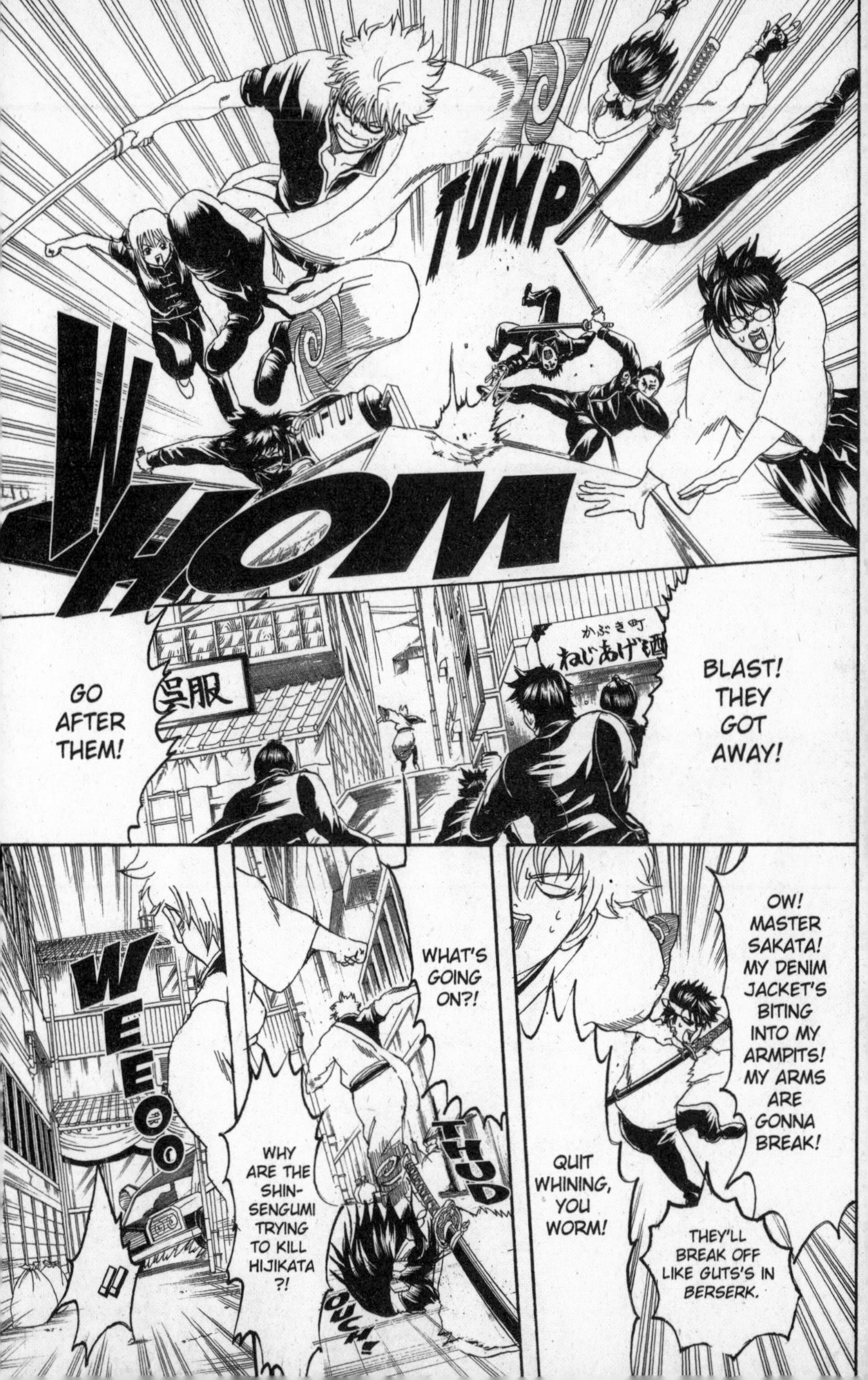
TUMP
WHOM
BLAST! THEY GOT AWAY!
かぶき町
ねじあげ酒
呉服
GO AFTER THEM!
OW! MASTER SAKATA! MY DENIM JACKET'S BITING INTO MY ARMPITS! MY ARMS ARE GONNA BREAK!
QUIT WHINING, YOU WORM!
THEY'LL BREAK OFF LIKE GUTS'S IN BERSERK.
WHAT'S GOING ON?!
THUD
WHY ARE THE SHIN-SENGUMI TRYING TO KILL HIJIKATA?!
OUCH!
WEEEOO
!!

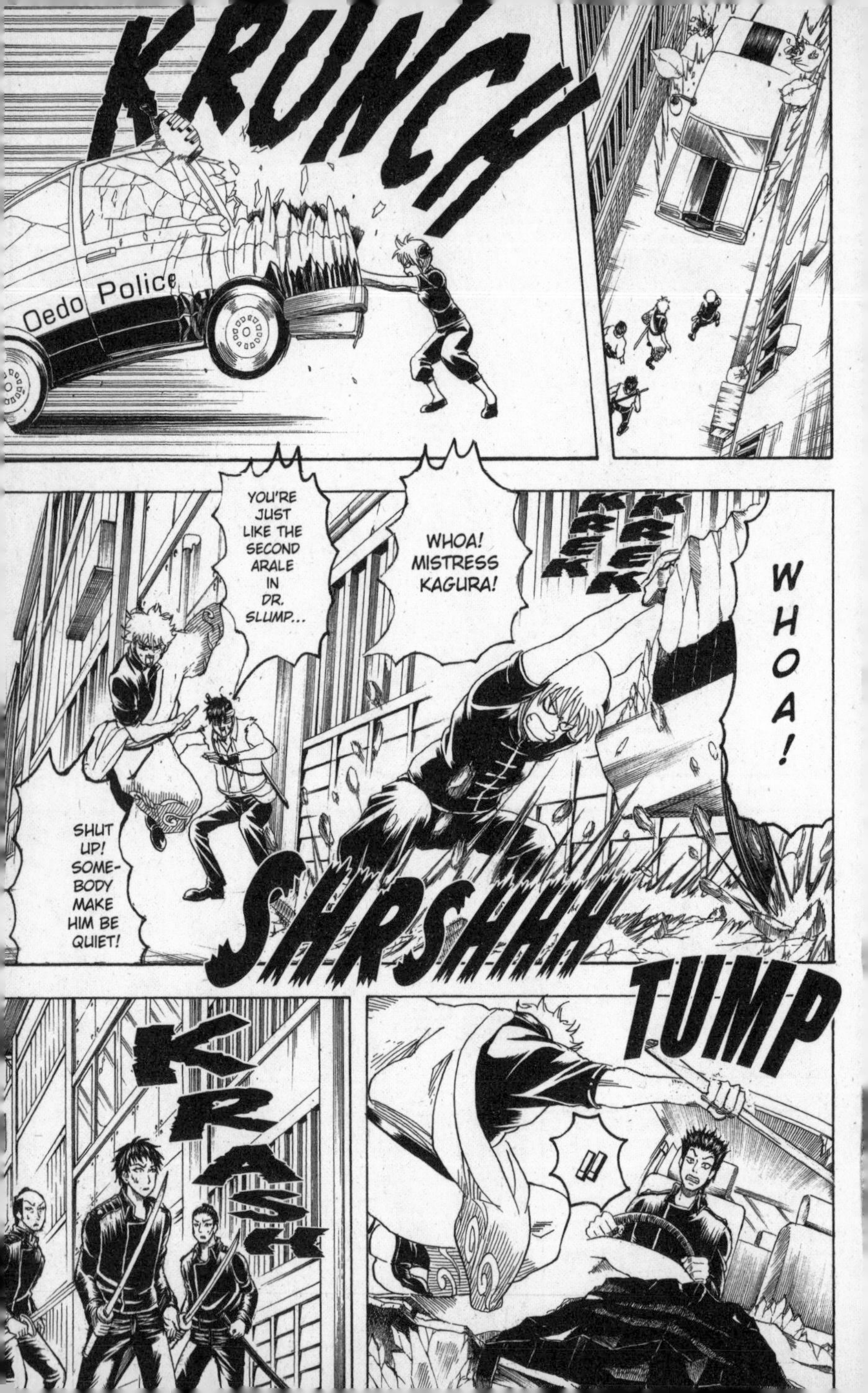
KRUNCH
Oedo Police
WHOA!
KREEK KREEK KREEK
WHOA! MISTRESS KAGURA!
YOU'RE JUST LIKE THE SECOND ARALE IN DR. SLUMP...
SHUT UP! SOME-BODY MAKE HIM BE QUIET!
SHRSHHH
TUMP
!!
KRASH

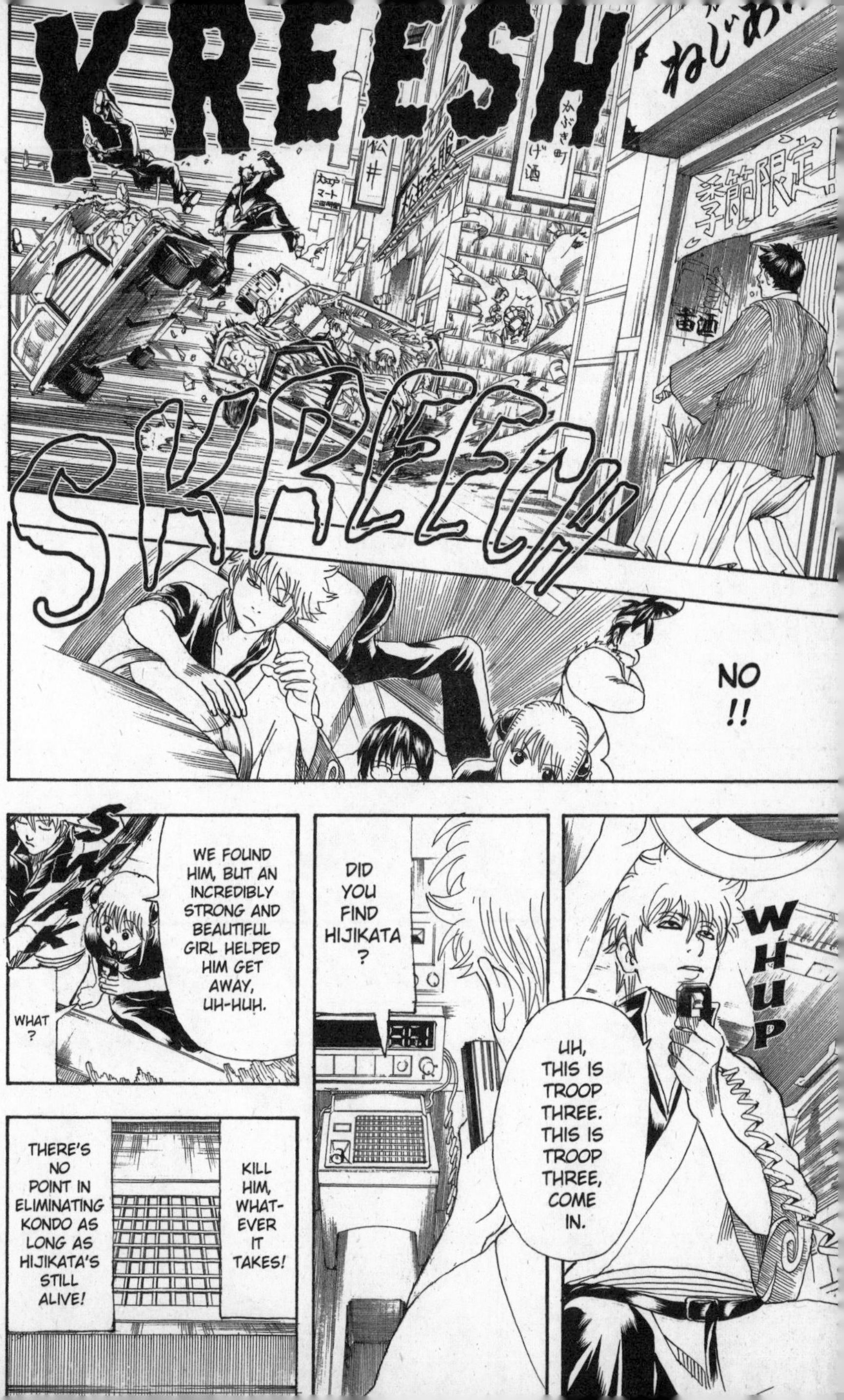
KREESH
SKREECH
NO!!
WHUP
UH, THIS IS TROOP THREE. THIS IS TROOP THREE, COME IN.
DID YOU FIND HIJIKATA?
WE FOUND HIM, BUT AN INCREDIBLY STRONG AND BEAUTIFUL GIRL HELPED HIM GET AWAY, UH-HUH.
WHAT?
KILL HIM, WHATEVER IT TAKES!
THERE'S NO POINT IN ELIMINATING KONDO AS LONG AS HIJIKATA'S STILL ALIVE!

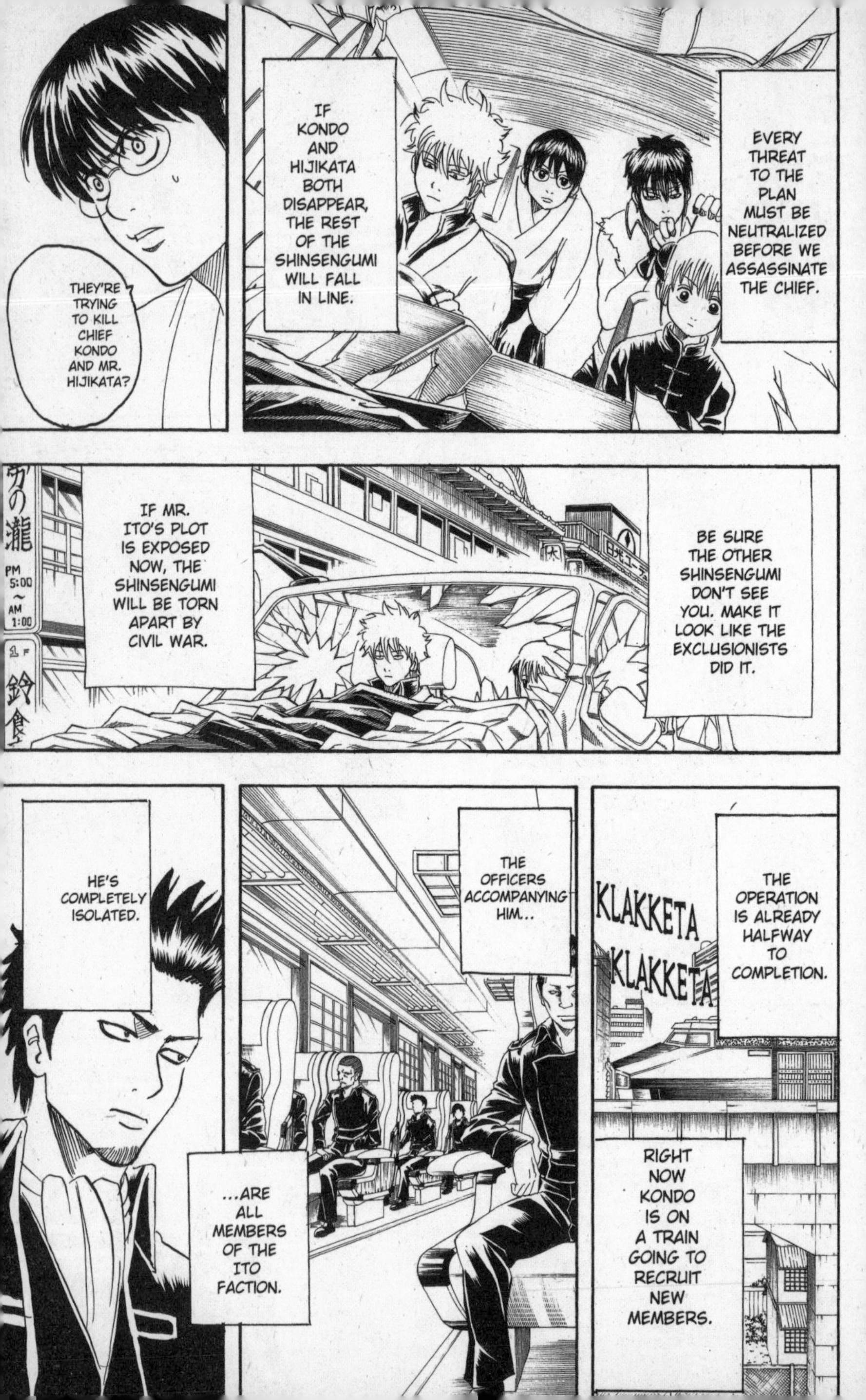
EVERY THREAT TO THE PLAN MUST BE NEUTRALIZED BEFORE WE ASSASSINATE THE CHIEF.
IF KONDO AND HIJIKATA BOTH DISAPPEAR, THE REST OF THE SHINSENGUMI WILL FALL IN LINE.
THEY'RE TRYING TO KILL CHIEF KONDO AND MR. HIJIKATA?
BE SURE THE OTHER SHINSENGUMI DON'T SEE YOU. MAKE IT LOOK LIKE THE EXCLUSIONISTS DID IT.
IF MR. ITO'S PLOT IS EXPOSED NOW, THE SHINSENGUMI WILL BE TORN APART BY CIVIL WAR.
PM 5:00 ~ AM 1:00
THE OPERATION IS ALREADY HALFWAY TO COMPLETION.
KLAKKETA
KLAKKETA
RIGHT NOW KONDO IS ON A TRAIN GOING TO RECRUIT NEW MEMBERS.
THE OFFICERS ACCOMPANYING HIM...
...ARE ALL MEMBERS OF THE ITO FACTION.
HE'S COMPLETELY ISOLATED.

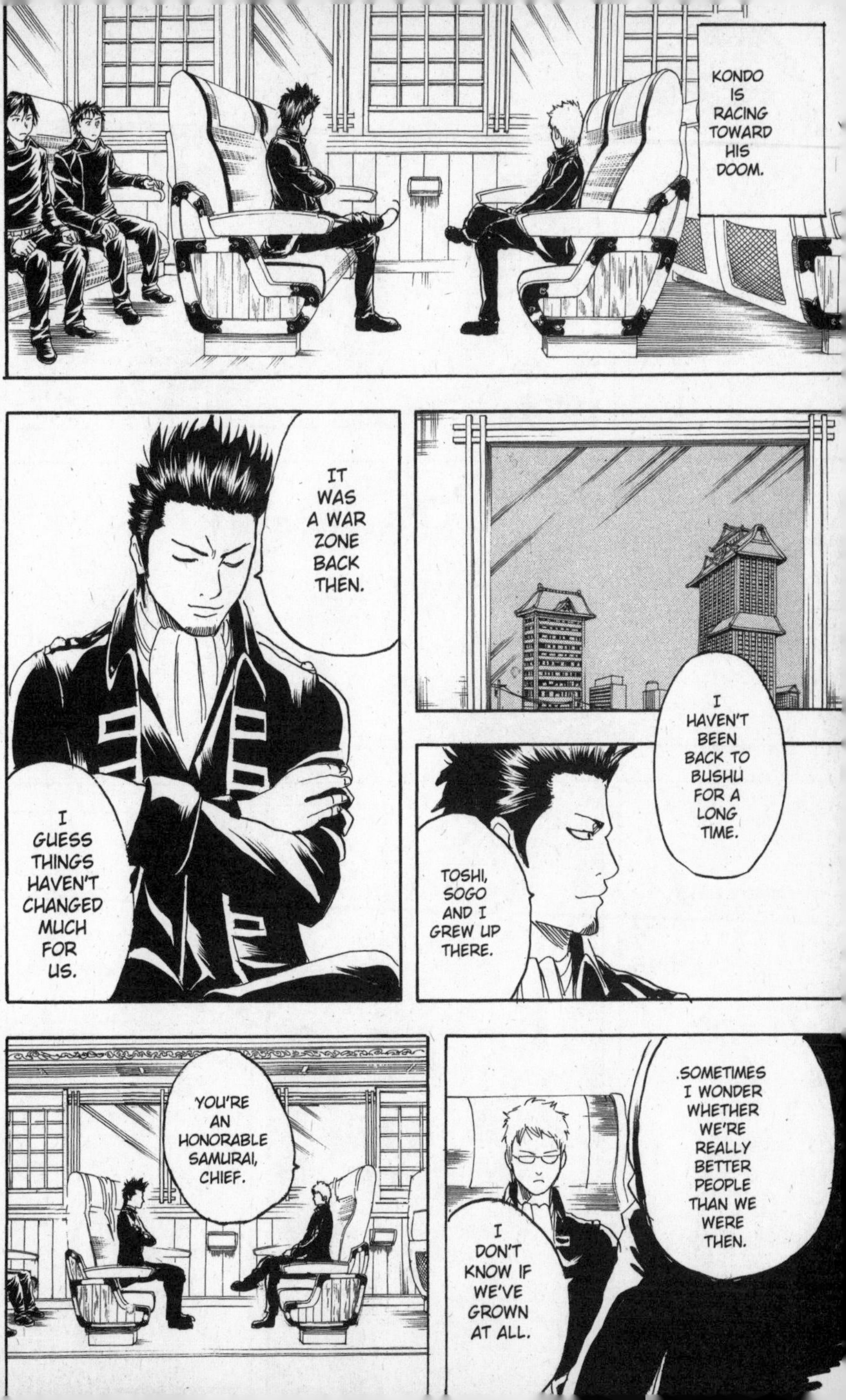
KONDO IS RACING TOWARD HIS DOOM.
I HAVEN'T BEEN BACK TO BUSHU FOR A LONG TIME.
TOSHI, SOGO AND I GREW UP THERE.
IT WAS A WAR ZONE BACK THEN.
I GUESS THINGS HAVEN'T CHANGED MUCH FOR US.
SOMETIMES I WONDER WHETHER WE'RE REALLY BETTER PEOPLE THAN WE WERE THEN.
I DON'T KNOW IF WE'VE GROWN AT ALL.
YOU'RE AN HONORABLE SAMURAI, CHIEF.

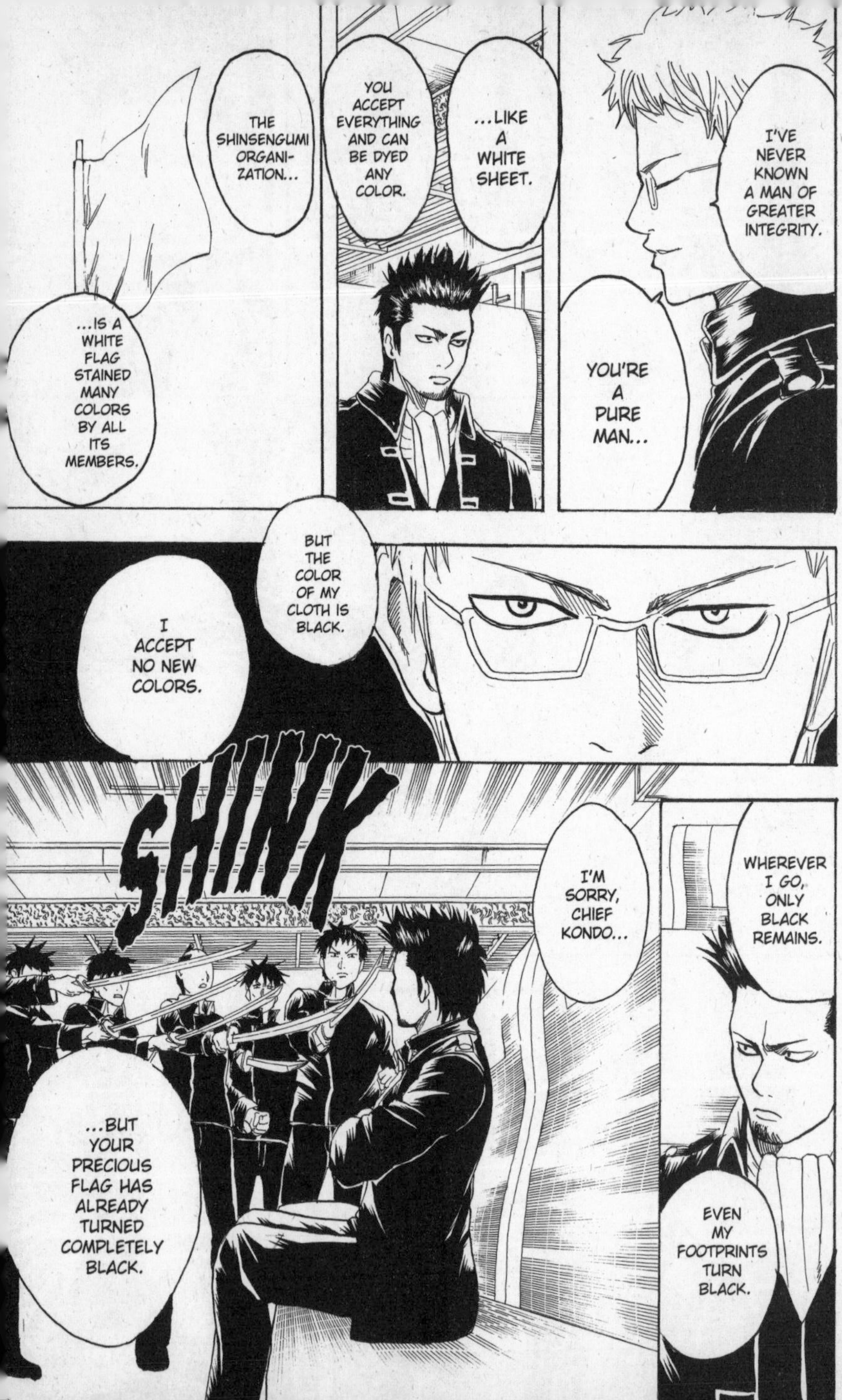
I'VE NEVER KNOWN A MAN OF GREATER INTEGRITY.
YOU'RE A PURE MAN...
...LIKE A WHITE SHEET.
YOU ACCEPT EVERYTHING AND CAN BE DYED ANY COLOR.
THE SHINSENGUMI ORGANIZATION...
...IS A WHITE FLAG STAINED MANY COLORS BY ALL ITS MEMBERS.
BUT THE COLOR OF MY CLOTH IS BLACK.
I ACCEPT NO NEW COLORS.
WHEREVER I GO, ONLY BLACK REMAINS.
EVEN MY FOOTPRINTS TURN BLACK.
I'M SORRY, CHIEF KONDO...
SHINK
...BUT YOUR PRECIOUS FLAG HAS ALREADY TURNED COMPLETELY BLACK.

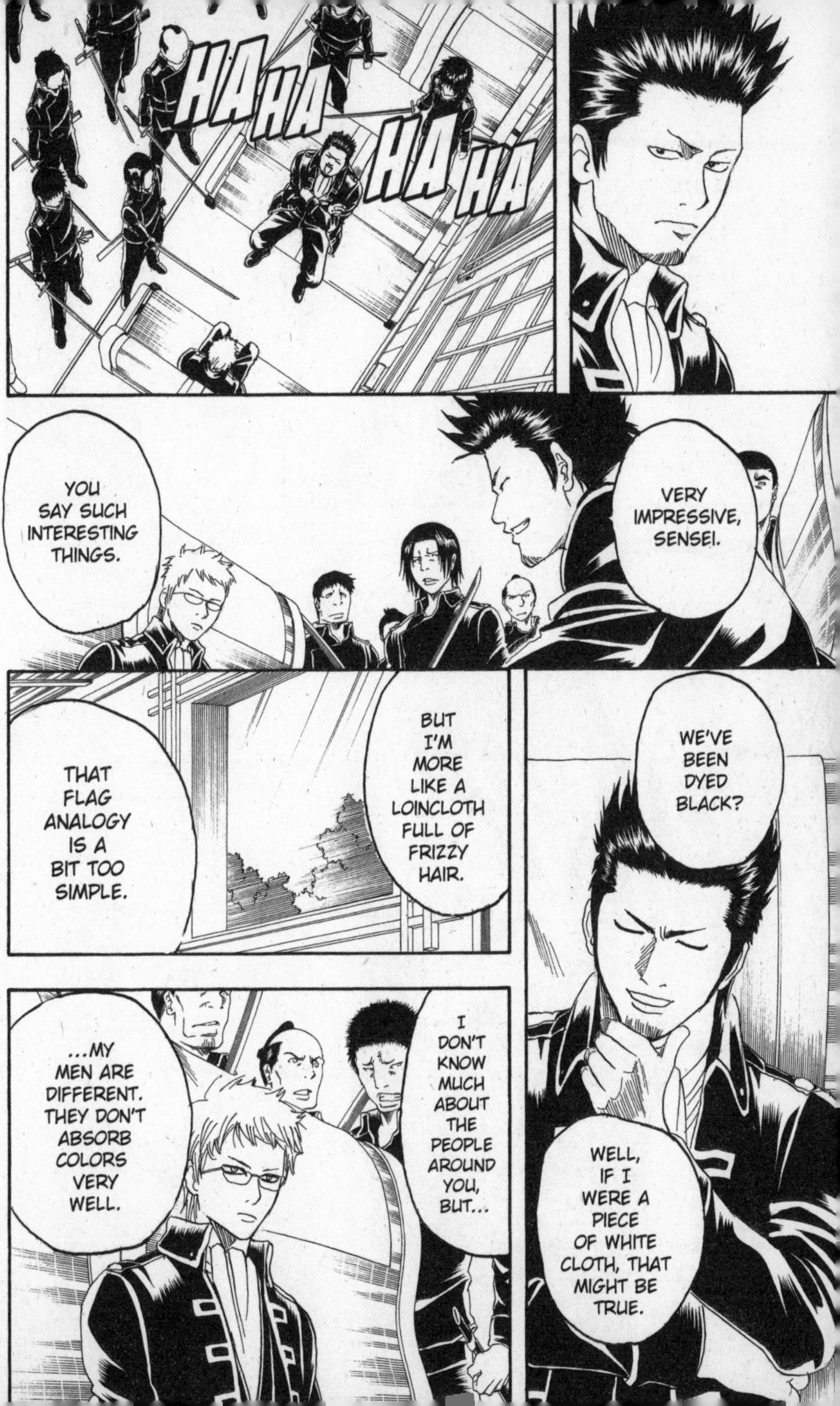
HA HA HA HA
YOU SAY SUCH INTERESTING THINGS.
VERY IMPRESSIVE, SENSEI.
WE'VE BEEN DYED BLACK?
WELL, IF I WERE A PIECE OF WHITE CLOTH, THAT MIGHT BE TRUE.
BUT I'M MORE LIKE A LOINCLOTH FULL OF FRIZZY HAIR.
THAT FLAG ANALOGY IS A BIT TOO SIMPLE.
I DON'T KNOW MUCH ABOUT THE PEOPLE AROUND YOU, BUT...
...MY MEN ARE DIFFERENT. THEY DON'T ABSORB COLORS VERY WELL.

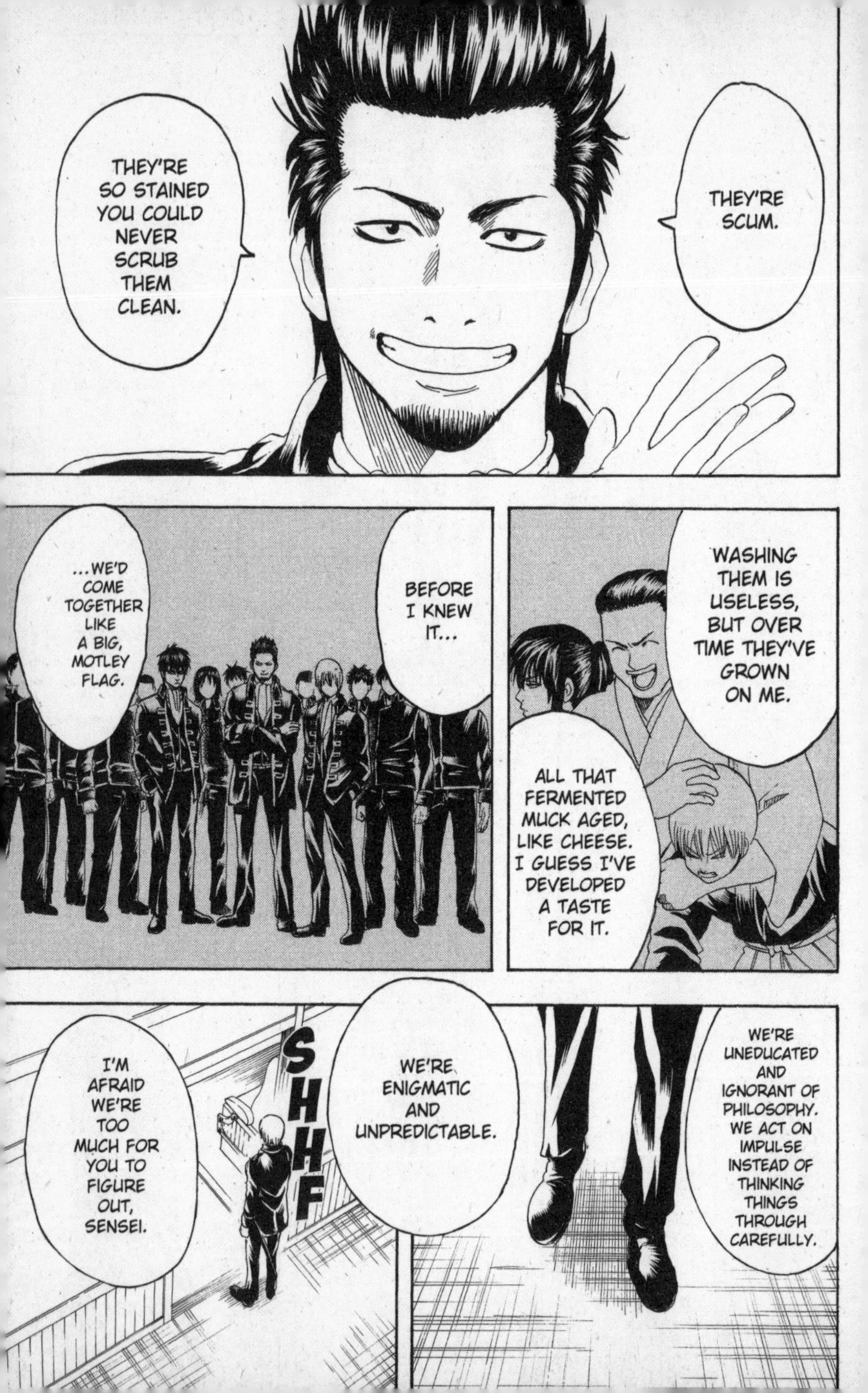
THEY'RE SCUM.
THEY'RE SO STAINED YOU COULD NEVER SCRUB THEM CLEAN.
WASHING THEM IS USELESS, BUT OVER TIME THEY'VE GROWN ON ME.
ALL THAT FERMENTED MUCK AGED, LIKE CHEESE. I GUESS I'VE DEVELOPED A TASTE FOR IT.
BEFORE I KNEW IT...
...WE'D COME TOGETHER LIKE A BIG, MOTLEY FLAG.
WE'RE UNEDUCATED AND IGNORANT OF PHILOSOPHY. WE ACT ON IMPULSE INSTEAD OF THINKING THINGS THROUGH CAREFULLY.
WE'RE ENIGMATIC AND UNPREDICTABLE.
SHHF
I'M AFRAID WE'RE TOO MUCH FOR YOU TO FIGURE OUT, SENSEI.

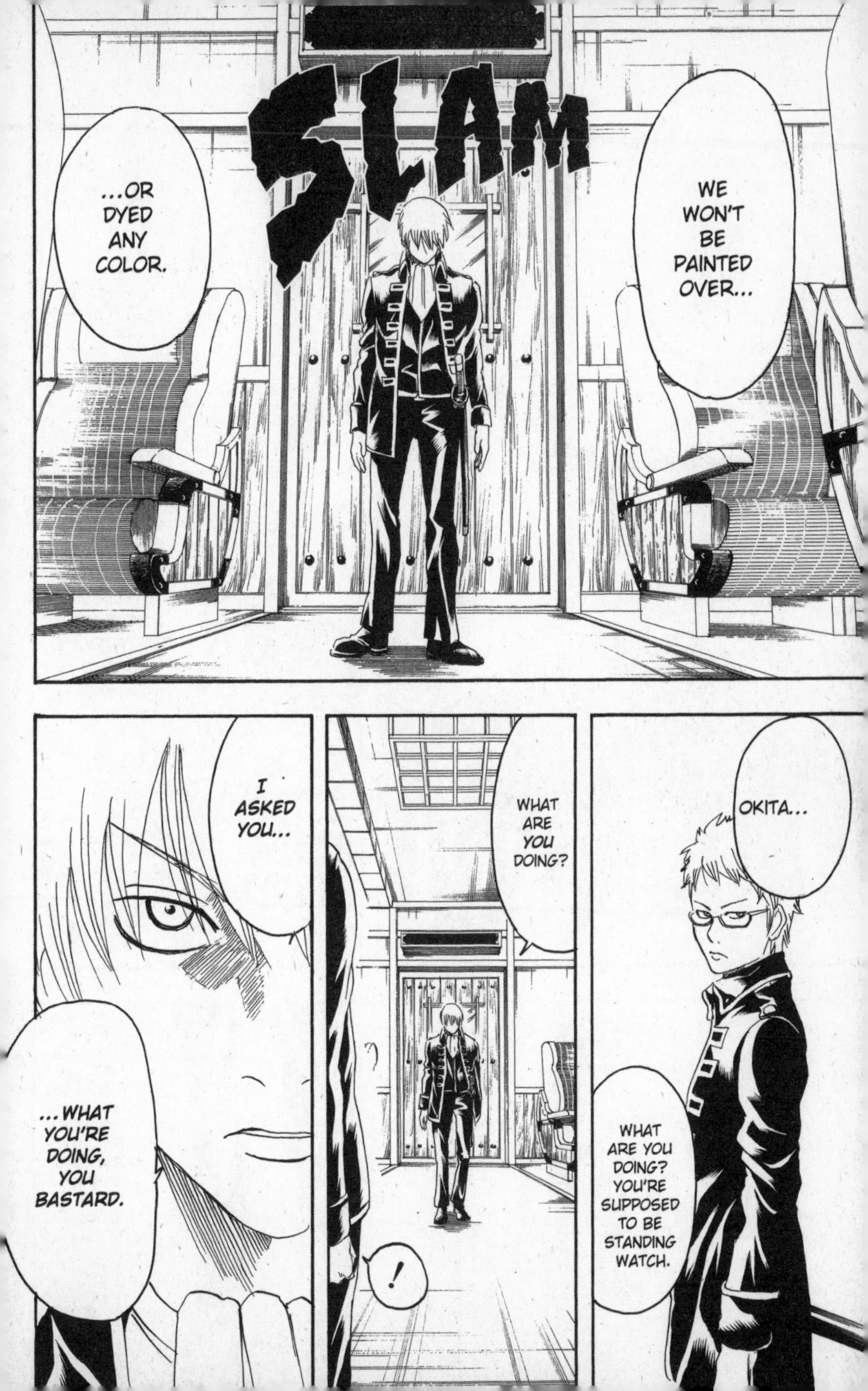
WE WON'T BE PAINTED OVER...
SLAM
...OR DYED ANY COLOR.
OKITA...
WHAT ARE YOU DOING? YOU'RE SUPPOSED TO BE STANDING WATCH.
WHAT ARE YOU DOING?
!
I ASKED YOU...
...WHAT YOU'RE DOING, YOU BASTARD.

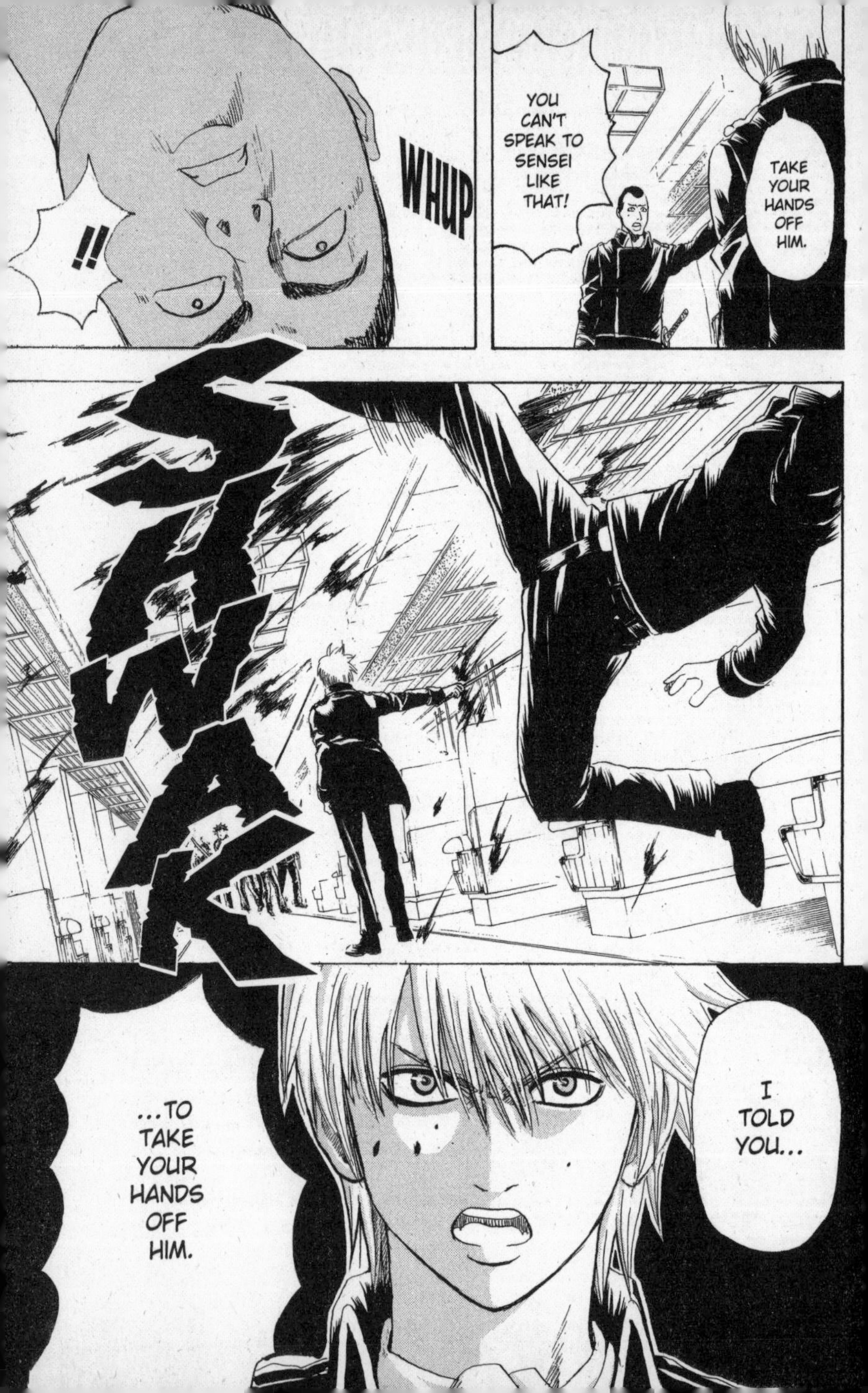

TAKE YOUR HANDS OFF HIM.
YOU CAN'T SPEAK TO SENSEI LIKE THAT!
WHUP
!!
WHAK
I TOLD YOU...
...TO TAKE YOUR HANDS OFF HIM.

SORACHI: (CONTINUED) ...I WOULDN'T HAVE FINISHED IF I DIDN'T DO IT THAT WAY.
ONISHI: YEAH, YOU WOULDN'T.
SORACHI: YUP.
ONISHI: YOU REALLY NEEDED TO BE FORCED LIKE THAT.
SORACHI: IT WAS HELL FOR ME. I GOT SCARED EVERY TIME THE PHONE RANG. I EVEN STARTED TO HEAR THE PHONE WHEN IT WASN'T RINGING. SERIOUSLY. (LAUGH) WHENEVER I HEAR ANY KIND OF ELECTRONIC SOUND, I AUTOMATICALLY THINK, "OH, ANOTHER PHONE CALL." I FELT LIKE I WAS HAVING A NERVOUS BREAKDOWN.
ONISHI: AND AFTER "SHIROKURO"...
SORACHI: AFTER THAT, DIDN'T YOU TELL ME TO START GIVING YOU THE DRAFTS FOR SERIALIZATION?
ONISHI: I TOLD YOU TO KEEP SERIALIZATIONS IN MIND WHEN YOU SENT THEM TO ME. IF IT WAS GOOD, I WOULD BRING IT UP AT THE NEXT MEETING. IF IT WASN'T VERY GOOD, WE'D USE IT AS ANOTHER ONE-SHOT THING.
SORACHI: OH YEAH. I WAS TOLD TO DRAW SOMETHING ABOUT SHINSENGUMI, AND I FLAT OUT REFUSED. BUT AFTER A WHILE, I DECIDED TO WORK WITH THE IDEA, SO I PUT TOGETHER SOME STUFF.
ONISHI: AT FIRST, YOU DIDN'T HAVE ALIENS AND HAD MONSTERS, RIGHT?
SORACHI: NO, I NEVER IMPLEMENTED THAT IDEA.
ONISHI: YOU DIDN'T?
SORACHI: I NEVER WANTED TO PUT MONSTERS IN IT. BUT YOU SAID, "WHY DON'T YOU HAVE MONSTERS AND THE SHINSENGUMI FIGHT EACH OTHER?" I DIDN'T WANT TO DO THAT, SO I PUT IN ALIENS INSTEAD.
ONISHI: AND THEN YOU SAID, "MAYBE I SHOULD HAVE GONE WITH MONSTERS AFTER ALL," AFTER THAT. (LAUGH)
SORACHI: NOT THE MONSTERS. I THOUGHT THAT MAYBE I SHOULD HAVE MADE THE SHINSENGUMI PEOPLE THE MAIN CHARACTERS. (LAUGH) I DIDN'T WANT TO BRING IT UP AT THE MEETING YET, BUT ONISHI SAID, "IT PROBABLY WON'T WORK." THAT'S WHY I JUST GAVE IT UP.
ONISHI: TO BE HONEST, I THOUGHT IT WOULD HAVE BEEN GREAT. (LAUGH)
SORACHI: (LAUGH) YOU ALWAYS SAY THAT AFTER IT'S TOO LATE. YOU DID THAT FOR "SHIROKURO" TOO.
ONISHI: WELL, IF I SAID IT, YOU NEVER WOULD HAVE EVEN TRIED TO BRING IT OUT.
SORACHI: SO THAT'S WHY YOU WERE DOING NOTHING BUT COMPLAINING WHEN I WAS DRAWING "SHIROKURO." I JUST KEPT THINKING THAT IF I FIXED IT UP, IT COULD BECOME REALLY GOOD.
ONISHI: MAYBE...
SORACHI: I DIDN'T WANT TO DO IT BECAUSE I KNEW THAT I COULD DRAW SOMETHING BETTER. BUT I GUESS I SHOULD HAVE PLANNED IT BETTER BEFORE THE SERIALIZATION STARTED.
ONISHI: IT ALWAYS ENDS UP BEING THE SAME NO MATTER HOW MUCH YOU TRY TO ELABORATE.
SORACHI: IF I DID, THE SHINSENGUMI PEOPLE WOULD HAVE BEEN THE MAIN CHARACTERS.
ONISHI: IT'S THE SAME.
SORACHI: I GUESS YOU'RE RIGHT...

"DEADLINES? WHAT'RE THEY? (LAUGH)" -SORACHI

[ABOUT WHAT HAPPENS DURING MEETINGS]

SORACHI: YOU KNOW, INTERVIEWS WITH OTHER COMIC AUTHORS ALWAYS GO REALLY SMOOTHLY. I'M SURE THEY'RE ABLE TO ANSWER THE QUESTIONS SO QUICKLY BECAUSE THEY'RE ALWAYS THINKING ABOUT WHAT TO SAY.
ONISHI: MAYBE.
SORACHI: THEY'RE THINKING ABOUT WHAT NOT TO SAY WHILE THEY'RE TALKING, RIGHT? I THINK THAT'S AMAZING.
ONISHI: BUT IT CAN BE GOOD TO BE A COMIC AUTHOR. YOU NEVER HAVE TO ADJUST YOURSELF TO FIT IN WITH OTHERS.
SORACHI: BECAUSE WE DON'T HAVE TO?
ONISHI: YOU DON'T. YOU NEVER HAVE TO BROWNNOSE ANYONE, AND YOU NEVER HAVE TO COMMUTE TO WORK ON A SET SCHEDULE OR ANYTHING.
SORACHI: YEAH, THAT'S GREAT.
ONISHI: AS LONG AS YOU MEET YOUR DEADLINES, YOU CAN DRAW YOUR COMICS AT YOUR OWN PACE.
SORACHI: SO THAT'S WHY YOU KEEP EMPHASIZING MEETING DEADLINES?
ONISHI: YES.
SORACHI: DEADLINES? WHAT'RE THEY? (LAUGH)
ONISHI: DON'T GIVE ME THAT. (LAUGH)
SORACHI: SO WHAT'S "DEAD" ABOUT THE "LINE"?
ONISHI: THERE'S A CUTOFF TIME FOR THE PRINTING OF AN ISSUE...
SORACHI: WELL, IF THAT'S WHAT YOU MEAN, I'VE NEVER MISSED A DEADLINE.
ONISHI: BUT THAT'S BECAUSE THERE'S ALWAYS SOMEONE TO HELP YOU OUT AND MANAGE TO GET YOU IN.
SORACHI: I'M REFERRING TO THE DEADLINE YOU WERE TALKING ABOUT IN THE BEGINNING.
SORACHI: IF YOU CAN NOT HAVING THE COMIC GO INTO PRINT FOR THE ISSUE MISSING A DEADLINE, THEN I TOTALLY UNDERSTAND THAT DEADLINES MUST ALWAYS BE MET. YOU DON'T HAVE TO WORRY ABOUT THAT.
ONISHI: REALLY?
SORACHI: SO HOW IS THIS INTERVIEW GOING TO BE PRINTED IN AKAMARU JUMP?
ONISHI: WITH WORDS... I'M YOUR MANAGING EDITOR, AND I'LL PLAY THE PART OF THE INTERVIEWER.
SORACHI: BUT MOST LIKELY NO ONE CARES ABOUT IT.
ONISHI: ABOUT WHAT?
SORACHI: ABOUT GIN TAMA. THEY PROBABLY COULD CARE LESS ABOUT THAT THING WITH THE SIX PAGES I TALKED ABOUT EARLIER.
ONISHI: I'M SURE THEY CARE.
SORACHI: REALLY?
ONISHI: EVERYONE WANTS TO KNOW. IF IT'S LIKE THE Q&A FORMAT WE HAD IN "GIN CHANNEL!" IT'LL FEEL PRETENTIOUS. IT'S LIKE WE HAD TO THINK CAREFULLY BEFORE WRITING IT DOWN.
SORACHI: SO YOU PREFER SOMETHING THAT DOESN'T FLOW WELL?
ONISHI: YEAH. SOMETHING THAT DOESN'T FLOW WELL BUT IS MORE NATURAL.
SORACHI: I'VE NEVER SEEN ANYTHING LIKE THAT.
ONISHI: THEY DO THAT ALL THE TIME IN MUSIC MAGAZINES. THEY HAVE THOSE 10,000- CHARACTER OR 30,000-CHARACTER INTERVIEWS AND STUFF. THAT'S WHEN THEY TALK ABOUT THEIR PERSONAL HISTORY, LIKE THEIR UPBRINGING.
SORACHI: DON'T YOU THINK THAT'S KIND OF PRETENTIOUS? IT'S GIVING MORE INFORMATION THAN PEOPLE WANT TO KNOW, AND IT GIVES THE IMPRESSION THAT WE DON'T CARE ABOUT THE READERS.
ONISHI: IF YOU WANT TO KEEP NITPICKING, THERE WON'T BE AN END TO IT. THAT'S WHY PEOPLE WHO WANT TO READ IT WILL. PEOPLE WHO DON'T, WON'T...
SORACHI: I MEANT THAT EVEN HAVING THE INTERVIEW IN THE FIRST PLACE MAKES ME LOOK PRETENTIOUS.
ONISHI: BUT DON'T YOU LIKE THE INTERVIEWS WITH OTHER COMIC AUTHORS?
SORACHI: I DO. I LIKE THE ONES THAT I'M NOT IN.
ONISHI: SEE? IT'S THE SAME THING.
SORACHI: I LIKE THE OTHER AUTHORS'. BUT THEY HAVE ACTUAL INTERVIEWS. THEY HAVE A STRAIGHTFORWARD ANSWER, AND IT'S ALWAYS VERY EDUCATIONAL.

CONTINUED ON PAGE 106

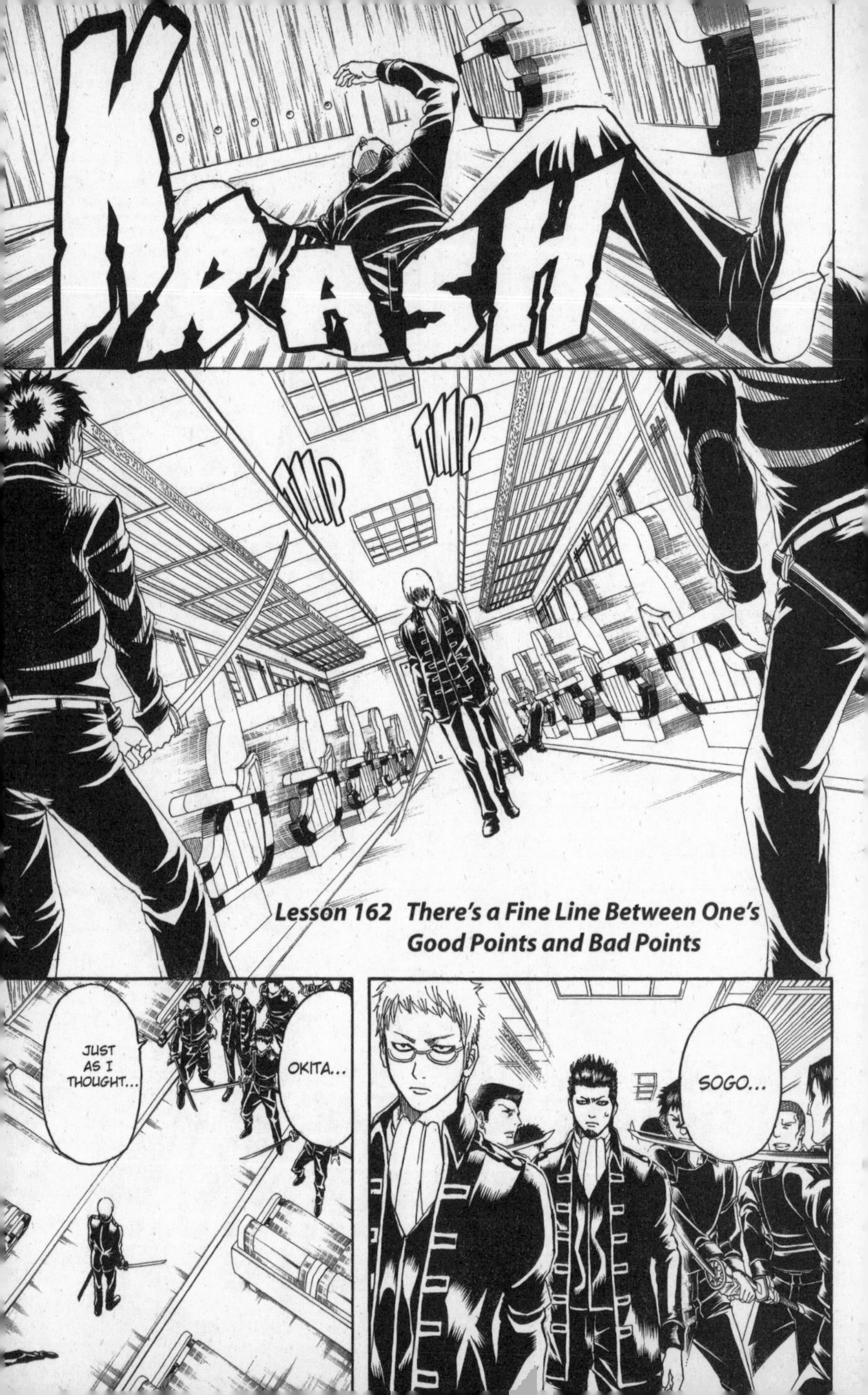
KRASH
TMP
TMP
Lesson 162 There's a Fine Line Between One's Good Points and Bad Points
SOGO...
OKITA...
JUST AS I THOUGHT...

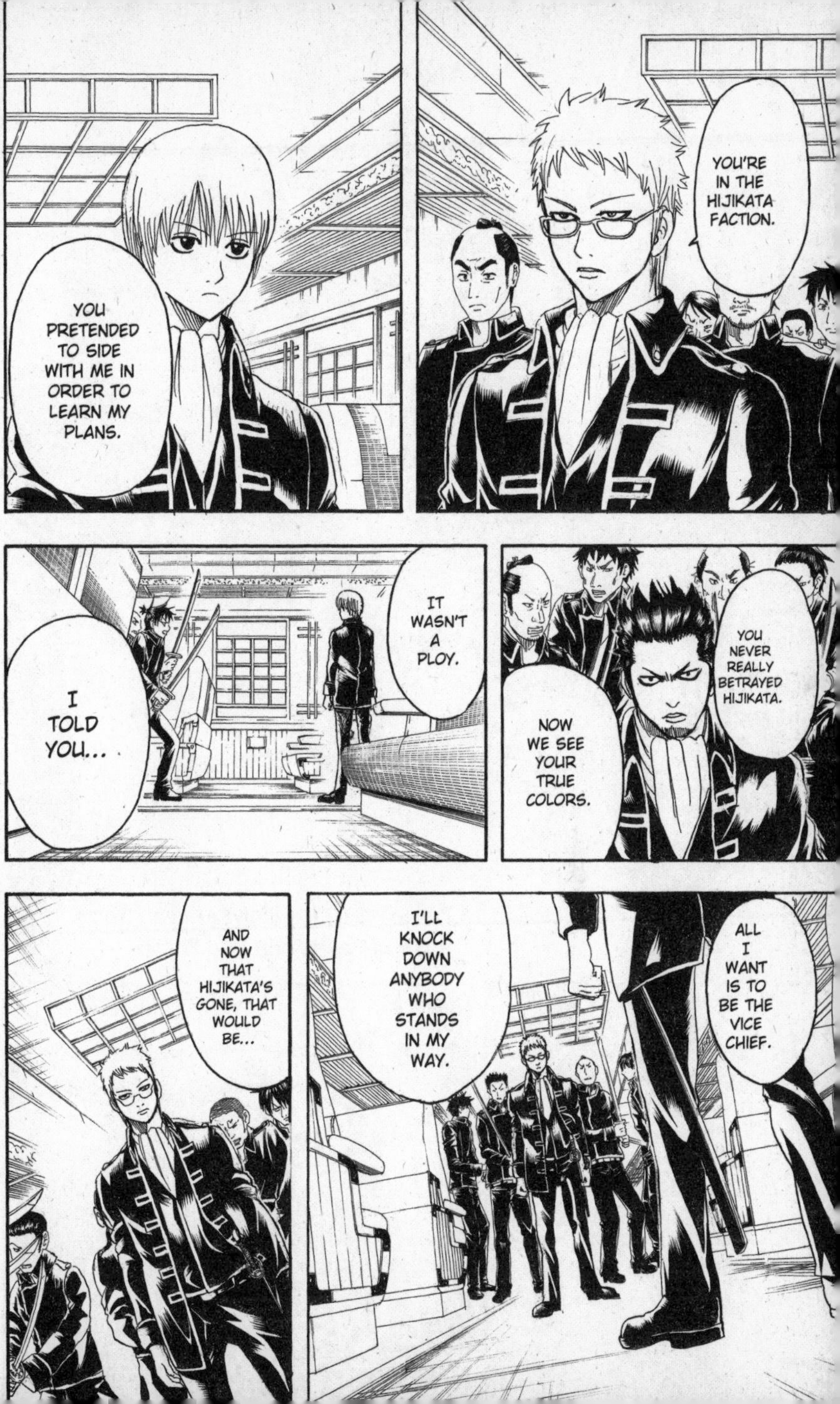
YOU'RE IN THE HIJIKATA FACTION.
YOU PRETENDED TO SIDE WITH ME IN ORDER TO LEARN MY PLANS.
YOU NEVER REALLY BETRAYED HIJIKATA.
NOW WE SEE YOUR TRUE COLORS.
IT WASN'T A PLOY.
I TOLD YOU...
ALL I WANT IS TO BE THE VICE CHIEF.
I'LL KNOCK DOWN ANYBODY WHO STANDS IN MY WAY.
AND NOW THAT HIJIKATA'S GONE, THAT WOULD BE...

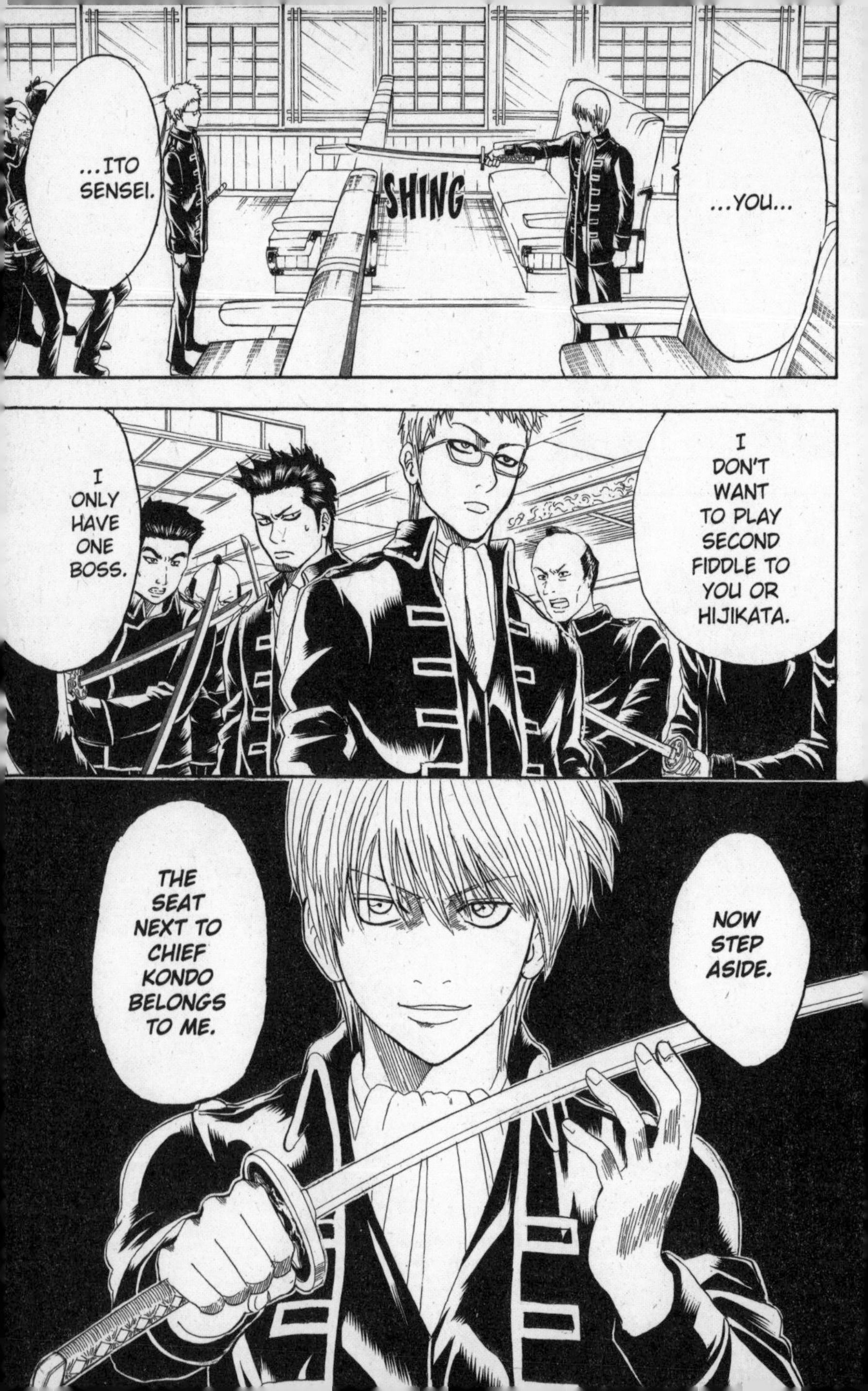
...YOU...
...ITO SENSEI.
SHING
I DON'T WANT TO PLAY SECOND FIDDLE TO YOU OR HIJIKATA.
I ONLY HAVE ONE BOSS.
THE SEAT NEXT TO CHIEF KONDO BELONGS TO ME.
NOW STEP ASIDE.

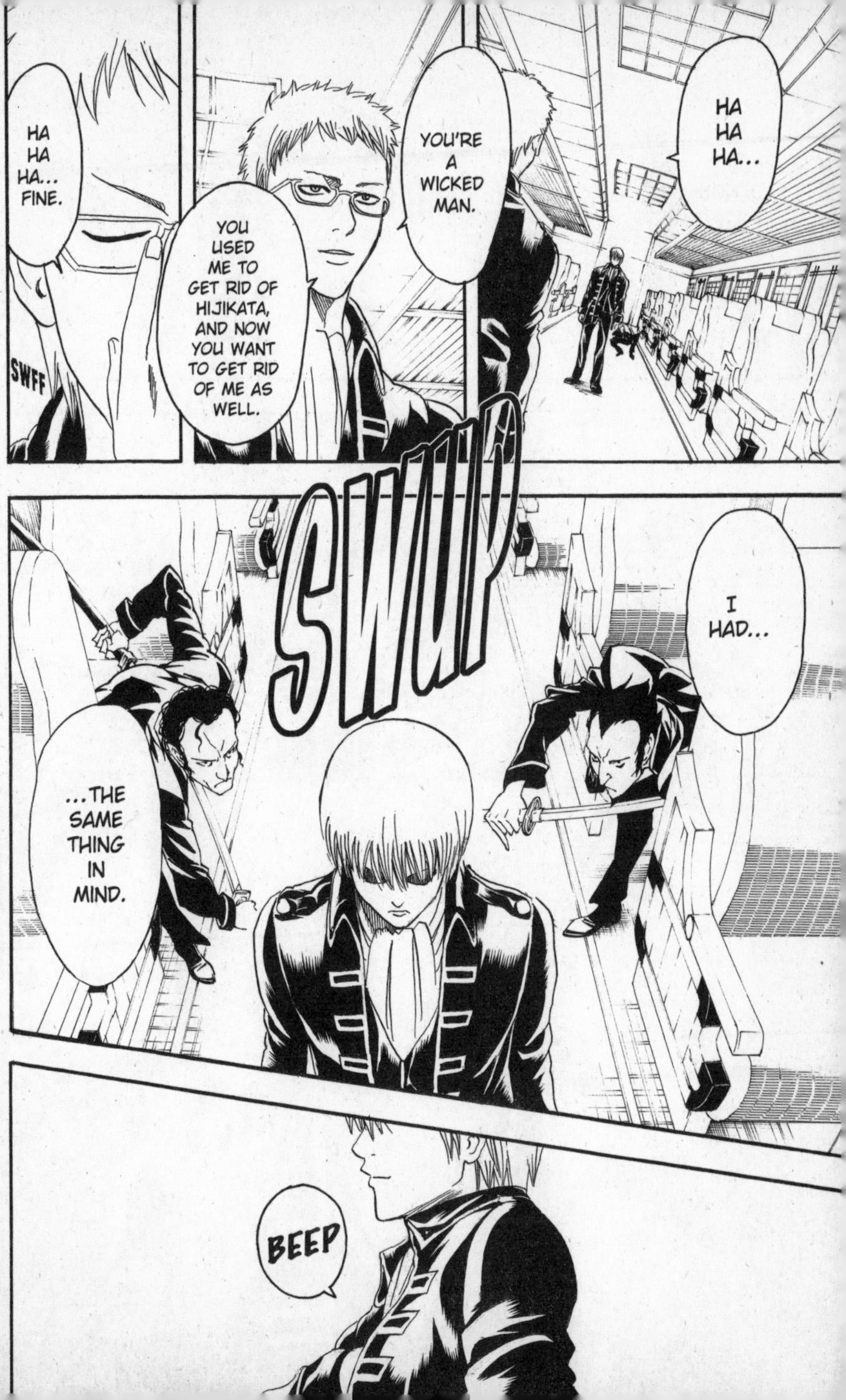

HA HA HA...
YOU'RE A WICKED MAN.
YOU USED ME TO GET RID OF HIJIKATA, AND NOW YOU WANT TO GET RID OF ME AS WELL.
HA HA HA... FINE.
SWFF
SWIP
I HAD...
...THE SAME THING IN MIND.
BEEP

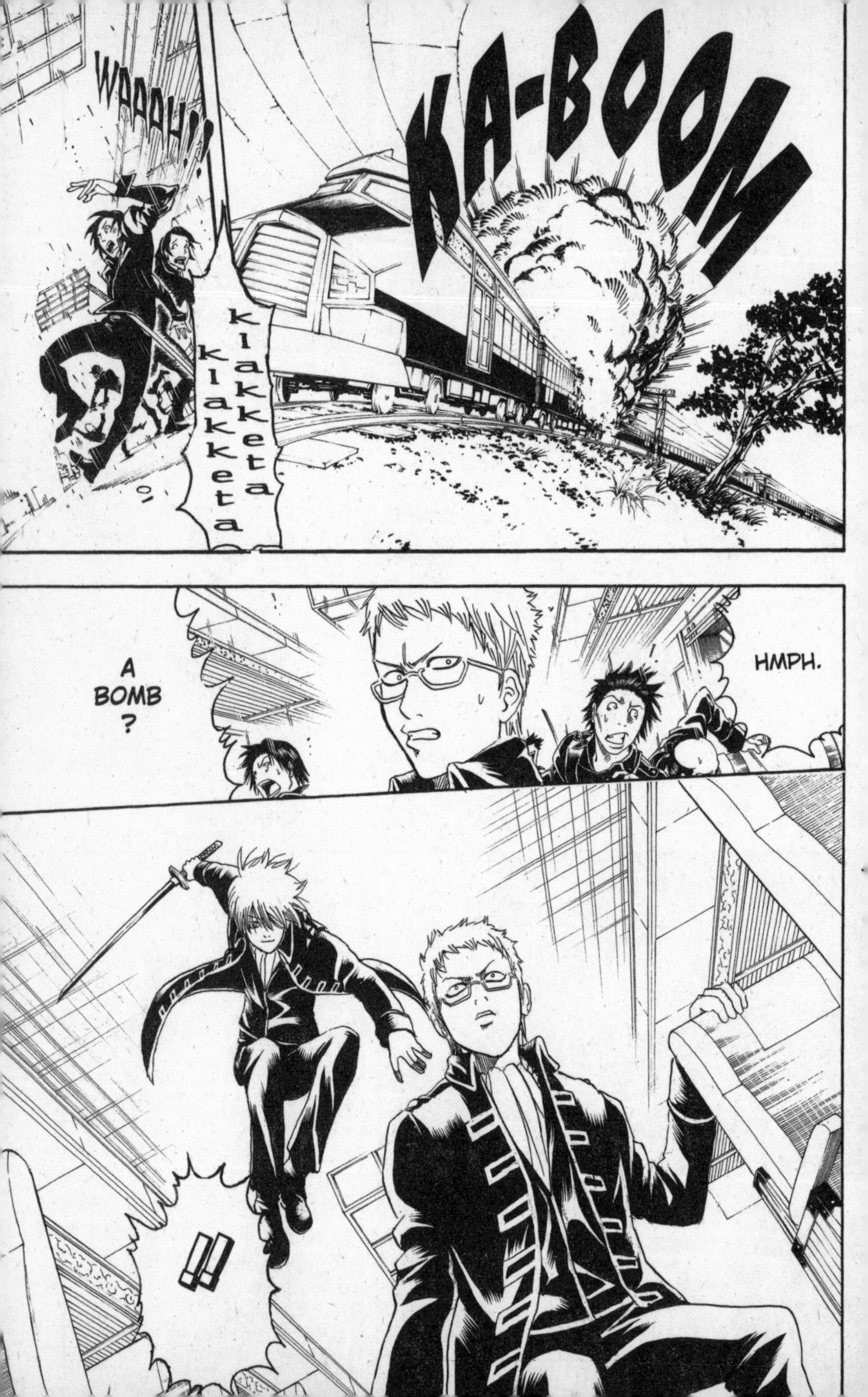
KA-BOOM
klakketa klakketa
WAAAH!!
HMPH.
A BOMB?
!!

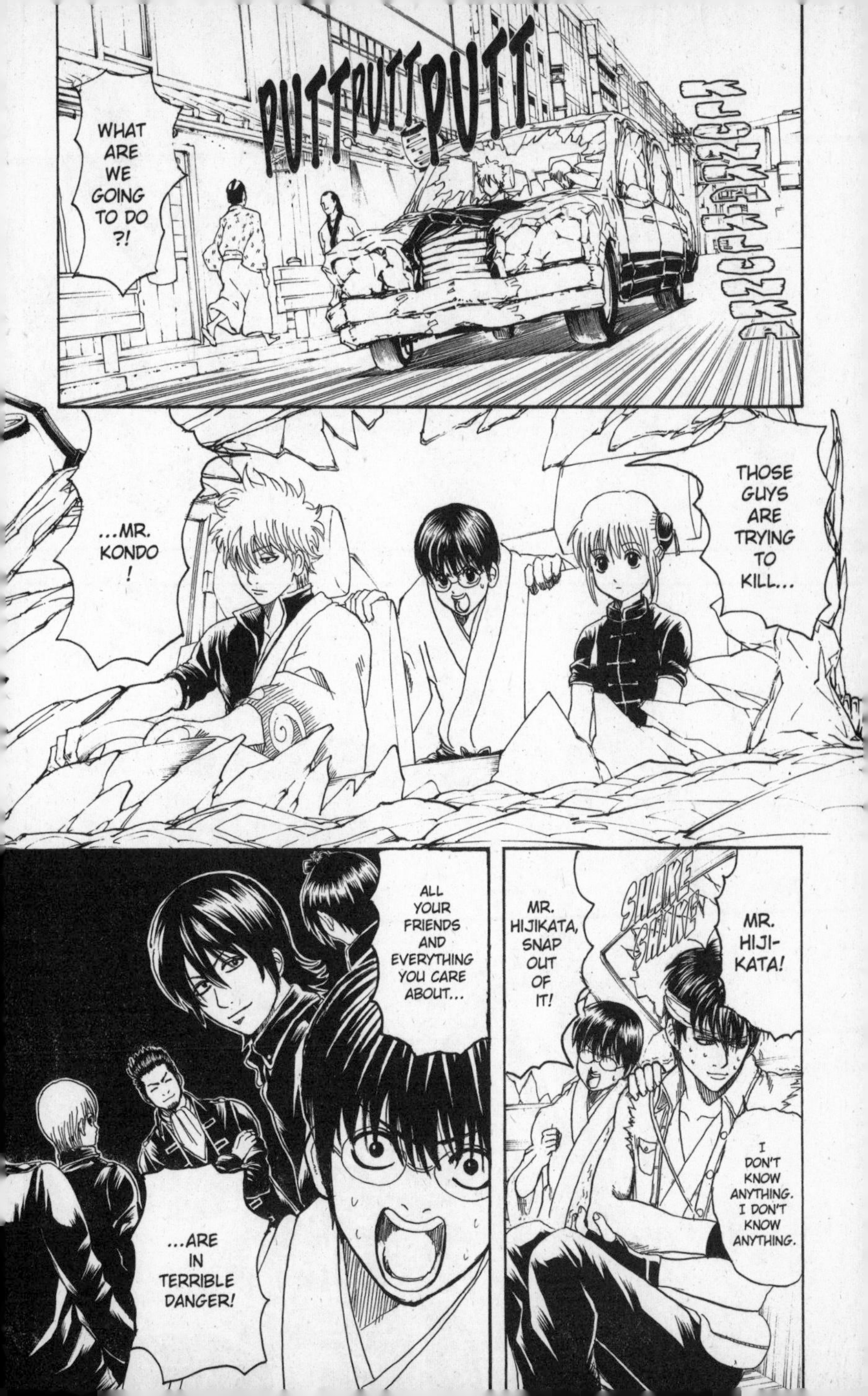
KLUNKA KLUNKA
PUTT PUTT PUTT
WHAT ARE WE GOING TO DO?!
THOSE GUYS ARE TRYING TO KILL...
...MR. KONDO!
MR. HIJI-KATA!
SHAKE SHAKE
MR. HIJIKATA, SNAP OUT OF IT!
I DON'T KNOW ANYTHING. I DON'T KNOW ANYTHING.
ALL YOUR FRIENDS AND EVERYTHING YOU CARE ABOUT...
...ARE IN TERRIBLE DANGER!

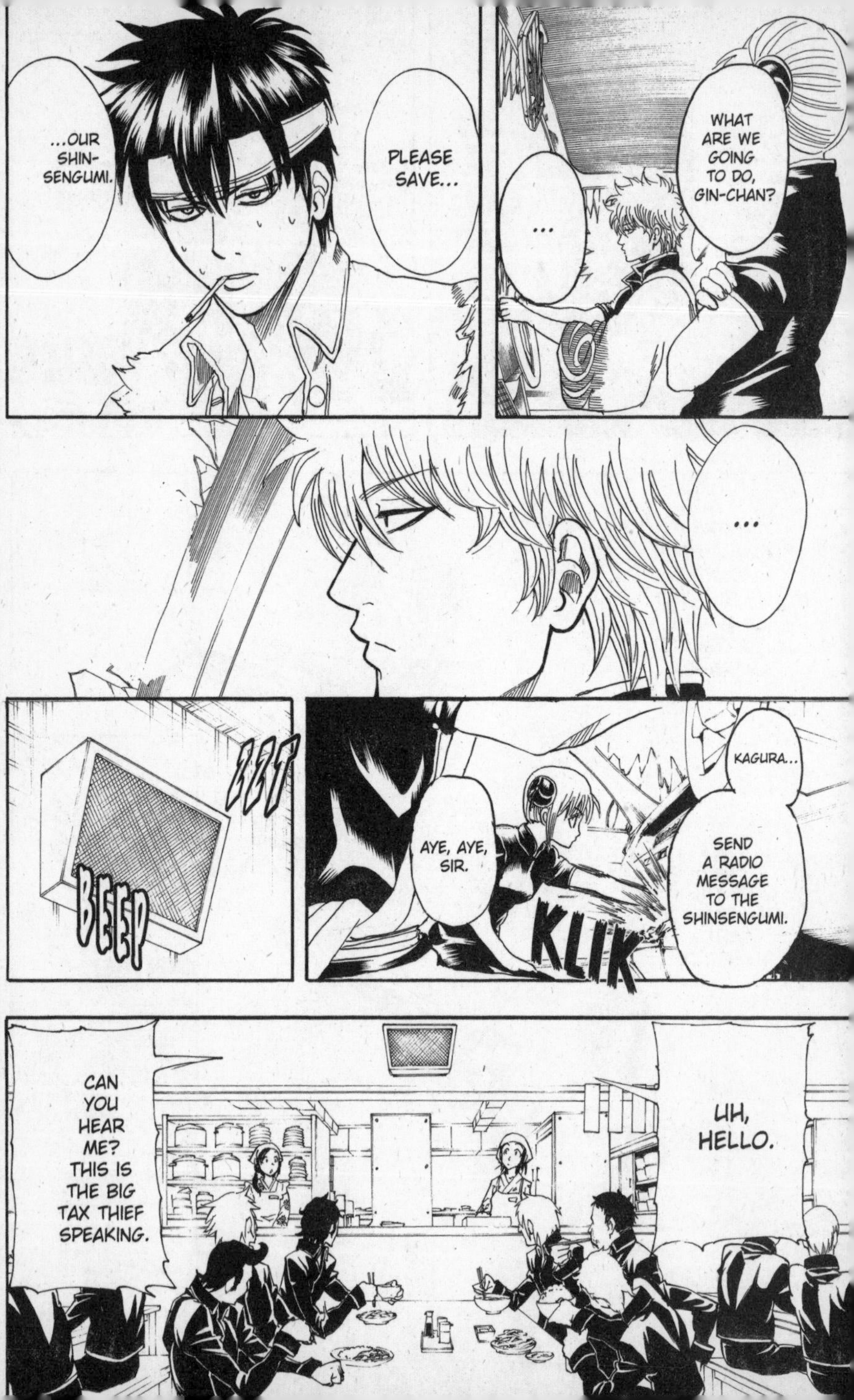
WHAT ARE WE GOING TO DO, GIN-CHAN?
...
PLEASE SAVE...
...OUR SHIN-SENGUMI.
...
KAGURA...
SEND A RADIO MESSAGE TO THE SHINSENGUMI.
AYE, AYE, SIR.
KLIK
BEEP
UH, HELLO.
CAN YOU HEAR ME? THIS IS THE BIG TAX THIEF SPEAKING.

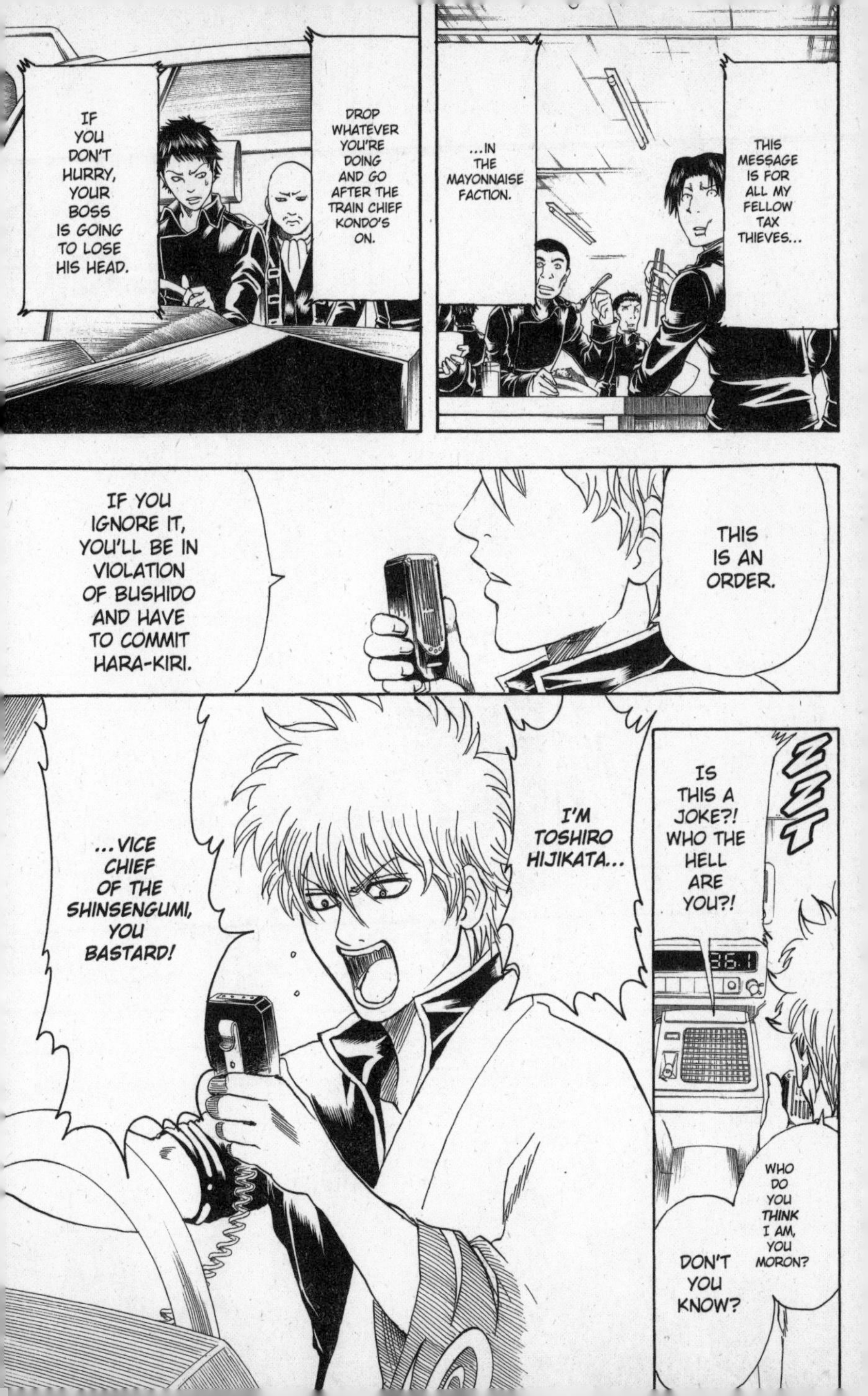
THIS MESSAGE IS FOR ALL MY FELLOW TAX THIEVES...
...IN THE MAYONNAISE FACTION.
DROP WHATEVER YOU'RE DOING AND GO AFTER THE TRAIN CHIEF KONDO'S ON.
IF YOU DON'T HURRY, YOUR BOSS IS GOING TO LOSE HIS HEAD.
THIS IS AN ORDER.
IF YOU IGNORE IT, YOU'LL BE IN VIOLATION OF BUSHIDO AND HAVE TO COMMIT HARA-KIRI.
IS THIS A JOKE?! WHO THE HELL ARE YOU?!
WHO DO YOU THINK I AM, YOU MORON?
DON'T YOU KNOW?
I'M TOSHIRO HIJIKATA...
...VICE CHIEF OF THE SHINSENGUMI, YOU BASTARD!

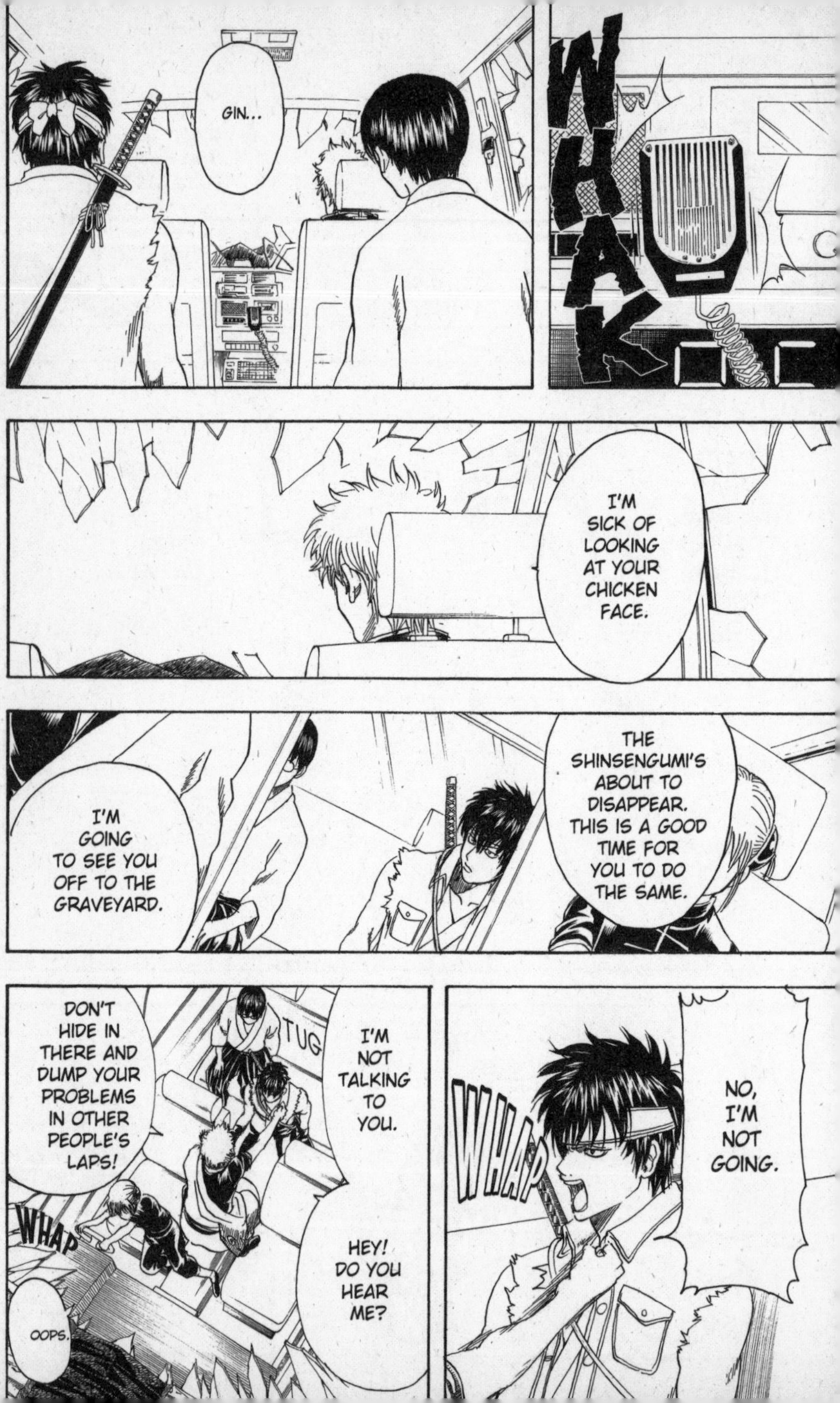
WHAK
GIN...
I'M SICK OF LOOKING AT YOUR CHICKEN FACE.
THE SHINSENGUMI'S ABOUT TO DISAPPEAR. THIS IS A GOOD TIME FOR YOU TO DO THE SAME.
I'M GOING TO SEE YOU OFF TO THE GRAVEYARD.
NO, I'M NOT GOING.
WHAP
TUG
I'M NOT TALKING TO YOU.
DON'T HIDE IN THERE AND DUMP YOUR PROBLEMS IN OTHER PEOPLE'S LAPS!
HEY! DO YOU HEAR ME?
WHAP
OOPS.

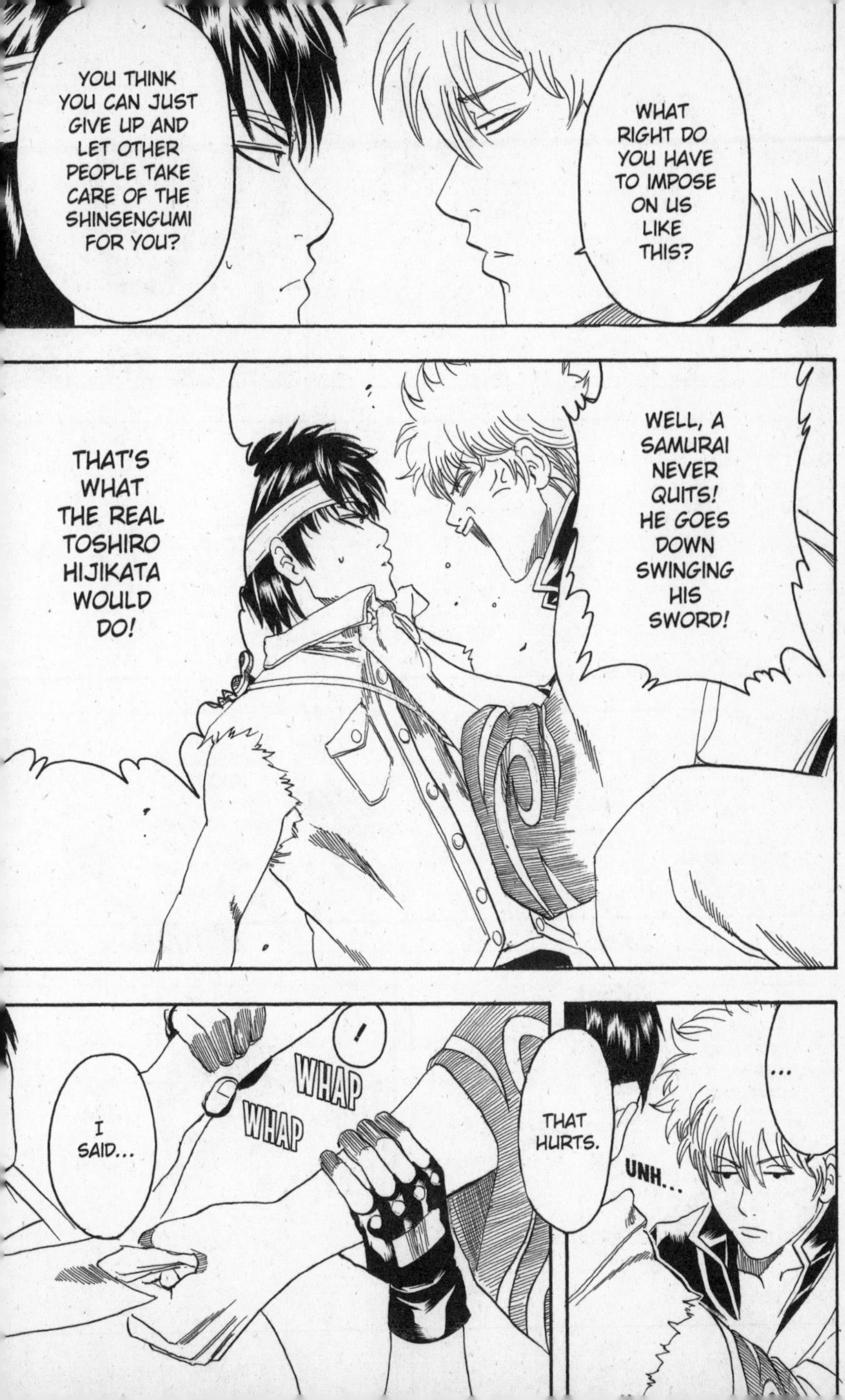
WHAT RIGHT DO YOU HAVE TO IMPOSE ON US LIKE THIS?
YOU THINK YOU CAN JUST GIVE UP AND LET OTHER PEOPLE TAKE CARE OF THE SHINSENGUMI FOR YOU?
WELL, A SAMURAI NEVER QUITS! HE GOES DOWN SWINGING HIS SWORD!
THAT'S WHAT THE REAL TOSHIRO HIJIKATA WOULD DO!
...
THAT HURTS.
UNH...
!
WHAP
WHAP
I SAID...

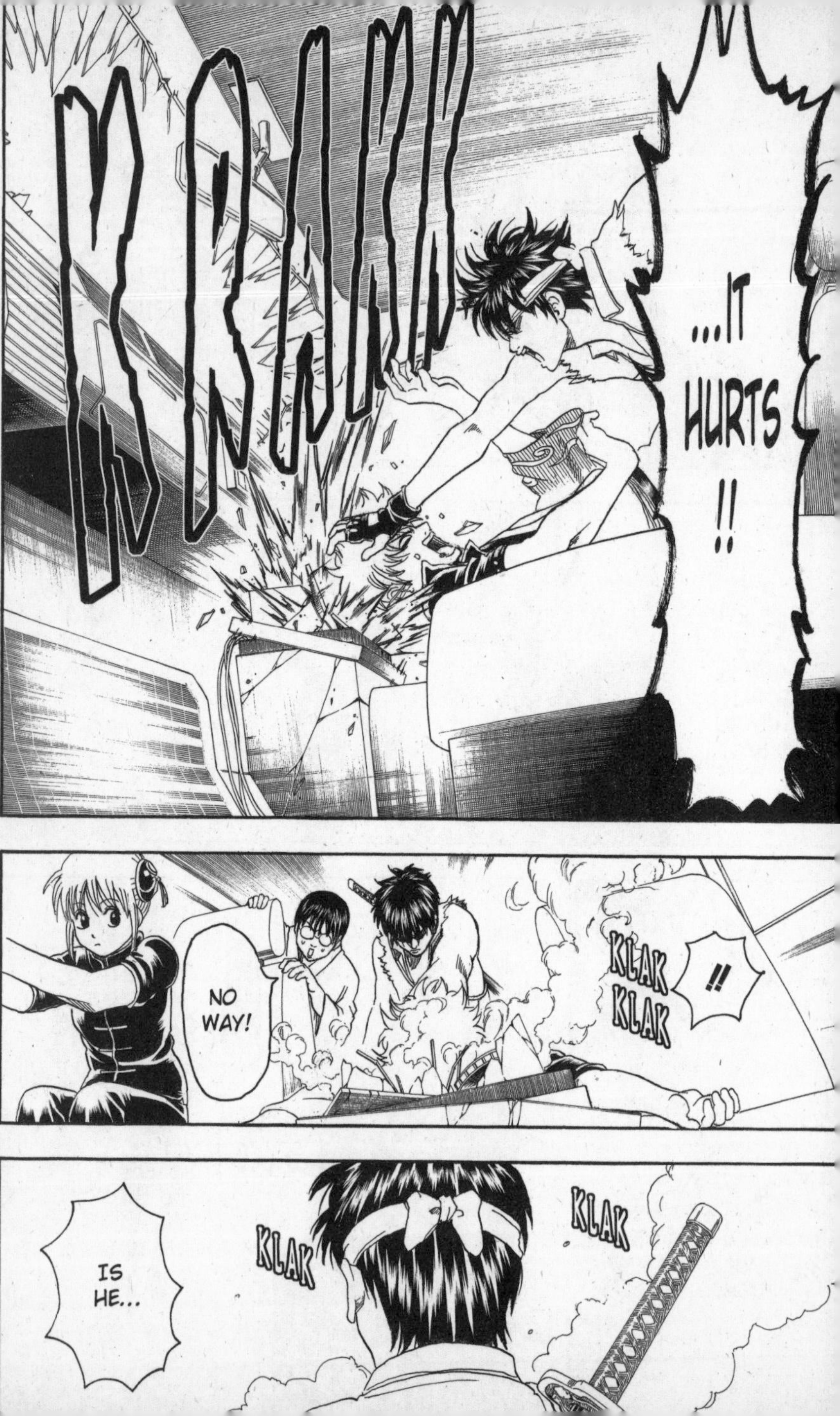
KRASH
...IT HURTS!!
!!
KLAK KLAK
NO WAY!
KLAK
KLAK
IS HE...

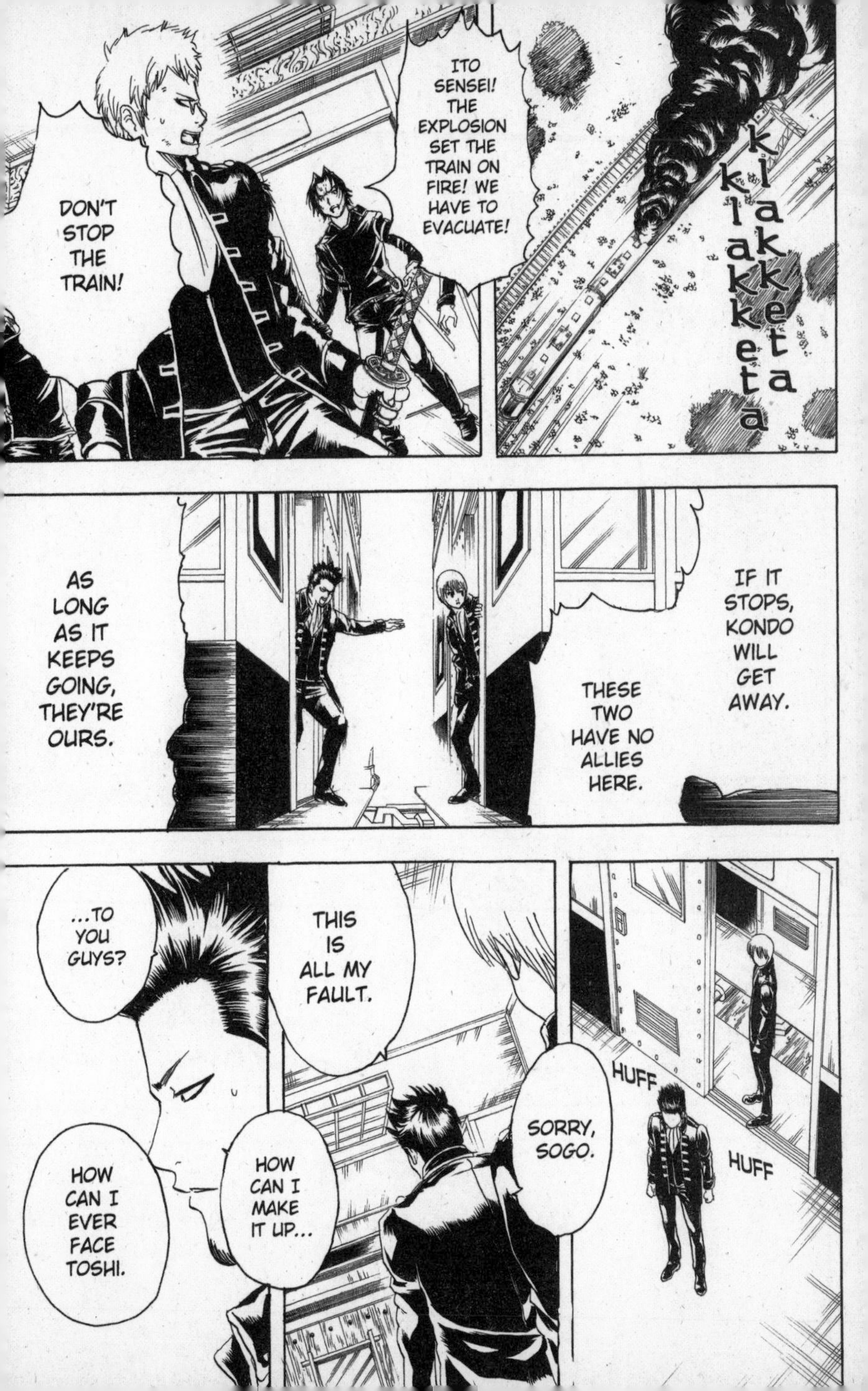
klakketa
klakketa
ITO SENSEI! THE EXPLOSION SET THE TRAIN ON FIRE! WE HAVE TO EVACUATE!
DON'T STOP THE TRAIN!
IF IT STOPS, KONDO WILL GET AWAY.
THESE TWO HAVE NO ALLIES HERE.
AS LONG AS IT KEEPS GOING, THEY'RE OURS.
HUFF
SORRY, SOGO.
HUFF
THIS IS ALL MY FAULT.
HOW CAN I MAKE IT UP...
...TO YOU GUYS?
HOW CAN I EVER FACE TOSHI.

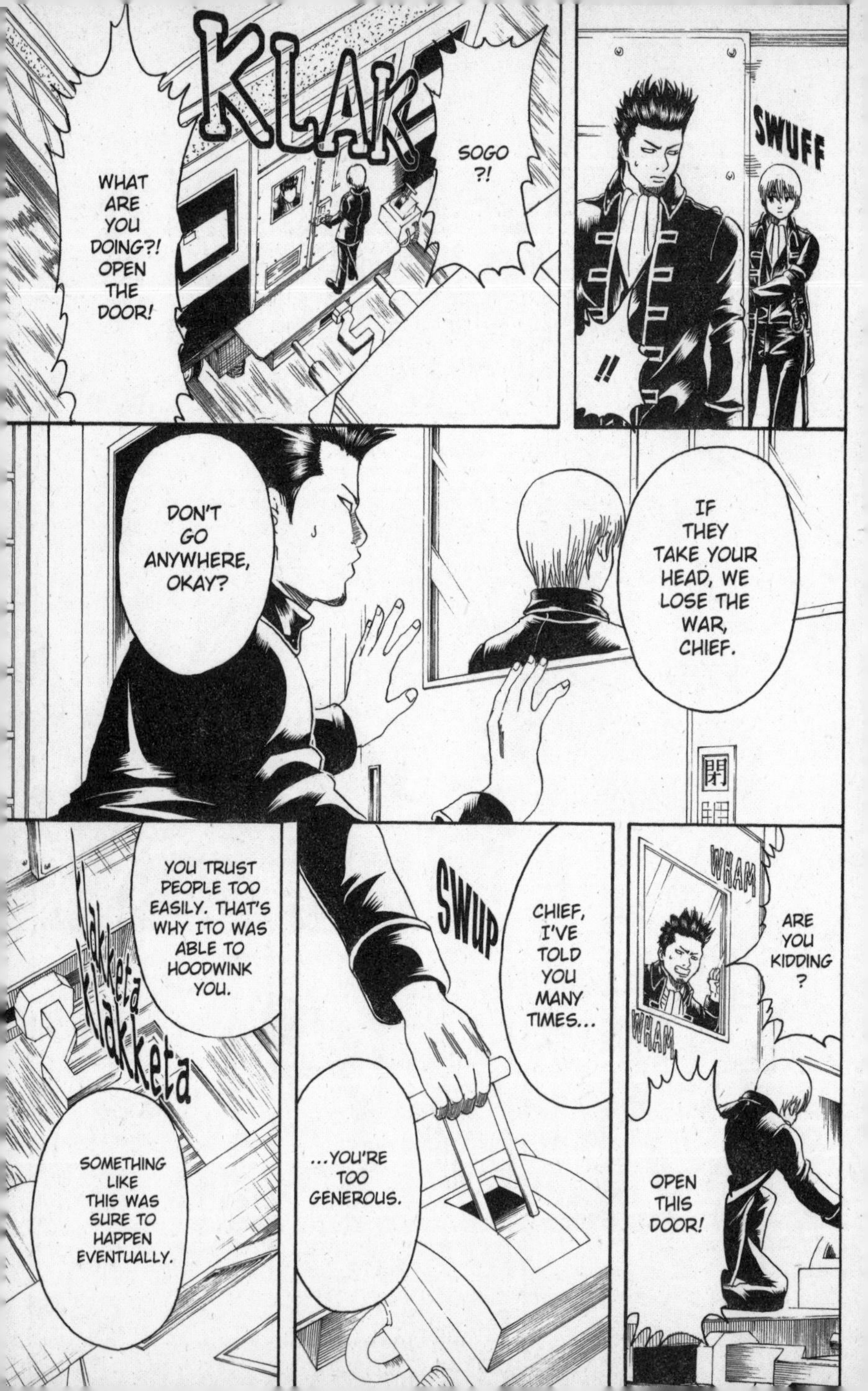
SWUFF
!!
KLAK
SOGO ?!
WHAT ARE YOU DOING?! OPEN THE DOOR!
IF THEY TAKE YOUR HEAD, WE LOSE THE WAR, CHIEF.
閉
DON'T GO ANYWHERE, OKAY?
WHAM
ARE YOU KIDDING ?
WHAM
OPEN THIS DOOR!
SWUP
CHIEF, I'VE TOLD YOU MANY TIMES...
...YOU'RE TOO GENEROUS.
YOU TRUST PEOPLE TOO EASILY. THAT'S WHY ITO WAS ABLE TO HOODWINK YOU.
klakketa klakketa
SOMETHING LIKE THIS WAS SURE TO HAPPEN EVENTUALLY.

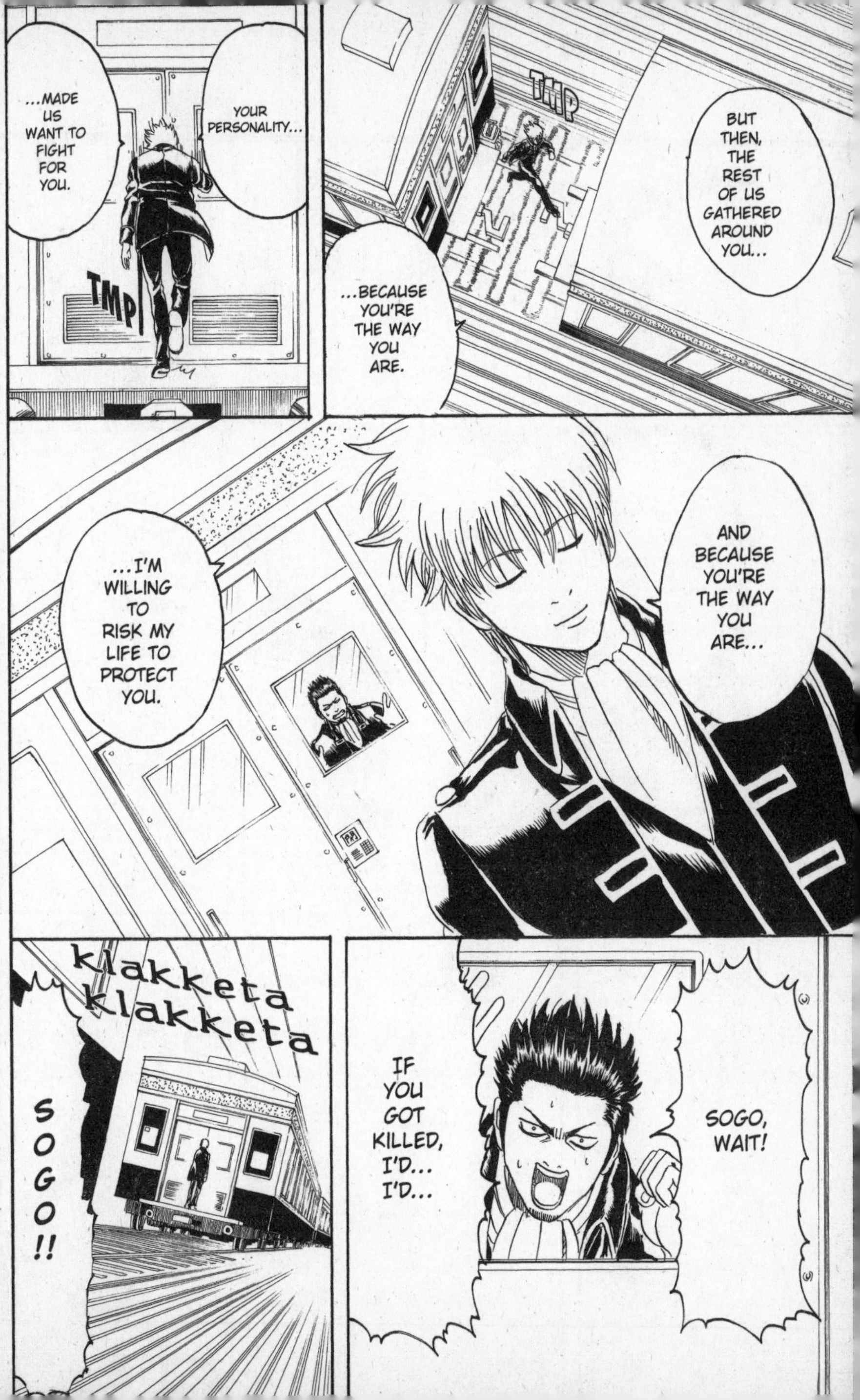
TMP
BUT THEN, THE REST OF US GATHERED AROUND YOU...
...BECAUSE YOU'RE THE WAY YOU ARE.
YOUR PERSONALITY...
...MADE US WANT TO FIGHT FOR YOU.
TMP
AND BECAUSE YOU'RE THE WAY YOU ARE...
...I'M WILLING TO RISK MY LIFE TO PROTECT YOU.
SOGO, WAIT!
IF YOU GOT KILLED, I'D... I'D...
klakketa klakketa
SOGO!!

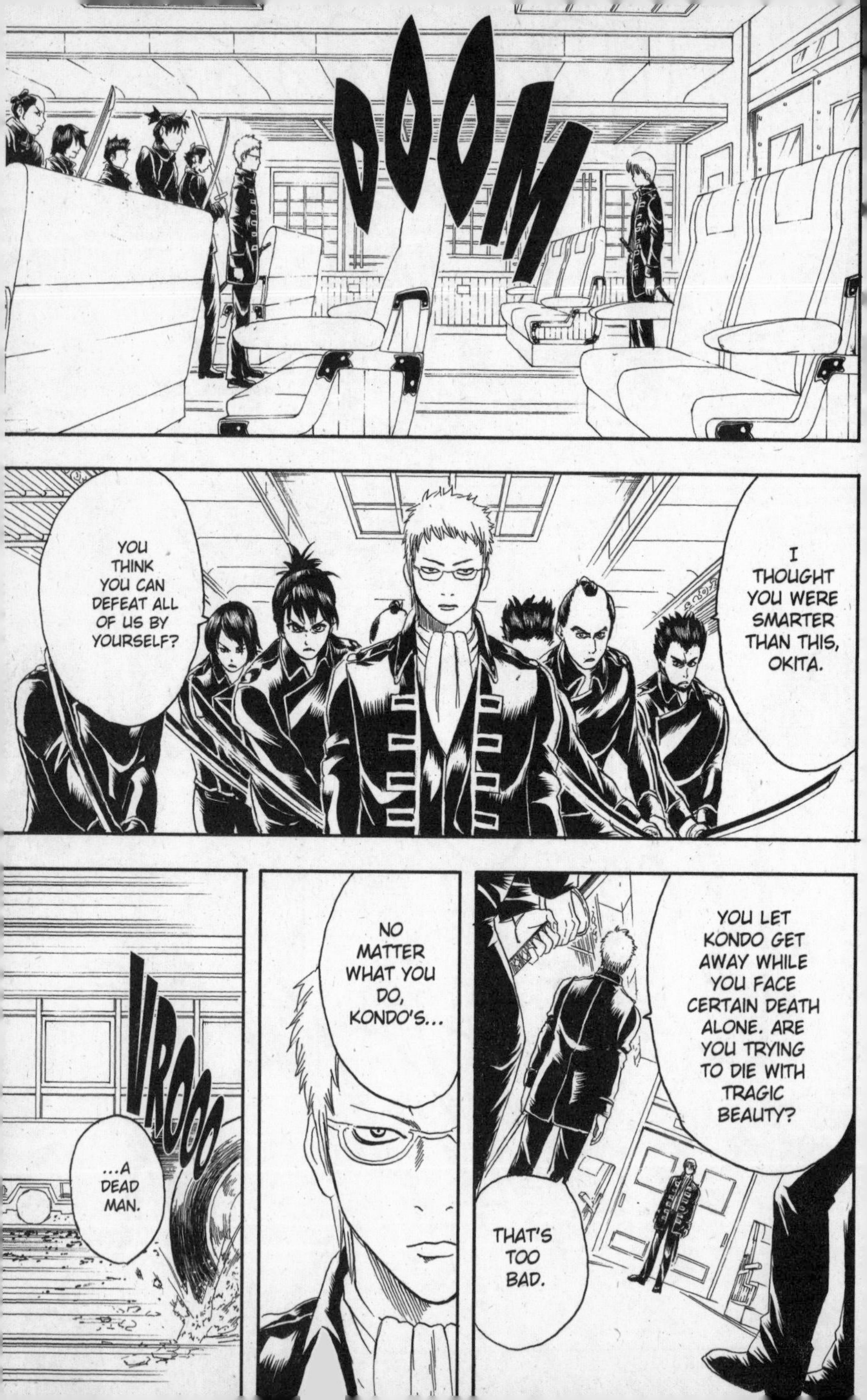
DOOM
I THOUGHT YOU WERE SMARTER THAN THIS, OKITA.
YOU THINK YOU CAN DEFEAT ALL OF US BY YOURSELF?
YOU LET KONDO GET AWAY WHILE YOU FACE CERTAIN DEATH ALONE. ARE YOU TRYING TO DIE WITH TRAGIC BEAUTY?
THAT'S TOO BAD.
NO MATTER WHAT YOU DO, KONDO'S...
VROOO
...A DEAD MAN.

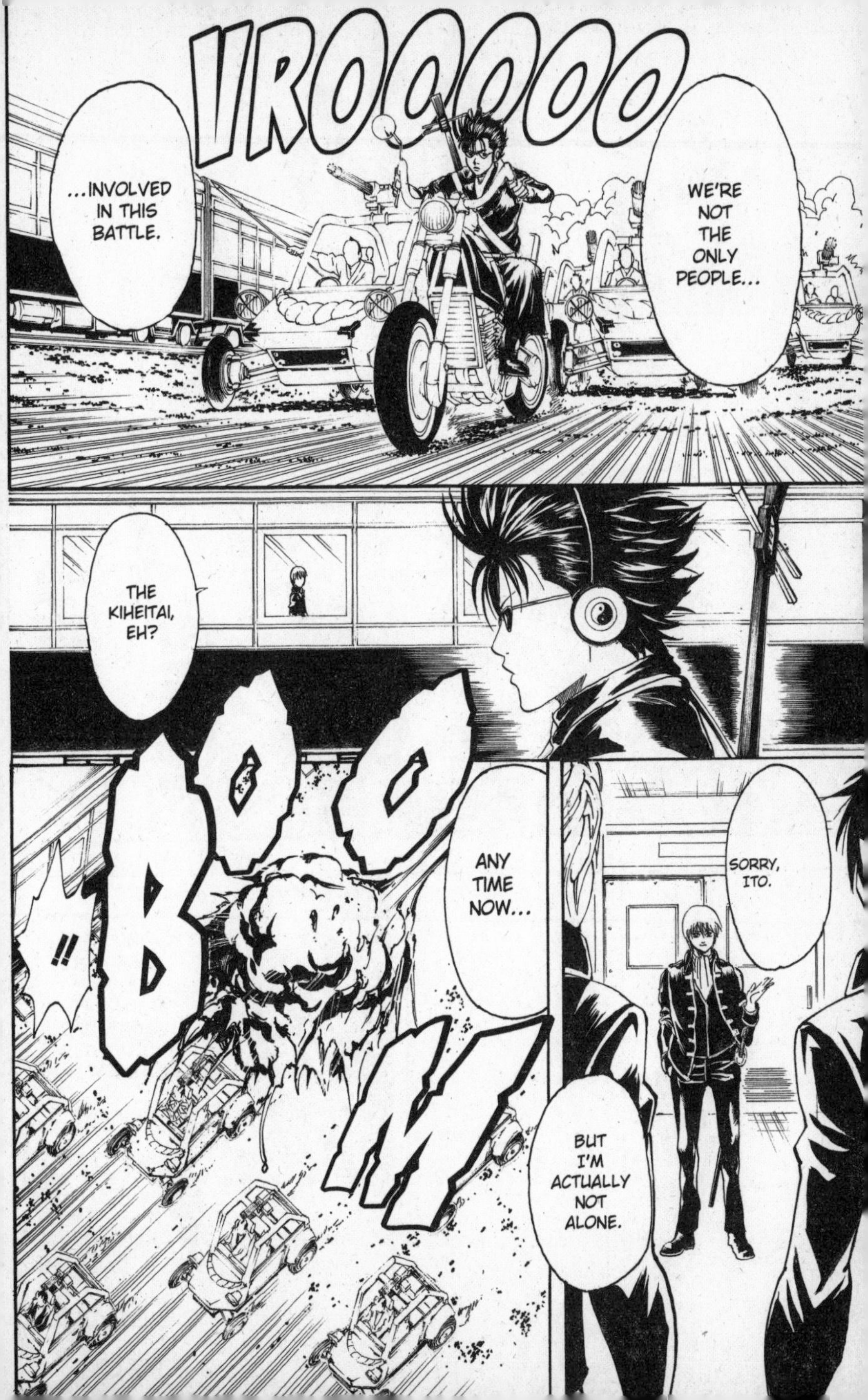
VROOOOOO
WE'RE NOT THE ONLY PEOPLE...
...INVOLVED IN THIS BATTLE.
THE KIHEITAI, EH?
SORRY, ITO.
BUT I'M ACTUALLY NOT ALONE.
ANY TIME NOW...
BOOM
!!

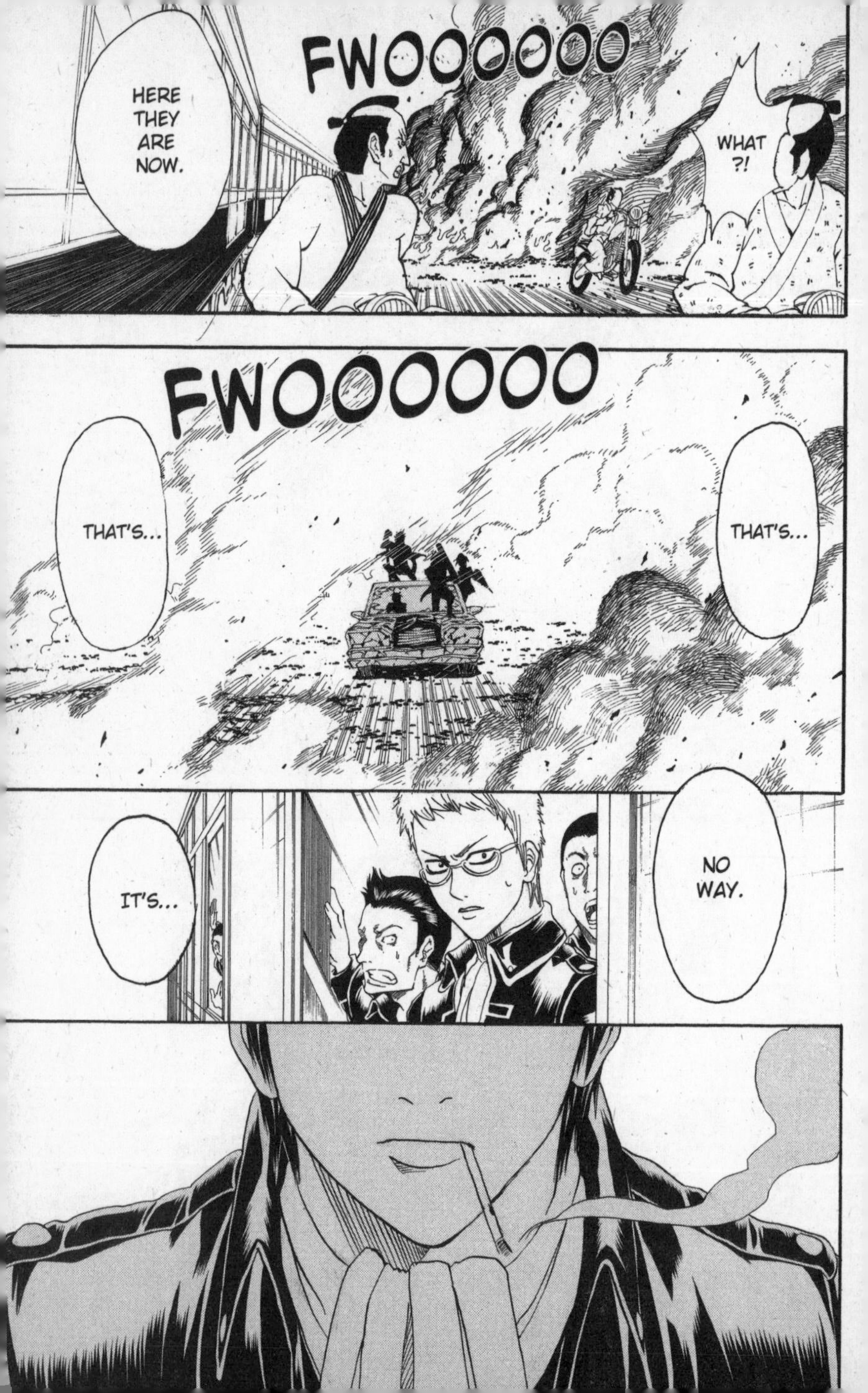
FWOOOOOO
WHAT ?!
HERE THEY ARE NOW.
FWOOOOOO
THAT'S...
THAT'S...
NO WAY.
IT'S...

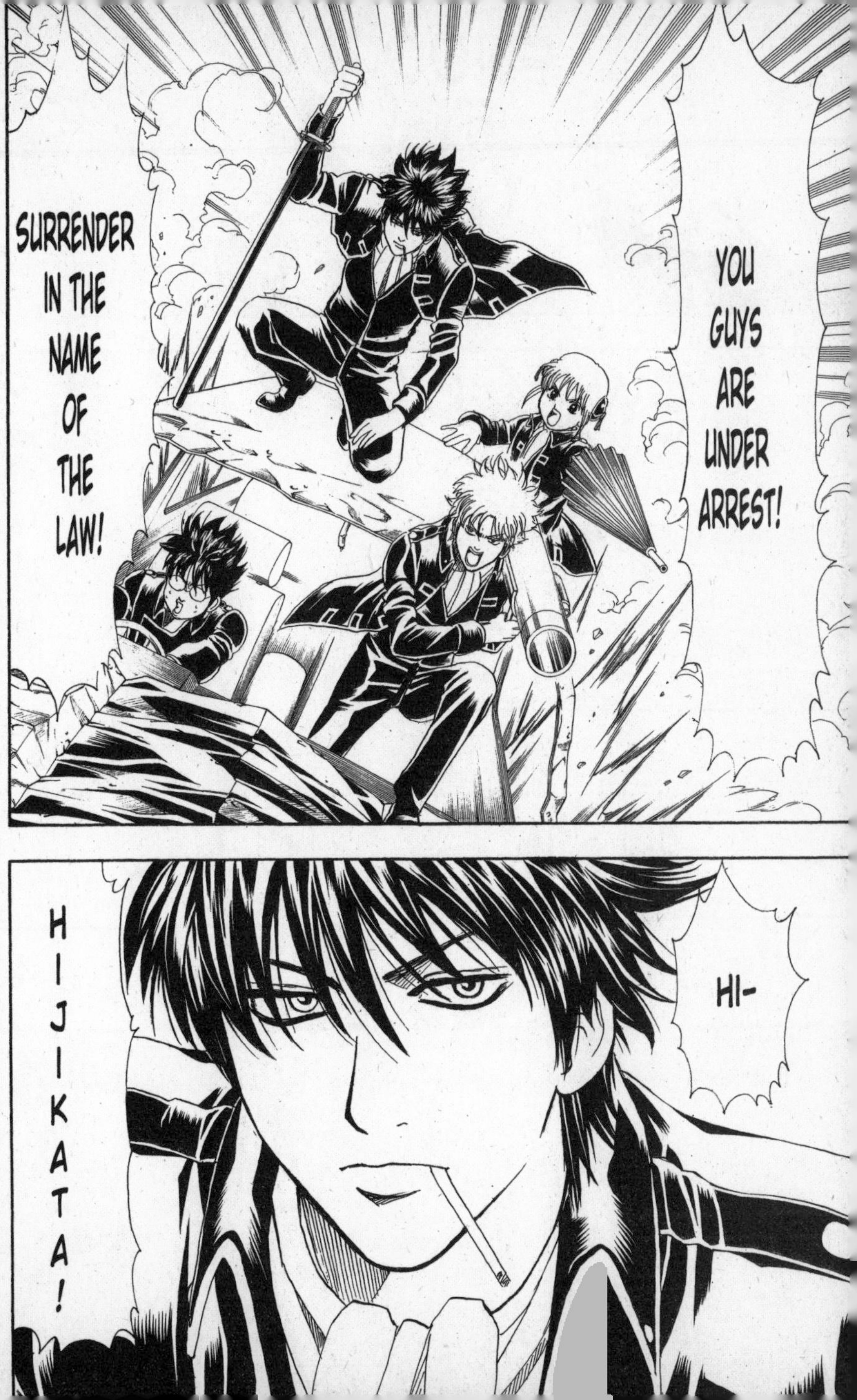
YOU GUYS ARE UNDER ARREST!
SURRENDER IN THE NAME OF THE LAW!
HI-
HIJIKATA!

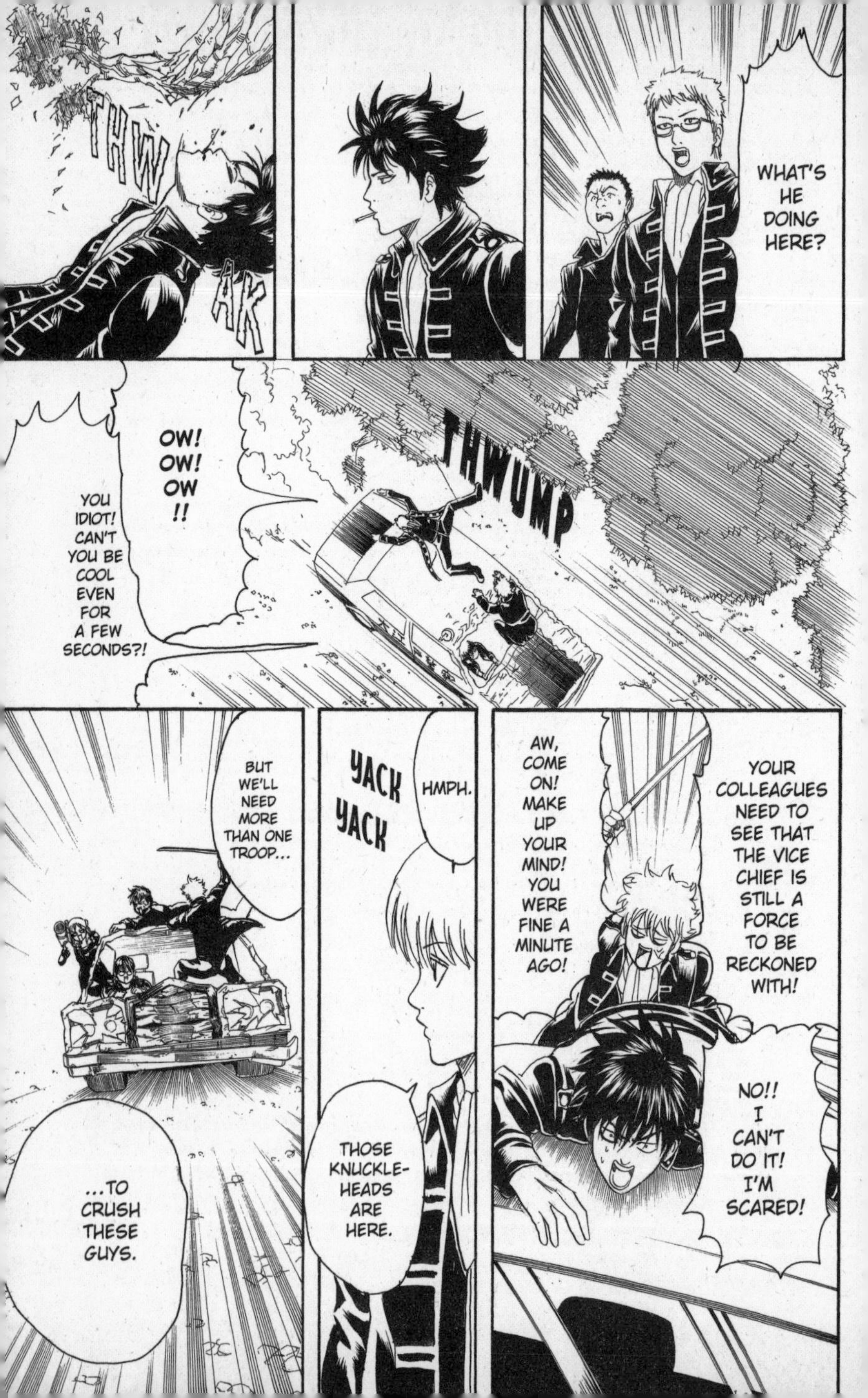
WHAT'S HE DOING HERE?
THWAK
THWUMP
OW! OW! OW !!
YOU IDIOT! CAN'T YOU BE COOL EVEN FOR A FEW SECONDS?!
YOUR COLLEAGUES NEED TO SEE THAT THE VICE CHIEF IS STILL A FORCE TO BE RECKONED WITH!
AW, COME ON! MAKE UP YOUR MIND! YOU WERE FINE A MINUTE AGO!
NO!! I CAN'T DO IT! I'M SCARED!
HMPH.
YACK YACK
THOSE KNUCKLE-HEADS ARE HERE.
BUT WE'LL NEED MORE THAN ONE TROOP...
...TO CRUSH THESE GUYS.

HIDEAKI SORACHI ROUGHLY 43,000 CHARACTER INTERVIEW

"SACCHAN, KYUBEI AND TAKASUGI ARE CHARACTERS THAT ARE REALLY HARD TO MANAGE." -SORACHI

ONISHI: SO YOU WANT A HUGE HEADLINE THAT SAYS, "I ILLUSTRATE THE DEVELOPMENT OF HUMANITY!" OR SOMETHING LIKE THAT? (LAUGH)

SORACHI: YEAH, I WANT A HUGE LEAD-IN MESSAGE AND THEN... YEAH. SO THAT'S HOW IT'LL BE?

ONISHI: I DON'T THINK THIS NEEDS TO BE AS SERIOUS AS THOSE INTERVIEWS. ANYWAY, SO HOW DO YOU PRODUCE YOUR STORIES?

SORACHI: FIRST, I TALK IT OVER WITH MY MANAGING EDITOR...

ONISHI: WE MEET FOR FOUR TO FIVE HOURS EACH WEEK.

SORACHI: IT WAS SEVEN HOURS THE OTHER WEEK.

ONISHI: REALLY? BUT THAT WAS BECAUSE WE TALKED ABOUT NOTHING, RIGHT?

SORACHI: I REMEMBER THAT IT STARTED OFF WITH A FIGHT. YOU SAID, "YOUR MANUSCRIPT IS LATE!" IT THEN DEVOLVED INTO SMALL TALK. MAYBE THAT'S WHAT CAUSED IT TO LAST FOR SEVEN HOURS. EVEN FOR COMIC AUTHORS, THAT MEETING TOOK WAY TOO LONG. I THINK THE AVERAGE TIME FOR MEETINGS IS ABOUT ONE OR TWO HOURS FOR OTHER PEOPLE.

ONISHI: I THINK IT REALLY DEPENDS. IN OUR CASE, WE MEET AT THE BEGINNING OF THE WEEK, AND THEN WE GO OVER THINGS OVER THE PHONE THROUGHOUT THE WEEK.

SORACHI: EVEN WHEN WE DO THE MEETINGS, I NEVER WANT TO DO WHAT YOU WANT.

ONISHI: YEAH, YOU NEVER IMPLEMENT MY SUGGESTIONS. EVER. (LAUGH) BUT THERE'S REALLY NO POINT IN GETTING RILED UP DURING THE MEETING...

SORACHI: EVEN WHEN WE GET EXCITED DURING THE MEETING, NOTHING ENDS UP GETTING USED.

ONISHI: YEAH. BECAUSE THAT EXCITEMENT ENDS WHEN THE MEETING ENDS. THAT EXCITEMENT DOESN'T GO INTO THE WORK.

SORACHI: IT'LL SEEM LIKE THE MEETING WAS ALREADY FUN, SO I FEEL LIKE THE COMIC DOESN'T NEED TO BE FUN. BUT THERE ARE TIMES WHEN I CAN CREATE SOMETHING REALLY INTERESTING WHEN I COMPLETELY IGNORE WHAT WE TALKED ABOUT DURING THE MEETING.

ONISHI: I THINK IT'S JUST A MATTER OF MOTIVATION. THE KIND WHERE YOU THINK, "I'M WILLING TO DO THE OPPOSITE TO DRAW THIS." THAT TYPE OF THING.

[HOW DO YOU MAKE YOUR CHARACTERS?]

ONISHI: HOW DO YOU MAKE INTERESTING CHARACTERS?

SORACHI: TO PUT IT SIMPLY, I "DROP THEM ON THE GROUND."

ONISHI: THE GROUND. YOU MEAN ON THE SIDE OF THE READERS?

SORACHI: YES. CHARACTERS IN THE COMIC ARE ALWAYS KIND OF UNSTEADY. THAT'S WHY I TRY TO MAKE THEM DOWN-TO-EARTH.

ONISHI: SO YOU'RE MAKING THE POINT OF "JUST BECAUSE THEY'RE COMIC CHARACTERS, THEY'RE STILL REGULAR PEOPLE." SO YOU SHOW THEM PICKING THEIR NOSE OR GOING FOR CHEAP SWEETS. THAT KIND OF THING?

SORACHI: I HAVE TO THINK OF REALLY MINUTE DETAILS. IT'S LIKE YOUR NEIGHBOR. I THINK I'VE SUCCEEDED IN CHARACTER CREATION IF YOU FEEL LIKE YOU KNOW WHAT YOU WOULD FIND IN THAT CHARACTER'S TRASH CAN. BUT THERE AREN'T THAT MANY CHARACTERS LIKE THAT IN GINTAMA. THERE ARE STILL PLENTY OF CHARACTERS THAT I DON'T UNDERSTAND MYSELF. LIKE SACCHAN, KYUBEI AND TAKASUGI. THOSE CHARACTERS ARE REALLY DIFFICULT TO USE.

ONISHI: MEANING YOU HAVEN'T REALLY GRASPED THEIR CHARACTERS YET?

SORACHI: WAIT. THIS CONVERSATION IS A REALLY GOOD FIT FOR THE INTERVIEW, DON'T YOU THINK? I CAN USE THAT FOR A LEAD-IN CAPTION.

ONISHI: "EVEN I HAVEN'T GRASPED WHO THESE CHARACTERS REALLY ARE!" LIKE THAT? SO IN CONTRAST, WHICH CHARACTERS ARE EASY TO USE THEN?

SORACHI: ZURA. (KATSURA)

ONISHI: ZURA, HUH. ZURA IS INTERESTING.

SORACHI: IT REALLY FEELS WORTHWHILE WHEN I GET TO BRING UP ZURA. IT HAS THE MOST IMPACT WHEN HE HAS A "DUMB" MOMENT. HE'S A VERY DEVELOPED CHARACTER, SO IT'S ALSO THE MOST FUN TO BREAK HIM DOWN. HEY, DON'T YOU THINK THIS PART SOUNDS LIKE A REAL INTERVIEW? (LAUGH) I REALLY LIKE POPS MATSUDAIRA TOO. EVEN THOUGH I DON'T REALLY UNDERSTAND HIM.

ONISHI: DID I TELL YOU ABOUT HOW A GINTAMA FAN CRIED WHILE ARGUING WITH ME?

SORACHI: ABOUT WHAT?

ONISHI: I WAS TALKING TO A FAN THAT REALLY LIKES GIN-SAN. I SAID THAT GIN-SAN USUALLY SAYS RANDOM STUFF HE DOESN'T MEAN. THAT FAN SCREAMED AT ME, SAYING, "NO, HE DOESN'T! TAKE THAT BACK!"

SORACHI: WHILE CRYING?

ONISHI: MORE LIKE ANGRY CRYING. THAT FAN ALSO SAID, "WHAT DO YOU KNOW ABOUT GIN-SAN?!"

SORACHI: WOW.

ONISHI: ALL I COULD SAY WAS, "YEAH, I SEE."

SORACHI: THAT'S GREAT. THAT MEANS THE CHARACTER TOOK ON A LIFE OF ITS OWN. GIN-SAN ISN'T SOMEONE WE CAN CONTROL ANYMORE.

ONISHI: IS THERE A PARTICULAR CHAPTER OF GINTAMA THAT YOU REALLY LIKE?

SORACHI: THE CHAPTER WITH THE SUKIYAKI (CHAPTER 100).

SORACHI: WHAT ABOUT YOU?

ONISHI: I LIKE THE CHAPTERS IN WHICH KATSURA MAKES AN APPEARANCE.

SORACHI: HOW ABOUT THE CHAPTERS WITH THE HEARTWARMING STORIES?

ONISHI: FOR THOSE, I DON'T THINK YOU HAVE ENOUGH PAGES. YOU DON'T GET TO ENJOY THE AFTEREFFECTS OF THE TOUCHING MOMENTS LONG ENOUGH.

SORACHI: FOR THE HEARTWARMING STORIES, I LIKE THE ONE WITH THE KAPPA (CHAPTER 18). IT HAD A GOOD AMOUNT OF HUMOR MIXED IN. THE FIREWORKS ONE (CHAPTER 56) WAS GOOD, BUT THE YOROZUYA GUYS (FREELANCERS) ENDED UP DOING NOTHING.

ONISHI: FOR THE THIRD ANNIVERSARY PROMOTION, WE GATHERED VOTES FROM READERS ABOUT THIS TOPIC TOO.

SORACHI: THE CHAPTER WITH MAYOLER 13 (CHAPTER 65) (MAYOLER: MADE-UP TERM IN THE COMIC REFERRING TO PEOPLE WHO LOVE MAYONNAISE, USUALLY HIJIKATA) WAS GOOD TOO. I ALWAYS RUN OUT OF PAGES. I WISH THAT I COULD GET MORE PAGES TO WRAP UP MY STORIES BETTER EVERY SINGLE TIME. THAT'S WHY I HAVE A LOT OF REGRETS FOR EVERY STORY. I'VE NEVER BEEN COMPLETELY SATISFIED WITH HOW I'VE WRAPPED UP A CHAPTER.

ONISHI: WHAT ABOUT THE FLOWER-VIEWING CHAPTER (CHAPTER 17)?

SORACHI: I THINK THAT COULD HAVE BEEN DONE BETTER. I ACTUALLY WANTED TO BRING OUT EVERY SINGLE CHARACTER.

ONISHI: OH, I SEE.

SORACHI: THINKING BACK, WE'VE NEVER REALLY TALKED ABOUT GINTAMA LIKE WE ARE DOING NOW. WE ALWAYS TALK ABOUT OTHER AUTHORS AND CURRENT EVENTS.

ONISHI: YEAH. I GUESS THERE ARE THINGS THAT YOU JUST DON'T SEE UNTIL YOU TAKE A STEP BACK.

[WHAT ELSE DO YOU WANT TO DRAW?]

ONISHI: WHAT ELSE DO YOU WANT TO DRAW ASIDE FROM GINTAMA?

SORACHI: I WANT TO DO STUFF THAT USES A SCHOOL AS THE SETTING.

ONISHI: WHY?

CONTINUED ON PAGE 126

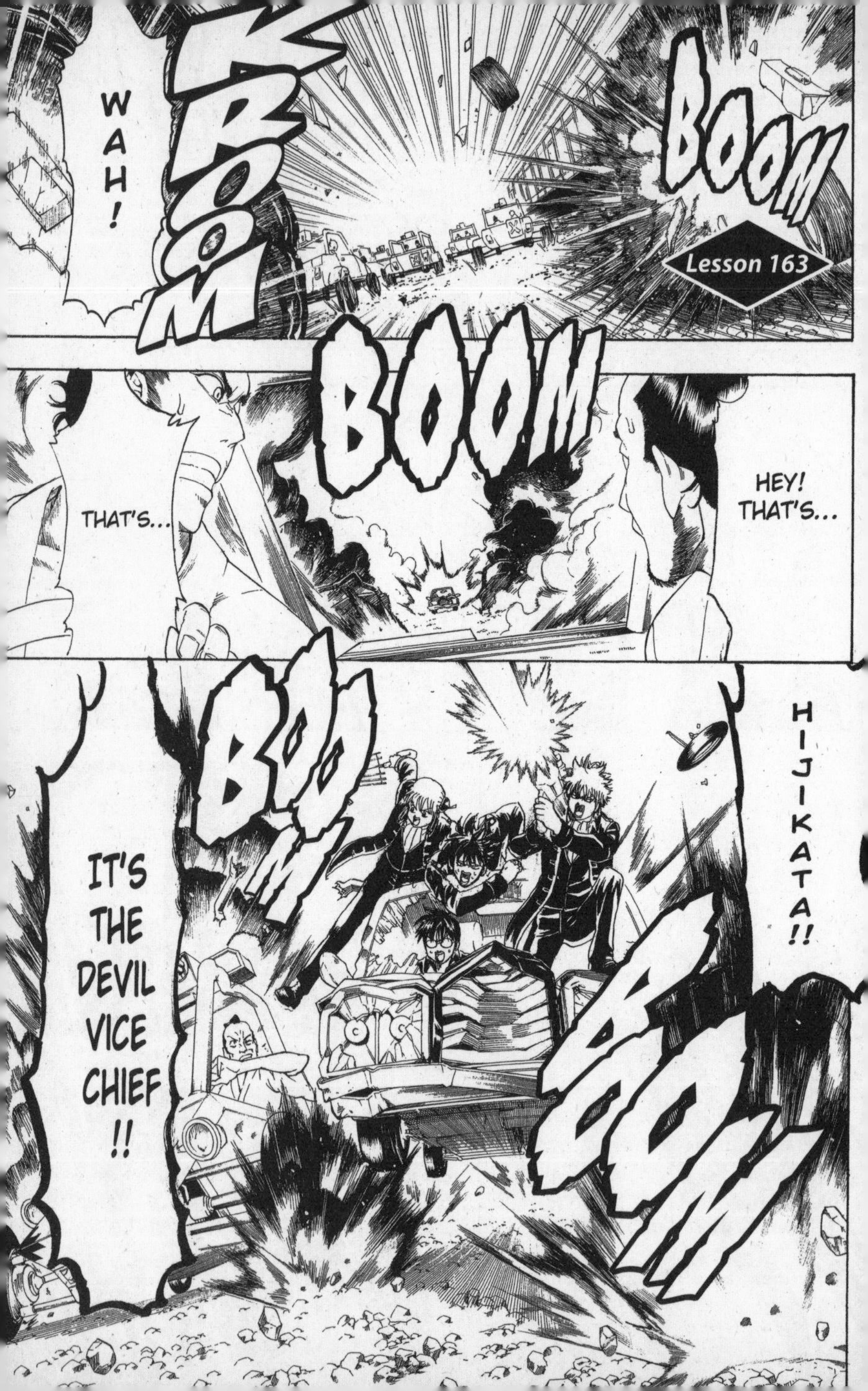
BOOM
Lesson 163
KBOOM
WAH!
HEY! THAT'S...
BOOM
THAT'S...
HIJIKATA!!
BOOM
BOOM
IT'S THE DEVIL VICE CHIEF!!

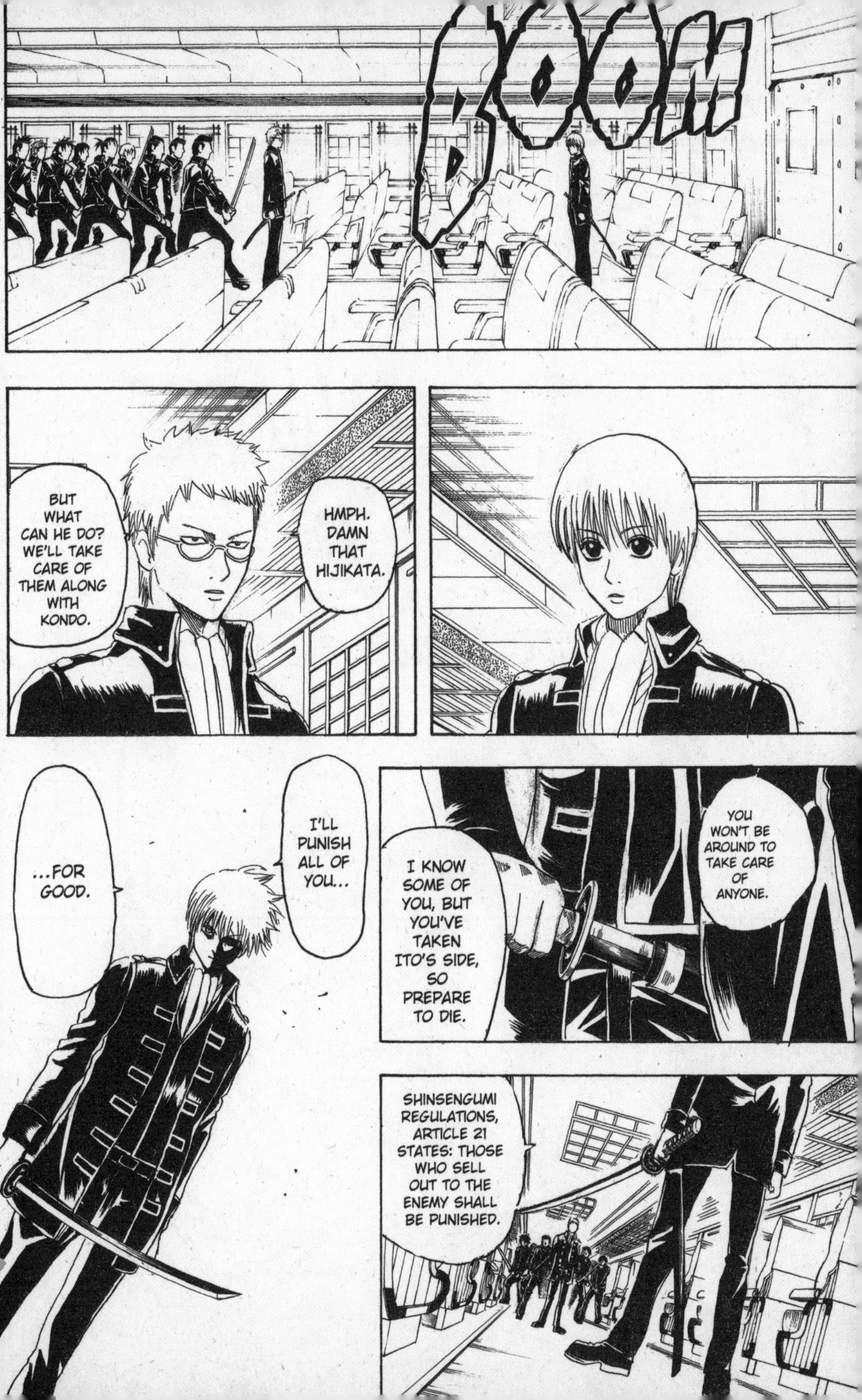
BOOM
HMPH. DAMN THAT HIJIKATA.
BUT WHAT CAN HE DO? WE'LL TAKE CARE OF THEM ALONG WITH KONDO.
YOU WON'T BE AROUND TO TAKE CARE OF ANYONE.
I KNOW SOME OF YOU, BUT YOU'VE TAKEN ITO'S SIDE, SO PREPARE TO DIE.
SHINSENGUMI REGULATIONS, ARTICLE 21 STATES: THOSE WHO SELL OUT TO THE ENEMY SHALL BE PUNISHED.
I'LL PUNISH ALL OF YOU...
...FOR GOOD.

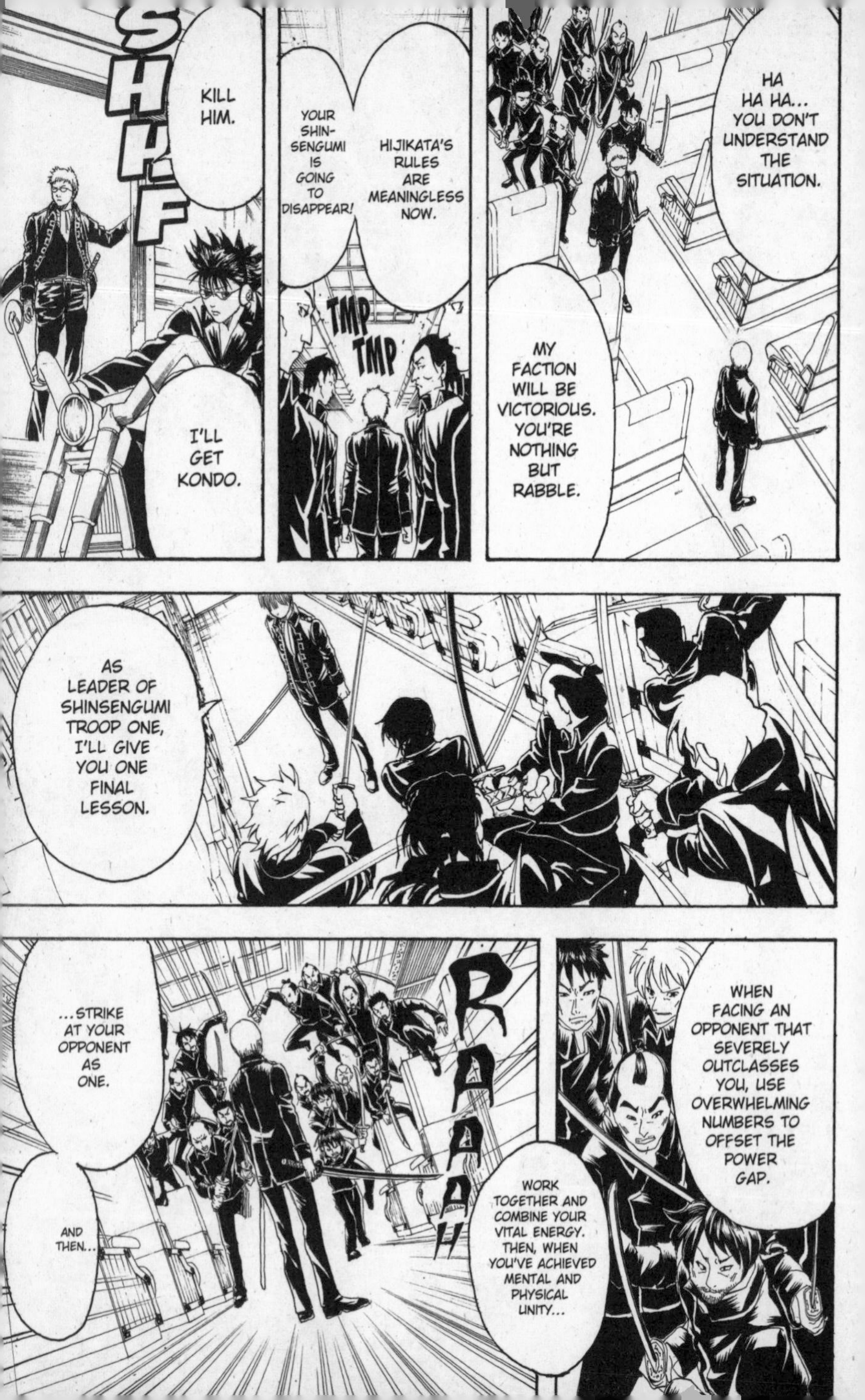
HA HA HA... YOU DON'T UNDERSTAND THE SITUATION.
MY FACTION WILL BE VICTORIOUS. YOU'RE NOTHING BUT RABBLE.
HIJIKATA'S RULES ARE MEANINGLESS NOW.
YOUR SHINSENGUMI IS GOING TO DISAPPEAR!
TMP TMP
KILL HIM.
SHUF
I'LL GET KONDO.
AS LEADER OF SHINSENGUMI TROOP ONE, I'LL GIVE YOU ONE FINAL LESSON.
WHEN FACING AN OPPONENT THAT SEVERELY OUTCLASSES YOU, USE OVERWHELMING NUMBERS TO OFFSET THE POWER GAP.
WORK TOGETHER AND COMBINE YOUR VITAL ENERGY. THEN, WHEN YOU'VE ACHIEVED MENTAL AND PHYSICAL UNITY...
RAAAH
...STRIKE AT YOUR OPPONENT AS ONE.
AND THEN...

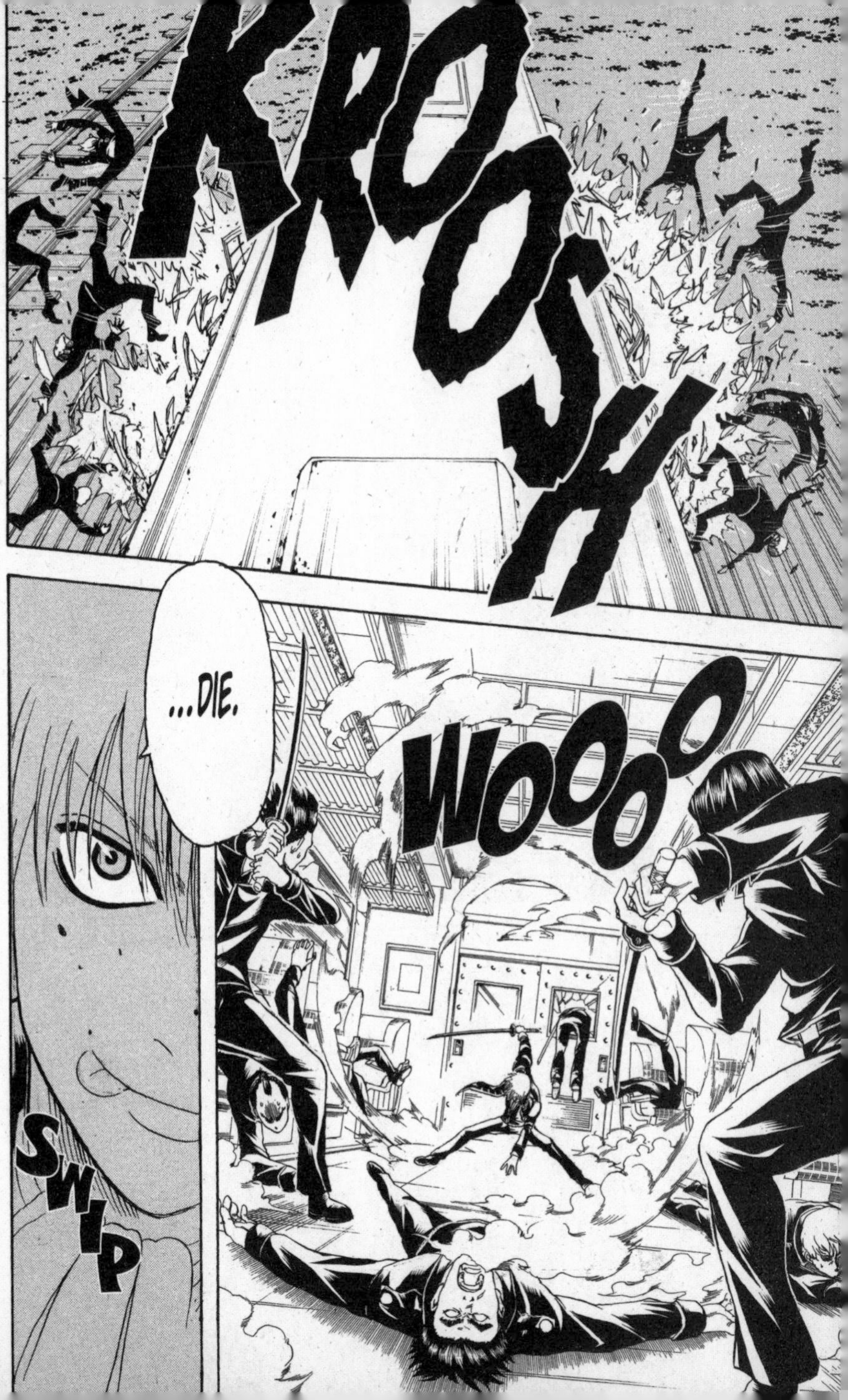
KROSH
WOOOO
...DIE.
SWIP

Lesson 163
A Uniform Makes You Look 20 Percent Better

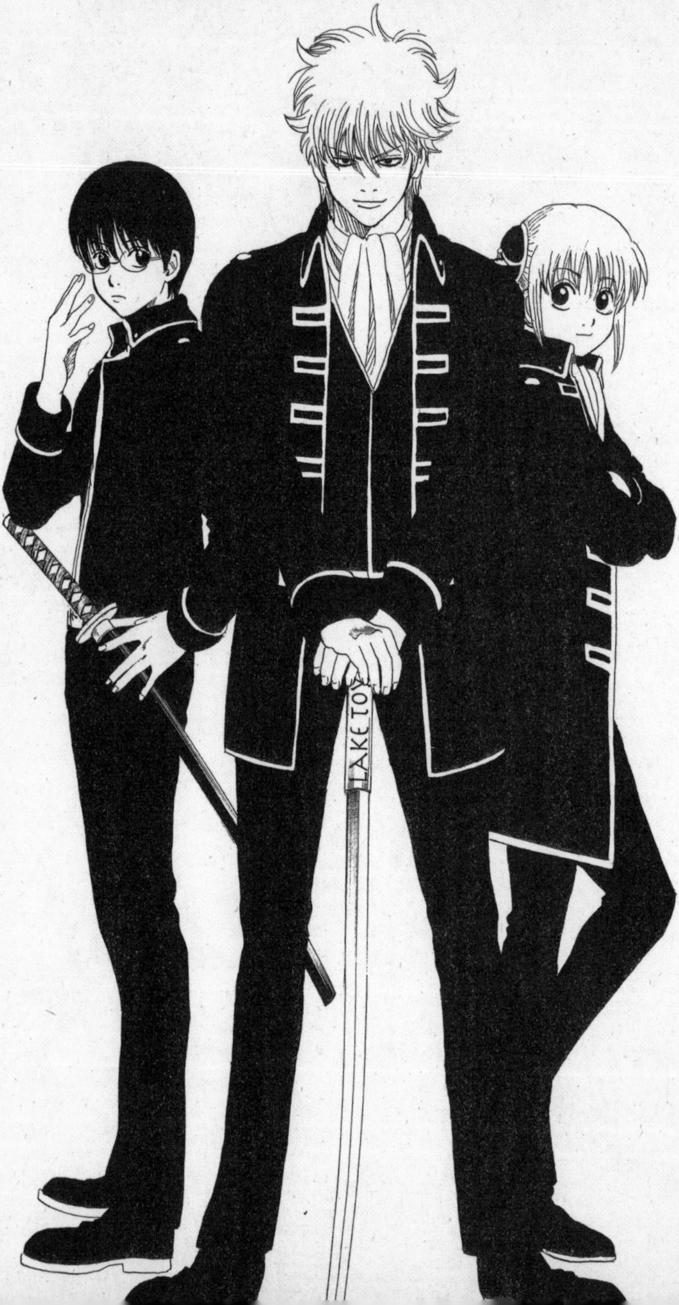

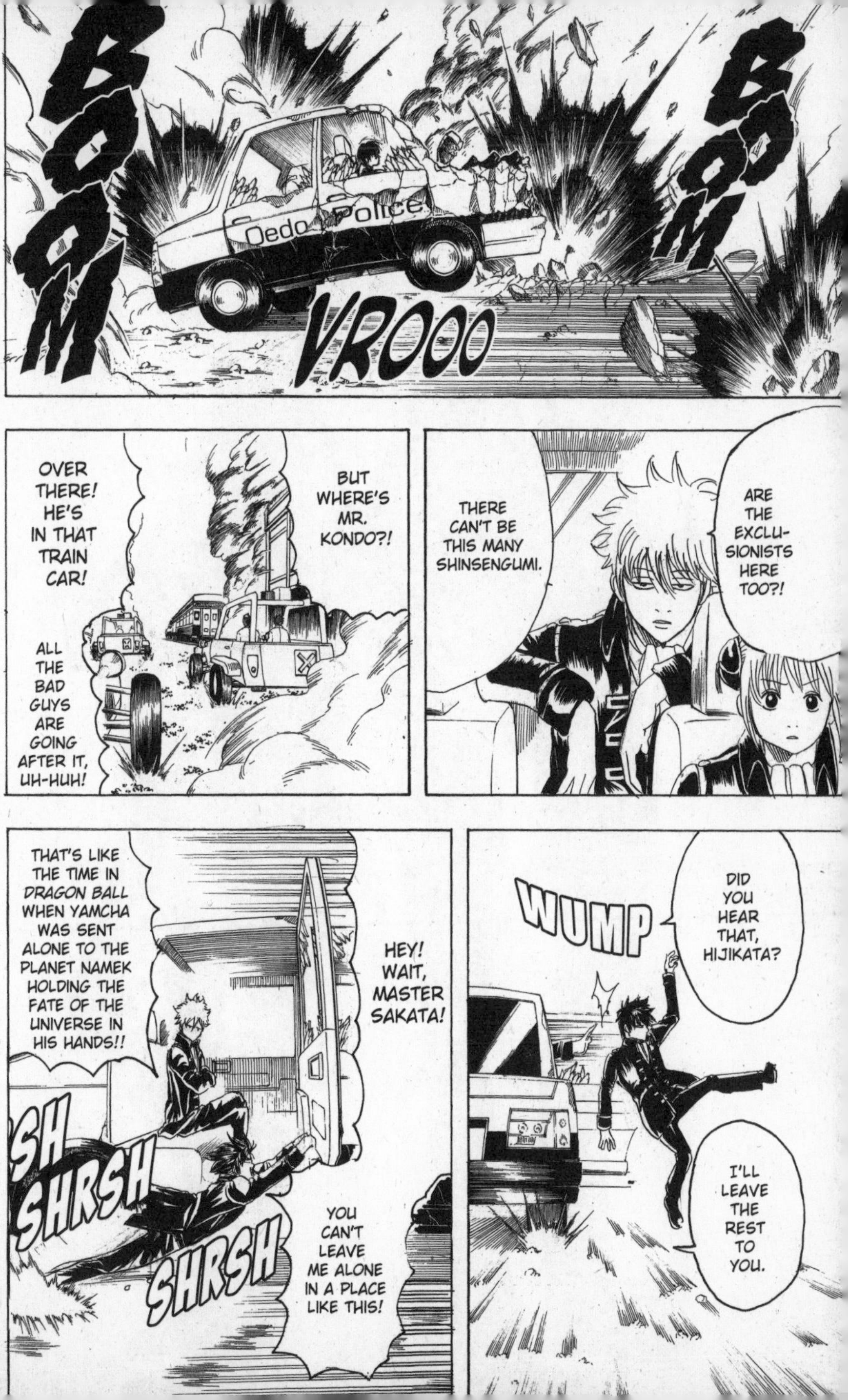
BOOM
BOOM
Oedo Police
VROOO
ARE THE EXCLUSIONISTS HERE TOO?!
THERE CAN'T BE THIS MANY SHINSENGUMI.
BUT WHERE'S MR. KONDO?!
OVER THERE! HE'S IN THAT TRAIN CAR!
ALL THE BAD GUYS ARE GOING AFTER IT, UH-HUH!
DID YOU HEAR THAT, HIJIKATA?
WUMP
I'LL LEAVE THE REST TO YOU.
HEY! WAIT, MASTER SAKATA!
THAT'S LIKE THE TIME IN DRAGON BALL WHEN YAMCHA WAS SENT ALONE TO THE PLANET NAMEK HOLDING THE FATE OF THE UNIVERSE IN HIS HANDS!!
YOU CAN'T LEAVE ME ALONE IN A PLACE LIKE THIS!
SHRSH
SHRSH

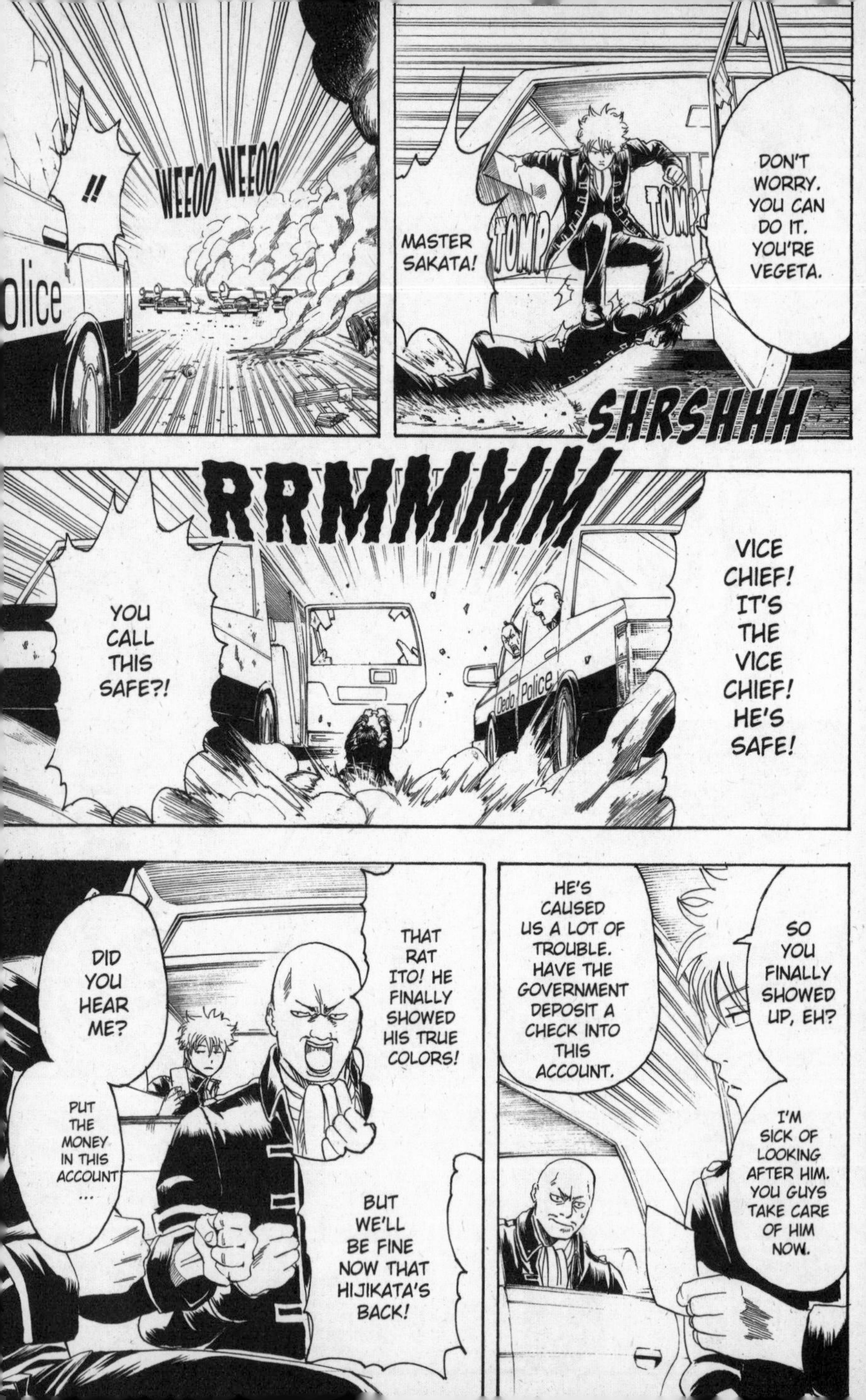
DON'T WORRY. YOU CAN DO IT. YOU'RE VEGETA.
TOMP TOMP
MASTER SAKATA!
SHRSHHH
!!
WEEOO WEEOO
olice
RRMMMM
VICE CHIEF! IT'S THE VICE CHIEF! HE'S SAFE!
Oedo Police
YOU CALL THIS SAFE?!
SO YOU FINALLY SHOWED UP, EH?
HE'S CAUSED US A LOT OF TROUBLE. HAVE THE GOVERNMENT DEPOSIT A CHECK INTO THIS ACCOUNT.
I'M SICK OF LOOKING AFTER HIM. YOU GUYS TAKE CARE OF HIM NOW.
THAT RAT ITO! HE FINALLY SHOWED HIS TRUE COLORS!
DID YOU HEAR ME?
BUT WE'LL BE FINE NOW THAT HIJIKATA'S BACK!
PUT THE MONEY IN THIS ACCOUNT ...

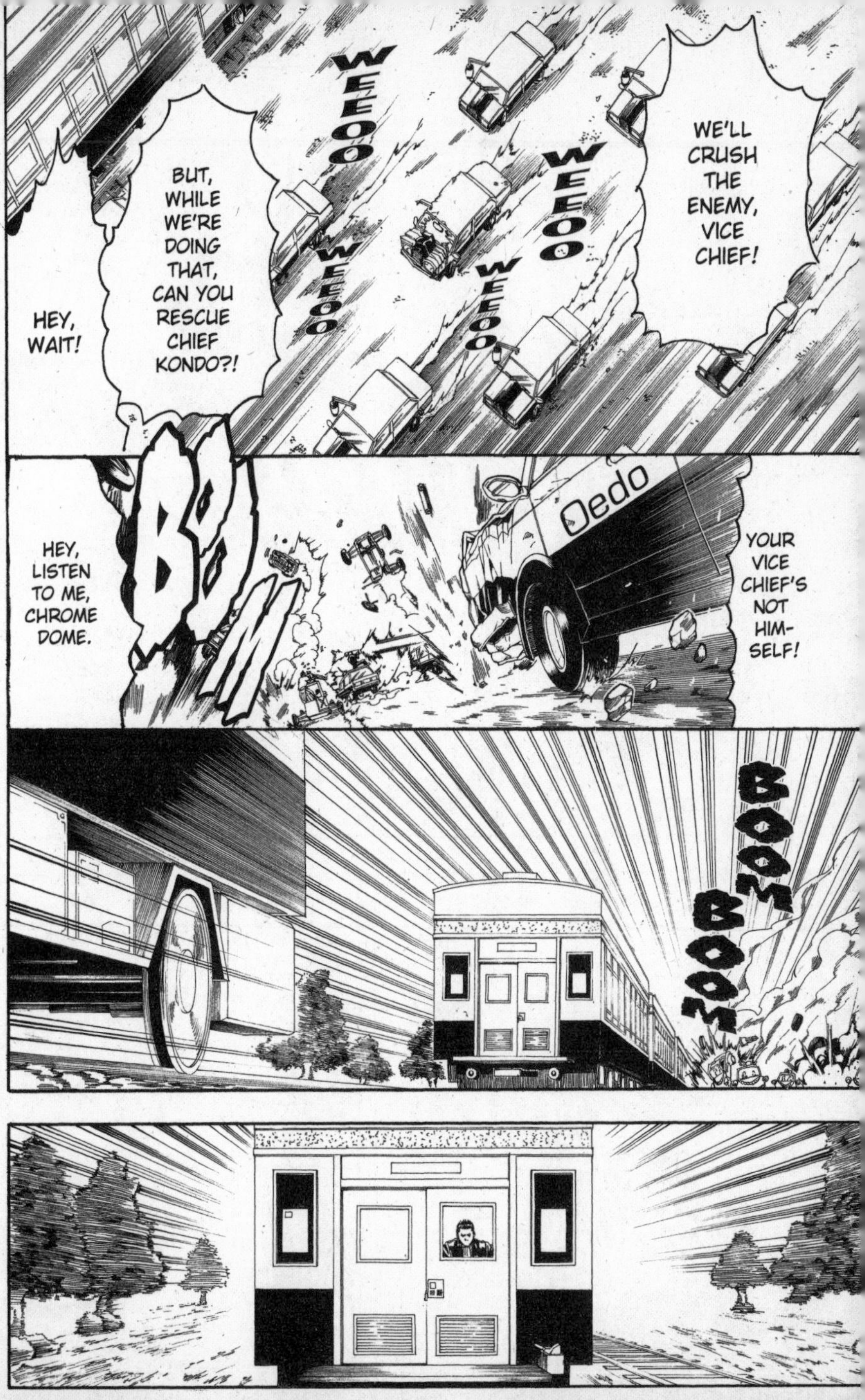
WE'LL CRUSH THE ENEMY, VICE CHIEF!
WEEOO
WEEOO
WEEOO
WEEOO
BUT, WHILE WE'RE DOING THAT, CAN YOU RESCUE CHIEF KONDO?!
HEY, WAIT!
YOUR VICE CHIEF'S NOT HIM-SELF!
Oedo
BOOM
HEY, LISTEN TO ME, CHROME DOME.
BOOM
BOOM

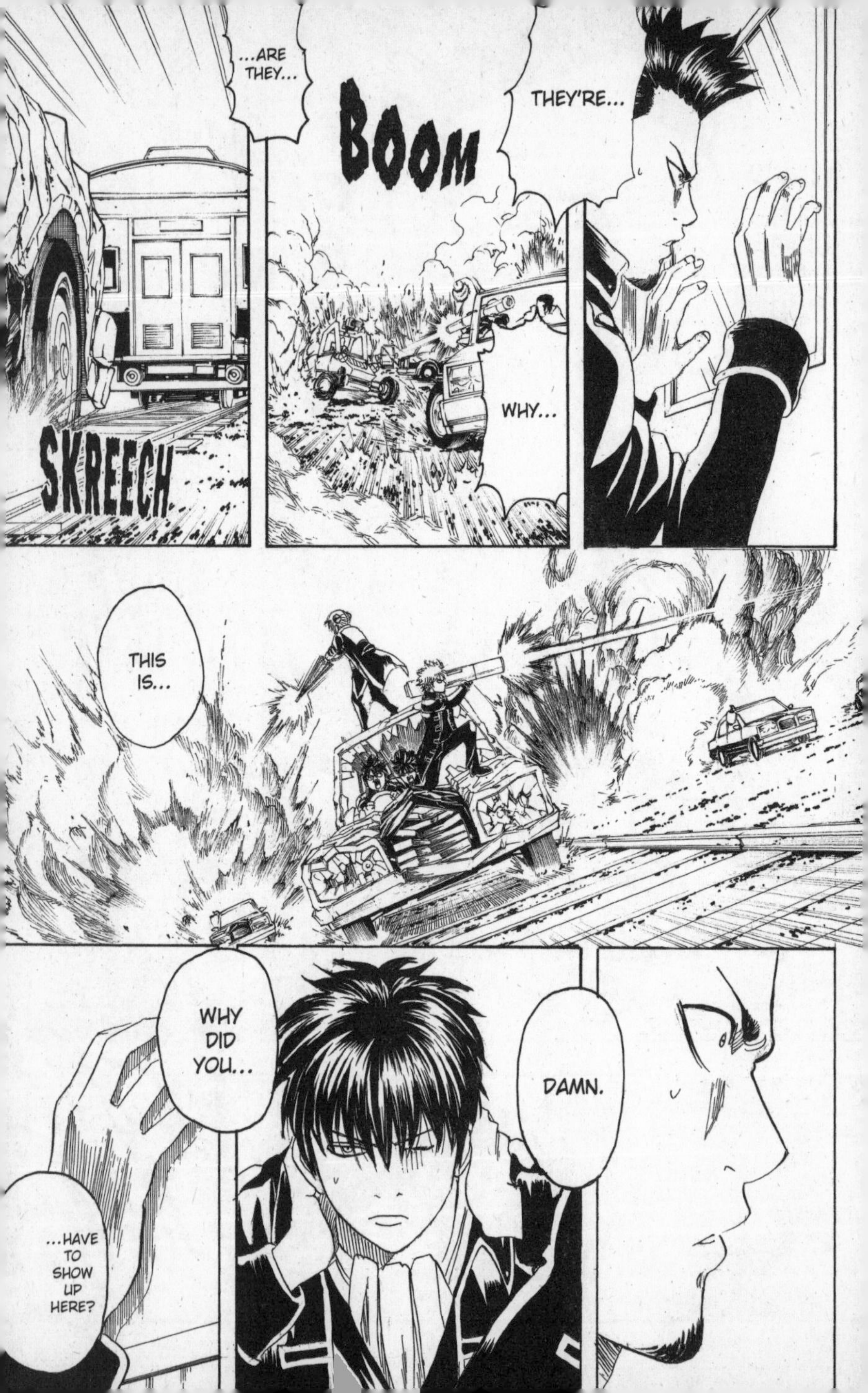
THEY'RE...
BOOM
WHY...
...ARE THEY...
SKREECH
THIS IS...
DAMN.
WHY DID YOU...
...HAVE TO SHOW UP HERE?

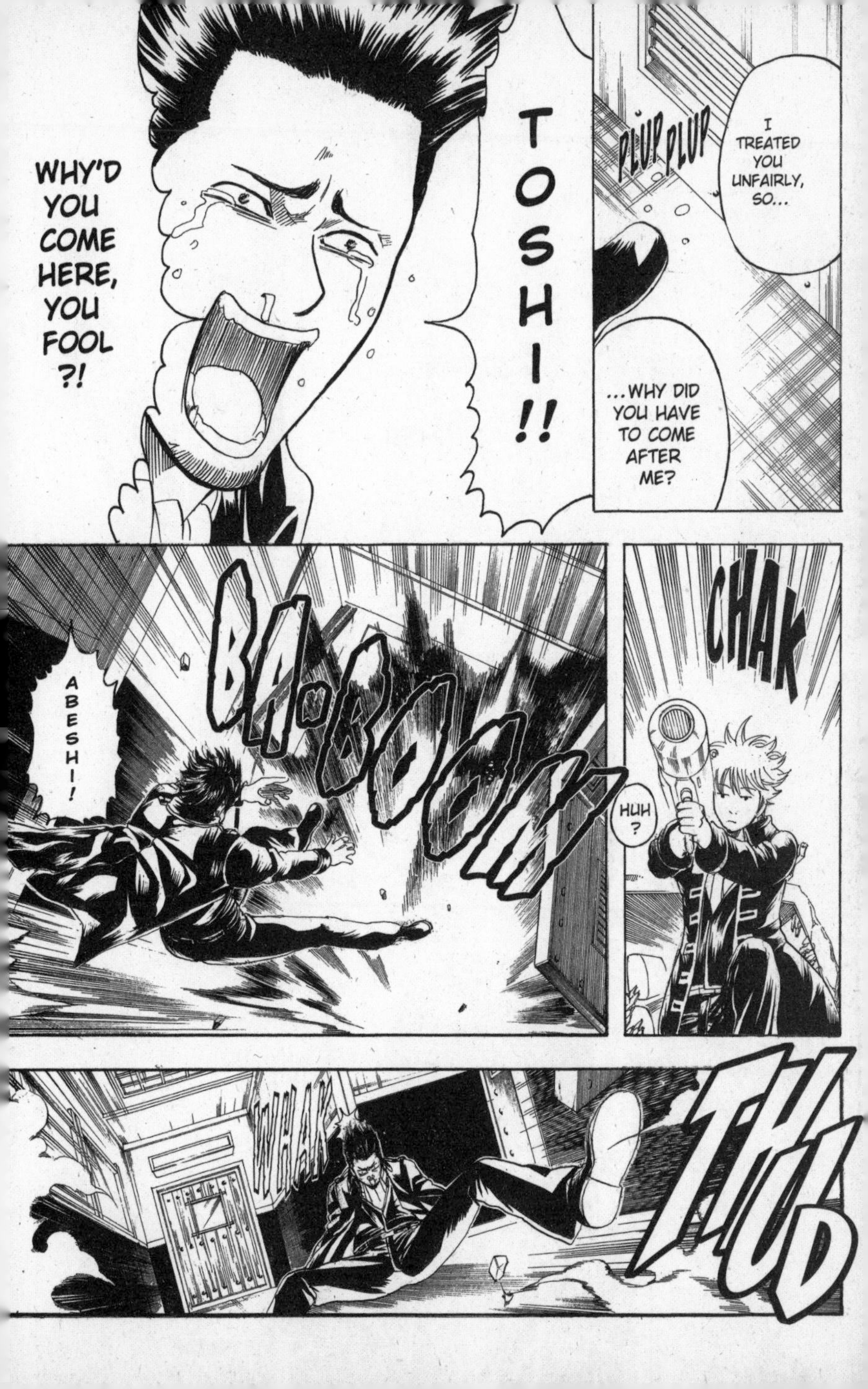
I TREATED YOU UNFAIRLY, SO...
PLUP PLUP
...WHY DID YOU HAVE TO COME AFTER ME?
TOSHI!!
WHY'D YOU COME HERE, YOU FOOL?!
CHAK
HUH?
BA-BOOM
ABESHI!
THUD

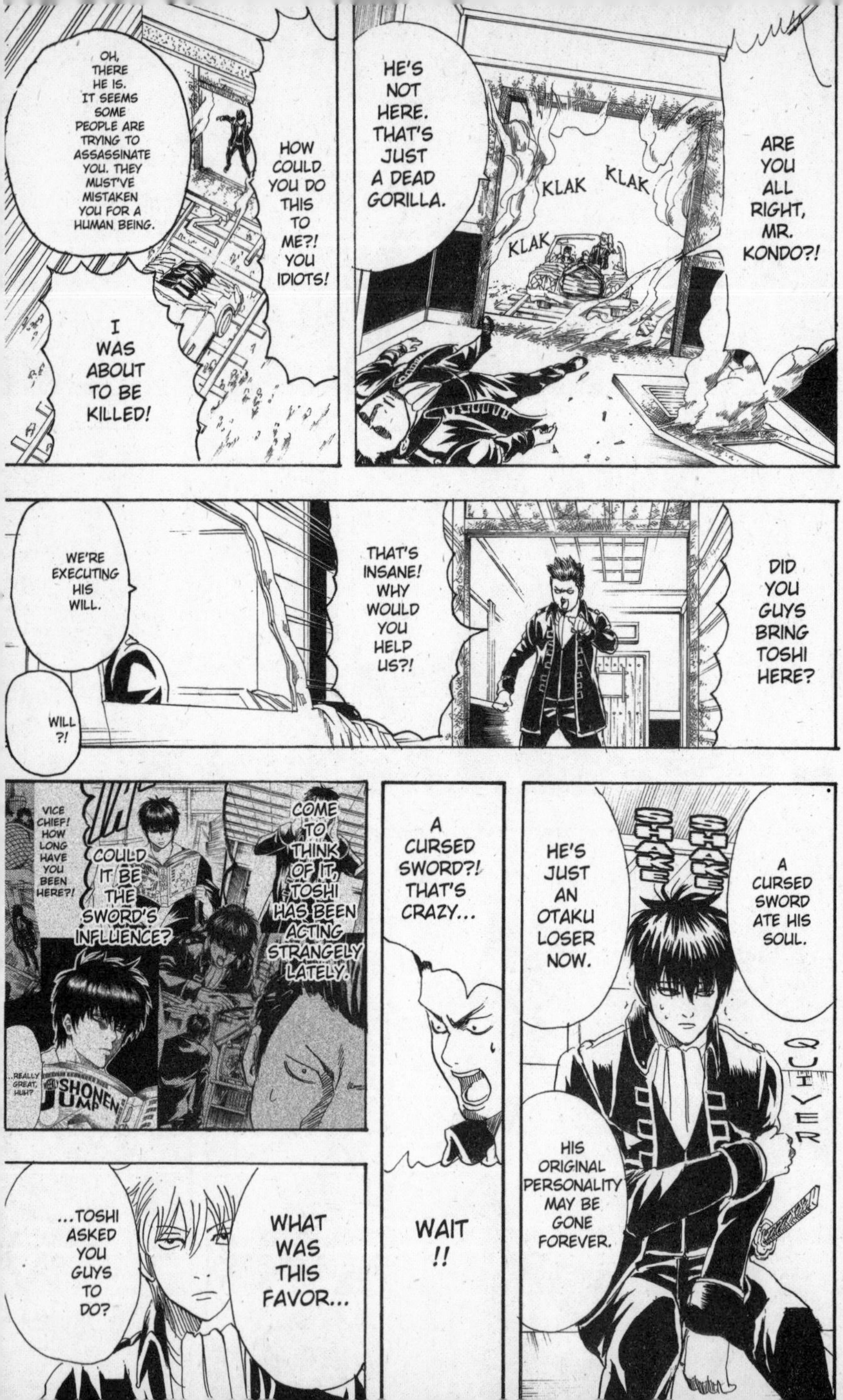
ARE YOU ALL RIGHT, MR. KONDO?!
KLAK KLAK
KLAK
HE'S NOT HERE. THAT'S JUST A DEAD GORILLA.
HOW COULD YOU DO THIS TO ME?! YOU IDIOTS!
OH, THERE HE IS. IT SEEMS SOME PEOPLE ARE TRYING TO ASSASSINATE YOU. THEY MUST'VE MISTAKEN YOU FOR A HUMAN BEING.
I WAS ABOUT TO BE KILLED!
DID YOU GUYS BRING TOSHI HERE?
THAT'S INSANE! WHY WOULD YOU HELP US?!
WE'RE EXECUTING HIS WILL.
WILL?!
A CURSED SWORD ATE HIS SOUL.
SHAKE
SHAKE
HE'S JUST AN OTAKU LOSER NOW.
QUIVER
HIS ORIGINAL PERSONALITY MAY BE GONE FOREVER.
A CURSED SWORD?! THAT'S CRAZY...
WAIT!!
COME TO THINK OF IT, TOSHI HAS BEEN ACTING STRANGELY LATELY.
COULD IT BE THE SWORD'S INFLUENCE?
VICE CHIEF! HOW LONG HAVE YOU BEEN HERE?!
...REALLY GREAT, HUH?
SHONEN JUMP
WHAT WAS THIS FAVOR...
...TOSHI ASKED YOU GUYS TO DO?

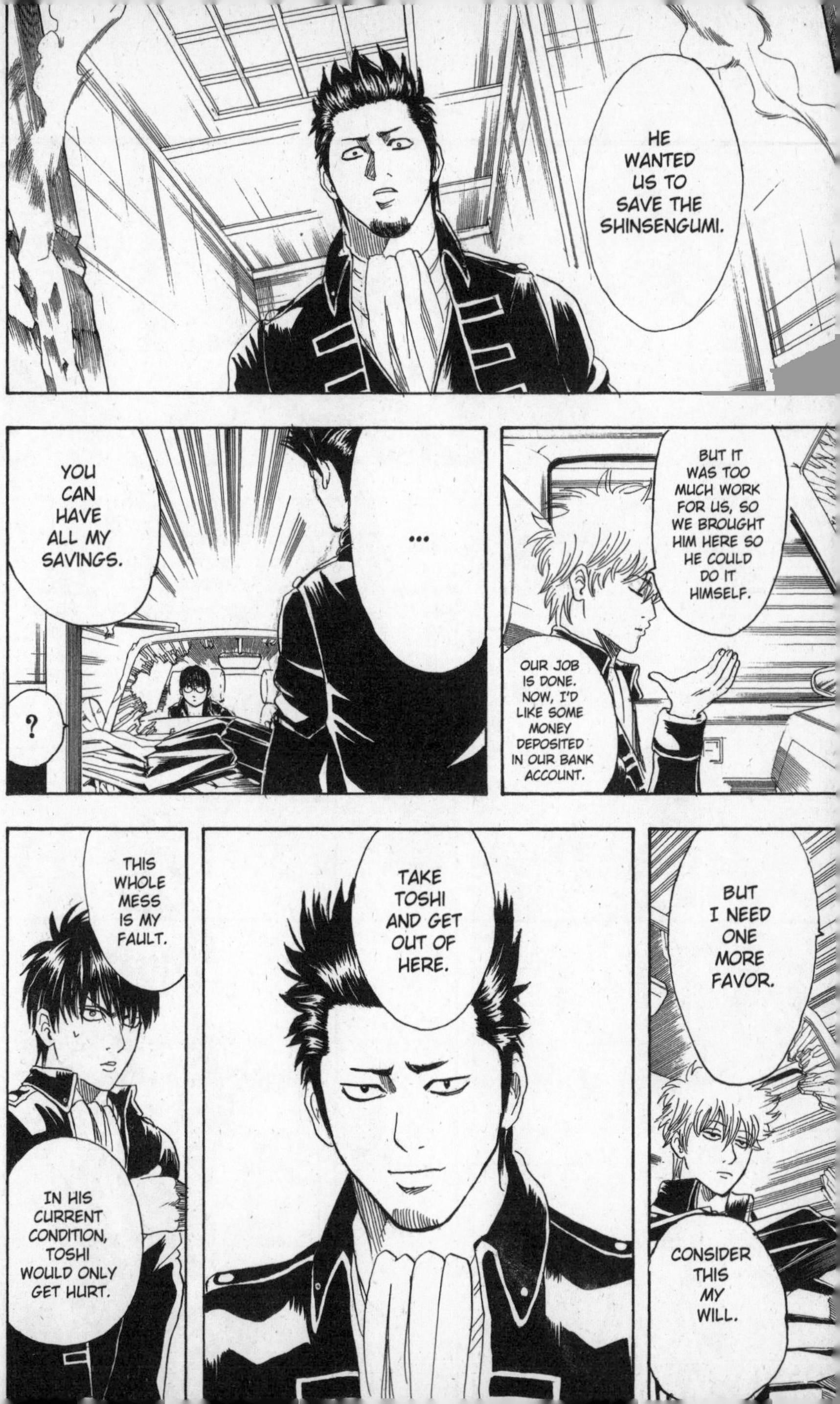
HE WANTED US TO SAVE THE SHINSENGUMI.
BUT IT WAS TOO MUCH WORK FOR US, SO WE BROUGHT HIM HERE SO HE COULD DO IT HIMSELF.
OUR JOB IS DONE. NOW, I'D LIKE SOME MONEY DEPOSITED IN OUR BANK ACCOUNT.
...
YOU CAN HAVE ALL MY SAVINGS.
?
BUT I NEED ONE MORE FAVOR.
CONSIDER THIS MY WILL.
TAKE TOSHI AND GET OUT OF HERE.
THIS WHOLE MESS IS MY FAULT.
IN HIS CURRENT CONDITION, TOSHI WOULD ONLY GET HURT.

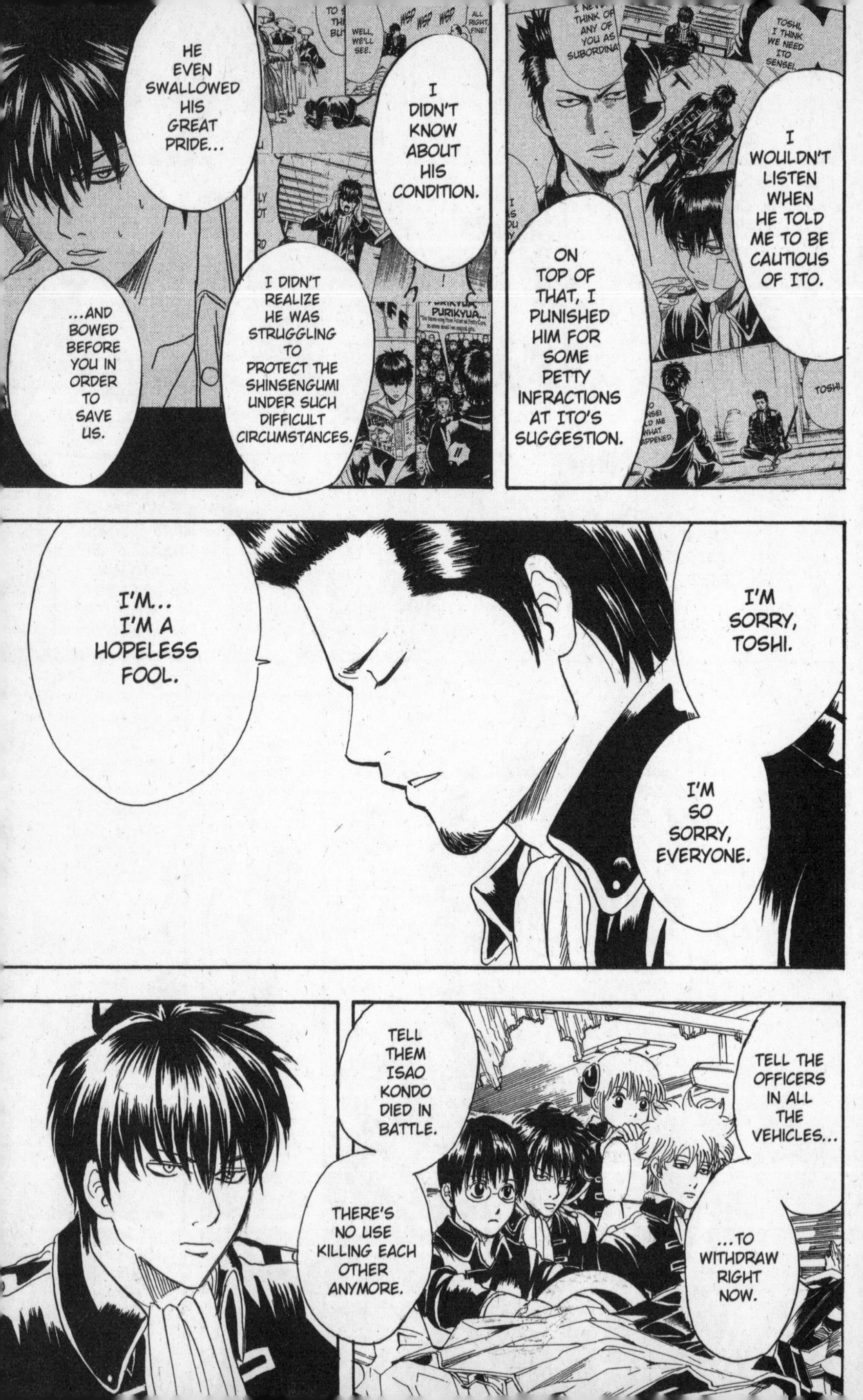
TOSHI, I THINK WE NEED ITO SENSEI.
I WOULDN'T LISTEN WHEN HE TOLD ME TO BE CAUTIOUS OF ITO.
TOSHI.
ON TOP OF THAT, I PUNISHED HIM FOR SOME PETTY INFRACTIONS AT ITO'S SUGGESTION.
ALL RIGHT, FINE!
WELL, WE'LL SEE.
I DIDN'T KNOW ABOUT HIS CONDITION.
I DIDN'T REALIZE HE WAS STRUGGLING TO PROTECT THE SHINSENGUMI UNDER SUCH DIFFICULT CIRCUMSTANCES.
HE EVEN SWALLOWED HIS GREAT PRIDE...
...AND BOWED BEFORE YOU IN ORDER TO SAVE US.
I'M SORRY, TOSHI.
I'M SO SORRY, EVERYONE.
I'M... I'M A HOPELESS FOOL.
TELL THE OFFICERS IN ALL THE VEHICLES...
...TO WITHDRAW RIGHT NOW.
TELL THEM ISAO KONDO DIED IN BATTLE.
THERE'S NO USE KILLING EACH OTHER ANYMORE.

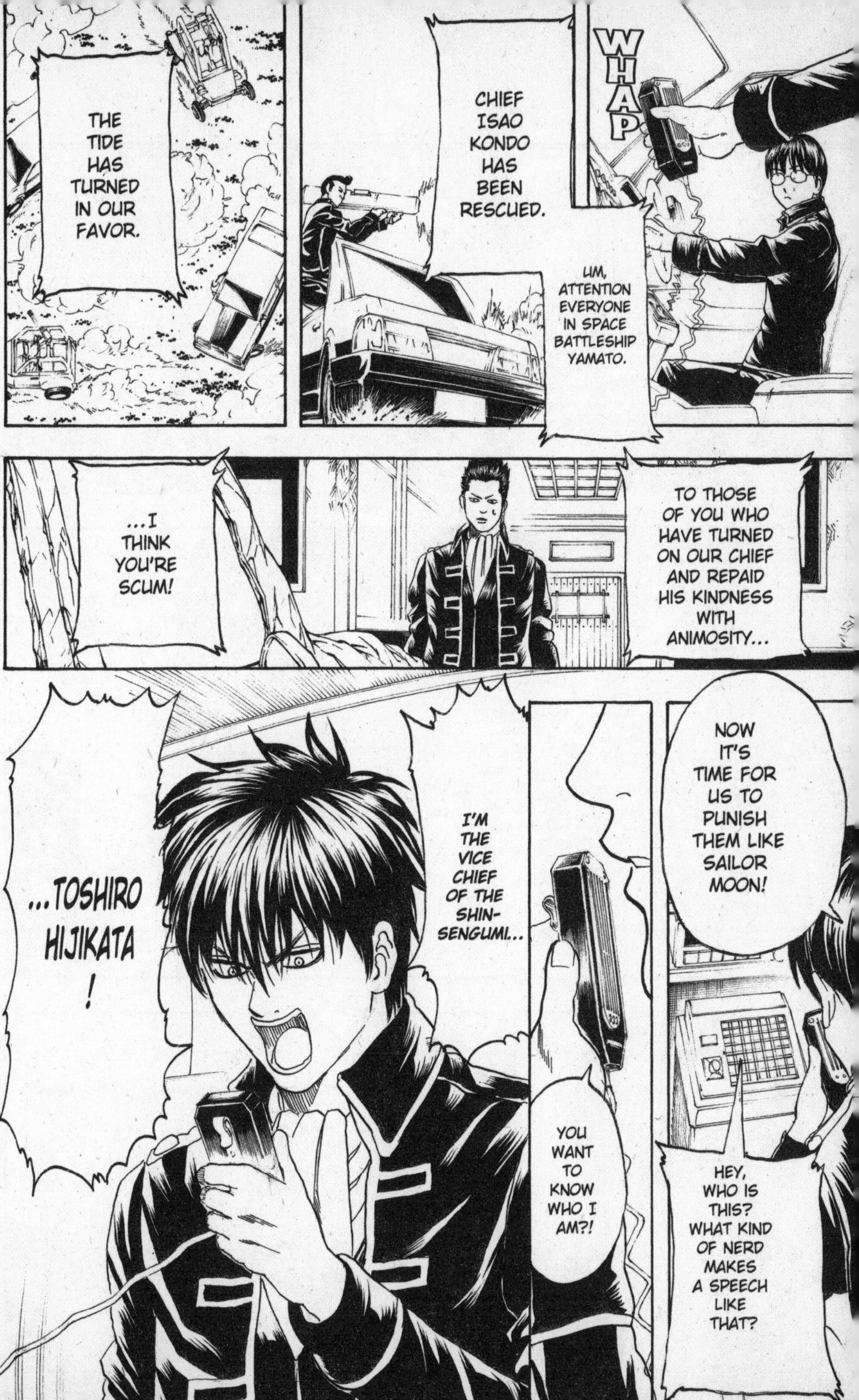
WHAP
UM, ATTENTION EVERYONE IN SPACE BATTLESHIP YAMATO.
CHIEF ISAO KONDO HAS BEEN RESCUED.
THE TIDE HAS TURNED IN OUR FAVOR.
TO THOSE OF YOU WHO HAVE TURNED ON OUR CHIEF AND REPAID HIS KINDNESS WITH ANIMOSITY...
...I THINK YOU'RE SCUM!
NOW IT'S TIME FOR US TO PUNISH THEM LIKE SAILOR MOON!
HEY, WHO IS THIS? WHAT KIND OF NERD MAKES A SPEECH LIKE THAT?
YOU WANT TO KNOW WHO I AM?!
I'M THE VICE CHIEF OF THE SHIN-SENGUMI...
...TOSHIRO HIJIKATA!

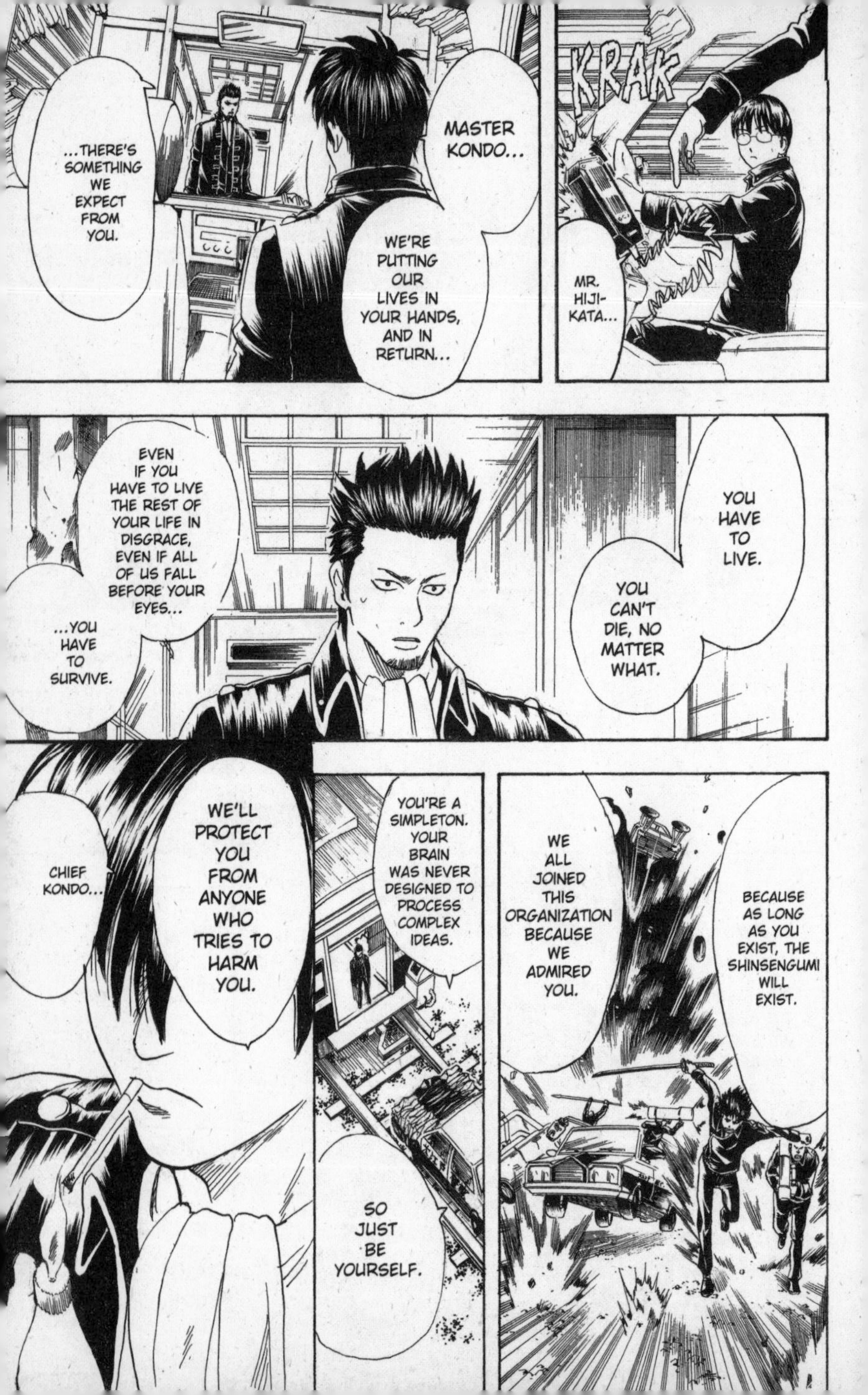
KRAK
MR. HIJI-KATA...
MASTER KONDO...
WE'RE PUTTING OUR LIVES IN YOUR HANDS, AND IN RETURN...
...THERE'S SOMETHING WE EXPECT FROM YOU.
YOU HAVE TO LIVE.
YOU CAN'T DIE, NO MATTER WHAT.
EVEN IF YOU HAVE TO LIVE THE REST OF YOUR LIFE IN DISGRACE, EVEN IF ALL OF US FALL BEFORE YOUR EYES...
...YOU HAVE TO SURVIVE.
BECAUSE AS LONG AS YOU EXIST, THE SHINSENGUMI WILL EXIST.
WE ALL JOINED THIS ORGANIZATION BECAUSE WE ADMIRED YOU.
YOU'RE A SIMPLETON. YOUR BRAIN WAS NEVER DESIGNED TO PROCESS COMPLEX IDEAS.
SO JUST BE YOURSELF.
WE'LL PROTECT YOU FROM ANYONE WHO TRIES TO HARM YOU.
CHIEF KONDO...

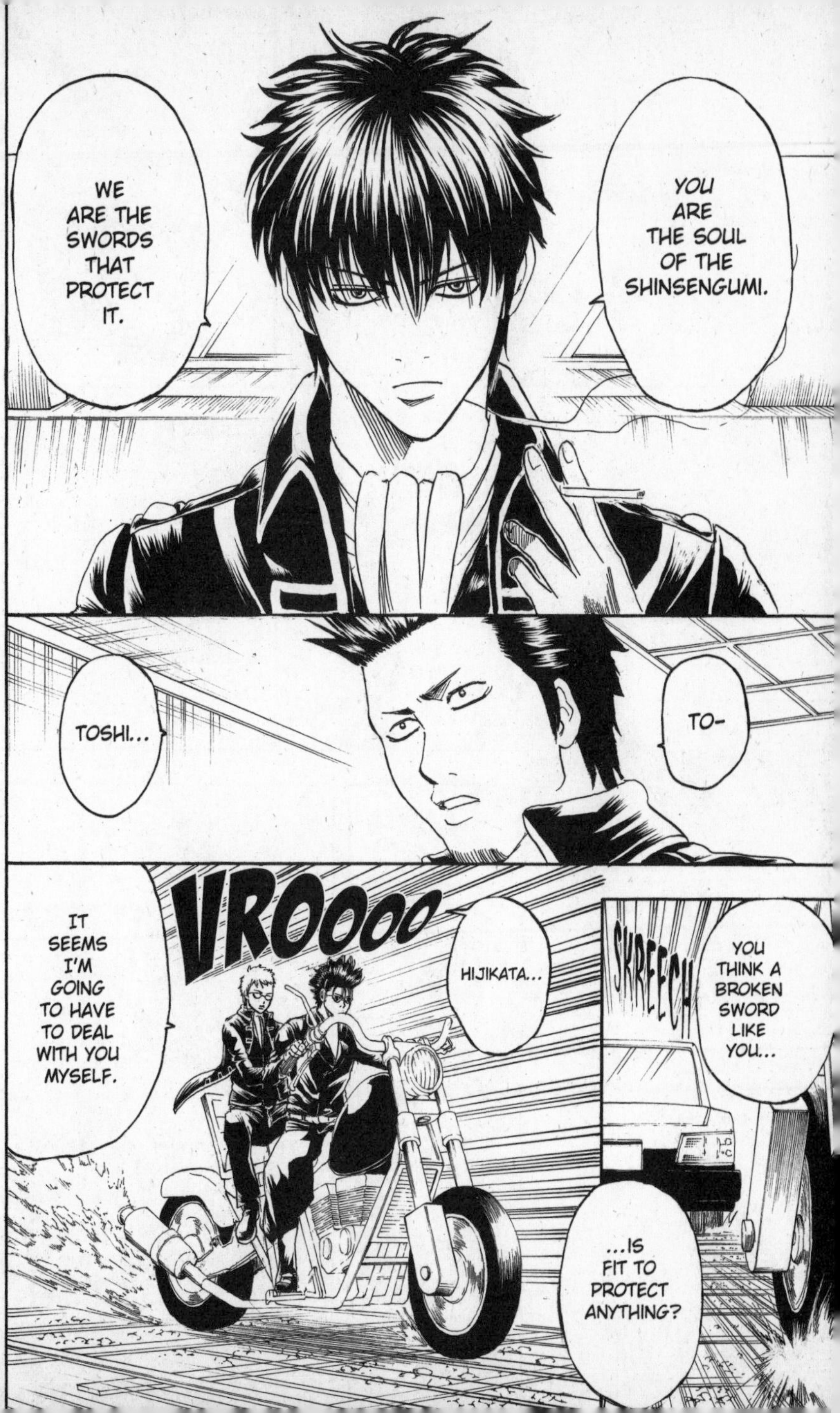
YOU ARE THE SOUL OF THE SHINSENGUMI.
WE ARE THE SWORDS THAT PROTECT IT.
TO-
TOSHI...
SKREECH
YOU THINK A BROKEN SWORD LIKE YOU...
...IS FIT TO PROTECT ANYTHING?
VROOOO
HIJIKATA...
IT SEEMS I'M GOING TO HAVE TO DEAL WITH YOU MYSELF.

I HAVE A SWORD RIGHT HERE.

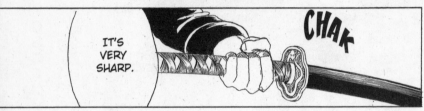

IT'S VERY SHARP.

CHAK

SHUT UP.

WHAT ARE YOU DOING?

DRAW YOUR SWORD.

UNH!

KREEK

I CAN DO IT. I CAN DRAW THIS SWORD IF I TRY.

BURN, MY COSMO,* BURN! *[FROM KNIGHTS OF THE ZODIAC]

NO, NO! NO! NO!

KREEK

KREEK

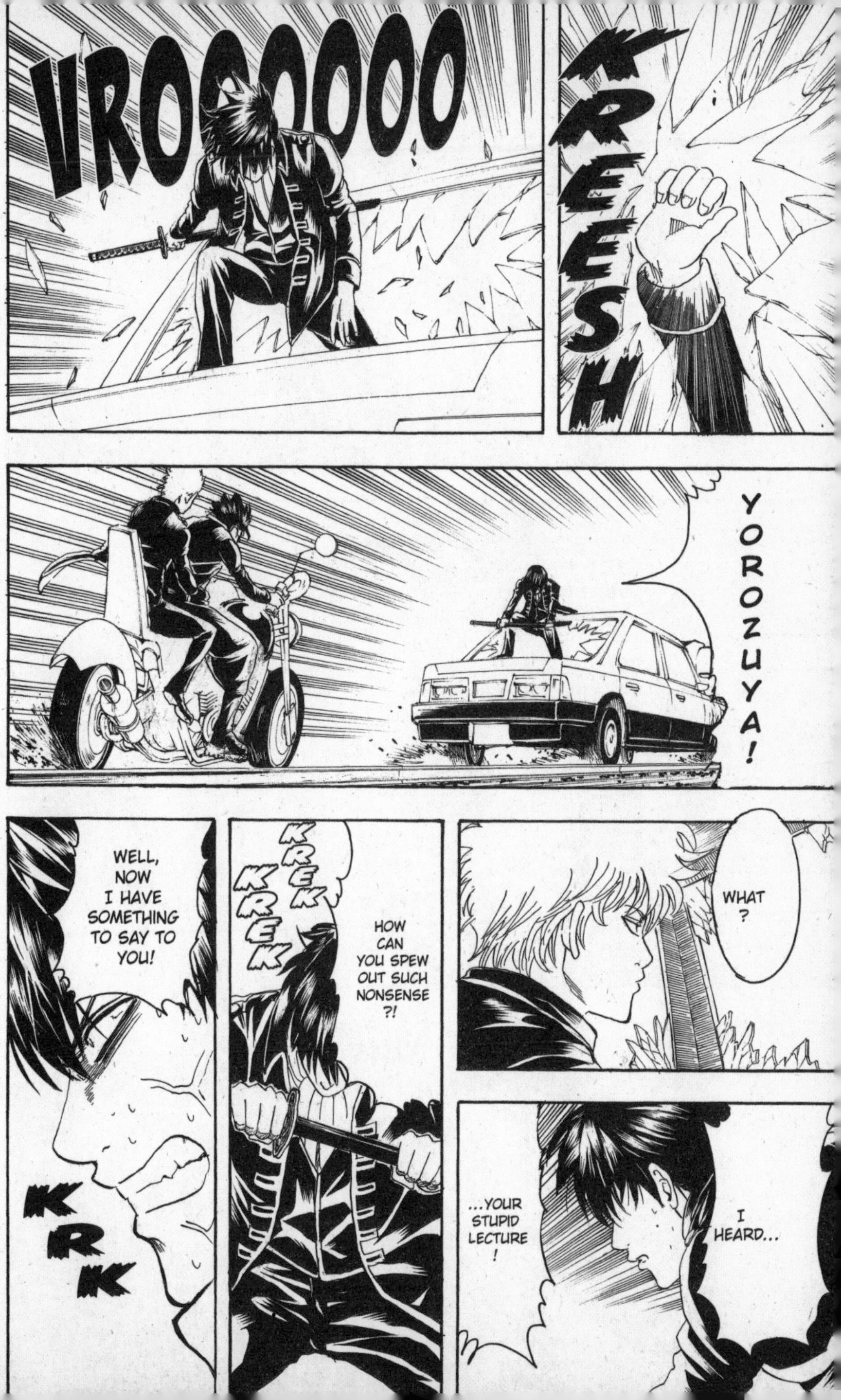
KREESH
VROOOOOO
YOROZUYA!
WHAT?
I HEARD...
...YOUR STUPID LECTURE!
KREK
KREK
HOW CAN YOU SPEW OUT SUCH NONSENSE?!
WELL, NOW I HAVE SOMETHING TO SAY TO YOU!
KRK

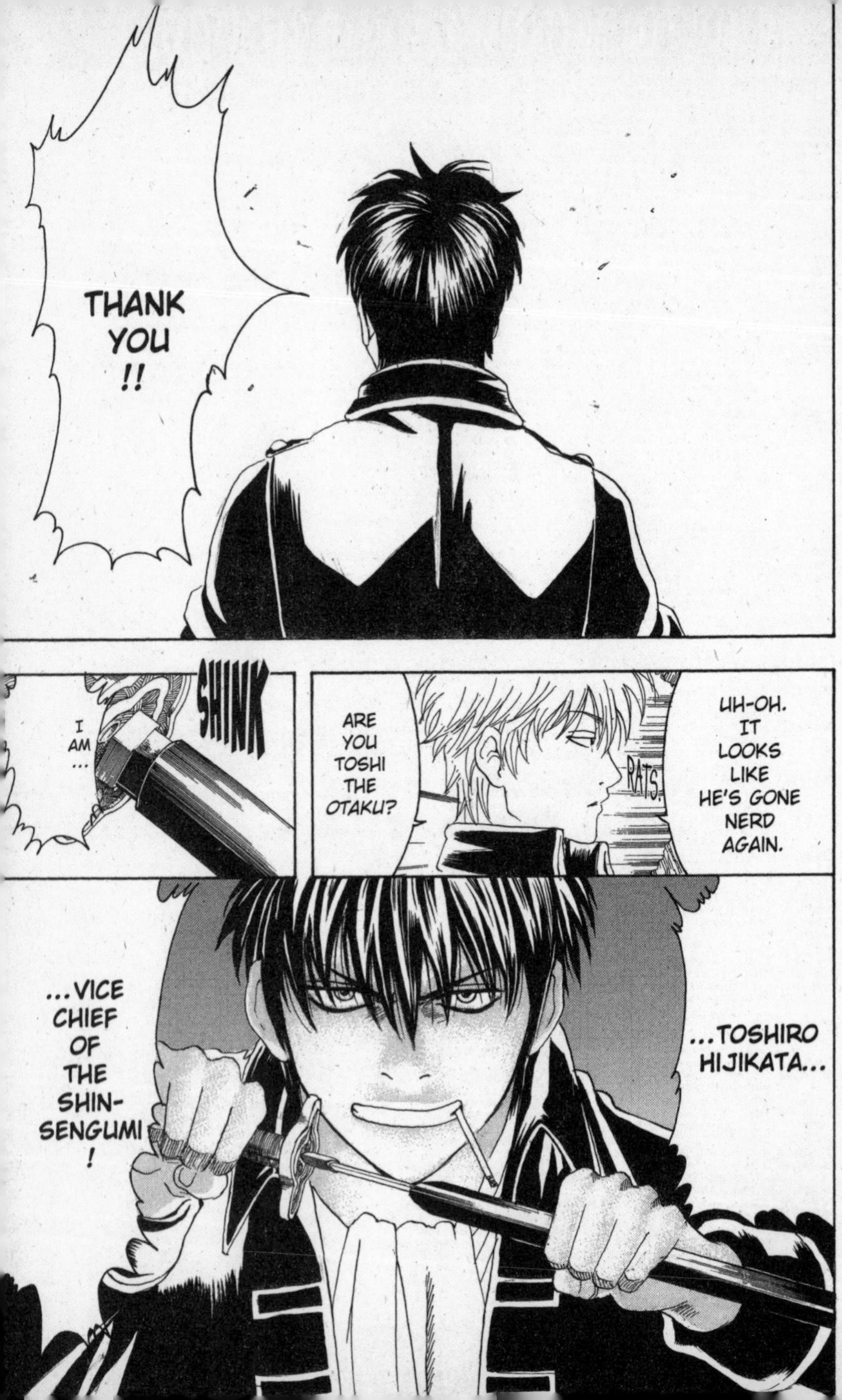
THANK YOU !!
UH-OH. IT LOOKS LIKE HE'S GONE NERD AGAIN.
RATS.
ARE YOU TOSHI THE OTAKU?
SHINK
I AM ...
...TOSHIRO HIJIKATA...
...VICE CHIEF OF THE SHIN-SENGUMI !

SORACHI: I FEEL LIKE I WON'T BE ABLE TO DO IT WELL IF I GET TOO OLD. AND I LIKE THE ATMOSPHERE OF PEOPLE ENJOYING CHATTING AND MAKING NOISE. JUST THINKING ABOUT CLASSROOMS I CAN CONSTRUCT CHARACTERS CREATIVELY...
ONISHI: THEN WE'LL DO A CAMPUS-BASED THING NEXT.
SORACHI: BUT JUST DOING SCHOOL STUFF WON'T MAKE IT INHERENTLY FUN.
ONISHI: DID YOU SAY THAT YOUR FAVORITE "MIYAZAKI FILM" WAS *KIKI'S DELIVERY SERVICE?*
SORACHI: YEAH. I LIKE *KIKI'S DELIVERY SERVICE*. BUT I NEVER THOUGHT THAT KIKI WAS CUTE OR ANYTHING.
ONISHI: THEN WHY DO YOU LIKE THE MOVIE?
SORACHI: I JUST LIKED THE STORY, AND I LOVED HOW THE TOWN LOOKED.
ONISHI: THE STORY WAS A PRETTY GENERIC DRAMA.
SORACHI: WHAT? I THOUGHT IT WAS GREAT.
ONISHI: THERE WEREN'T ANY FIGHTS. THE PLANE NEVER CRASHED.
SORACHI: I GUESS. BUT I DO LIKE *CASTLE IN THE SKY*, TOO.
ONISHI: SO YOU DON'T LIKE THINGS WITH SUPERHEROES IN IT.
SORACHI: I DON'T.
ONISHI: YOU LIKE STUFF WHERE ORDINARY PEOPLE ARE TRYING THEIR BEST TO GET THROUGH LIFE. THAT KIND OF THING?
SORACHI: YOU'RE RIGHT IN HOW I ALWAYS LIKE THE SIDE CHARACTERS IN THE MIYAZAKI FILMS. I RARELY LIKE THE MAIN CHARACTERS. BUT I REALLY LIKED SHEETA. WHAT PART OF IT DID YOU LIKE, ONISHI?
ONISHI: THE PART THAT GETS ME EXCITED?
SORACHI: THAT'S A REALLY STUPID ANSWER. (LAUGH) YOU LIKE THE DIRECTION, RIGHT? DID YOU LIKE HOW SIMPLE IT WAS?
ONISHI: LIKE THE PART WHERE THE CASTLE MOVED!
SORACHI: YEAH. *CASTLE IN THE SKY* WAS LIKE THAT.
SORACHI: BUT IT FEELS LIKE A GOOD ROMANTIC ADVENTURE. SO THIS INTERVIEW IS ABOUT MIYAZAKI FILMS NOW? (LAUGH) NOW BACK TO WHY I DECIDED TO START DRAWING COMICS. I WOULD SAY THAT IT'S THANKS TO *CASTLE IN THE SKY*. WHEN I SAW THE LAST SCENE WHERE LAPUTA WAS FLYING, IT FELT REALLY HEART WRENCHING. IT REALLY GIVES YOU THAT FEELING OF "DON'T LEAVE ME BEHIND!" I WONDER IF PEOPLE WILL GET WHAT I'M SAYING...
ONISHI: DID YOU TRY TO WRITE UP A SEQUEL BY YOURSELF?
SORACHI: (LAUGH) NO. WHETHER IT BE TV SHOWS OR COMICS, EVERYTHING HAS TO HAVE AN END. FROM THE READER'S STANDPOINT, THEY ALWAYS GET LEFT BEHIND IN THE END. IT LEAVES YOU FEELING "WAIT JUST A MINUTE." IN THAT CASE, I'D RATHER BE THE ONE WRITING THE STORY. I THINK THAT'S PART OF MY MOTIVATION FOR DRAWING COMICS. IS THERE ANY OTHER WAY TO SOLVE THAT DILEMMA?
ONISHI: MY WAY OF SOLVING THAT DILEMMA IS TO WATCH THE SEQUEL.
SORACHI: BUT THAT SEQUEL WILL HAVE AN END, TOO (LAUGH). YOU DON'T HAVE A CHOICE BUT TO DO IT YOURSELF. DON'T YOU JUST FEEL EMPTY AFTER YOU WATCH A GOOD MOVIE?
ONISHI: WHY?
SORACHI: ALL YOU CAN DO IS WATCH IT.
ONISHI: EVERYONE IS LIKE THAT.
SORACHI: DON'T YOU WANT TO GET TO THE POINT WHERE YOU CAN THINK, "I WANT TO MAKE A GREAT MOVIE"?
ONISHI: NORMAL PEOPLE DON'T THINK LIKE THAT. I THINK IT'S ONLY YOU.
SORACHI: I KNOW FOR A FACT THAT I CAN'T MAKE ANYTHING GREAT, BUT I STILL WANT TO BE IN THIS INDUSTRY FOR AS LONG AS I LIVE.
ONISHI: THEN YOUR GOAL IN LIFE IS TO BE A MOVIE DIRECTOR?
SORACHI: NO. I DON'T WANT TO BE ONE. BUT DON'T YOU WANT TO CONTINUE TO CREATE SOMETHING WITH YOUR OWN HANDS? THE MORE I WATCH, THE SADDER I GET.

"BUT YOU USUALLY DON'T TALK WITH OTHER PEOPLE, DO YOU?" -ONISHI

SORACHI: MAYBE THAT'S WHY I'M A COMIC AUTHOR.
ONISHI: I DON'T THINK MOST PEOPLE THINK LIKE THAT. THEY USUALLY JUST SAY STUFF LIKE, "THAT WAS A GREAT MOVIE," AND THAT'S THE END OF IT.
SORACHI: AND DON'T YOU WANT TO USE THAT FEELING AS MOTIVATION TO CREATE SOMETHING? WHEN THEY JUST SAY, "MAN, I HAVE TO GO BACK TO WORK TOMORROW," DON'T YOU THINK THAT MAKES YOU FEEL EMPTY INSIDE? WOULDN'T IT BE GREAT IF YOU COULD SAY, "ALL RIGHT. I'M GOING TO MAKE SOMETHING BETTER THAN THAT STARTING TOMORROW."
ONISHI: (LAUGH) IT WOULD BE. BUT NORMAL PEOPLE DON'T THINK LIKE THAT.
SORACHI: SO PEOPLE DON'T WANT TO BE ABLE TO CREATE SOMETHING THAT CAN DEEPLY MOVE OTHER PEOPLE IN THE SAME WAY?
ONISHI: THEY DON'T. BUT YOU DO. THAT'S WHY YOU'RE A COMIC AUTHOR.
SORACHI: I THOUGHT EVERYONE GETS EXCITED LIKE THAT WHENEVER THEY SEE SOMETHING GREAT...

[WHAT'S A FUTURE GOAL?]

ONISHI: YOUR FUTURE GOAL.
SORACHI: I WANT TO BE ABLE TO KEEP DRAWING COMICS.
ONISHI: UNTIL YOU'RE HOW OLD?
SORACHI: UNTIL I DIE.
ONISHI: OH.
SORACHI: YUP... WHAT?
ONISHI: I MEAN, AT WHAT AGE DO YOU WANT TO RETIRE?
SORACHI: I DON'T WANT TO.
ONISHI: SO YOU WANT TO KEEP DRAWING.
SORACHI: YEAH. BUT I HATE THIS CURRENT SITUATION OF ALWAYS BEING BACKED INTO A CORNER WITH DEADLINES. BUT I GUESS THAT WON'T HAPPEN.
ONISHI: WELL...
SORACHI: YEAH. IT'LL END BADLY. YOU KNOW THAT MY NEXT WORK IS GOING TO FLOP (LAUGH). AND THEN I'LL JUST END UP OPENING A CAFÉ BEFORE DRIFTING INTO OBLIVION.
ONISHI: (LAUGH) WHY A CAFÉ?
SORACHI: I DON'T KNOW. I THOUGHT IT WOULD FIT MY IMAGE. THE IMAGE OF "I USED TO DRAW COMICS FOR A LIVING" KIND OF THING.
ONISHI: "CAFÉ OWNED BY FORMER COMIC AUTHOR, HIDEAKI SORACHI." SO IT'S A COMIC BOOK CAFÉ (LAUGH)?
SORACHI: NO. IT'S THE KIND WHERE YOU GET TO CHAT WITH THE OWNER.
ONISHI: BUT YOU USUALLY DON'T TALK WITH OTHER PEOPLE, DO YOU?
SORACHI: I THINK A LOT OF FLEDGLING COMIC AUTHORS WILL COME.
ONISHI: ALL THE WAY TO HOKKAIDO?
SORACHI: I DON'T THINK I WANT TO GO BACK TO HOKKAIDO. I JUST WANT TO CONTINUE CREATING SOMETHING. IT CAN BE COMICS. IT CAN BE SCRIPTWRITING. I DON'T HAVE ANYTHING ELSE I REALLY WANT TO DO.
ONISHI: SO YOU JUST WANT TO KEEP WRITING STORIES?
SORACHI: YEAH. I WANT TO DO SOMETHING SIMILAR TO WHAT I'M DOING NOW.
ONISHI: SO YOU'LL BE DRAWING GROUNDWORK SKETCHES RIGHT BEFORE YOU DIE? (LAUGH)
SORACHI: THAT COULD BE OKAY TOO. I GET REALLY TIRED WHILE I'M DOING THE GROUNDWORK SKETCHES. BUT I FEEL THE HAPPIEST WHEN READERS SAY THAT WHAT I WROTE WAS INTERESTING. MY ONLY INTERESTS ARE COMICS AFTER ALL.
ONISHI: YOU NEVER GET SICK, HUH?
SORACHI: I DO. BUT...

CONTINUED ON PAGE 146

Lesson 164
Don't Play on the Railroad Tracks

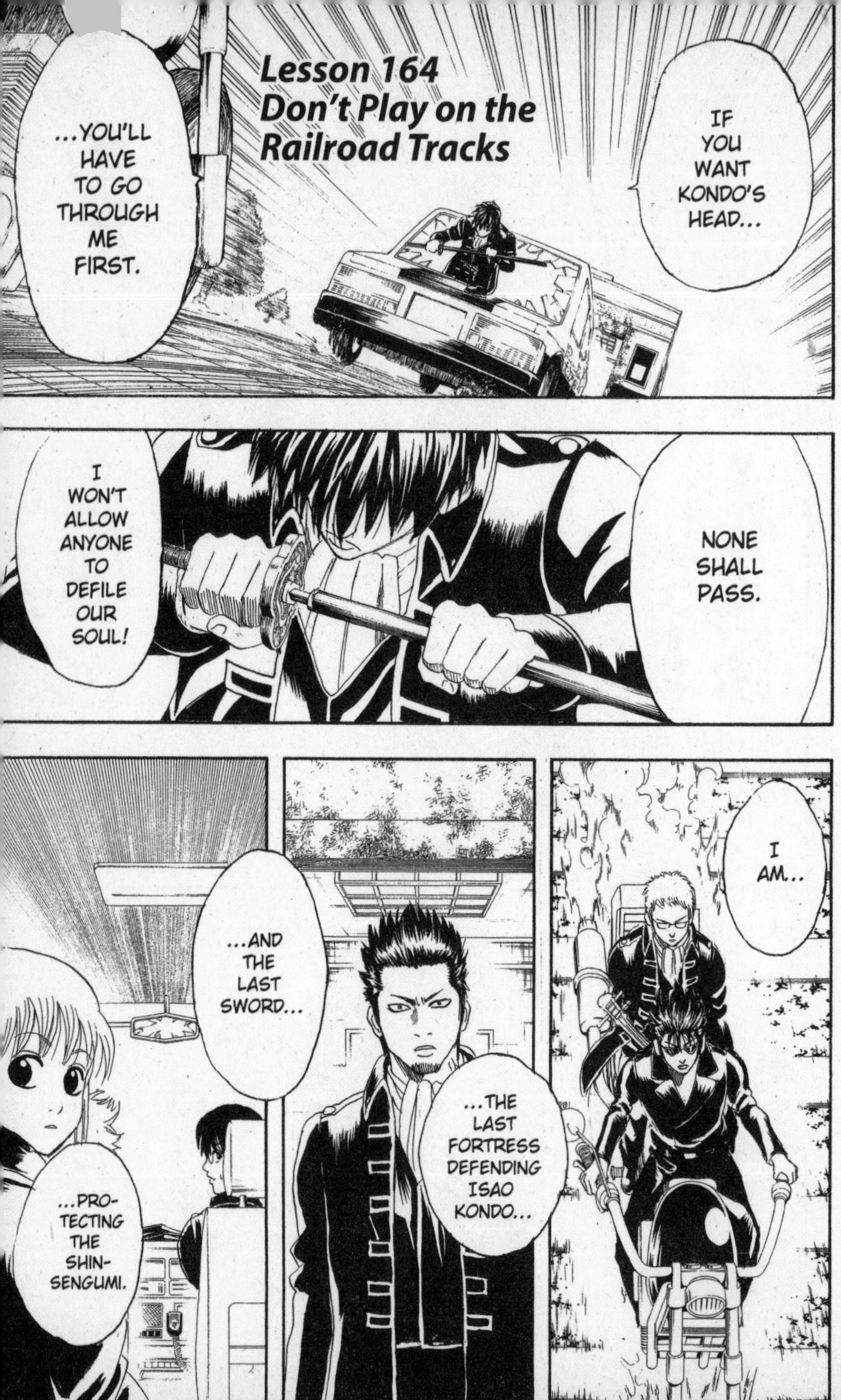
IF YOU WANT KONDO'S HEAD...
...YOU'LL HAVE TO GO THROUGH ME FIRST.
NONE SHALL PASS.
I WON'T ALLOW ANYONE TO DEFILE OUR SOUL!
I AM...
...THE LAST FORTRESS DEFENDING ISAO KONDO...
...AND THE LAST SWORD...
...PROTECTING THE SHINSENGUMI.

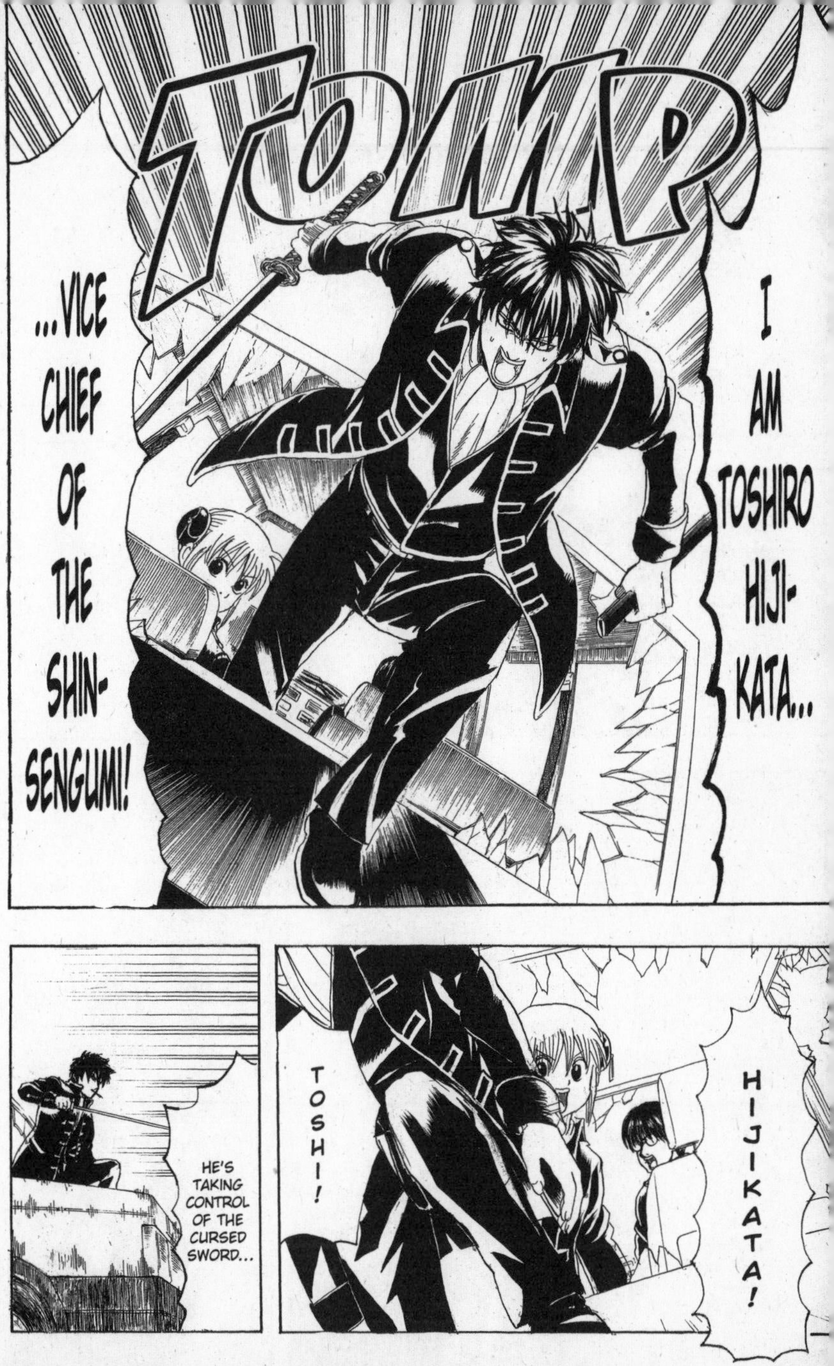
TOMP
I AM TOSHIRO HIJI-KATA...
...VICE CHIEF OF THE SHIN-SENGUMI!
HIJIKATA!
TOSHI!
HE'S TAKING CONTROL OF THE CURSED SWORD...

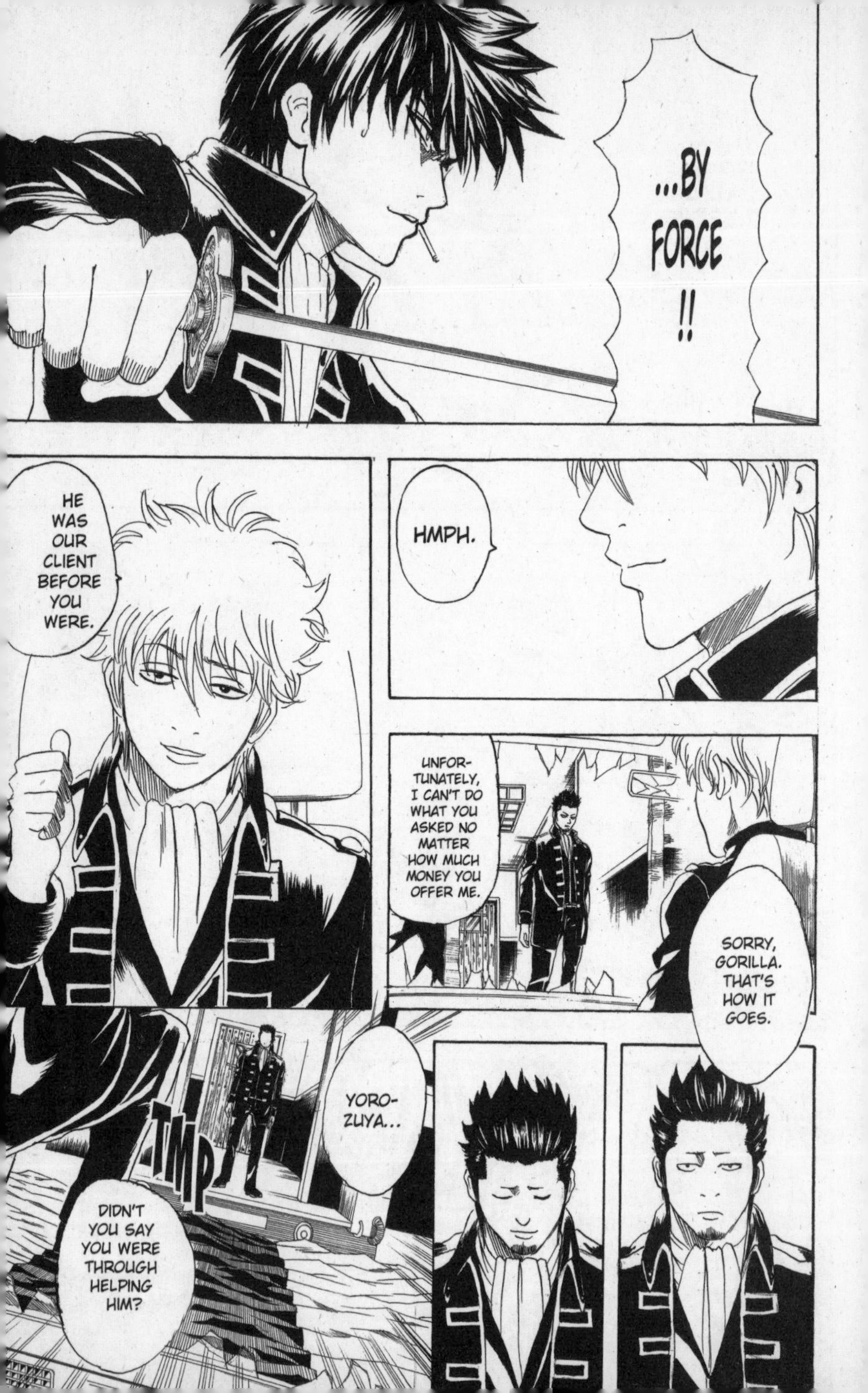
...BY FORCE !!
HMPH.
UNFORTUNATELY, I CAN'T DO WHAT YOU ASKED NO MATTER HOW MUCH MONEY YOU OFFER ME.
SORRY, GORILLA. THAT'S HOW IT GOES.
HE WAS OUR CLIENT BEFORE YOU WERE.
YORO-ZUYA...
TMP
DIDN'T YOU SAY YOU WERE THROUGH HELPING HIM?

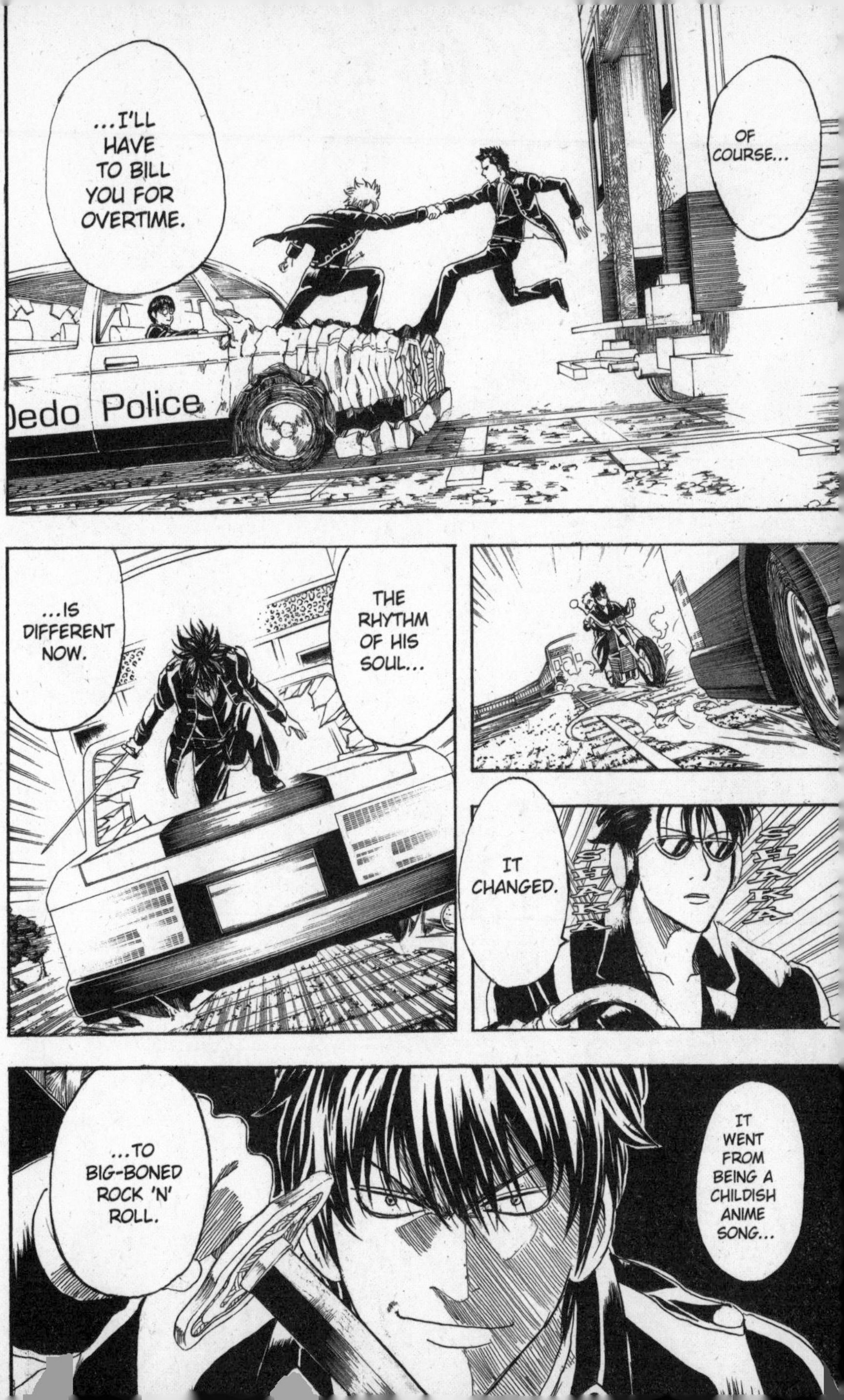
OF COURSE...
...I'LL HAVE TO BILL YOU FOR OVERTIME.
IT CHANGED.
SHAKA SHAKA
THE RHYTHM OF HIS SOUL...
...IS DIFFERENT NOW.
IT WENT FROM BEING A CHILDISH ANIME SONG...
...TO BIG-BONED ROCK 'N' ROLL.

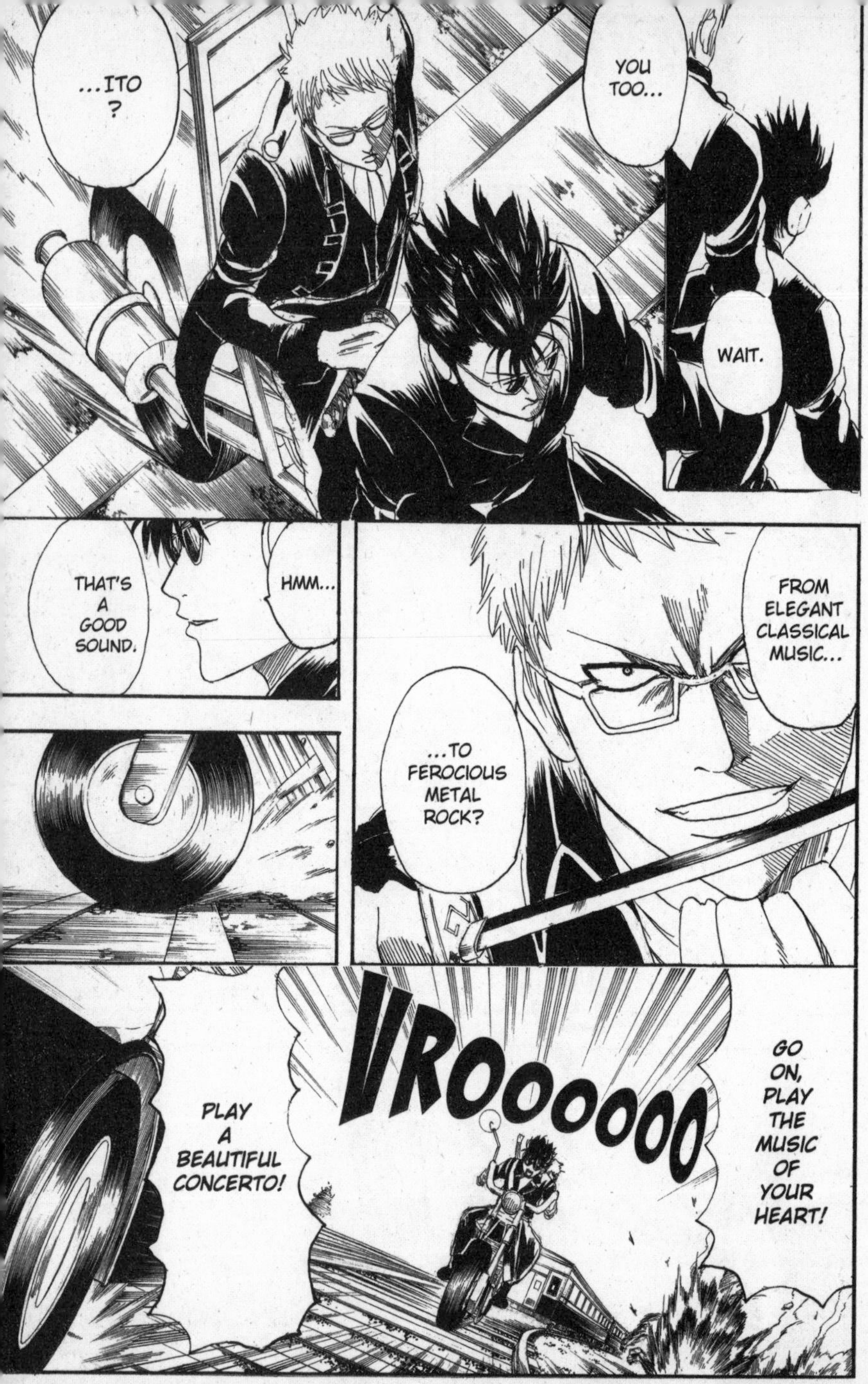
YOU TOO...
WAIT.
...ITO ?
FROM ELEGANT CLASSICAL MUSIC...
...TO FEROCIOUS METAL ROCK?
HMM...
THAT'S A GOOD SOUND.
GO ON, PLAY THE MUSIC OF YOUR HEART!
VROOOOOO
PLAY A BEAUTIFUL CONCERTO!

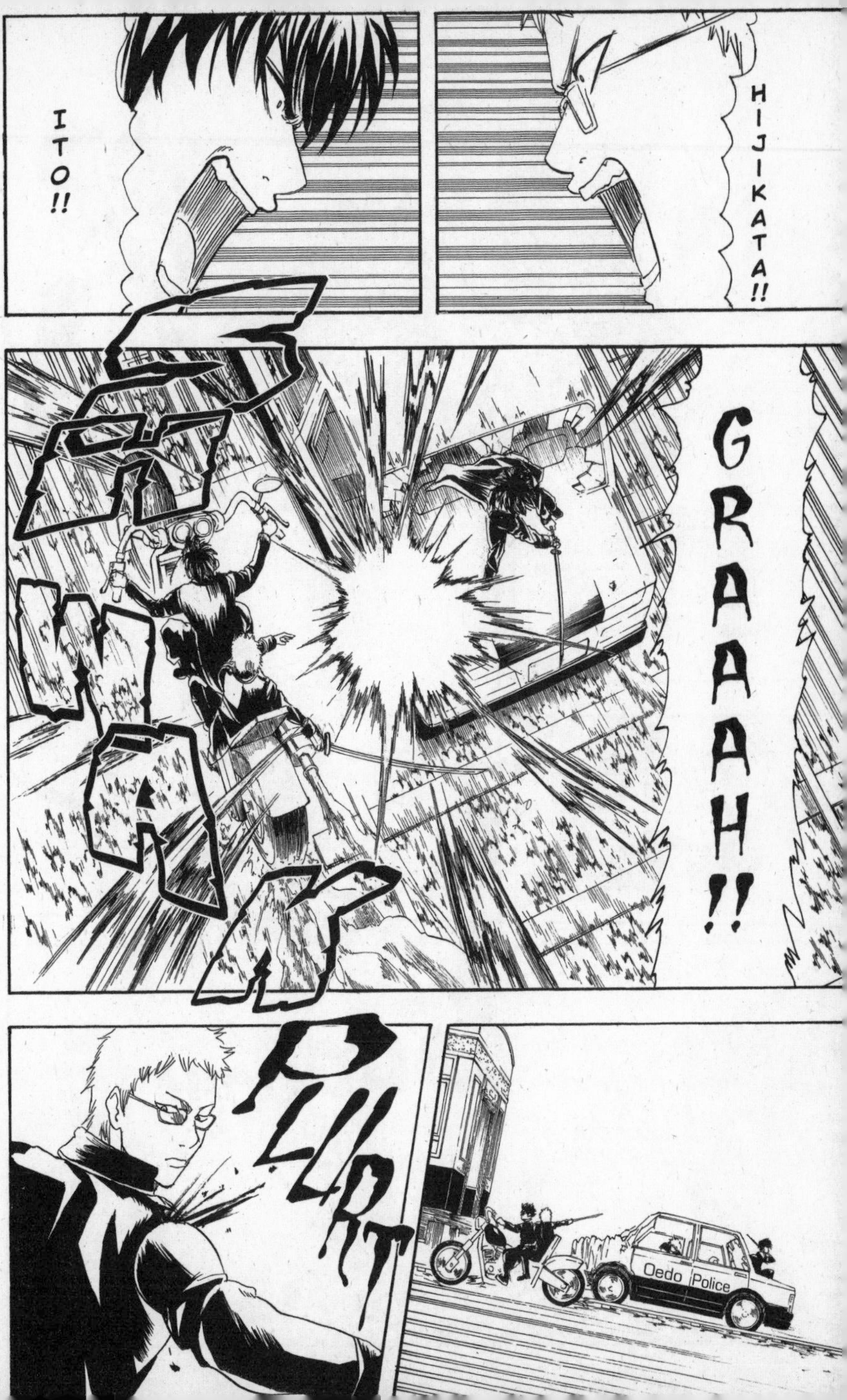
HIJIKATA!!
ITO!!
GRAAH!!
SHWAK
PLURT
Oedo Police

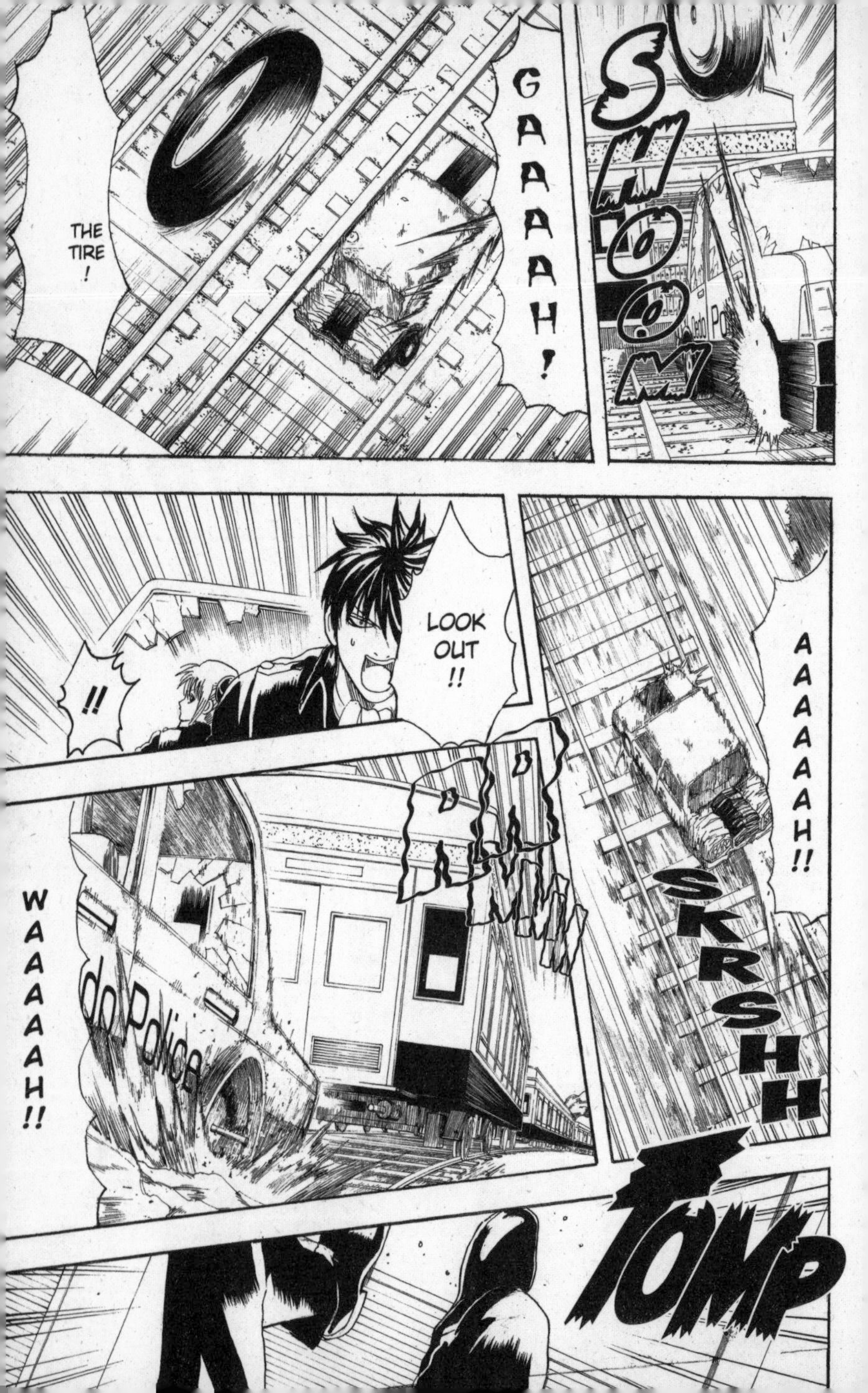
SHOOOOM
GAAAAAH!
THE TIRE!
AAAAAAAAH!!
SKRSHH
LOOK OUT!!
!!
WAAAAAAAH!!
TOMP

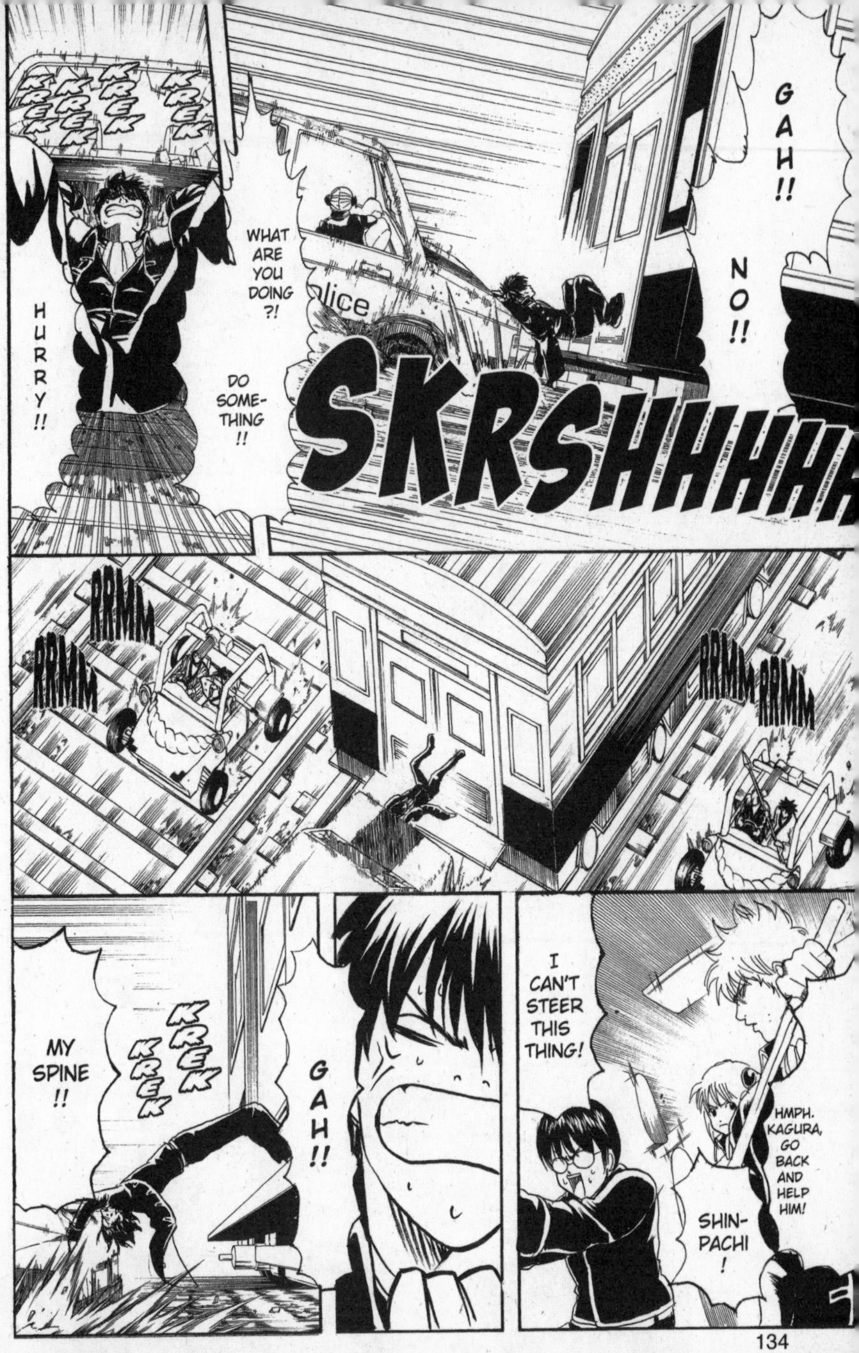
GAH!!
NO!!
olice
SKRSHHHHH
WHAT ARE YOU DOING ?!
DO SOMETHING !!
KREK KREK KREK KREK
HURRY!!
RRMM RRMM
RRMM RRMM
I CAN'T STEER THIS THING!
HMPH. KAGURA, GO BACK AND HELP HIM!
SHIN-PACHI !
GAH!!
KREK KREK
MY SPINE !!

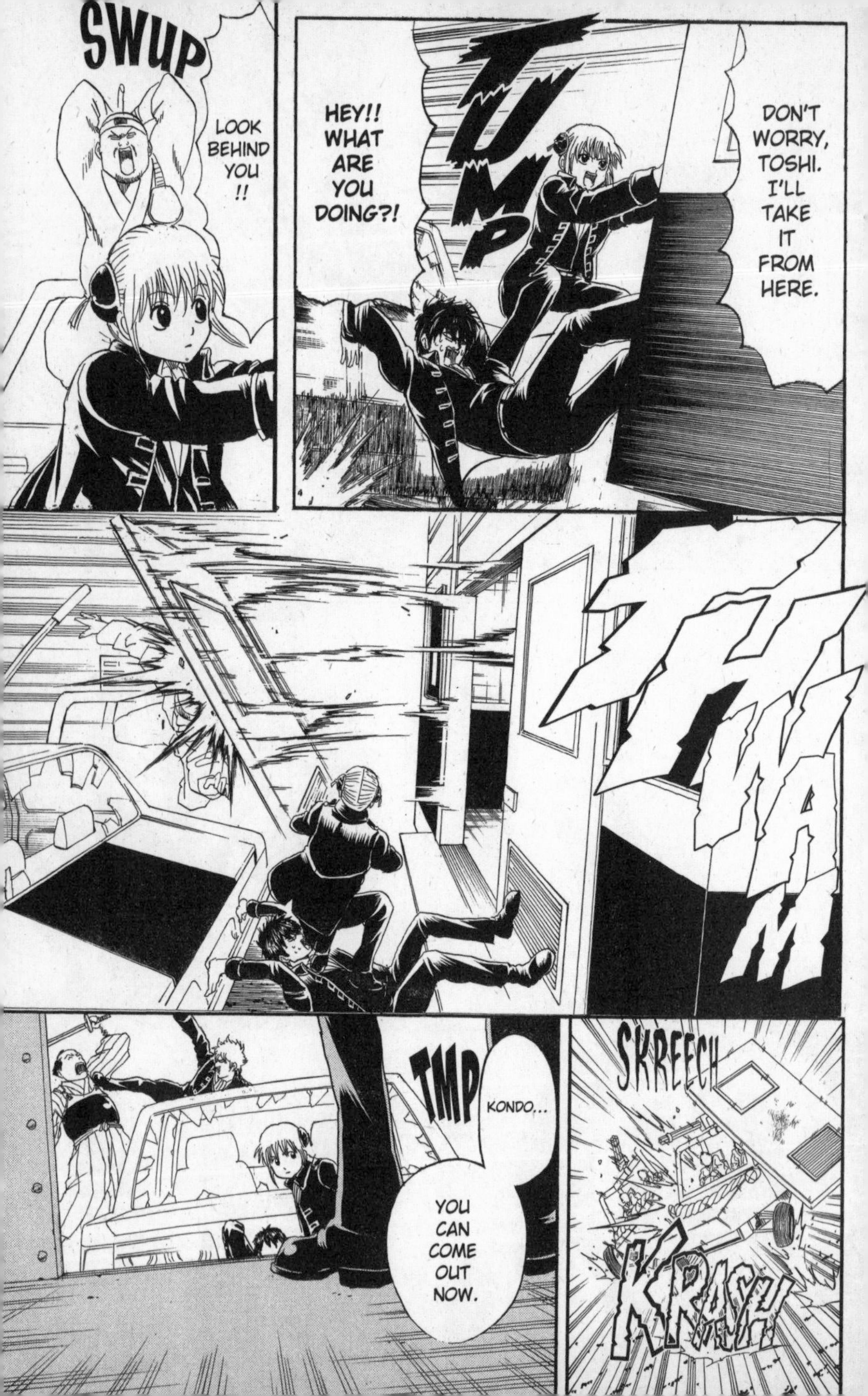
DON'T WORRY, TOSHI. I'LL TAKE IT FROM HERE.
JUMP
HEY!! WHAT ARE YOU DOING?!
SWUP
LOOK BEHIND YOU !!
WHAM
SKREECH
KRASH
TMP
KONDO...
YOU CAN COME OUT NOW.

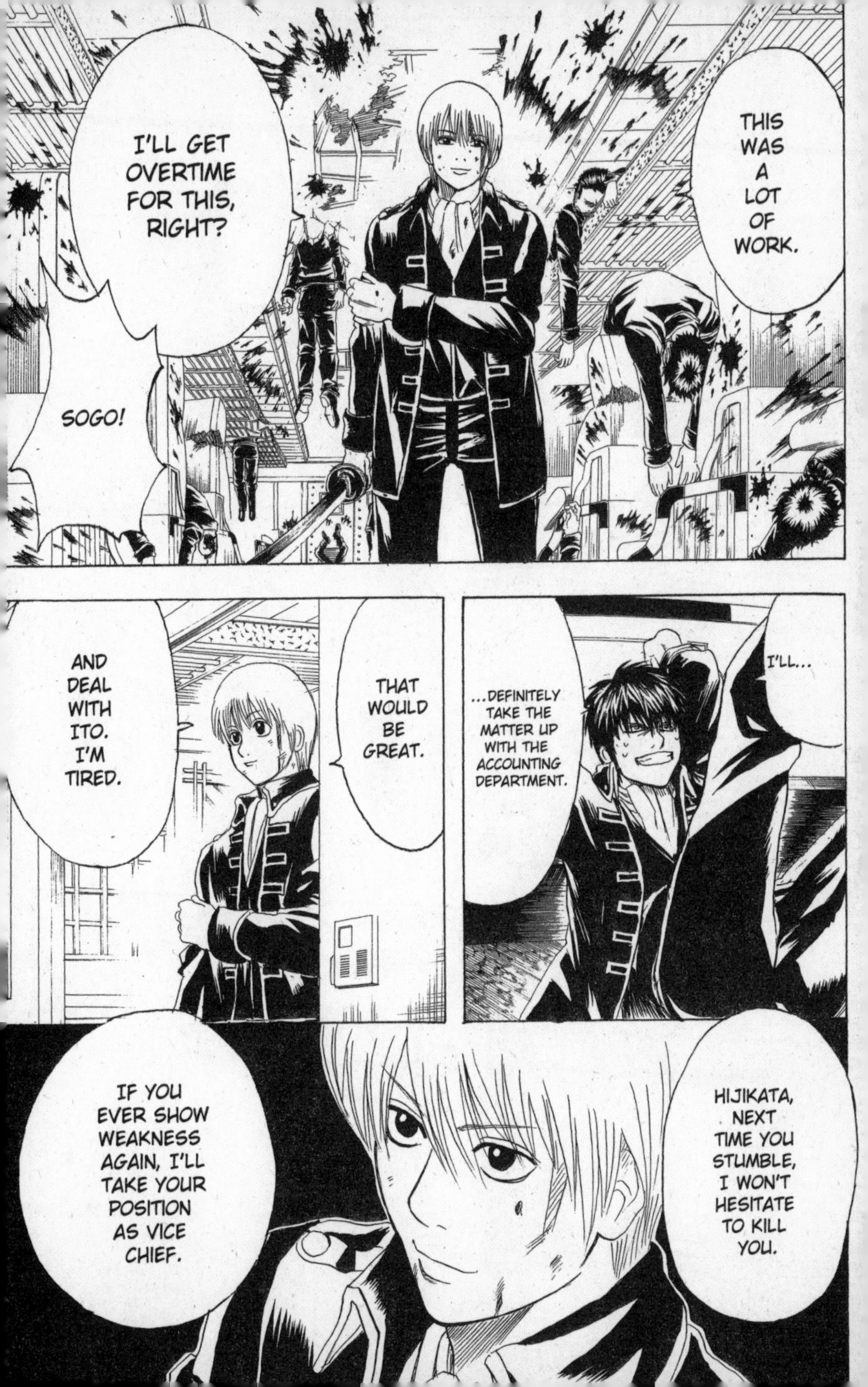
THIS WAS A LOT OF WORK.
I'LL GET OVERTIME FOR THIS, RIGHT?
SOGO!
I'LL...
...DEFINITELY TAKE THE MATTER UP WITH THE ACCOUNTING DEPARTMENT.
THAT WOULD BE GREAT.
AND DEAL WITH ITO. I'M TIRED.
HIJIKATA, NEXT TIME YOU STUMBLE, I WON'T HESITATE TO KILL YOU.
IF YOU EVER SHOW WEAKNESS AGAIN, I'LL TAKE YOUR POSITION AS VICE CHIEF.

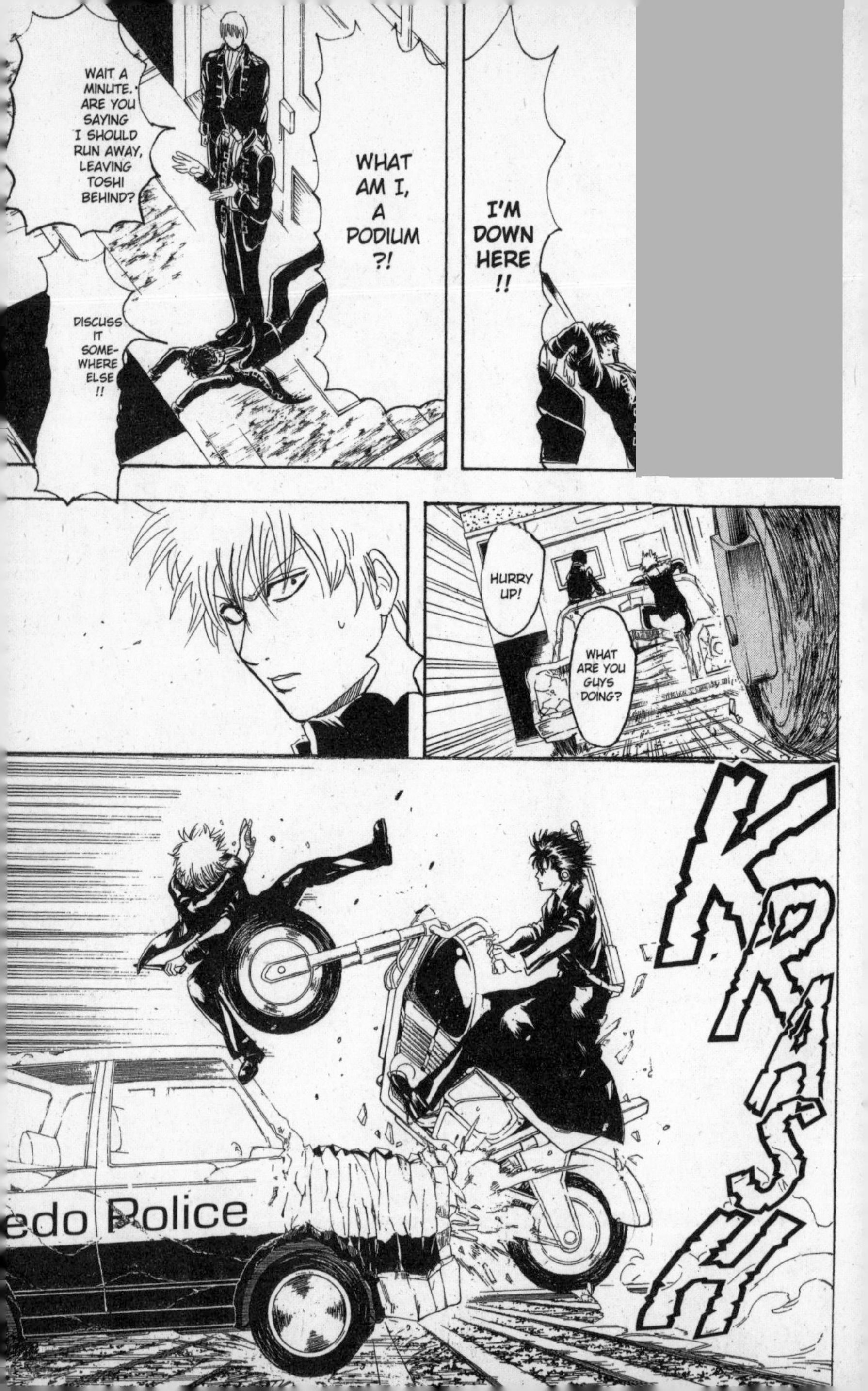
I'M DOWN HERE !!
WAIT A MINUTE. ARE YOU SAYING I SHOULD RUN AWAY, LEAVING TOSHI BEHIND?
WHAT AM I, A PODIUM ?!
DISCUSS IT SOMEWHERE ELSE !!
HURRY UP!
WHAT ARE YOU GUYS DOING?
KRASH
edo Police

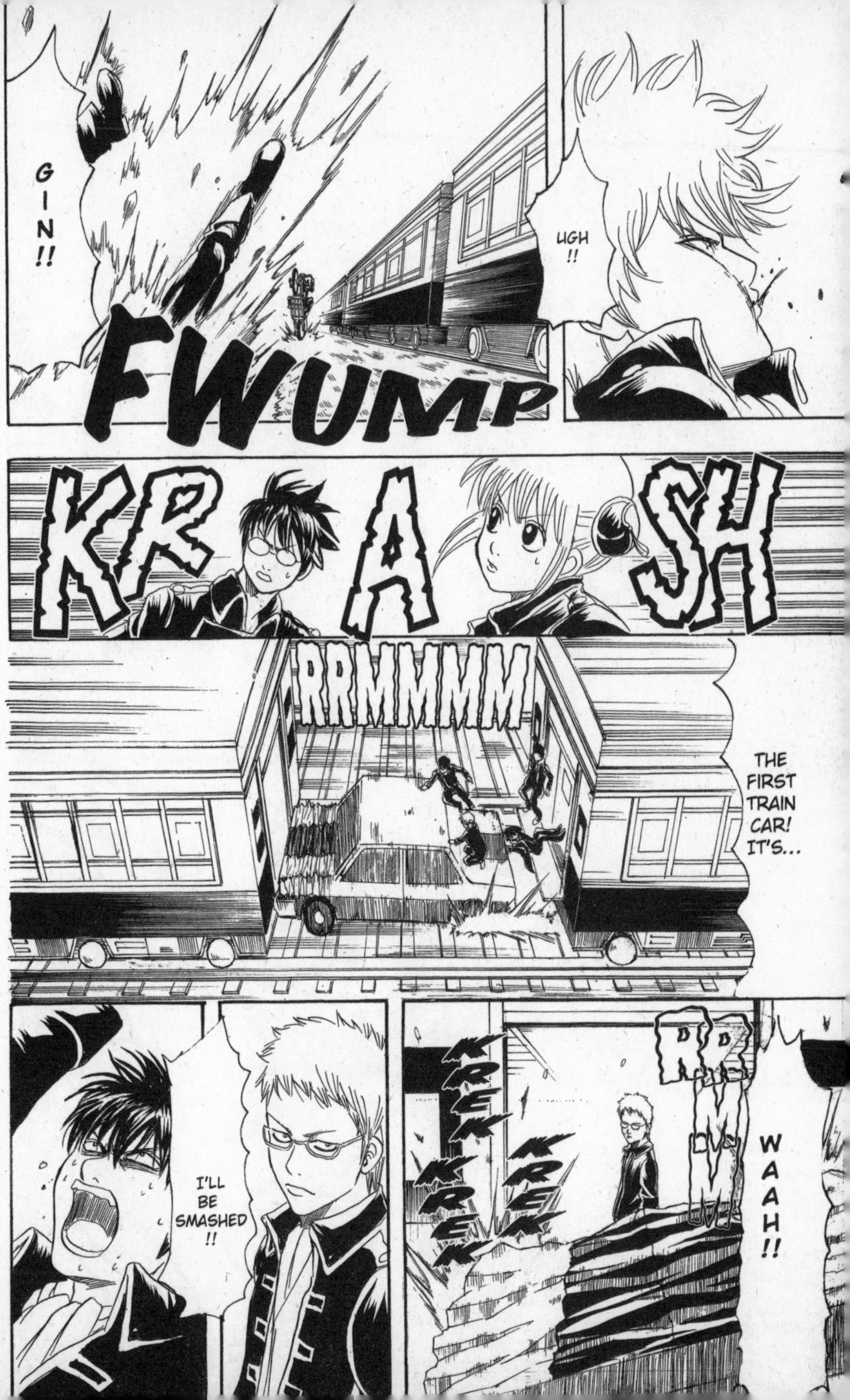

UGH !!
GIN!!
FWUMP
KRASH
RRMMMM
THE FIRST TRAIN CAR! IT'S...
WAAH!!
KREK KREK
KREK
I'LL BE SMASHED !!

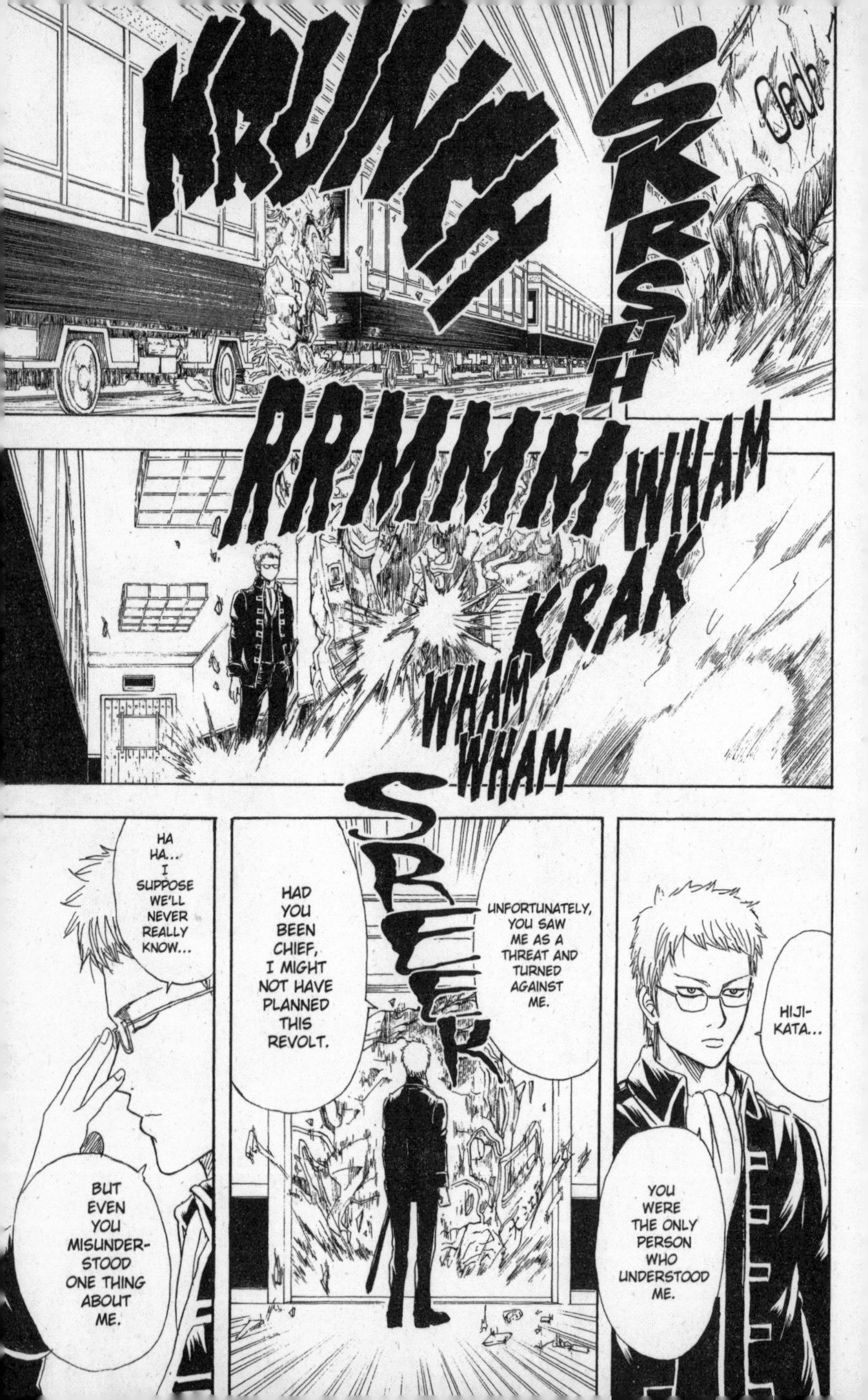

SKRSHH
Oedo
KRUNCH
RRMMM
WHAM
KRAK
WHAM
WHAM
HIJI-KATA...
YOU WERE THE ONLY PERSON WHO UNDERSTOOD ME.
UNFORTUNATELY, YOU SAW ME AS A THREAT AND TURNED AGAINST ME.
HAD YOU BEEN CHIEF, I MIGHT NOT HAVE PLANNED THIS REVOLT.
SREEEK
HA HA... I SUPPOSE WE'LL NEVER REALLY KNOW...
BUT EVEN YOU MISUNDER-STOOD ONE THING ABOUT ME.

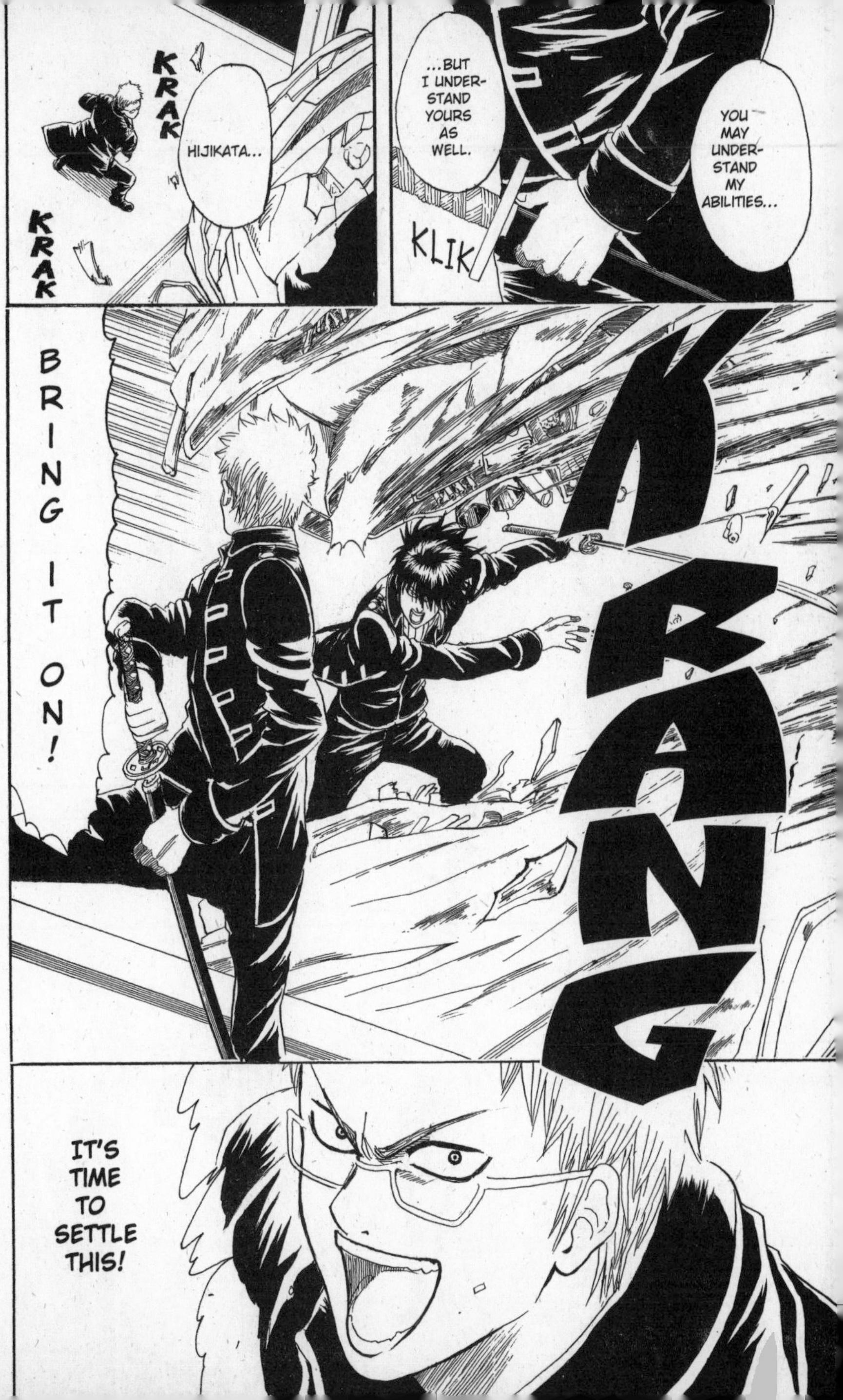
YOU MAY UNDERSTAND MY ABILITIES...
KLIK
...BUT I UNDERSTAND YOURS AS WELL.
HIJIKATA...
KRAK
KRAK
KRANG
BRING IT ON!
IT'S TIME TO SETTLE THIS!

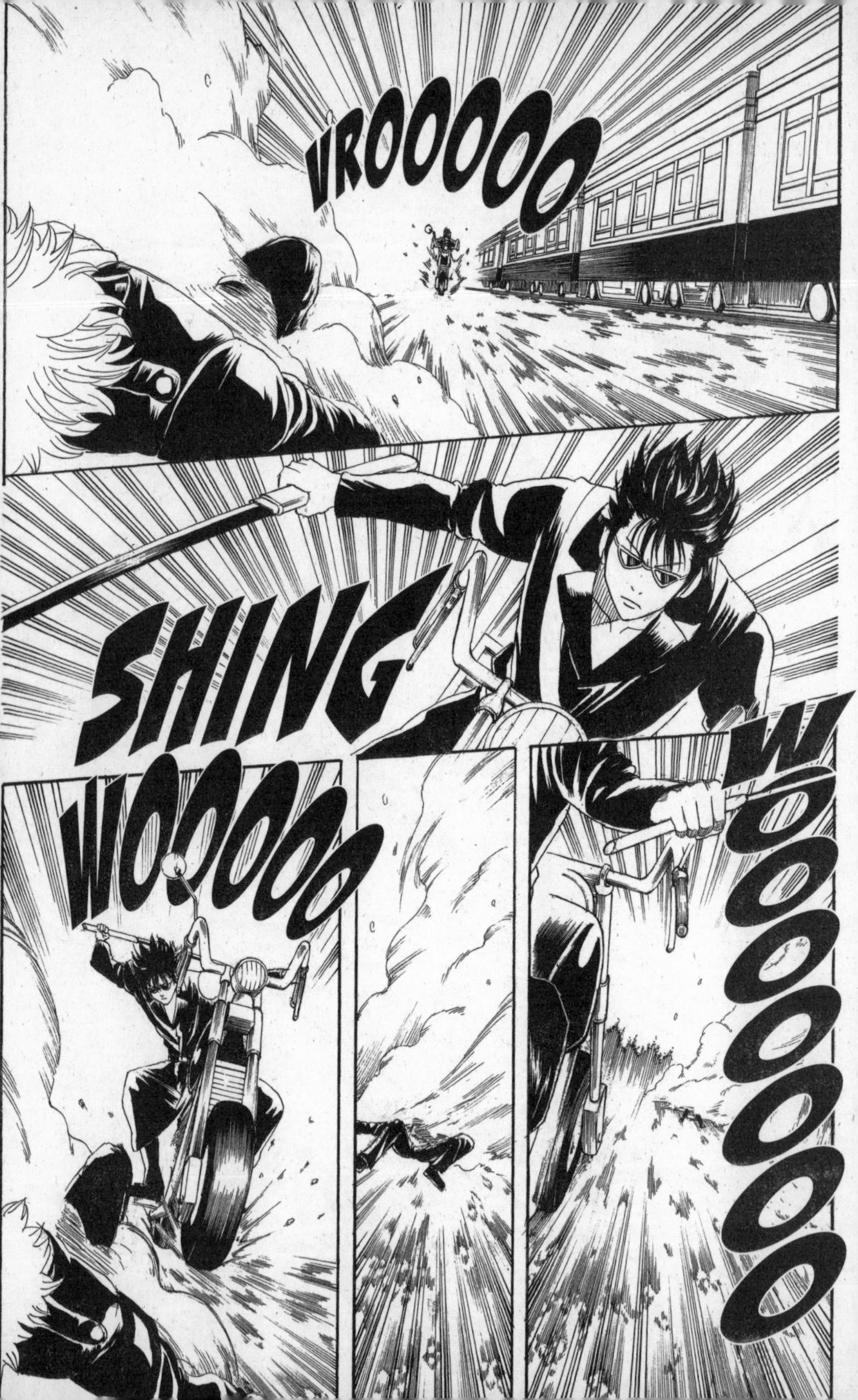
VROOOOO
SHING
WOOOOOOOO
WOOOOO

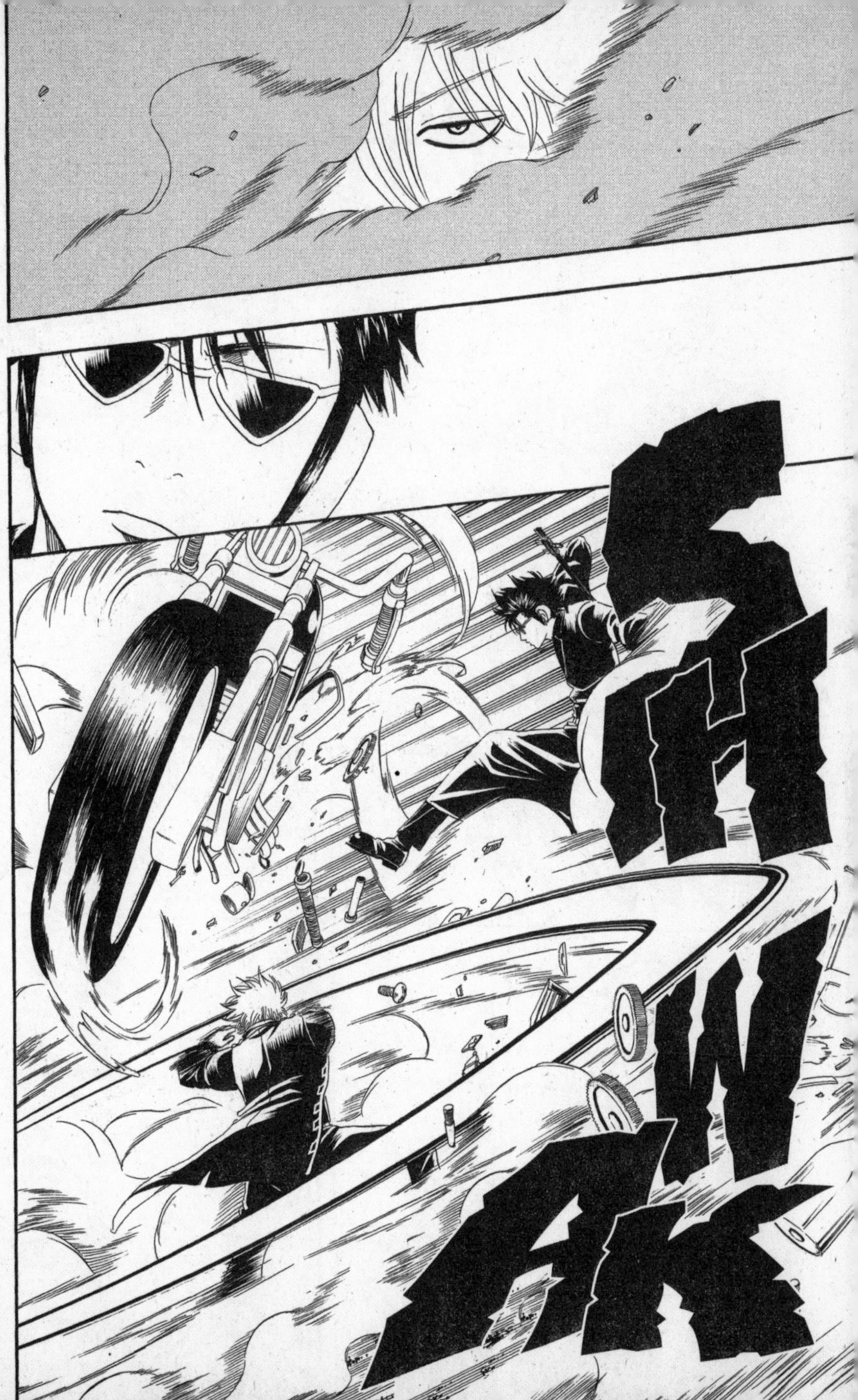
CHWAK

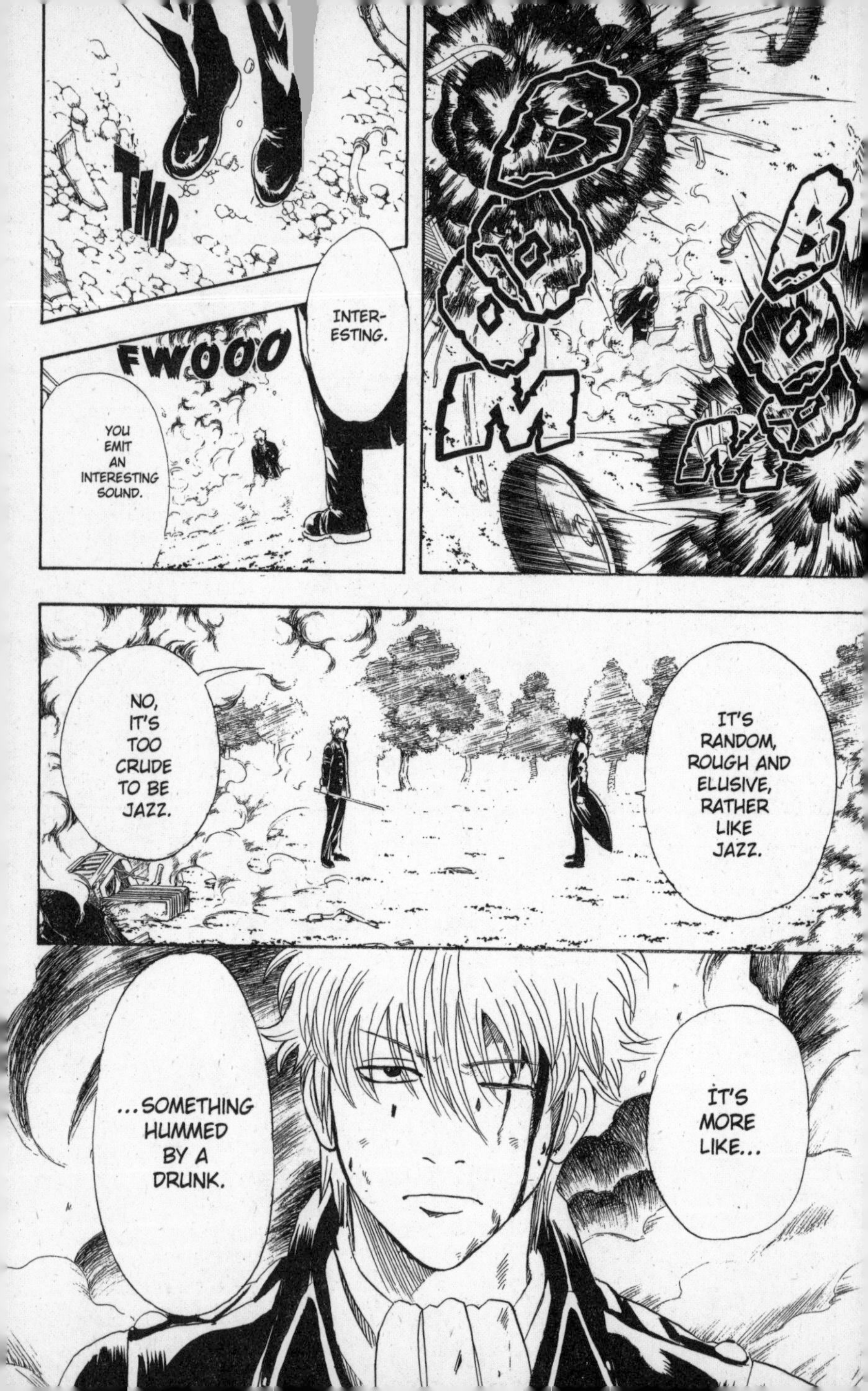
BOOM
BOOM
TMP
INTER-ESTING.
FWOOO
YOU EMIT AN INTERESTING SOUND.
IT'S RANDOM, ROUGH AND ELUSIVE, RATHER LIKE JAZZ.
NO, IT'S TOO CRUDE TO BE JAZZ.
IT'S MORE LIKE...
...SOMETHING HUMMED BY A DRUNK.

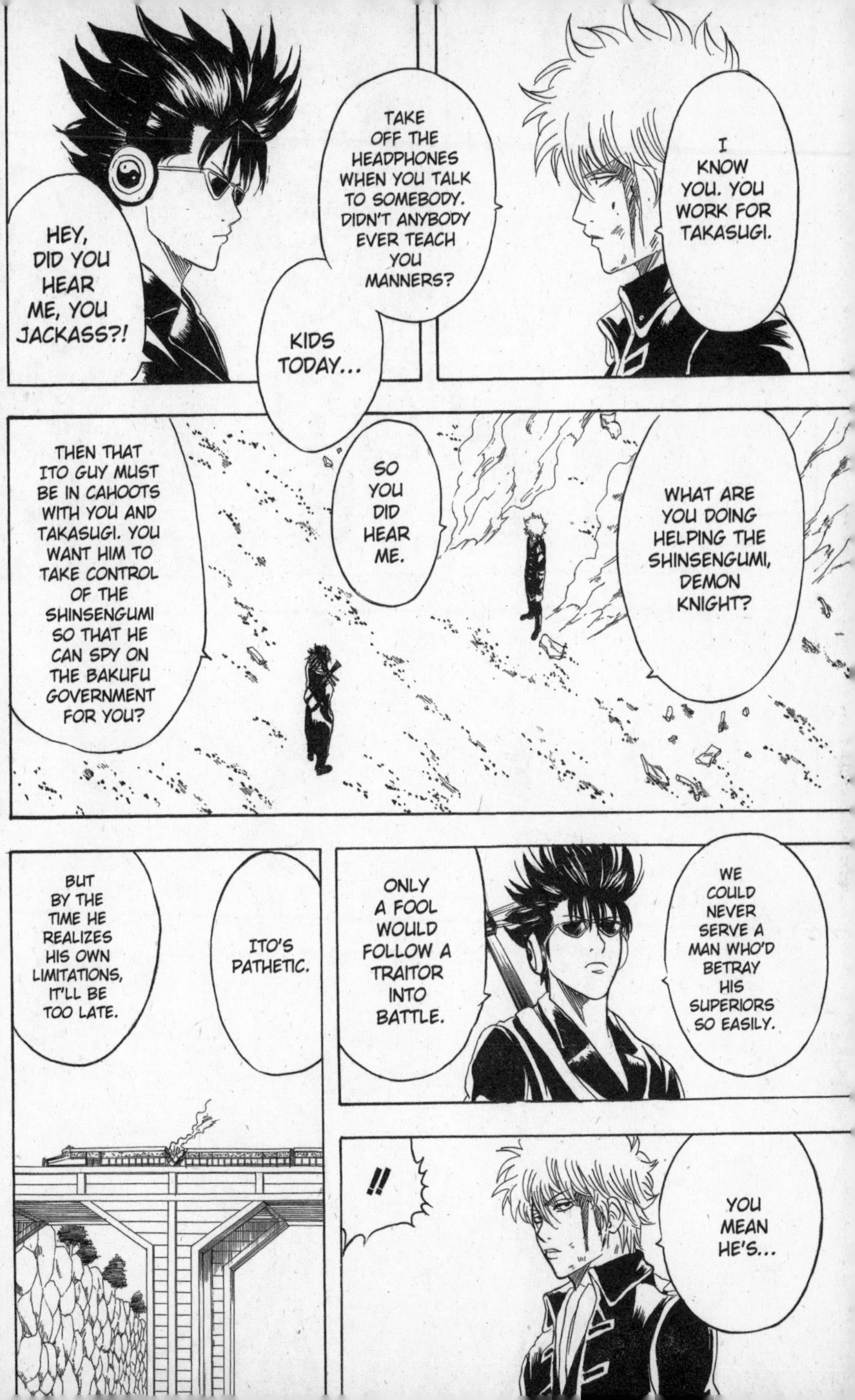
I KNOW YOU. YOU WORK FOR TAKASUGI.
TAKE OFF THE HEADPHONES WHEN YOU TALK TO SOMEBODY. DIDN'T ANYBODY EVER TEACH YOU MANNERS?
KIDS TODAY...
HEY, DID YOU HEAR ME, YOU JACKASS?!
WHAT ARE YOU DOING HELPING THE SHINSENGUMI, DEMON KNIGHT?
SO YOU DID HEAR ME.
THEN THAT ITO GUY MUST BE IN CAHOOTS WITH YOU AND TAKASUGI. YOU WANT HIM TO TAKE CONTROL OF THE SHINSENGUMI SO THAT HE CAN SPY ON THE BAKUFU GOVERNMENT FOR YOU?
WE COULD NEVER SERVE A MAN WHO'D BETRAY HIS SUPERIORS SO EASILY.
ONLY A FOOL WOULD FOLLOW A TRAITOR INTO BATTLE.
ITO'S PATHETIC.
BUT BY THE TIME HE REALIZES HIS OWN LIMITATIONS, IT'LL BE TOO LATE.
YOU MEAN HE'S...
!!

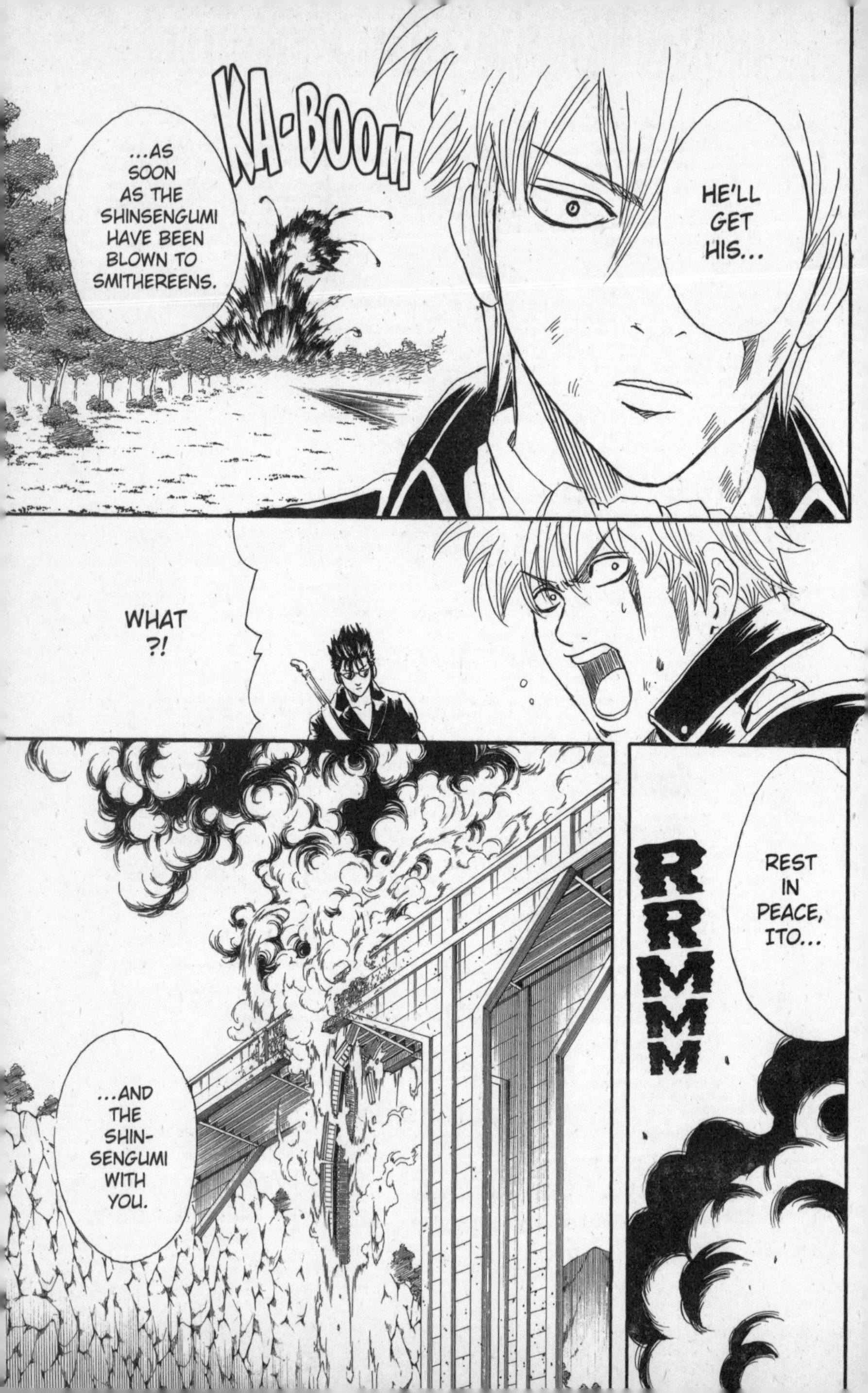
HE'LL GET HIS...
KA-BOOM
...AS SOON AS THE SHINSENGUMI HAVE BEEN BLOWN TO SMITHEREENS.
WHAT?!
REST IN PEACE, ITO...
RRMMM
...AND THE SHIN-SENGUMI WITH YOU.

SORACHI: (CONTINUED) ...I GET BETTER RIGHT AWAY.
ONISHI: WHEN? (LAUGH)
SORACHI: I GOT SICK SO MANY TIMES. YOU DIDN'T KNOW? YOU KNOW THE TIME WHEN KATSURA WENT TO THE DRIVING SCHOOL (CHAPTER 125)? THE CONTENTS WERE JUST MESSED UP BECAUSE I HAD A FEVER WHEN I WROTE IT.
ONISHI: (LAUGH)
SORACHI: I HAD A FEVER OF 100.4 F AT THE TIME. I COULDN'T STOP COUGHING, AND EVERYTHING LOOKED HAZY TO ME AS I DREW UP THE GROUNDWORK SKETCH. I STARTED FEELING FUNKY AND PANICKED BECAUSE THE DEADLINE WAS CLOSING IN ON ME. I'M SURE EVERYONE WOULD FEEL THE SAME WAY. EXCEPT IN MY CASE, THE DEADLINES CLOSE IN ON ME FROM ALL SIDES.
ONISHI: IT MUST HAVE BEEN TOUGH.

[ANY CHILDHOOD STORIES?]

ONISHI: ANY CHILDHOOD STORIES?
SORACHI: IT MIGHT SOUND WEIRD COMING FROM ME, BUT I WAS PRETTY POPULAR WHILE I WAS IN ELEMENTARY SCHOOL.
ONISHI: EVERYONE LIKED YOU BECAUSE YOU MADE THEM LAUGH?
SORACHI: YEAH. THE CLASSROOM REVOLVED AROUND ME. BUT ONLY THROUGH ELEMENTARY SCHOOL.
ONISHI: I'M SURE YOU WERE A SMART ALECK WHEN THE TEACHERS ASKED YOU QUESTIONS.
SORACHI: IT WAS NOTHING SMART LIKE THAT. BUT WHEN I GOT UP TO MIDDLE SCHOOL, THERE WERE PEOPLE THAT WERE BETTER AT IT THAN ME IN DIFFERENT WAYS, SO I STOPPED RIGHT THERE.
ONISHI: YOU DIDN'T WANT TO STAND OUT, BUT YOU DID AT THE SAME TIME?
SORACHI: I'M A SHY GUY. BUT I JUST WANT TO GET EVERYONE TO LAUGH.
ONISHI: KIND OF A "LOOK AT ME" TYPE OF ATTITUDE?
SORACHI: NOT LIKE THAT. BUT I NEVER STOPPED WANTING TO MAKE EVERYONE LAUGH.

"ISN'T THIS GOING TO MAKE US LOOK REALLY BAD?" -SORACHI

ONISHI: SO YOU DO LIKE THE ATTENTION.
SORACHI: WELL, IF YOU PUT IT LIKE THAT...
ONISHI: BUT YOU WANTED A WAY TO EXPRESS YOURSELF SO YOU'RE DRAWING COMICS EVEN NOW, RIGHT?
SORACHI: LOOKING BACK, I GUESS THAT'S RIGHT. IT SEEMS LIKE A TERRIBLE MOTIVATION TO DRAW COMICS THOUGH. NOW I FEEL ALL DIRTY.
ONISHI: I THINK EVERYONE WORKS UNDER A SIMILAR KIND OF MOTIVATION. THEY WANT TO GET ACKNOWLEDGED FOR THEIR WORK, AND IN THE END, THEY MAKE SOMETHING OF THEMSELVES. SOME PEOPLE TURN INTO COMIC AUTHORS WHILE SOME OTHERS BECOME CRIMINALS. SPEAKING OF WHICH, WE ALWAYS TALK ABOUT CURRENT EVENTS, DON'T WE?
SORACHI: YEAH, WE DO. WE GO BACK AND FORTH WITH LINES LIKE, "THIS GUY IS PROBABLY LIKE THIS."
ONISHI: YEAH. WE TALK TO EACH OTHER ABOUT THE SUSPECTS AND WHAT KIND OF PEOPLE THEY ARE.
SORACHI: OUR MEETINGS FOR ACTUAL WORK LAST ABOUT 15 MINUTES, BUT WE TALK ABOUT STUFF LIKE THIS FOR A REALLY LONG TIME.
ONISHI: THE MEETINGS ALWAYS GO OFF ON A TANGENT.
SORACHI: I'M GETTING THE FEELING THAT THIS INTERVIEW IS REALLY BAD.
ONISHI: DON'T WORRY ABOUT IT. IT'S LIKE A SECRET INTERVIEW ANYWAY.
SORACHI: ISN'T THIS GOING TO MAKE US LOOK REALLY BAD?
ONISHI: DON'T WORRY ABOUT IT.
ONISHI: IT'S JUST A TINY LITTLE PROJECT THAT'LL BE PRINTED IN THE CORNER OF A PAGE IN *AKAMARU JUMP*.
SORACHI: WRITTEN WORDS ARE SCARY. THEY CAN'T TELL WHAT OUR EMOTIONS ARE, SO THEY'LL JUST TAKE THE PRINTED WORDS AT FACE VALUE.
ONISHI: THEN JUST BE HONEST WHEN YOU TALK.
SORACHI: THAT'S WHAT I THINK I'M DOING. BUT I THINK IT'LL BE EVEN WORSE FOR MY IMAGE IF I GET TOO HONEST.
ONISHI: TRYING TO IMAGINE THE MENTALITY OF A CRIMINAL CAN BE REALLY EDUCATIONAL FOR A COMIC AUTHOR.
SORACHI: IT DOESN'T HAVE TO BE ABOUT A CRIMINAL.
ONISHI: THERE'S ALWAYS SOME KIND OF DEEP-SEATED REASON.
SORACHI: YEAH.
ONISHI: SO WE THINK ABOUT "WHAT DROVE THAT PERSON TO GO THAT FAR?" THINKING ABOUT IT LIKE THAT IS REALLY SIMILAR TO CREATING A CHARACTER.
SORACHI: YEAH. CHARACTERS THAT HAVE THAT DEEP-SEATED REASON TO TURN TO CRIME, BUT DON'T, SOMETIMES BECOME THE MAIN CHARACTERS OF A COMIC.
ONISHI: YEAH. IT'S THE JOB OF THE COMIC AUTHOR TO TAKE THAT WEIRD PORTION OF A CHARACTER AND TURN THAT INTO A REASONING OR LOGIC PROCESS OF THAT CHARACTER. WHEN ASKING "WHY DOES THAT CHARACTER DO THAT?" YOU DON'T JUST SAY "BECAUSE HE'S WEIRD." YOU HAVE TO FIND THE THINKING THAT THE CHARACTER HAS.
SORACHI: BUT IF YOU LOOK AT IT LIKE THAT, PARENTS ARE REALLY IMPORTANT. IN MY CASE, I REALLY TRUST MY FOLKS.
ONISHI: PEOPLE ALWAYS TURN TO THAT.
ONISHI: THEY'LL ASK, "WHAT WOULD MY PARENTS THINK IF I DID THIS?" SOMETIMES IT'S NOT ALWAYS ABOUT LOGIC.
SORACHI: YEAH.
ONISHI: THERE ARE A LOT OF PARTS WHERE IT GOES LIKE, "I WANT TO DO THIS, BUT MY PARENTS OR FRIENDS WOULD BE SADDENED IF I DID."
SORACHI: MY GENERATION OF PEOPLE ARE SLOWLY BECOMING PARENTS. I GUESS THAT PART IS STARTING TO CHANGE. THERE HAS ALWAYS BEEN CRIME IN SOCIETY. IT'S SOMETHING THAT WE ALL HAVE TO THINK ABOUT. IT'S JUST THE PROBLEMS THEMSELVES THAT ARE CHANGING... WAIT, WHAT WERE WE TALKING ABOUT?
ONISHI: MODERN SOCIETY.
SORACHI: YOU'RE GOING TO PUT THIS IN PRINT TOO?
ONISHI: IF IT SOUNDS FUNNY.
SORACHI: I REALLY DON'T WANT PEOPLE READING ABOUT THIS CONVERSATION BETWEEN US.
ONISHI: THAT'S HOW INTERVIEWS ARE. ANYWAY, WE DIGRESSED AGAIN. SO WHAT ELSE DID YOU DO WHEN YOU WERE IN ELEMENTARY SCHOOL?
SORACHI: I WAS REALLY ACTIVE BACK THEN. I WAS REALLY GOOD AT SPORTS.
ONISHI: WEREN'T YOU ON THE BASKETBALL TEAM DURING MIDDLE SCHOOL?
SORACHI: YEAH. BUT I STARTED TO BECOME LESS AND LESS ATHLETIC, SO I KNEW THAT THIS STUFF WASN'T FOR ME. YOU KNOW HOW THERE STARTS TO BE A LOT OF REALLY ATHLETIC PEOPLE POPPING UP HERE AND THERE IN MIDDLE SCHOOL? THAT'S WHEN I DECIDED TO GO INTO COMEDY INSTEAD.
ONISHI: OH, YOU MEAN YOUR WAY OF LIFE?
SORACHI: AND I'M REALLY THANKFUL FOR THAT.
ONISHI: WELL, IT BROUGHT YOU INTO THE WORK YOU'RE DOING NOW.
SORACHI: YEAH.
ONISHI: WHAT DID YOUR PARENTS GET MAD AT YOU FOR? AND HOW DID THEY DISCIPLINE YOU WHEN YOU WERE SMALL?

CONTINUED ON PAGE 166

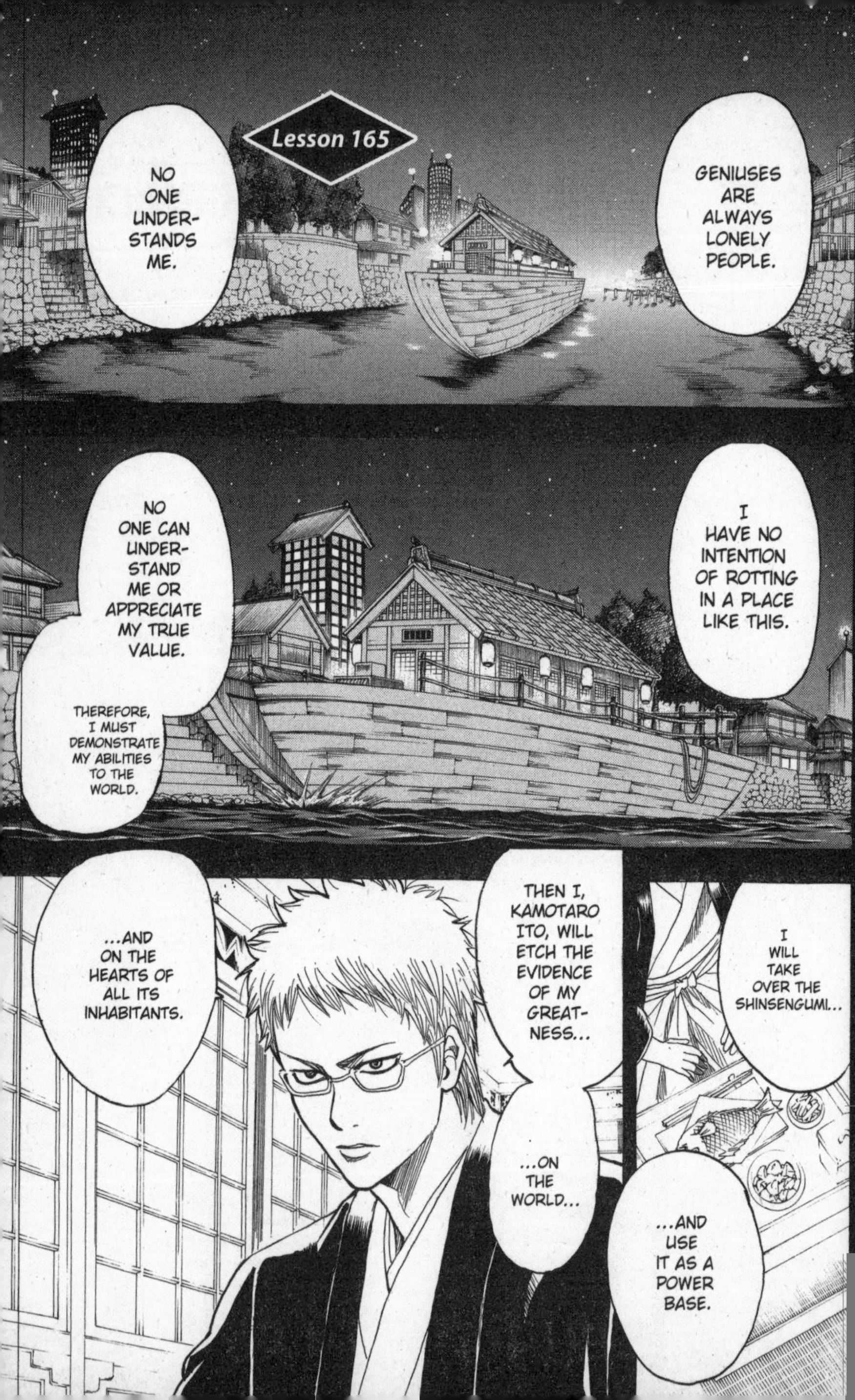
Lesson 165
GENIUSES ARE ALWAYS LONELY PEOPLE.
NO ONE UNDER-STANDS ME.
I HAVE NO INTENTION OF ROTTING IN A PLACE LIKE THIS.
NO ONE CAN UNDER-STAND ME OR APPRECIATE MY TRUE VALUE.
THEREFORE, I MUST DEMONSTRATE MY ABILITIES TO THE WORLD.
I WILL TAKE OVER THE SHINSENGUMI...
...AND USE IT AS A POWER BASE.
THEN I, KAMOTARO ITO, WILL ETCH THE EVIDENCE OF MY GREAT-NESS...
...ON THE WORLD...
...AND ON THE HEARTS OF ALL ITS INHABITANTS.

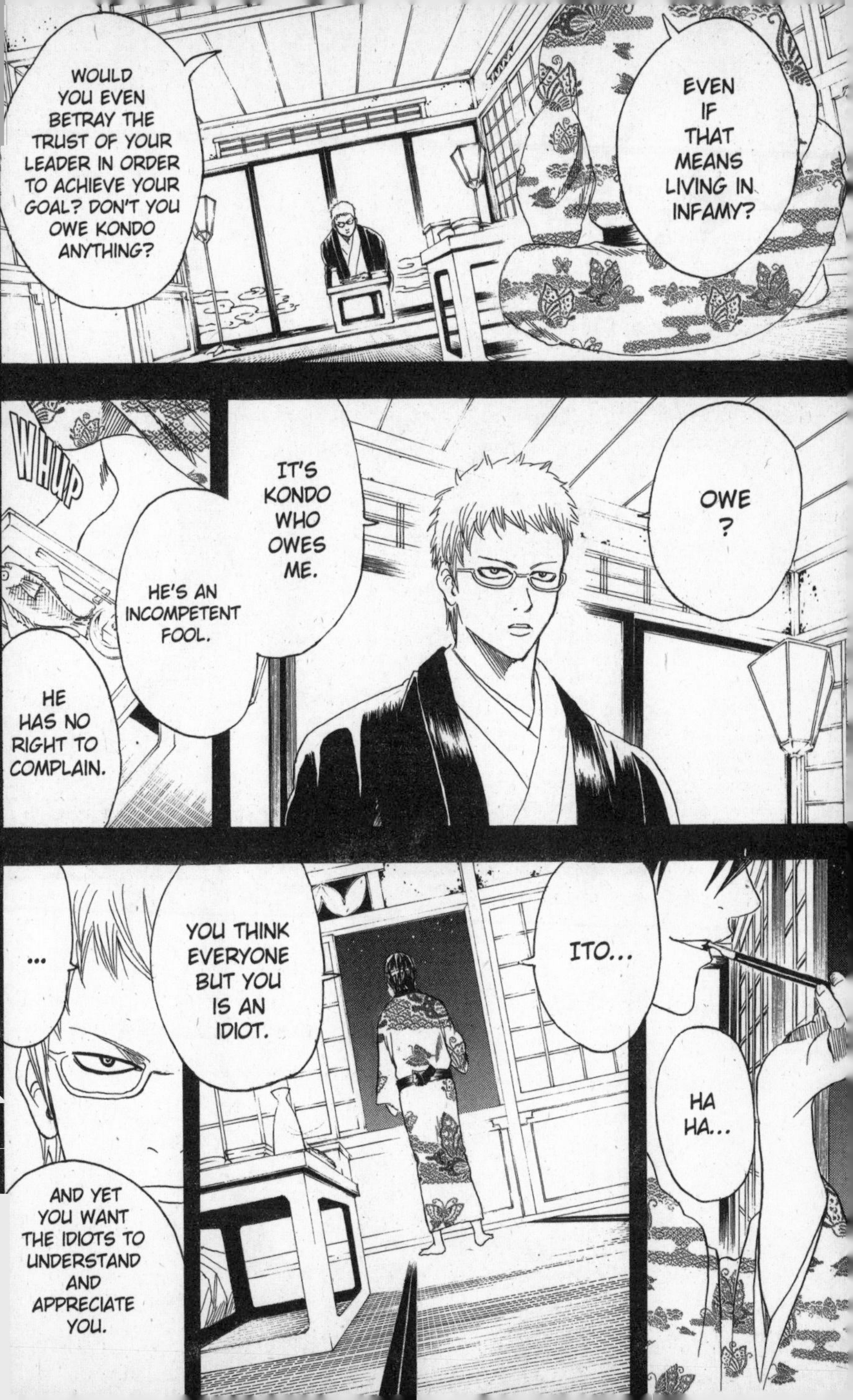
EVEN IF THAT MEANS LIVING IN INFAMY?
WOULD YOU EVEN BETRAY THE TRUST OF YOUR LEADER IN ORDER TO ACHIEVE YOUR GOAL? DON'T YOU OWE KONDO ANYTHING?
OWE?
IT'S KONDO WHO OWES ME.
WHUP
HE'S AN INCOMPETENT FOOL.
HE HAS NO RIGHT TO COMPLAIN.
ITO...
HA HA...
YOU THINK EVERYONE BUT YOU IS AN IDIOT.
...
AND YET YOU WANT THE IDIOTS TO UNDERSTAND AND APPRECIATE YOU.

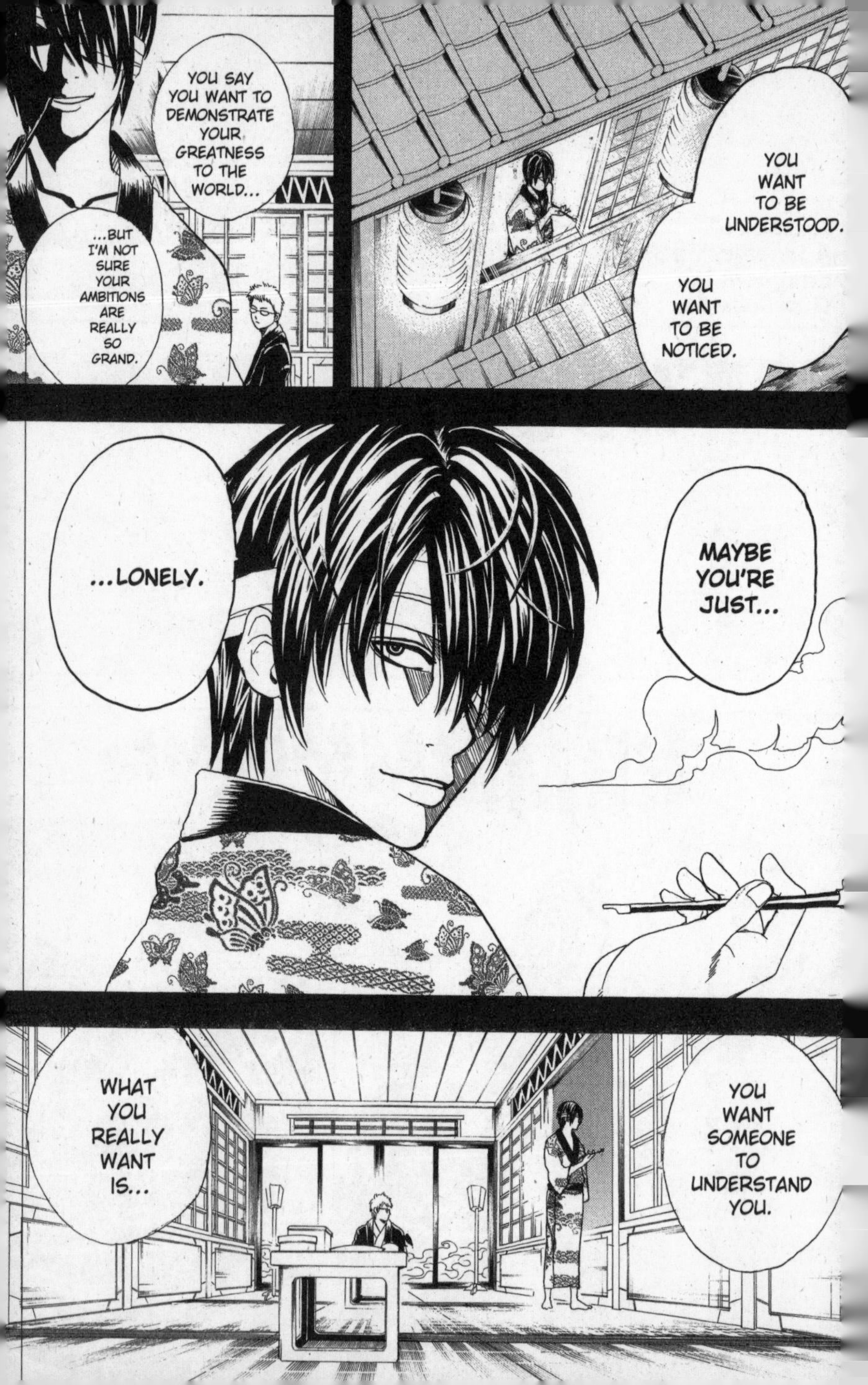
YOU WANT TO BE UNDERSTOOD.
YOU WANT TO BE NOTICED.
YOU SAY YOU WANT TO DEMONSTRATE YOUR GREATNESS TO THE WORLD...
...BUT I'M NOT SURE YOUR AMBITIONS ARE REALLY SO GRAND.
MAYBE YOU'RE JUST...
...LONELY.
YOU WANT SOMEONE TO UNDERSTAND YOU.
WHAT YOU REALLY WANT IS...

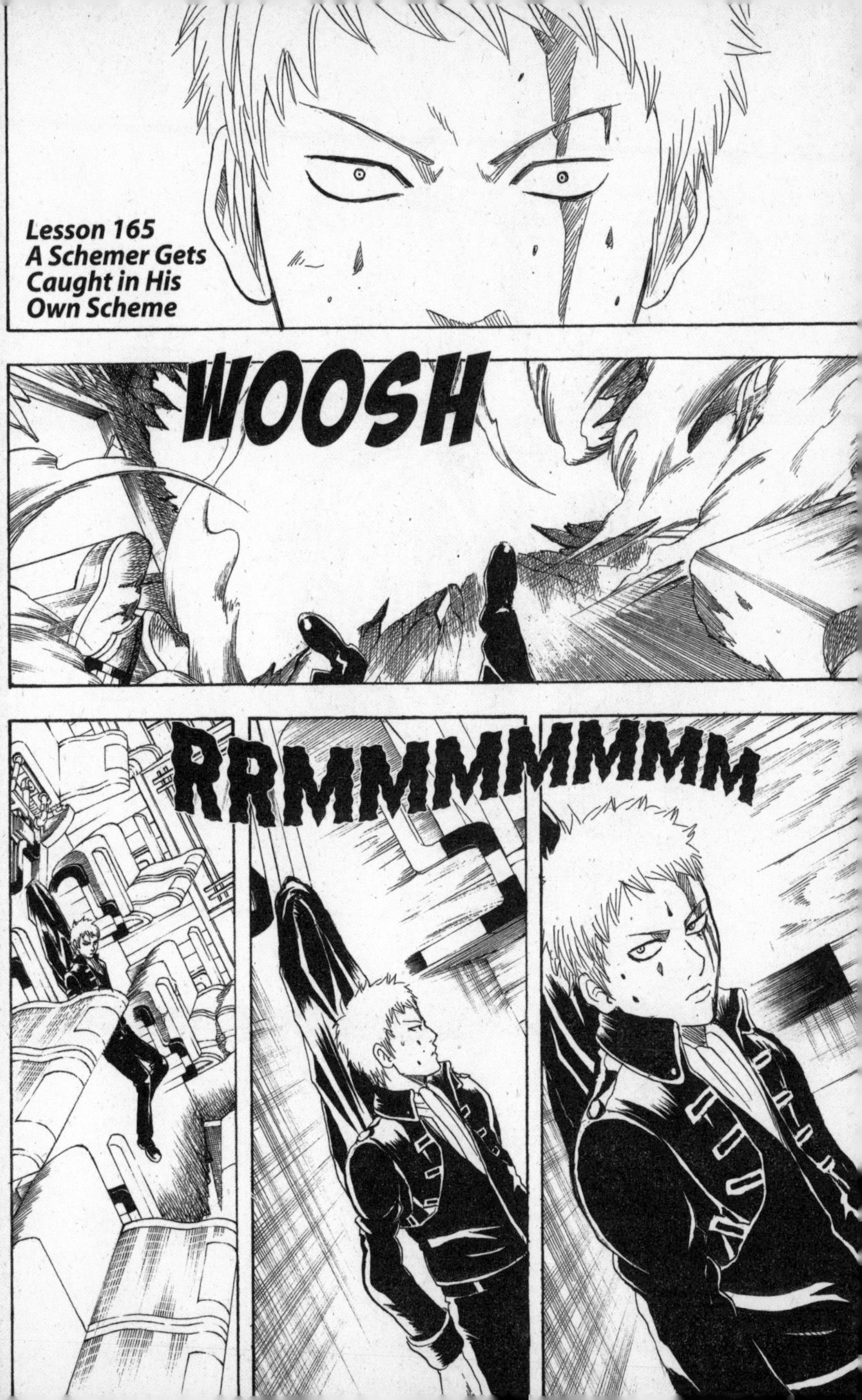
Lesson 165
A Schemer Gets Caught in His Own Scheme
WOOSH
RRMMMMMMMM

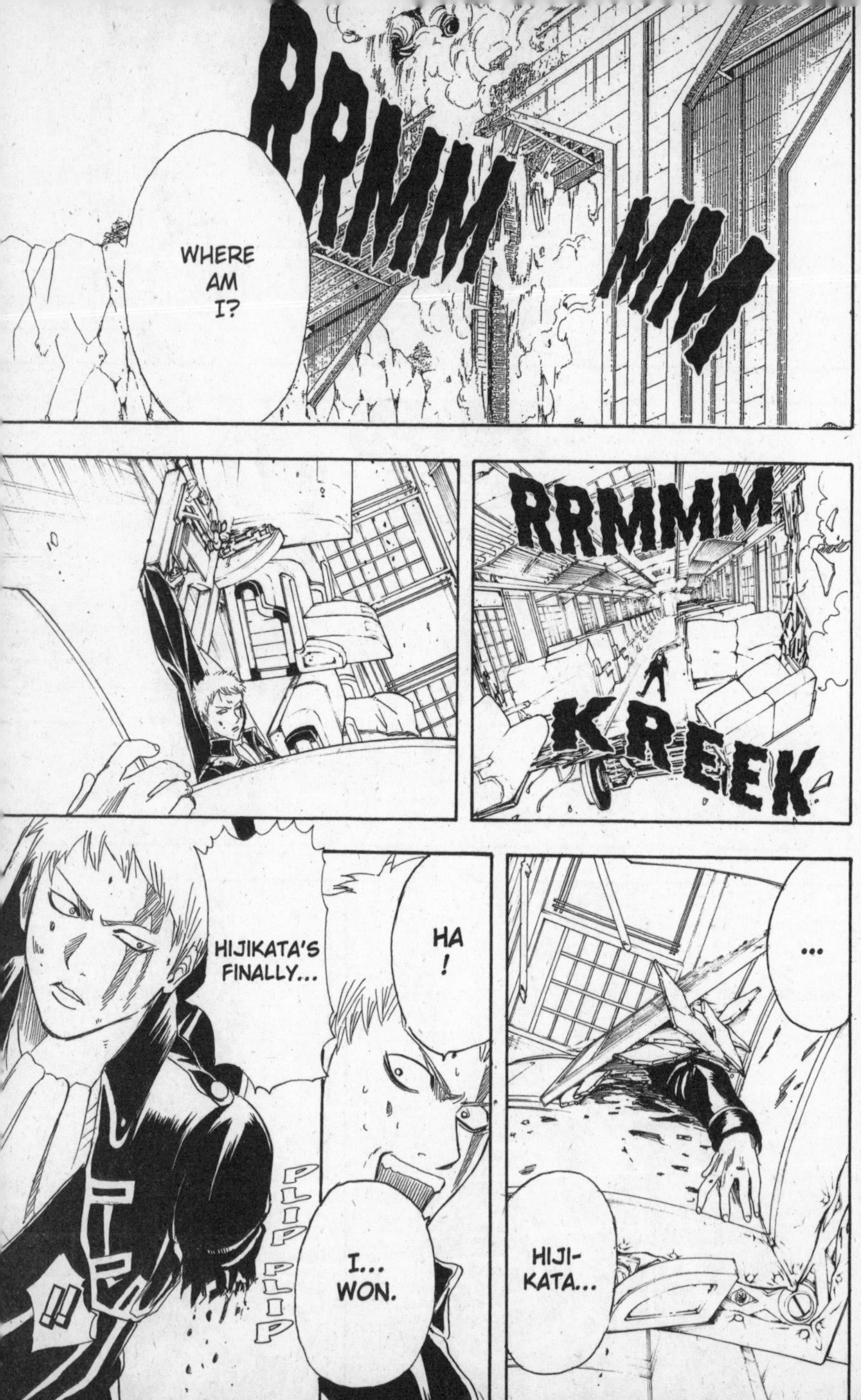
RRMM MM
WHERE AM I?
RRMMM
KREEK
...
HIJI-KATA...
HA!
I... WON.
PLIP PLIP
HIJIKATA'S FINALLY...
!!

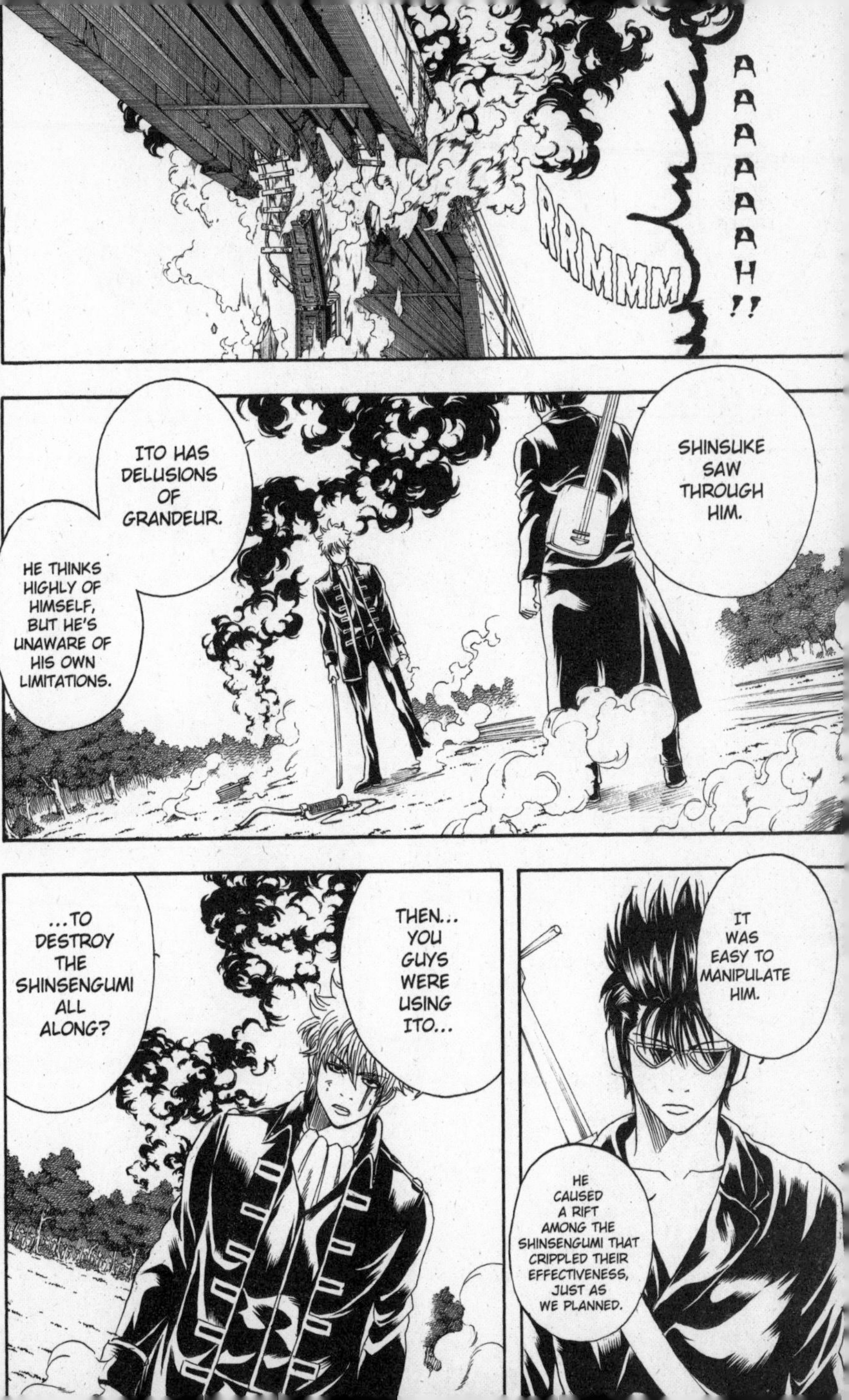
AAAAAAH!!
RRMMMM
SHINSUKE SAW THROUGH HIM.
ITO HAS DELUSIONS OF GRANDEUR.
HE THINKS HIGHLY OF HIMSELF, BUT HE'S UNAWARE OF HIS OWN LIMITATIONS.
IT WAS EASY TO MANIPULATE HIM.
HE CAUSED A RIFT AMONG THE SHINSENGUMI THAT CRIPPLED THEIR EFFECTIVENESS, JUST AS WE PLANNED.
THEN... YOU GUYS WERE USING ITO...
...TO DESTROY THE SHINSENGUMI ALL ALONG?

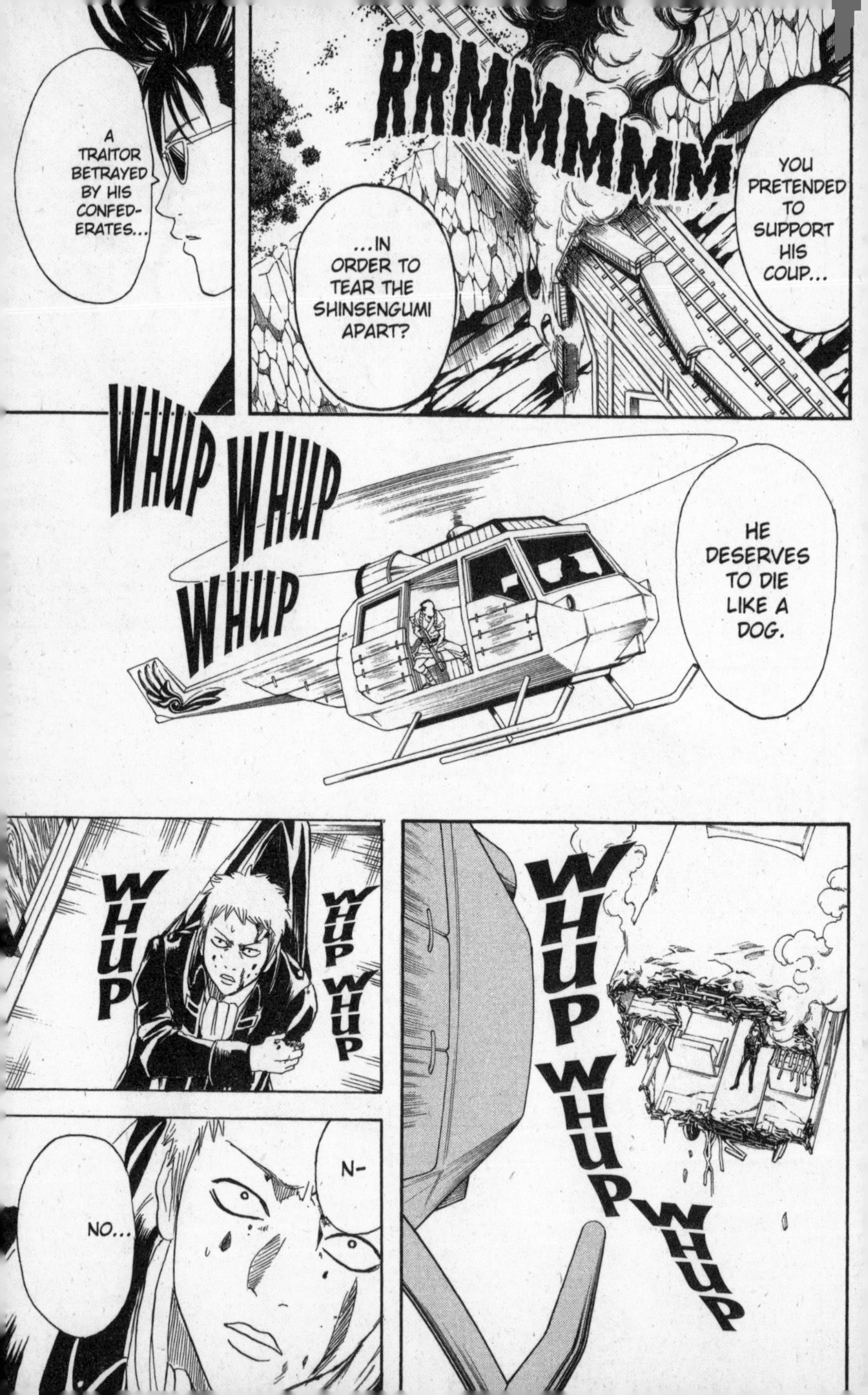
RRMMMMMM
YOU PRETENDED TO SUPPORT HIS COUP...
...IN ORDER TO TEAR THE SHINSENGUMI APART?
A TRAITOR BETRAYED BY HIS CONFEDERATES...
HE DESERVES TO DIE LIKE A DOG.
WHUP WHUP WHUP
WHUP WHUP WHUP WHUP
WHUP WHUP WHUP
N-
NO...

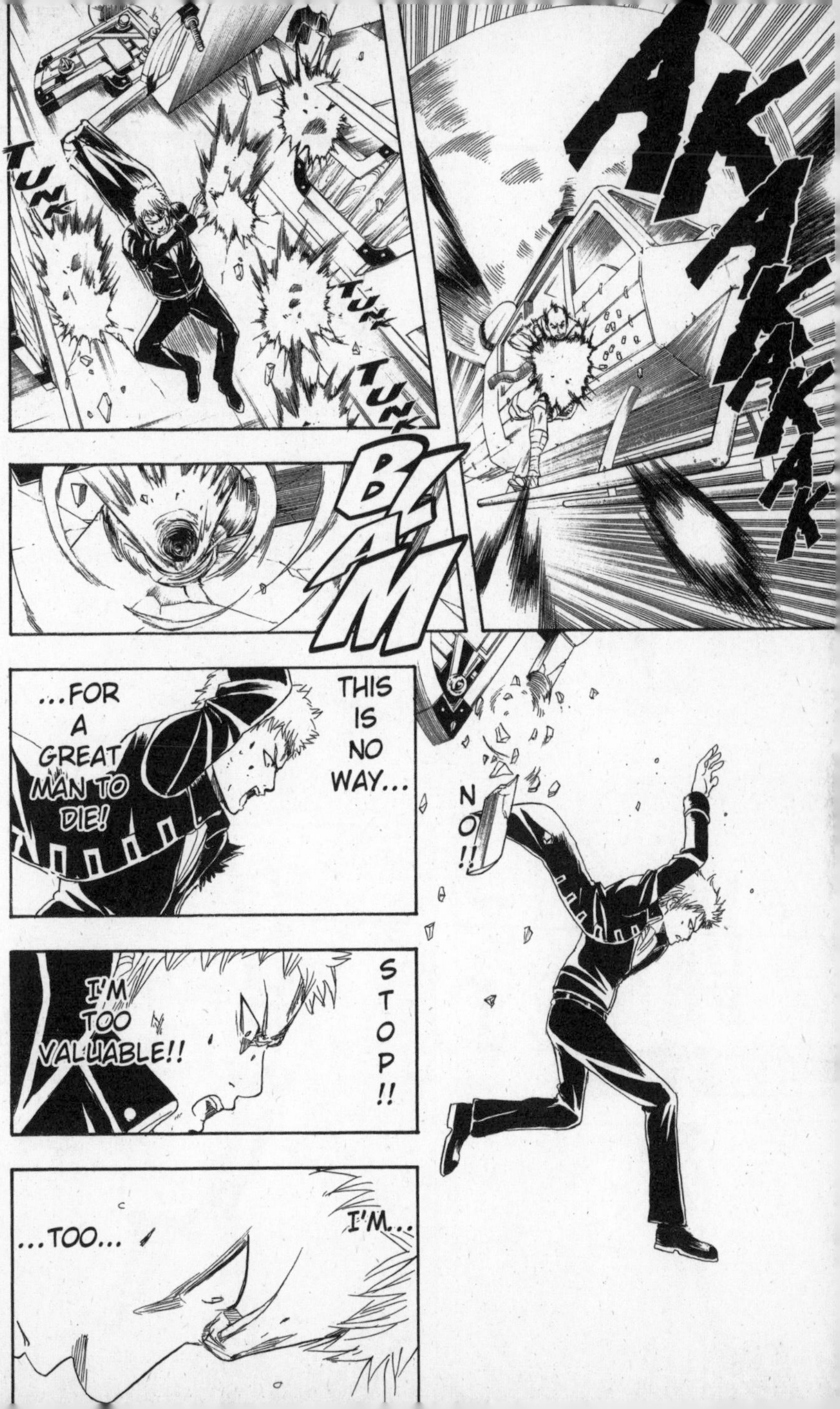
AKAKAKAK
TUNK
TUNK
TUNK
BLAM
NO!!
THIS IS NO WAY...
...FOR A GREAT MAN TO DIE!
STOP!!
I'M TOO VALUABLE!!
I'M...
...TOO...

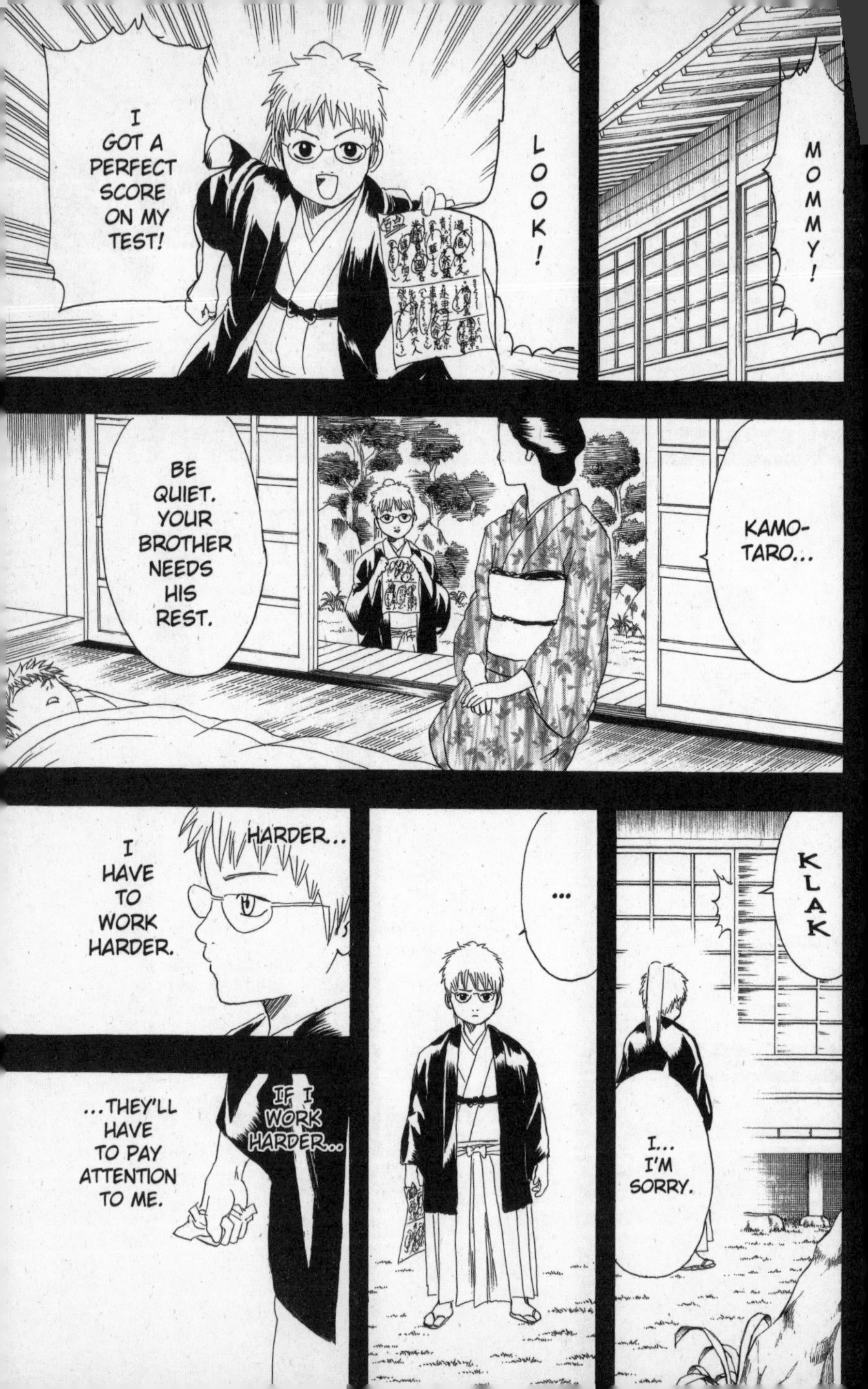
MOMMY!
LOOK!
I GOT A PERFECT SCORE ON MY TEST!
KAMO-TARO...
BE QUIET. YOUR BROTHER NEEDS HIS REST.
KLAK
I... I'M SORRY.
...
HARDER...
I HAVE TO WORK HARDER.
IF I WORK HARDER...
...THEY'LL HAVE TO PAY ATTENTION TO ME.

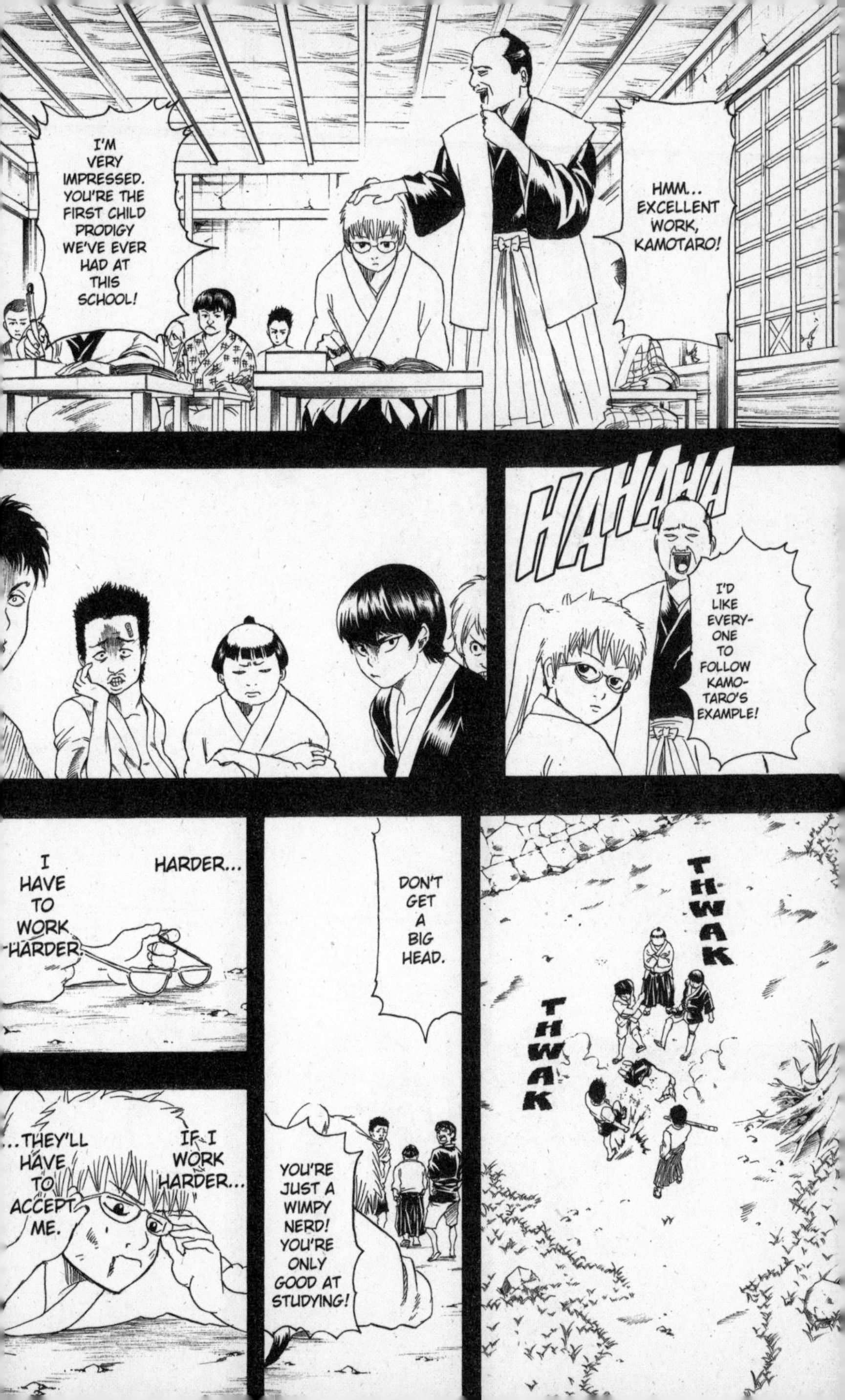
HMM... EXCELLENT WORK, KAMOTARO!
I'M VERY IMPRESSED. YOU'RE THE FIRST CHILD PRODIGY WE'VE EVER HAD AT THIS SCHOOL!
HAHAHA
I'D LIKE EVERY-ONE TO FOLLOW KAMO-TARO'S EXAMPLE!
THWAK
THWAK
DON'T GET A BIG HEAD.
YOU'RE JUST A WIMPY NERD! YOU'RE ONLY GOOD AT STUDYING!
HARDER...
I HAVE TO WORK HARDER.
IF I WORK HARDER...
...THEY'LL HAVE TO ACCEPT ME.

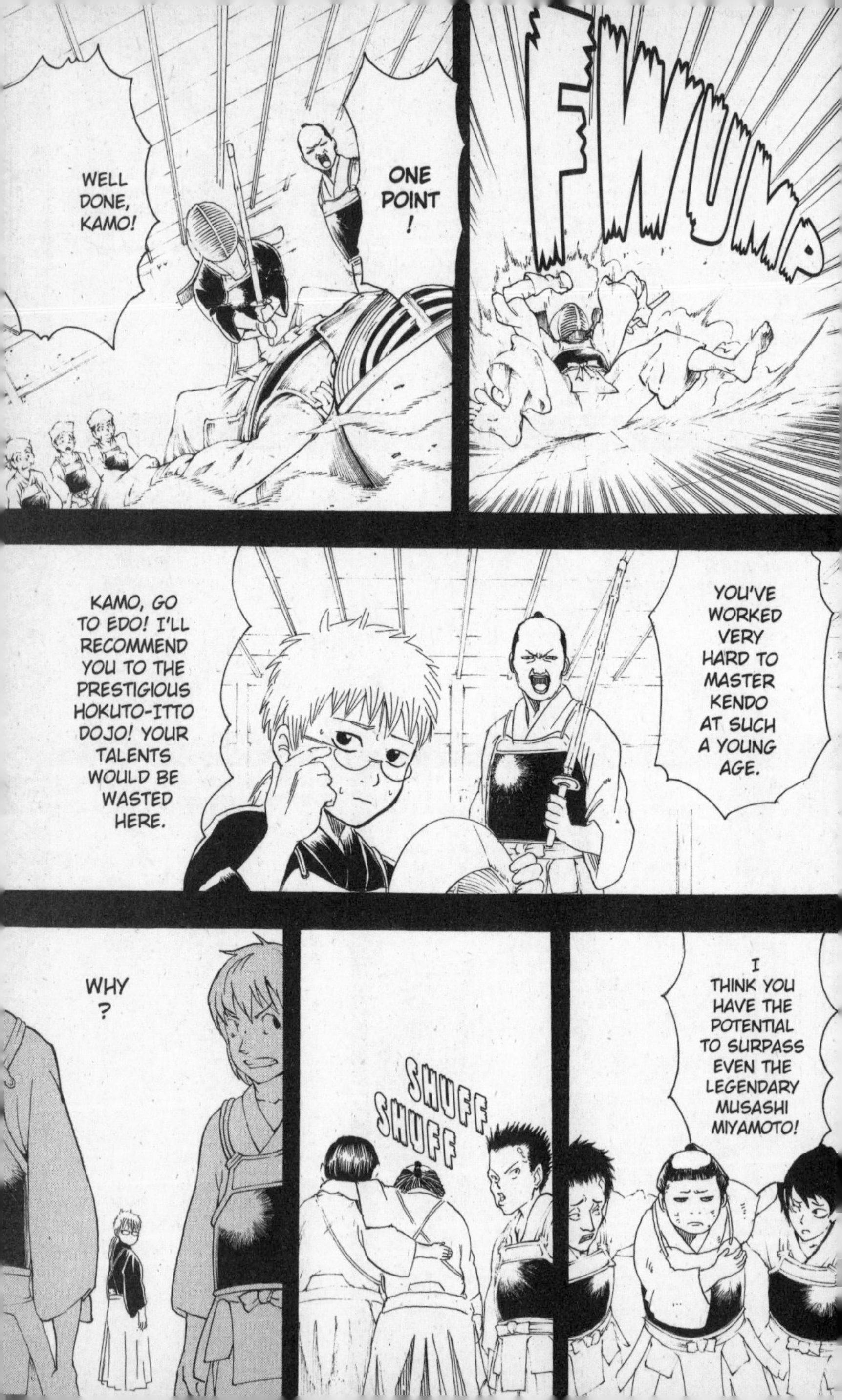
FWUMP
ONE POINT !
WELL DONE, KAMO!
YOU'VE WORKED VERY HARD TO MASTER KENDO AT SUCH A YOUNG AGE.
KAMO, GO TO EDO! I'LL RECOMMEND YOU TO THE PRESTIGIOUS HOKUTO-ITTO DOJO! YOUR TALENTS WOULD BE WASTED HERE.
I THINK YOU HAVE THE POTENTIAL TO SURPASS EVEN THE LEGENDARY MUSASHI MIYAMOTO!
SHUFF
SHUFF
WHY ?

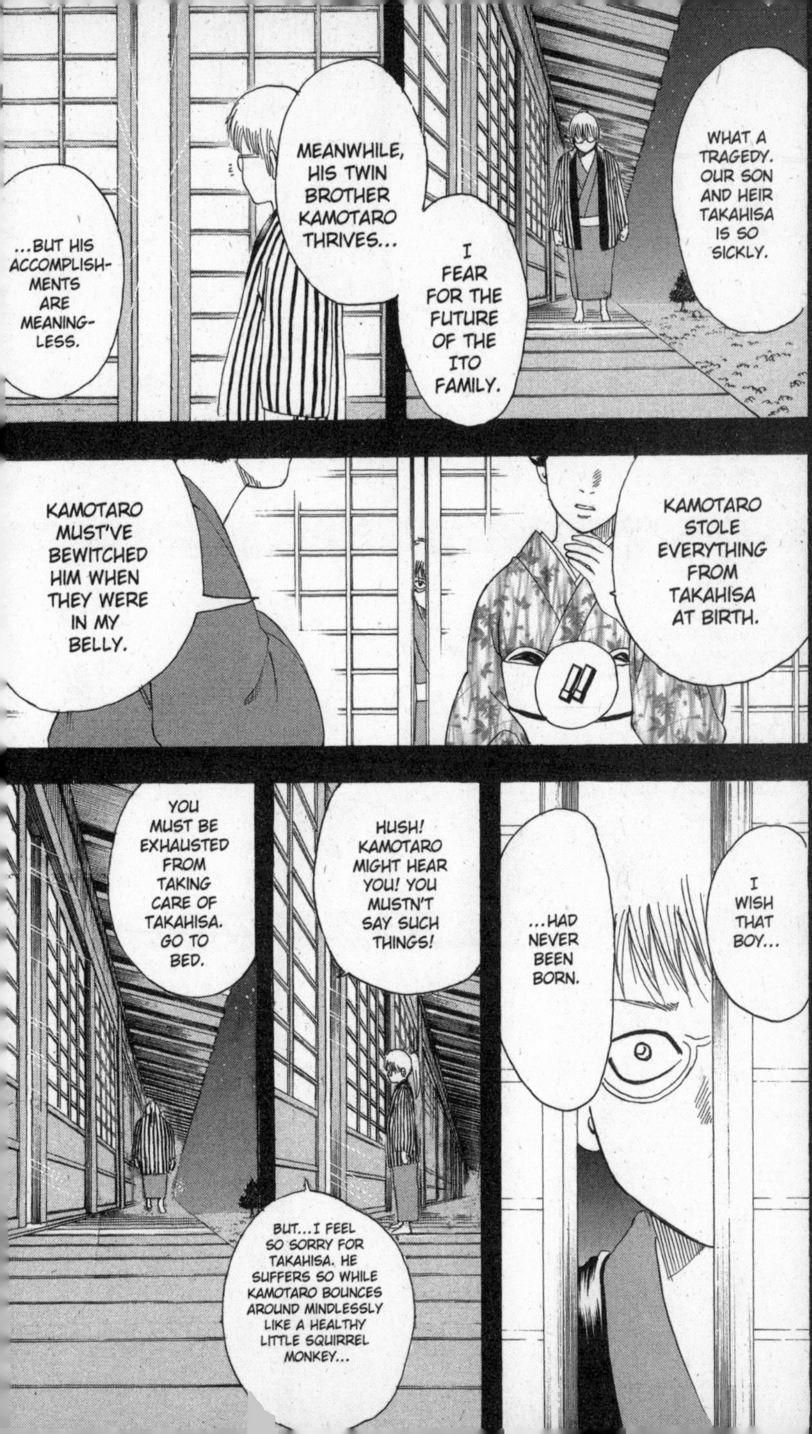
WHAT A TRAGEDY. OUR SON AND HEIR TAKAHISA IS SO SICKLY.
I FEAR FOR THE FUTURE OF THE ITO FAMILY.
MEANWHILE, HIS TWIN BROTHER KAMOTARO THRIVES...
...BUT HIS ACCOMPLISHMENTS ARE MEANINGLESS.
KAMOTARO STOLE EVERYTHING FROM TAKAHISA AT BIRTH.
!!
KAMOTARO MUST'VE BEWITCHED HIM WHEN THEY WERE IN MY BELLY.
I WISH THAT BOY...
...HAD NEVER BEEN BORN.
HUSH! KAMOTARO MIGHT HEAR YOU! YOU MUSTN'T SAY SUCH THINGS!
BUT...I FEEL SO SORRY FOR TAKAHISA. HE SUFFERS SO WHILE KAMOTARO BOUNCES AROUND MINDLESSLY LIKE A HEALTHY LITTLE SQUIRREL MONKEY...
YOU MUST BE EXHAUSTED FROM TAKING CARE OF TAKAHISA. GO TO BED.

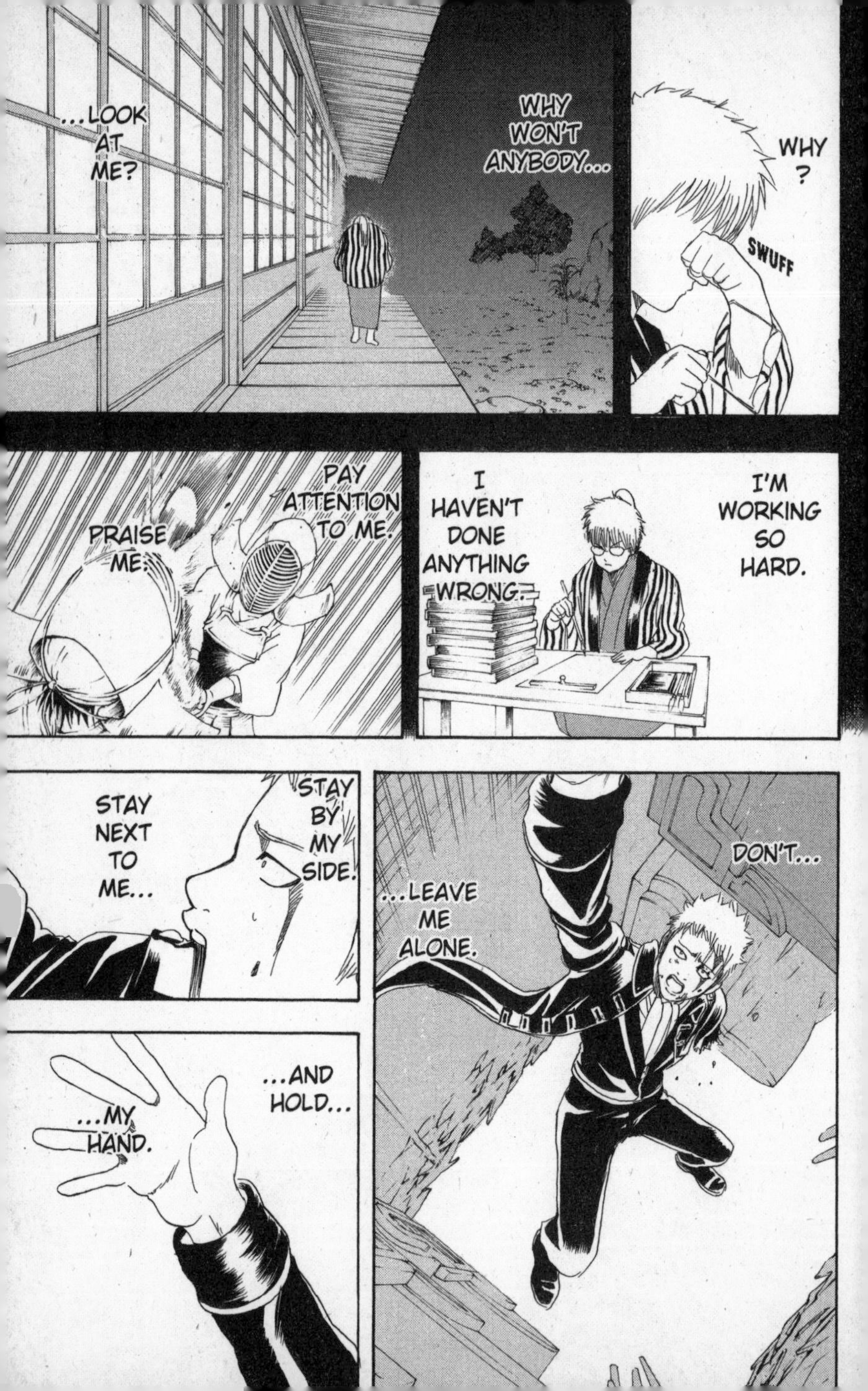
WHY?
SWUFF
WHY WON'T ANYBODY...
...LOOK AT ME?
I'M WORKING SO HARD.
I HAVEN'T DONE ANYTHING WRONG.
PAY ATTENTION TO ME.
PRAISE ME.
DON'T...
...LEAVE ME ALONE.
STAY BY MY SIDE.
STAY NEXT TO ME...
...AND HOLD...
...MY HAND.

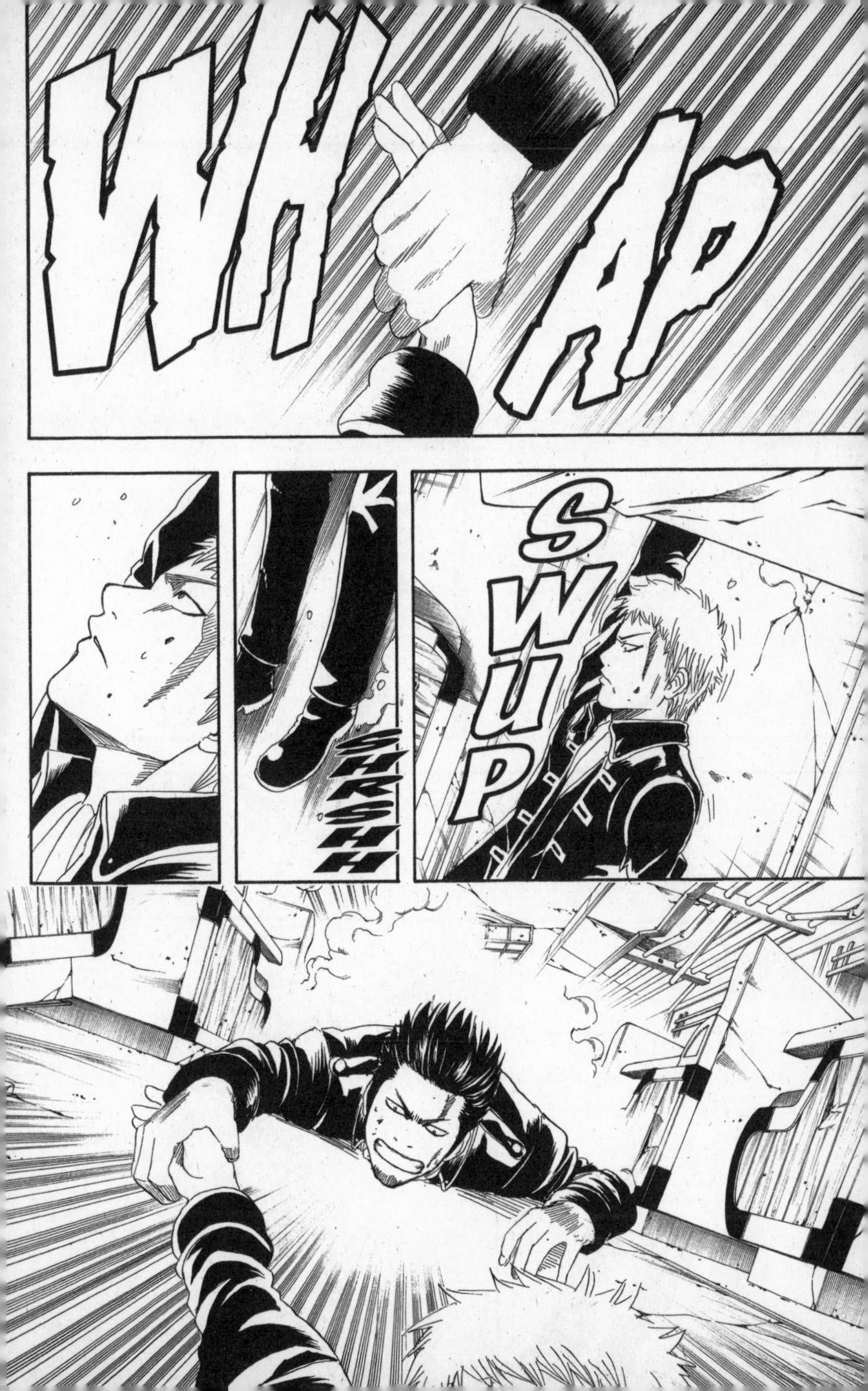
WHAP
SWUP
SHRSHH

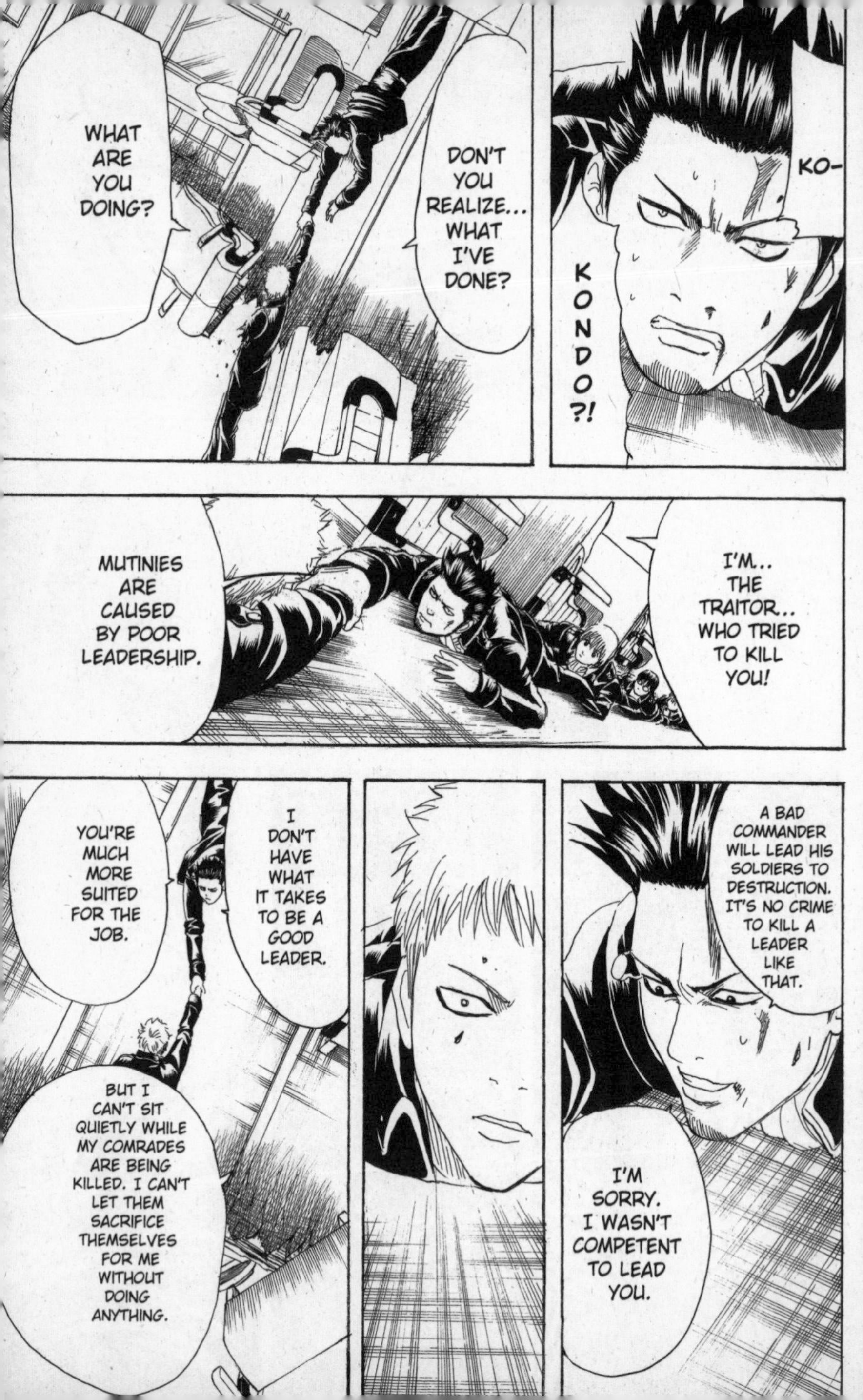
KO-
KONDO?!
DON'T YOU REALIZE... WHAT I'VE DONE?
WHAT ARE YOU DOING?
I'M... THE TRAITOR... WHO TRIED TO KILL YOU!
MUTINIES ARE CAUSED BY POOR LEADERSHIP.
A BAD COMMANDER WILL LEAD HIS SOLDIERS TO DESTRUCTION. IT'S NO CRIME TO KILL A LEADER LIKE THAT.
I'M SORRY. I WASN'T COMPETENT TO LEAD YOU.
I DON'T HAVE WHAT IT TAKES TO BE A GOOD LEADER.
YOU'RE MUCH MORE SUITED FOR THE JOB.
BUT I CAN'T SIT QUIETLY WHILE MY COMRADES ARE BEING KILLED. I CAN'T LET THEM SACRIFICE THEMSELVES FOR ME WITHOUT DOING ANYTHING.

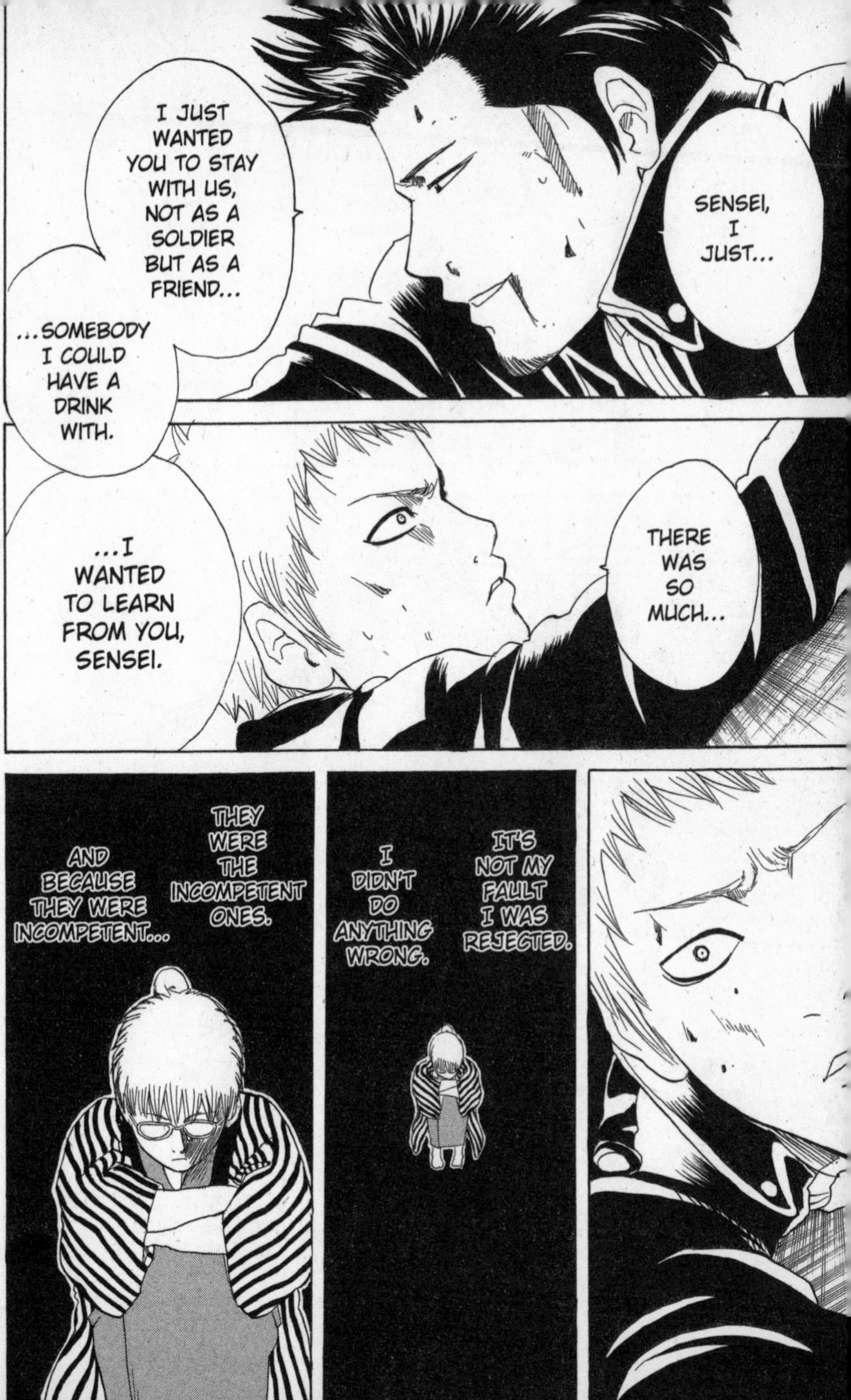
SENSEI, I JUST...
I JUST WANTED YOU TO STAY WITH US, NOT AS A SOLDIER BUT AS A FRIEND...
...SOMEBODY I COULD HAVE A DRINK WITH.
THERE WAS SO MUCH...
...I WANTED TO LEARN FROM YOU, SENSEI.
IT'S NOT MY FAULT I WAS REJECTED.
I DIDN'T DO ANYTHING WRONG.
THEY WERE THE INCOMPETENT ONES.
AND BECAUSE THEY WERE INCOMPETENT...

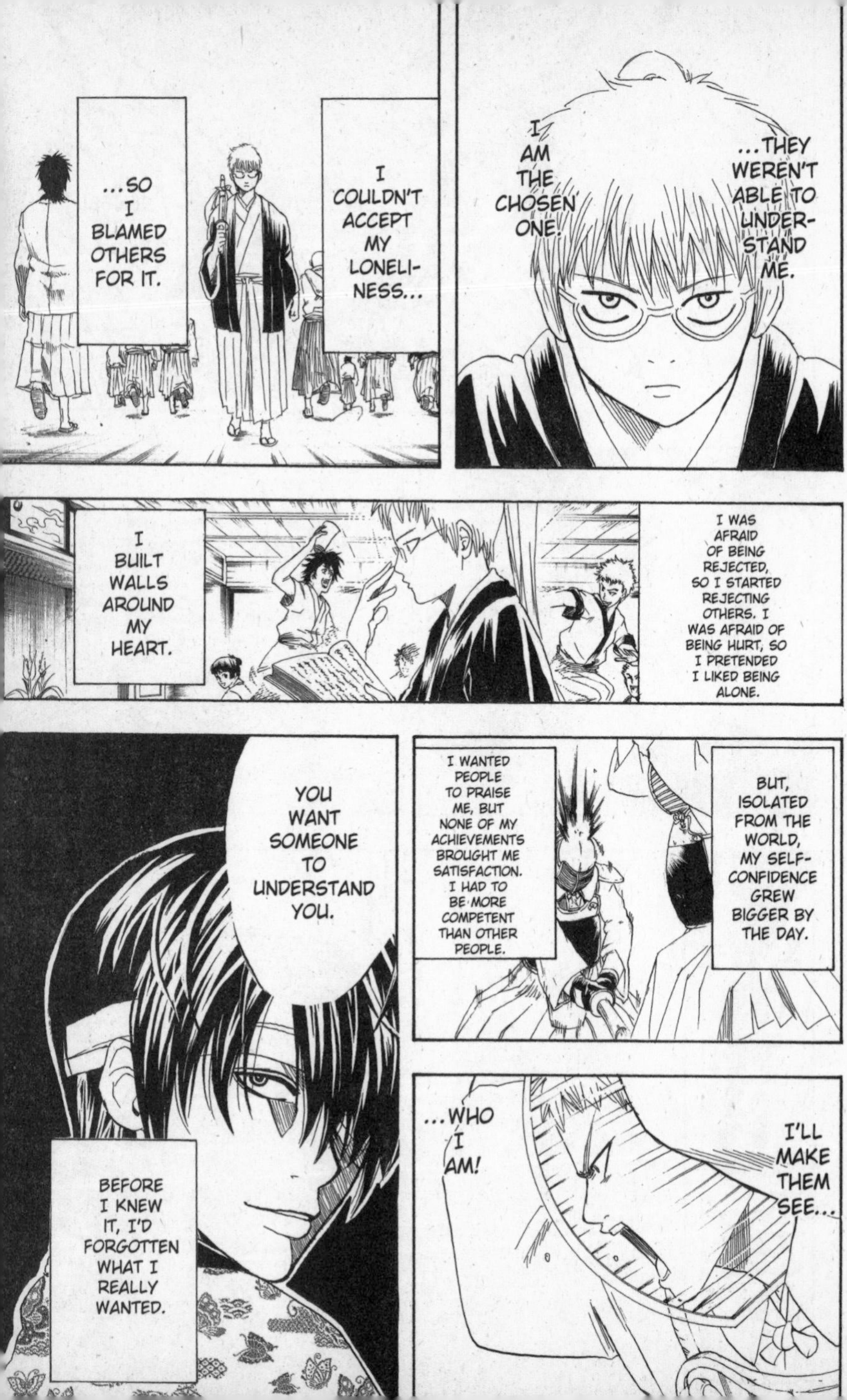
...THEY WEREN'T ABLE TO UNDER-STAND ME.
I AM THE CHOSEN ONE.
I COULDN'T ACCEPT MY LONELI-NESS...
...SO I BLAMED OTHERS FOR IT.
I WAS AFRAID OF BEING REJECTED, SO I STARTED REJECTING OTHERS. I WAS AFRAID OF BEING HURT, SO I PRETENDED I LIKED BEING ALONE.
I BUILT WALLS AROUND MY HEART.
BUT, ISOLATED FROM THE WORLD, MY SELF-CONFIDENCE GREW BIGGER BY THE DAY.
I WANTED PEOPLE TO PRAISE ME, BUT NONE OF MY ACHIEVEMENTS BROUGHT ME SATISFACTION. I HAD TO BE MORE COMPETENT THAN OTHER PEOPLE.
I'LL MAKE THEM SEE...
...WHO I AM!
YOU WANT SOMEONE TO UNDERSTAND YOU.
BEFORE I KNEW IT, I'D FORGOTTEN WHAT I REALLY WANTED.

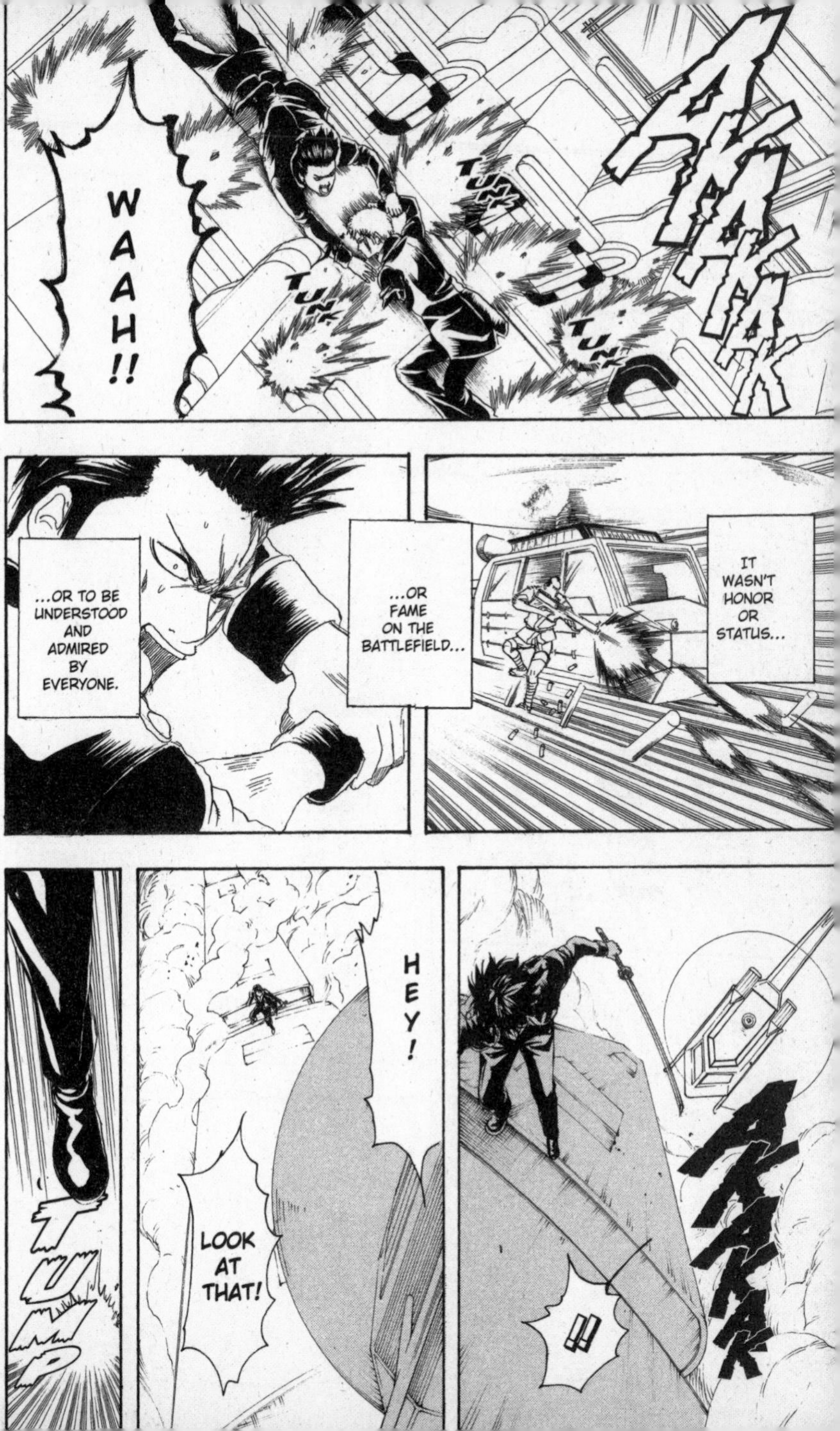
AKAKAK
TUNK
TUNK
TUNK
WAAAH!!
IT WASN'T HONOR OR STATUS...
...OR FAME ON THE BATTLEFIELD...
...OR TO BE UNDERSTOOD AND ADMIRED BY EVERYONE.
AKAKAK
!!
HEY!
LOOK AT THAT!
TUMP

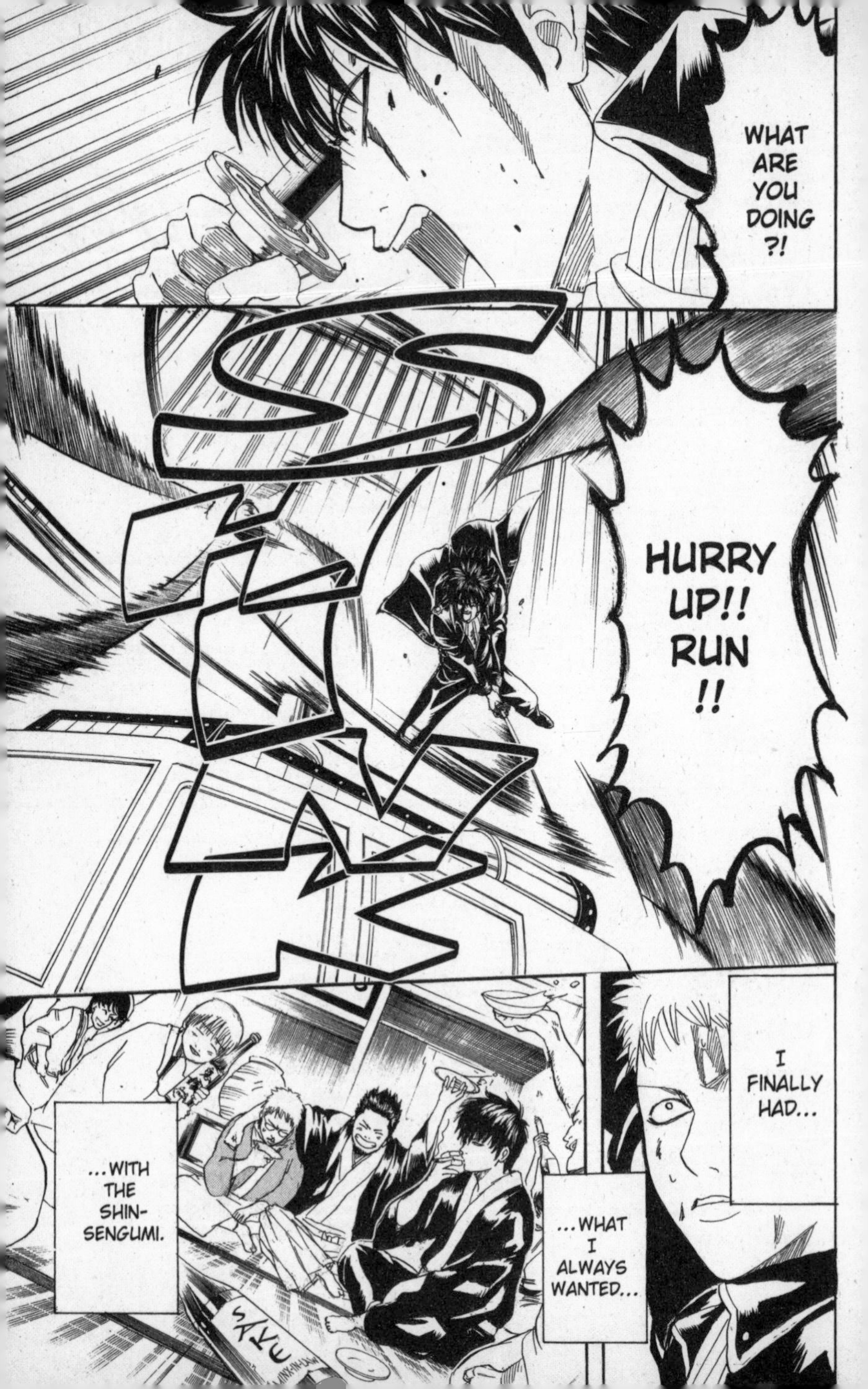
WHAT ARE YOU DOING ?!
HURRY UP!! RUN !!
I FINALLY HAD...
...WHAT I ALWAYS WANTED...
...WITH THE SHIN-SENGUMI.
SAKE

SORACHI: WAIT, YOU'RE ASKING ME?
ONISHI: "ARE YOU ASKING ME?" WHO IS THIS INTERVIEW FOR? (LAUGH)
SORACHI: MY TEACHERS GOT MAD AT ME A LOT MORE THAN MY PARENTS.
ONISHI: WHY?
SORACHI: I SCREWED AROUND WAY TOO MUCH... LIKE DURING MARATHONS, I TOOK SHORTCUTS, AND I GOT PUNCHED IN THE STOMACH FOR IT.
ONISHI: WHAT?
SORACHI: I CALLED MY P.E. TEACHER "GORILLA" AT THE TIME. I TOOK A SHORTCUT AND WAS RUNNING REALLY SLOW. THAT'S WHEN I SAW HIM WALK UP TO ME. I CHANGED MY PLAN AND JUST SAID, "MY STOMACH HURTS." BUT IT WAS TOO LATE SINCE HE COULD SEE RIGHT THROUGH MY LIE. THAT'S WHEN HE PUNCHED ME IN THE STOMACH AT FULL FORCE.
ONISHI: YOU'RE REALLY BRAVE IN THE WEIRDEST WAYS.

[FOR THE KIDS THAT ARE STRIVING TO BECOME COMIC AUTHORS...]

ONISHI: DO YOU HAVE ANYTHING FOR THE KIDS THAT ARE STRIVING TO BECOME COMIC AUTHORS?
SORACHI: YOU CAN'T JUST READ COMICS.
ONISHI: THEN WHAT DO THEY HAVE TO DO?
SORACHI: IF THEY WANT TO BE COMIC AUTHORS, THEN THAT MEANS THEY LIKE COMICS. BUT YOU'LL NEED SOMETHING ELSE ASIDE FROM THAT.
ONISHI: YEAH.
SORACHI: YOU HAVE TO JOIN YOUR SCHOOL'S CLUBS THAT INTEREST YOU... AND YOU HAVE TO KNOW HOW TO LIVE A NORMAL LIFE TOO. FOR EXAMPLE, YOU HAVE TO KNOW WHAT THE LIFE OF A REGULAR HIGH SCHOOLER IS LIKE. AT THE SAME TIME, YOU NEED TO HAVE A CROOKED VIEWPOINT ON THE MATTER.
ONISHI: SO, "KNOW WHAT A NORMAL LIFE CONSISTS OF, BUT HAVE A CROOKED WAY OF LOOKING AT IT."
SORACHI: THAT MAKES ME SOUND REALLY PRETENTIOUS, SO PLEASE DON'T PUT THAT IN PRINT.
ONISHI: I CAN JUST WRITE IT IN A WAY SO YOU WON'T SOUND LIKE A JERK.
SORACHI: PLEASE DON'T...
ONISHI: FINE. I'LL JUST TAG A "I REALLY SHOULDN'T BE THE ONE TO SAY SO, BUT..." TYPE OF LINE IN FRONT OF IT.
SORACHI: I DON'T WANT THAT.
ONISHI: I HOPE THEY'LL TURN THE COMIC AUTHOR INTERVIEWS INTO A KIND OF SERIES.
SORACHI: WHY? DO YOU LIKE IT THAT MUCH?
ONISHI: EVERYONE LOVES COMIC AUTHOR INTERVIEWS.

"YOU HAVE TO ILLUSTRATE 'HUMANS.' THAT'S WHY YOU HAVE TO CONTINUE TO PURSUE WHAT IT MEANS." –ONISHI

ONISHI: BUT WE DON'T HAVE MANY OPPORTUNITIES.
SORACHI: THEN MINE WON'T BE VERY USEFUL. MAYBE WE SHOULD TALK ABOUT MORE SERIOUS STUFF.
ONISHI: IT DOESN'T NEED TO BE USEFUL. EVERYONE SEEMS TO LIKE READING THE DIARY BLOGS ON MIXI. BUT I HATE IT. (NOTE: MIXI IS A POPULAR SOCIAL-NETWORKING SITE)
SORACHI: (LAUGH) SO YOU GET ANNOYED WHEN YOU READ YOUR FRIENDS' DIARIES?
ONISHI: IT'S ALWAYS PEOPLE THAT DON'T RESPOND TO EMAILS THAT UPDATE THEIR BLOGS ON MIXI EVERY SINGLE DAY. IT MAKES ME DO A DOUBLE TAKE. I JUST WANT TO SHOUT, "IT DOESN'T TAKE THAT LONG TO RESPOND TO MY EMAIL," AT THEM. (LAUGH)
SORACHI: WHAT DOES THAT HAVE TO DO WITH MIXI? (LAUGH)
ONISHI: (LAUGH)
SORACHI: GOING BACK TO THE LAST QUESTION, MOST PEOPLE WHO WANT TO BECOME COMIC AUTHORS USUALLY START BY DRAWING. THAT'S WHY THEY ALWAYS END UP TRYING TO LEARN HOW TO DRAW. I KNOW THAT'S IMPORTANT TOO.
ONISHI: BUT YOU WANT THEM TO OBSERVE PEOPLE TOO?
SORACHI: YOU CAN'T BECOME A COMIC AUTHOR JUST BY DRAWING COMICS.
ONISHI: YEAH. YOU HAVE TO ILLUSTRATE "HUMANS." THAT'S WHY YOU HAVE TO CONTINUE TO PURSUE WHAT IT MEANS.
SORACHI: IF YOU THINK ABOUT IT, PEOPLE WHO HAVE NO INTEREST IN BECOMING A COMIC AUTHOR CAN ACTUALLY BE THE ONES THAT CREATE SOME REALLY GREAT COMICS.

[OBSERVING GIN TAMA]

ONISHI: WHAT DO YOU HAVE PLANNED FOR FUTURE DEVELOPMENTS?
SORACHI: FOR WHAT? *GIN TAMA?*
ONISHI: YEAH.
SORACHI: I CAN'T SAY THAT HERE.
ONISHI: JUST TELL ME WHAT YOU HAVE IN MIND WITHOUT GIVING TOO MUCH AWAY.
SORACHI: I WANT TO END IT BY VOLUME 30.
ONISHI: VOLUME 30?
SORACHI: IF YOU DON'T END IT IN 30 VOLUMES, PEOPLE WON'T WANT TO BUY THE FULL SET.
ONISHI: OF COURSE NOT. WHAT ABOUT *KOCHIKAME*? (NOTE: A LONG-RUNNING AND ONGOING COMIC THAT HAS SURPASSED THE 100TH-VOLUME MARK YEARS AGO.)
SORACHI: IF A MANGA HAS THAT KIND OF ENERGY THEN IT MIGHT BE POSSIBLE. BUT CASUAL STUFF LIKE *GIN TAMA* ISN'T GOING TO LAST LIKE THAT. TO BE HONEST, I THINK I'M STRETCHING IT ALREADY. DON'T YOU THINK IT'LL BE PERFECT IF *GIN TAMA* ENDS AT VOLUME 15?
ONISHI: BUT THERE ARE A LOT OF FANS THAT WANT YOU TO KEEP DRAWING IT FOREVER.
SORACHI: IF I KEEP MAKING MESSY STORIES LIKE THAT EVERY TIME, PAST VOLUME 30, IT'LL BE LIKE SAZAE-SAN. (NOTE: A LONG-RUNNING AND ONGOING CARTOON THAT HAS BEEN ON THE AIR FOR DECADES.)
ONISHI: BUT SAZAE-SAN ISN'T MESSY. EVERYONE WATCHES IT.
SORACHI: IT'S DIFFERENT. PEOPLE WATCH THAT SHOW ONLY BECAUSE IT'S SUNDAY AT THAT TIME SLOT. SO, THEY WATCH IT ANYWAY BECAUSE THERE'S NOTHING BETTER ON.
ONISHI: I DISAGREE. WHEN I WAS SMALL, I REALLY LOOKED FORWARD TO IT. EACH SHOW HAD THREE EPISODES SO IT MADE ME GO, "ALL RIGHT! ANOTHER EPISODE!"
SORACHI: FOR ME, I WENT, "MAN, I GOT SCHOOL TOMORROW." SO I DIDN'T EVEN FEEL LIKE WATCHING IT.
ONISHI: I WATCHED IT.
SORACHI: DON'T YOU GET DEPRESSED STARTING AT AROUND THE TIME THAT SAZAE-SAN STARTS?
ONISHI: I DO... IN A WAY. THEN WHAT ABOUT THE *GIN TAMA* ANIME?
SORACHI: I'M REALLY HAPPY THAT *GIN TAMA* GOT TURNED INTO AN ANIME. IN THE BEGINNING, I WAS TOLD THAT THERE WERE TALKS ABOUT TURNING IT INTO AN ANIME. BUT THEY NEVER GAVE ME ANY DETAILS, SO I DIDN'T THINK IT WOULD HAPPEN. WHEN I WENT TO THE JUMP FESTA ANIME TOUR '05, I SAW THE CROWD'S REACTION AND I REALIZED THAT *GIN TAMA* WAS ACTUALLY BETTER KNOWN THAN I THOUGHT.

CONTINUED ON PAGE 186

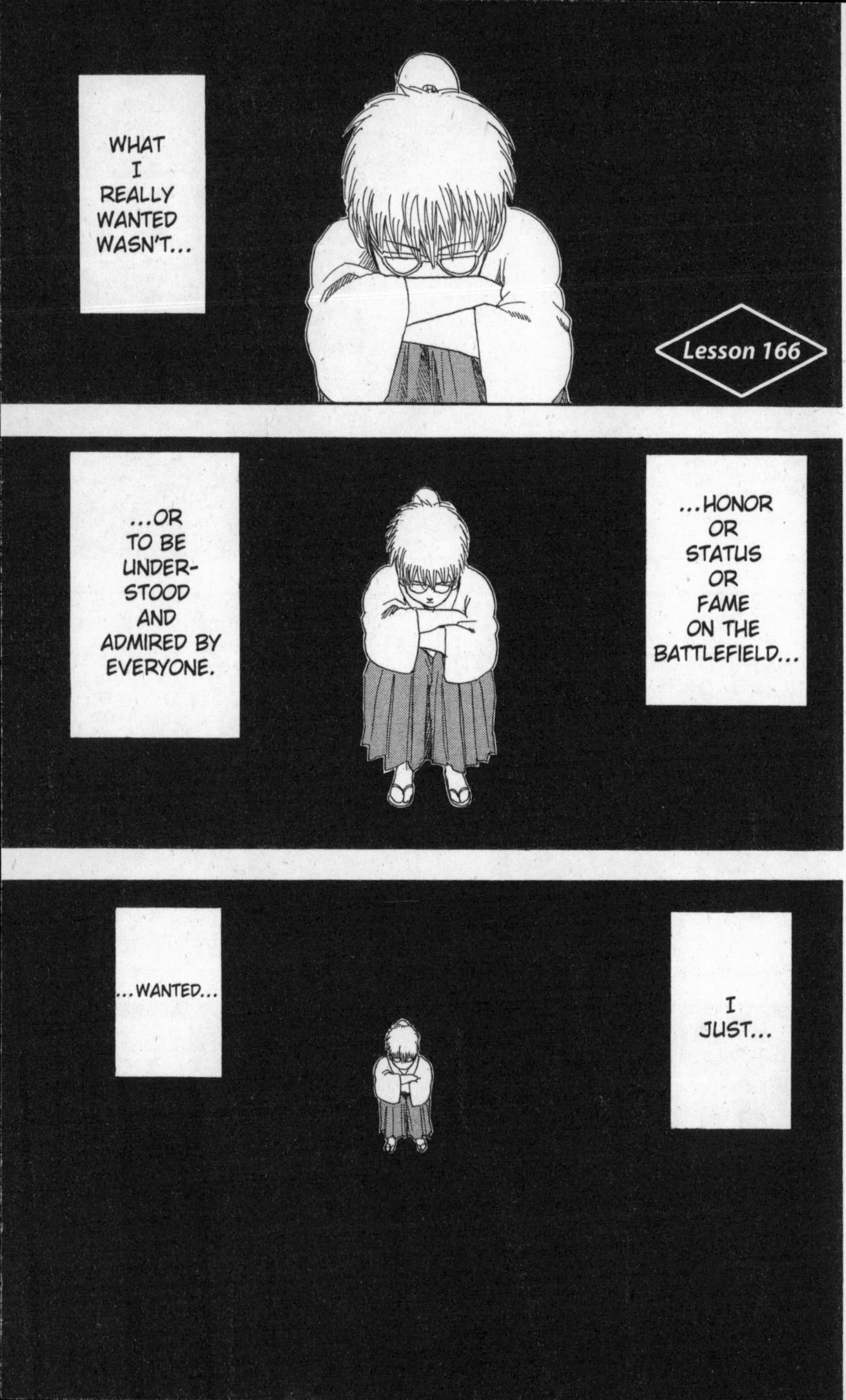
Lesson 166
WHAT I REALLY WANTED WASN'T...
...HONOR OR STATUS OR FAME ON THE BATTLEFIELD...
...OR TO BE UNDER-STOOD AND ADMIRED BY EVERYONE.
I JUST...
...WANTED...

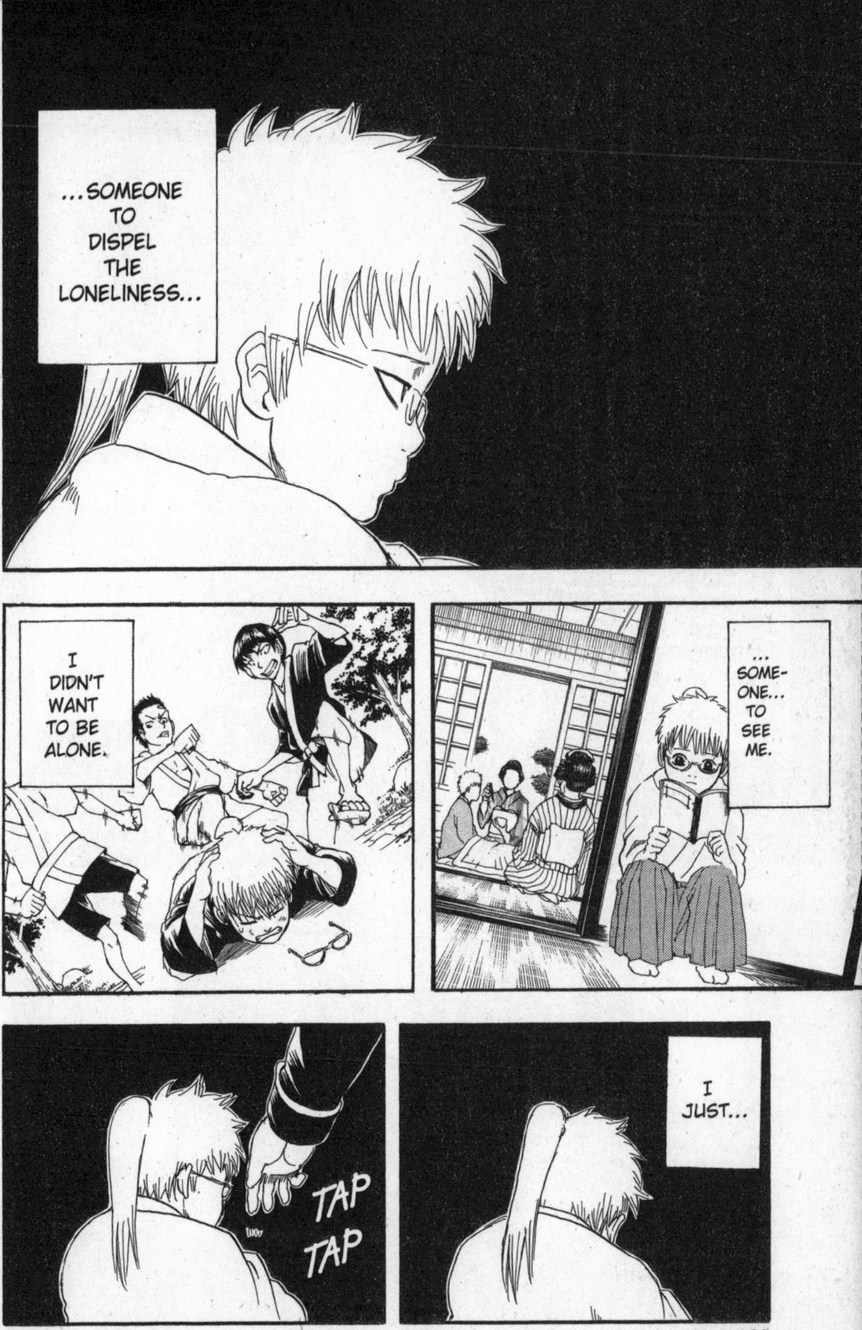
...SOMEONE TO DISPEL THE LONELINESS...
... SOME-ONE... TO SEE ME.
I DIDN'T WANT TO BE ALONE.
I JUST...
TAP TAP

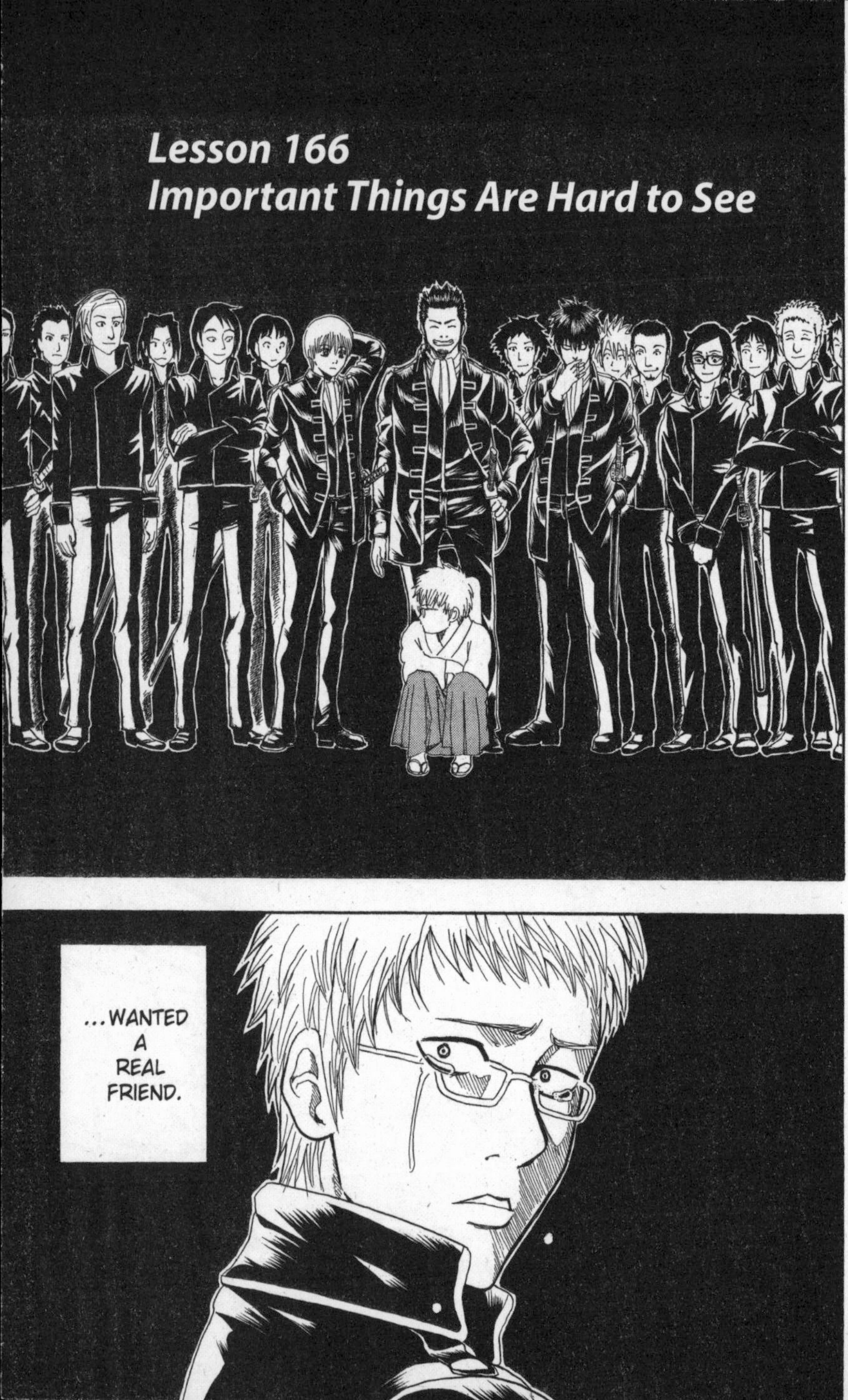
Lesson 166
Important Things Are Hard to See
...WANTED A REAL FRIEND.

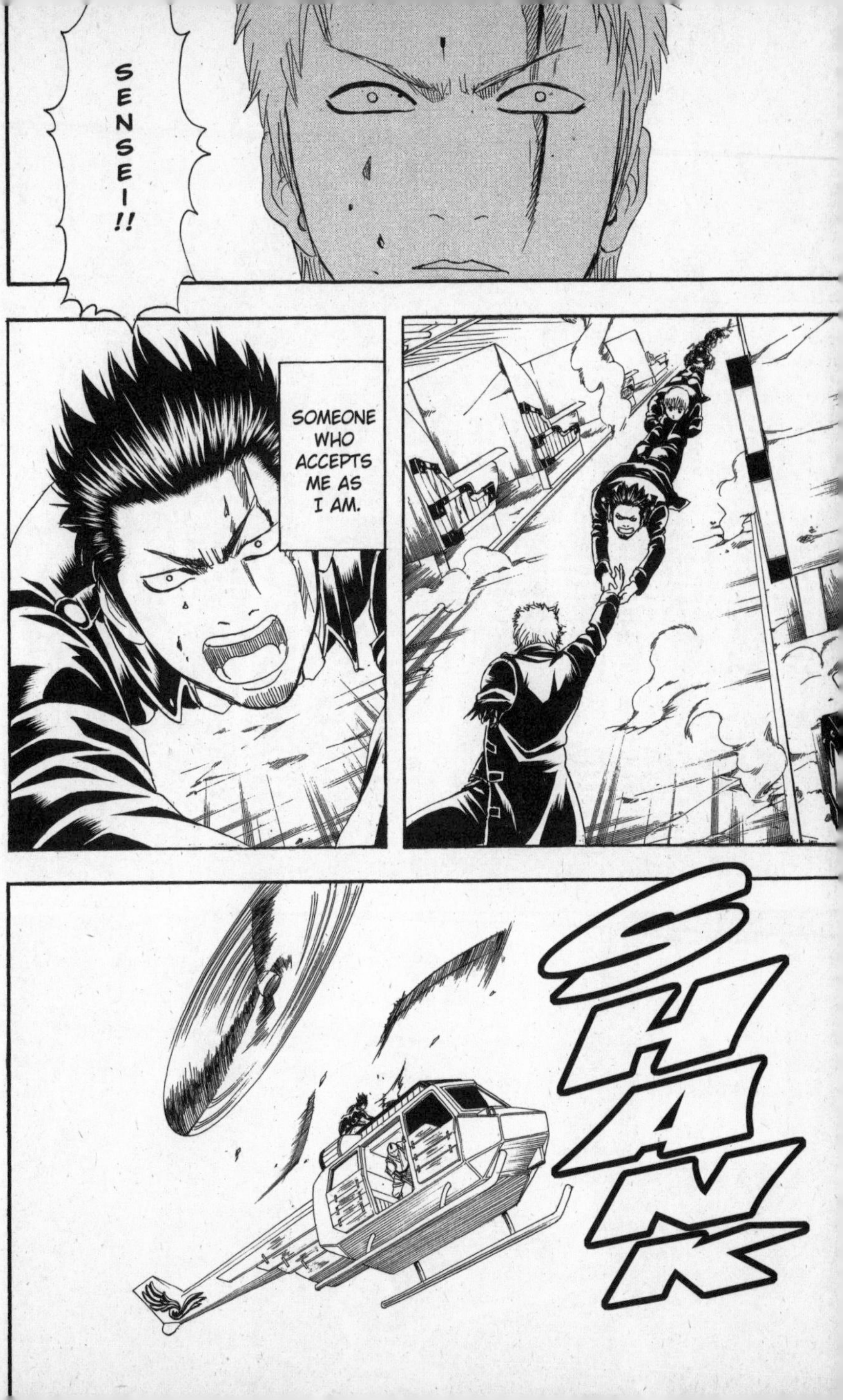
SENSEI!!
SOMEONE WHO ACCEPTS ME AS I AM.
SHANK

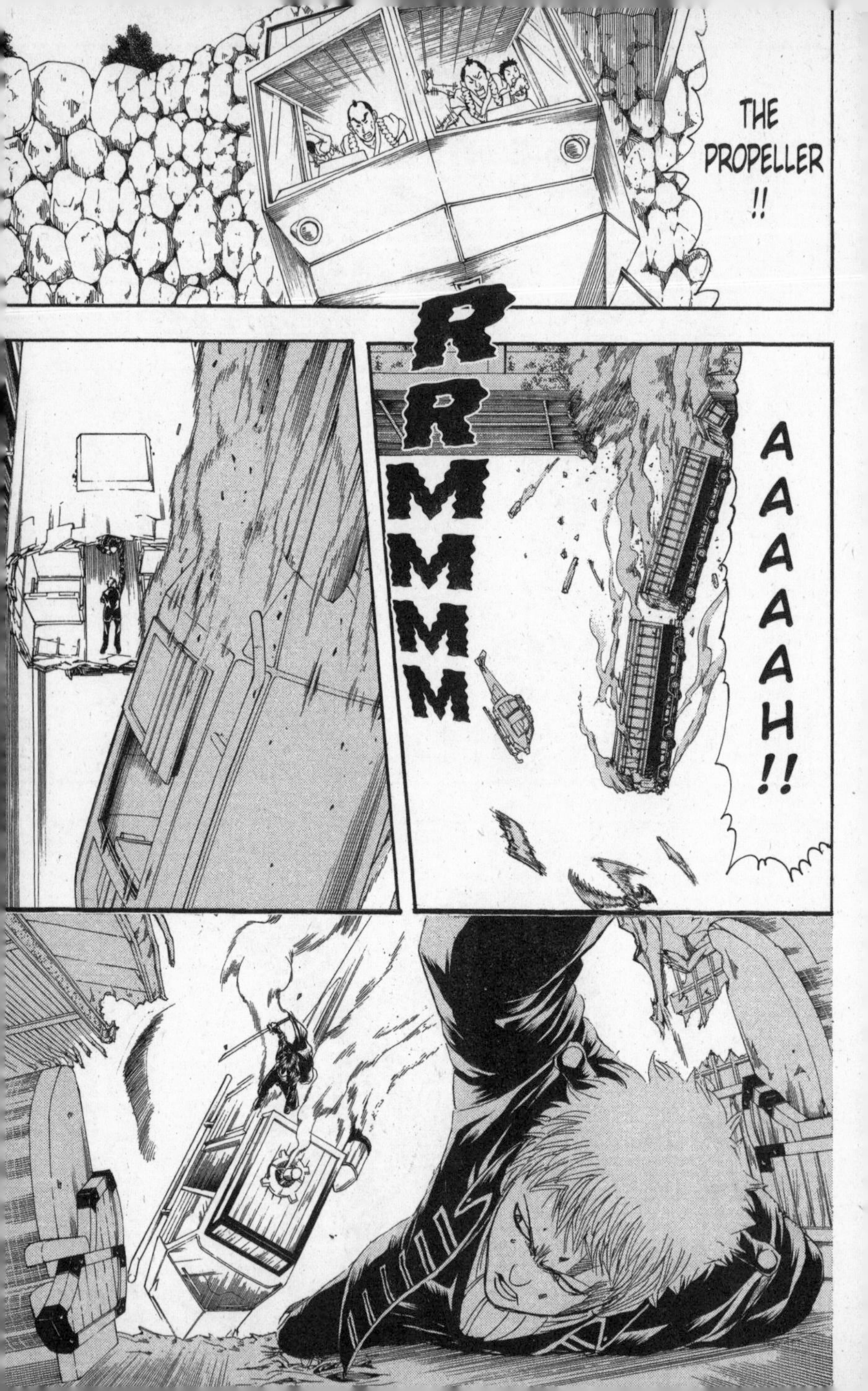
THE PROPELLER !!
RRMMMM
AAAAAH!!

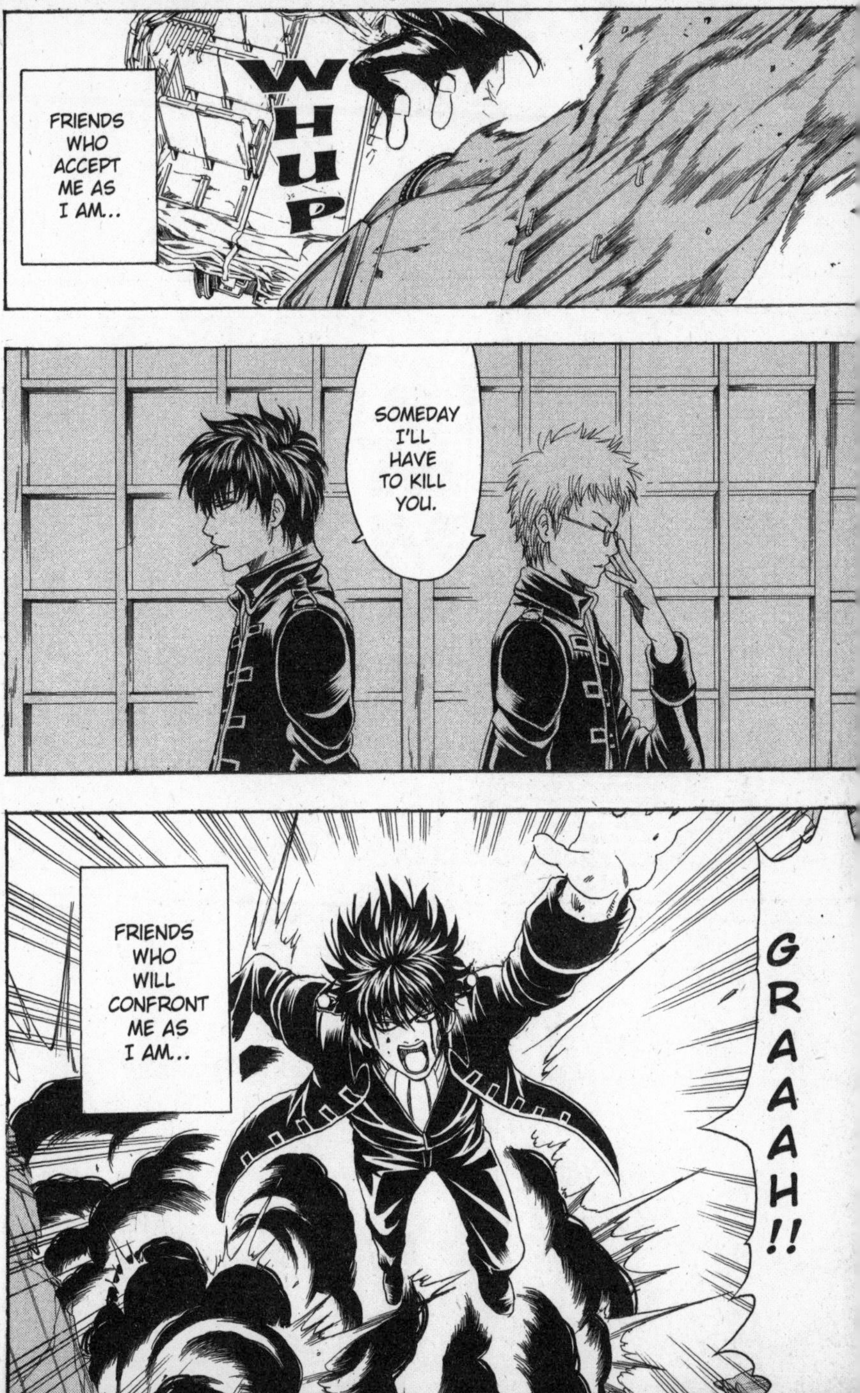
WHUP
FRIENDS WHO ACCEPT ME AS I AM...
SOMEDAY I'LL HAVE TO KILL YOU.
GRAAAH!!
FRIENDS WHO WILL CONFRONT ME AS I AM...

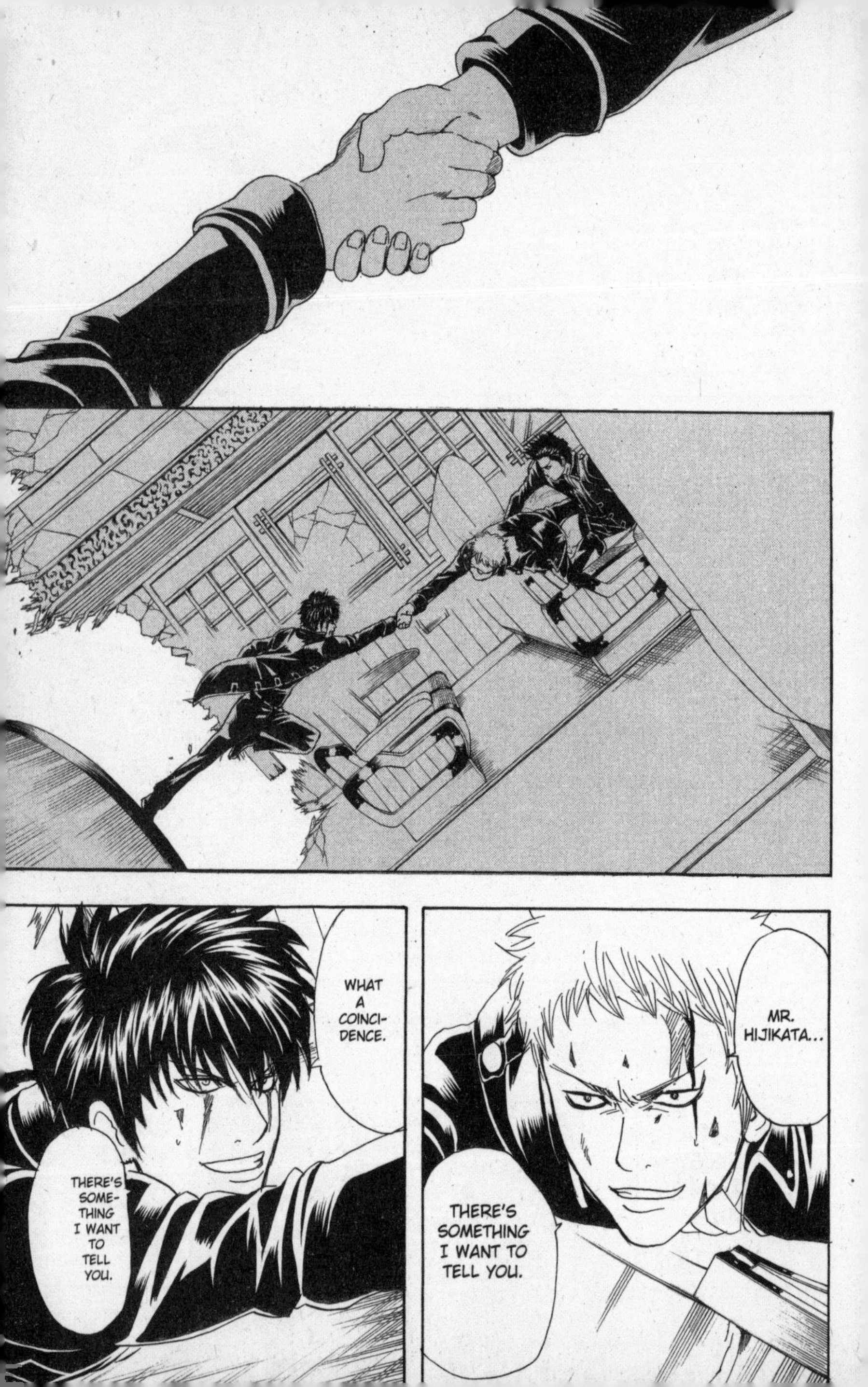
MR. HIJIKATA...
THERE'S SOMETHING I WANT TO TELL YOU.
WHAT A COINCIDENCE.
THERE'S SOMETHING I WANT TO TELL YOU.

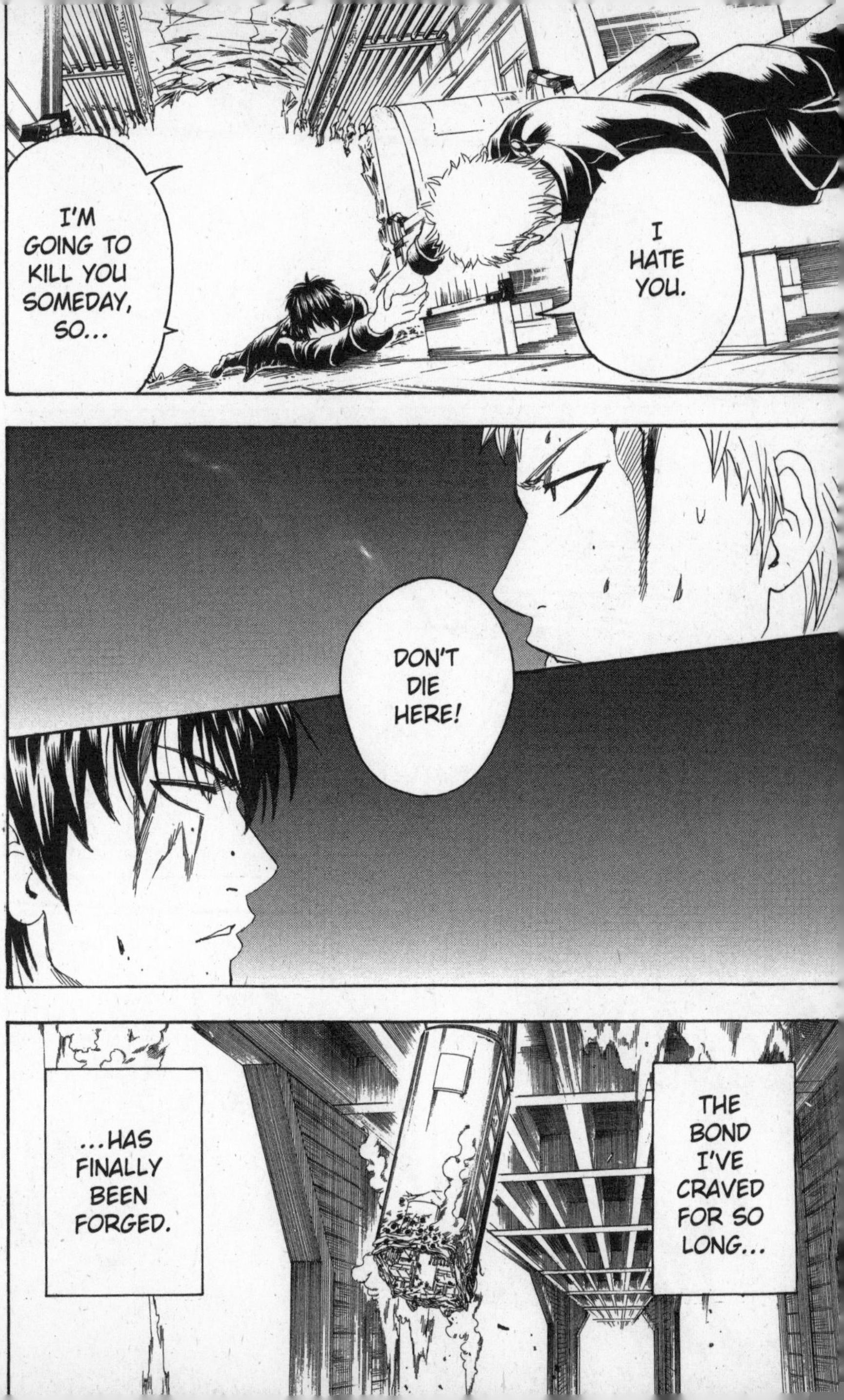
I HATE YOU.
I'M GOING TO KILL YOU SOMEDAY, SO...
DON'T DIE HERE!
THE BOND I'VE CRAVED FOR SO LONG...
...HAS FINALLY BEEN FORGED.

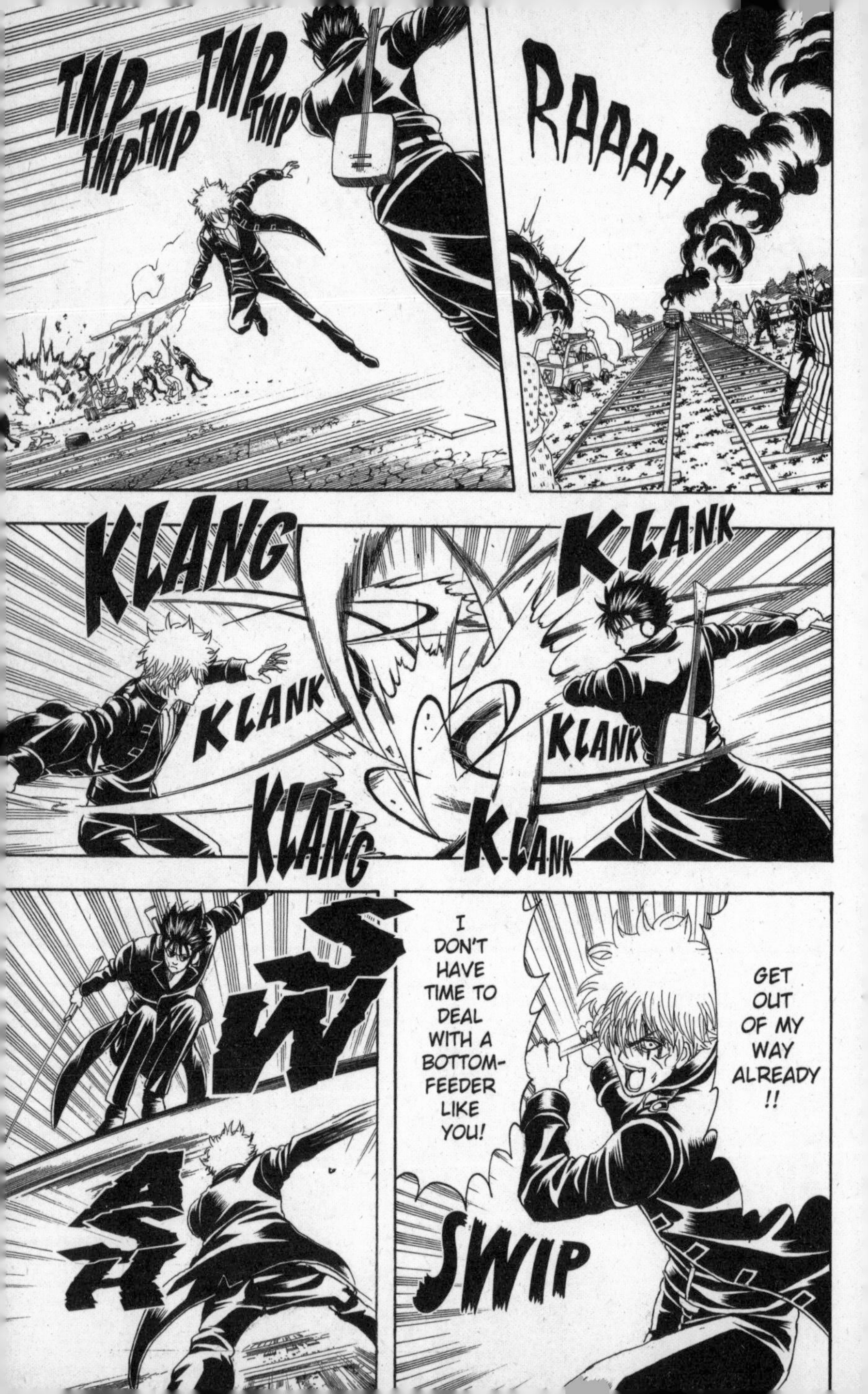
RAAAH
TMP TMP
TMP TMP
TMP TMP
KLANK
KLANG
KLANK
KLANK
KLANK
KLANG
GET OUT OF MY WAY ALREADY!!
I DON'T HAVE TIME TO DEAL WITH A BOTTOM-FEEDER LIKE YOU!
SWIP

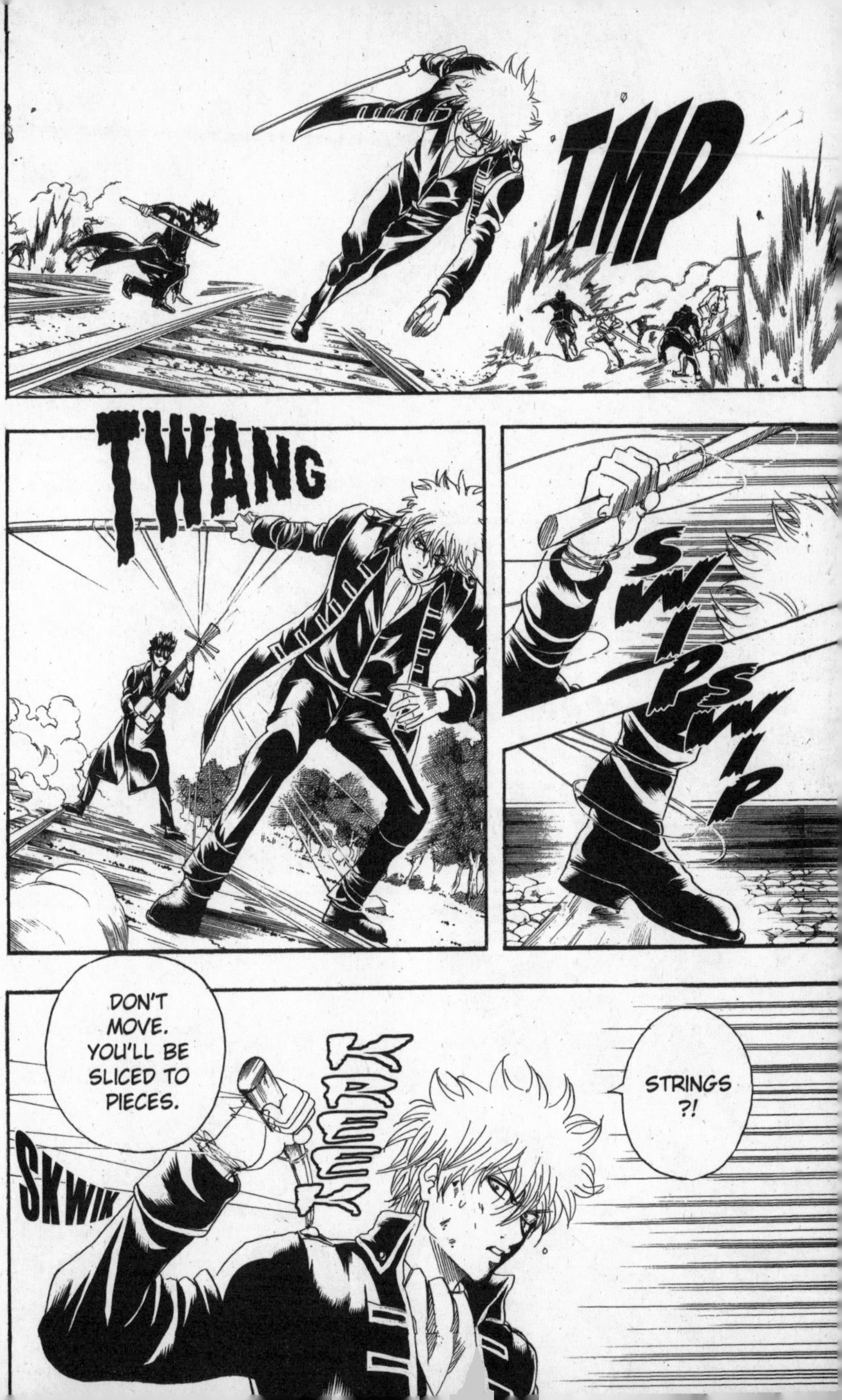
TMP
SWIP SWIP
TWANG
STRINGS ?!
KREEEK
DON'T MOVE. YOU'LL BE SLICED TO PIECES.
SKWIK

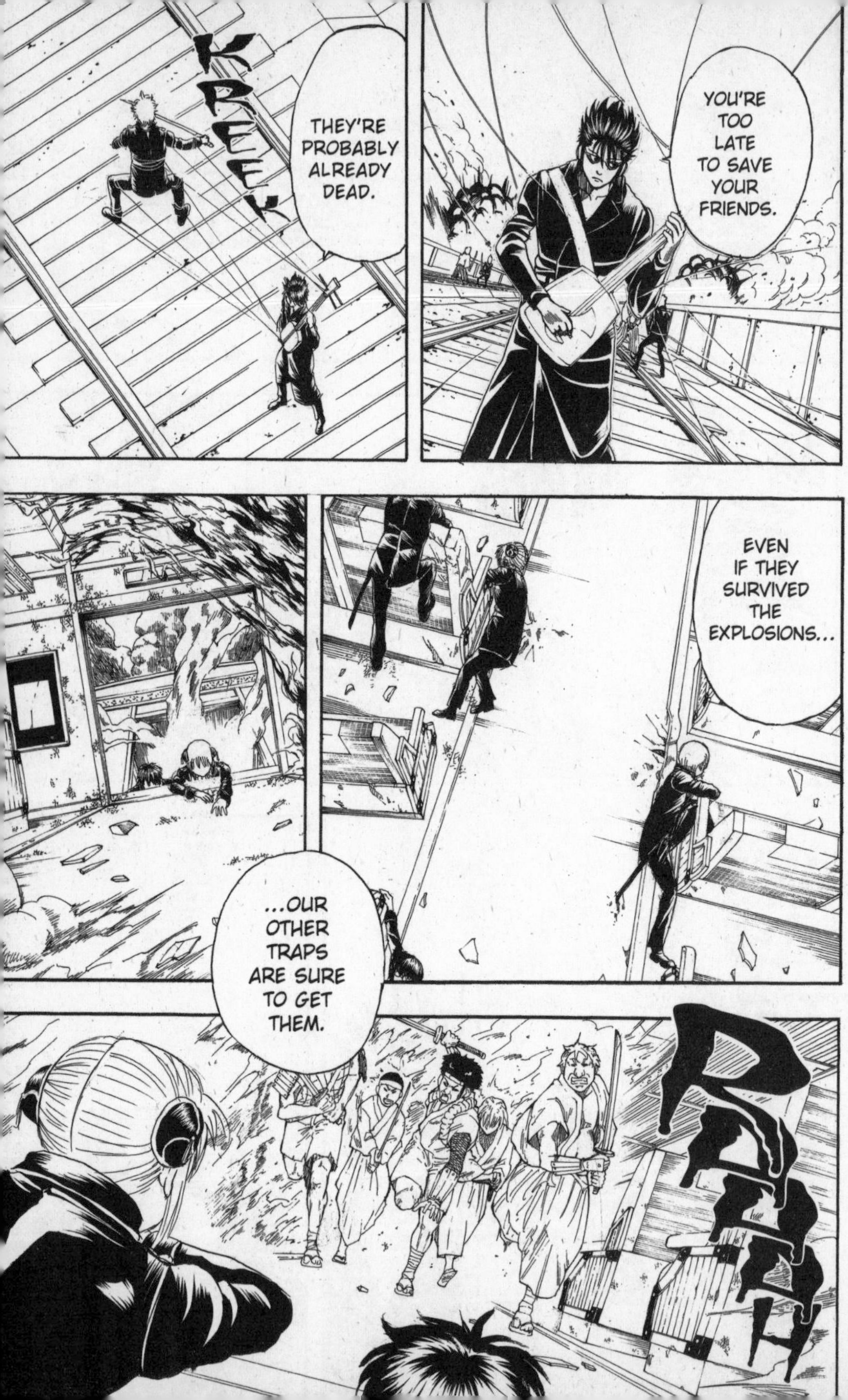
YOU'RE TOO LATE TO SAVE YOUR FRIENDS.
KREEK
THEY'RE PROBABLY ALREADY DEAD.
EVEN IF THEY SURVIVED THE EXPLOSIONS...
...OUR OTHER TRAPS ARE SURE TO GET THEM.

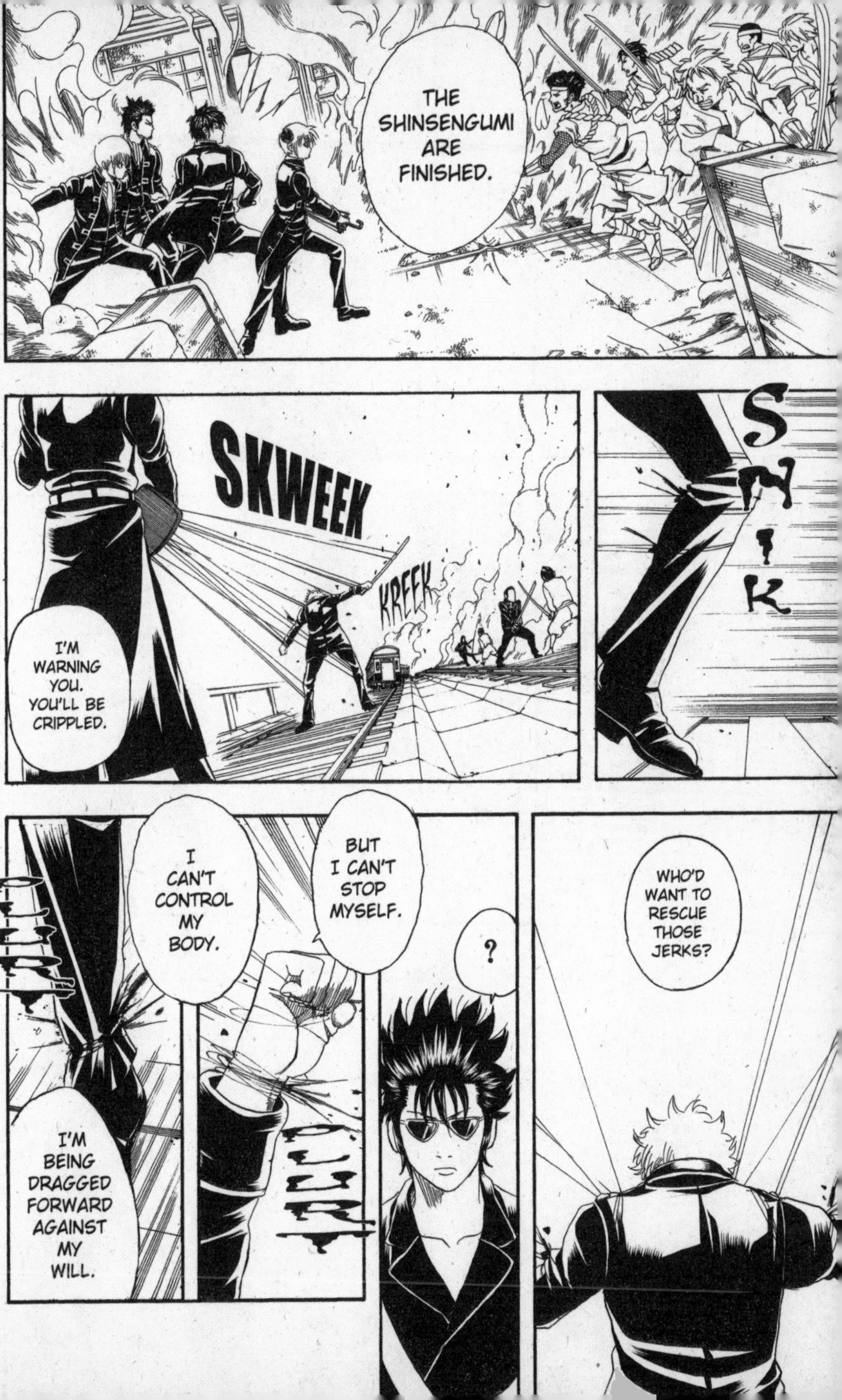
THE SHINSENGUMI ARE FINISHED.
SNIK
SKWEEK
KREEK
I'M WARNING YOU. YOU'LL BE CRIPPLED.
WHO'D WANT TO RESCUE THOSE JERKS?
?
BUT I CAN'T STOP MYSELF.
I CAN'T CONTROL MY BODY.
I'M BEING DRAGGED FORWARD AGAINST MY WILL.

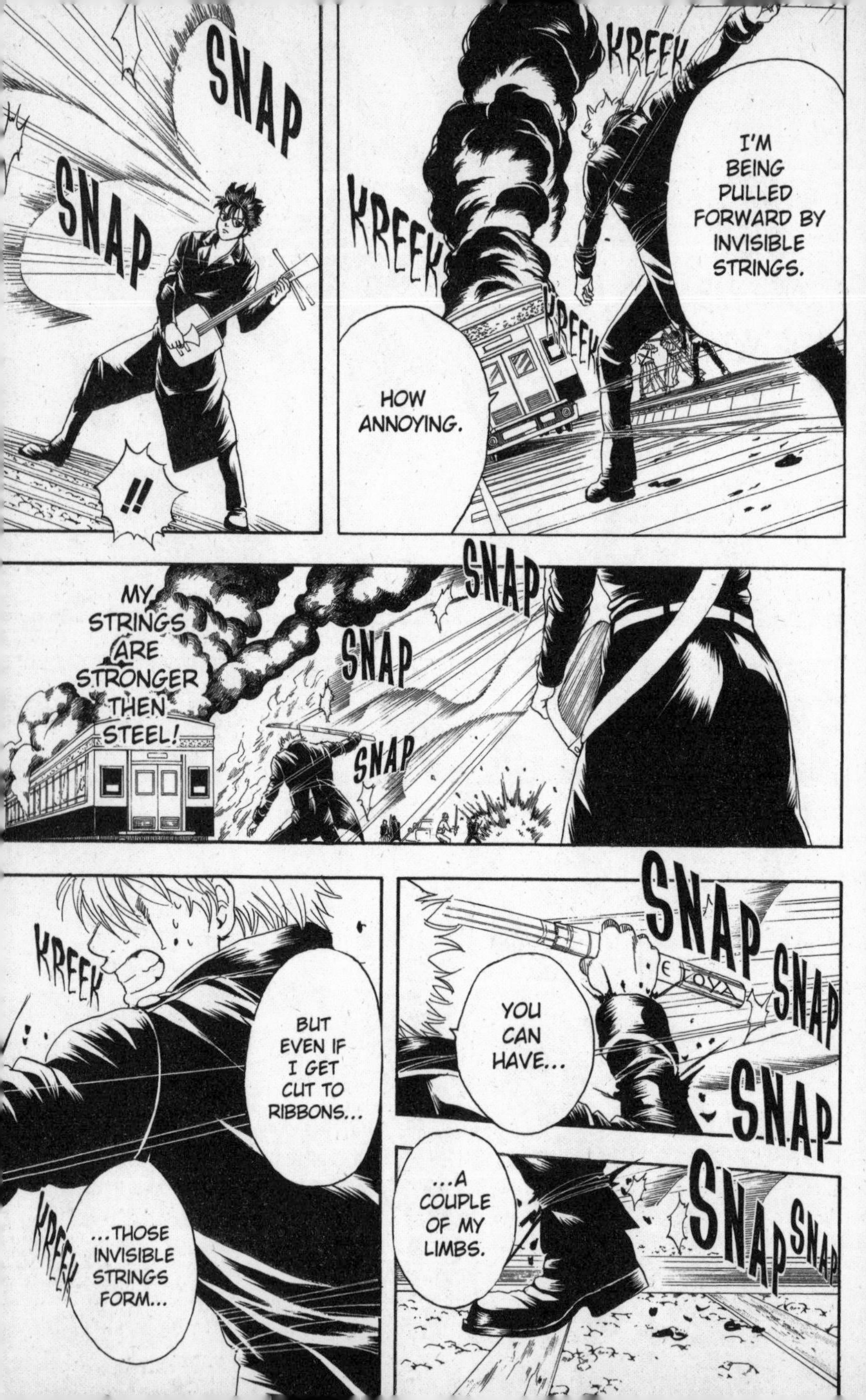
KREEK
I'M BEING PULLED FORWARD BY INVISIBLE STRINGS.
KREEK
KREEK
HOW ANNOYING.
SNAP
SNAP
!!
SNAP
SNAP
SNAP
MY STRINGS ARE STRONGER THEN STEEL!
SNAP
SNAP
SNAP
YOU CAN HAVE...
SNAP
SNAP
...A COUPLE OF MY LIMBS.
KREEK
BUT EVEN IF I GET CUT TO RIBBONS...
KREEK
...THOSE INVISIBLE STRINGS FORM...

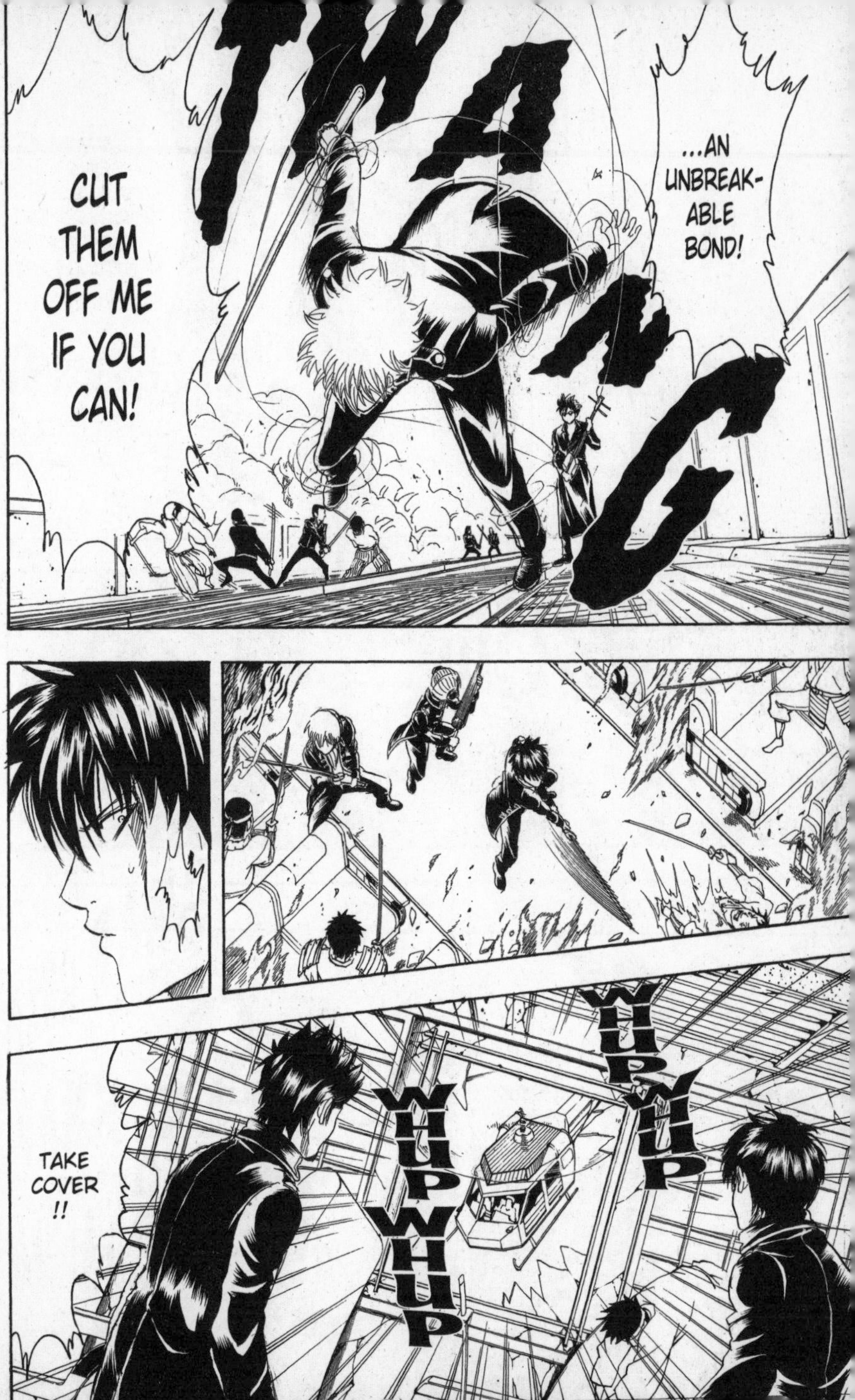
...AN UNBREAKABLE BOND!
THWANG
CUT THEM OFF ME IF YOU CAN!
WHUP WHUP
WHUP WHUP WHUP
TAKE COVER !!

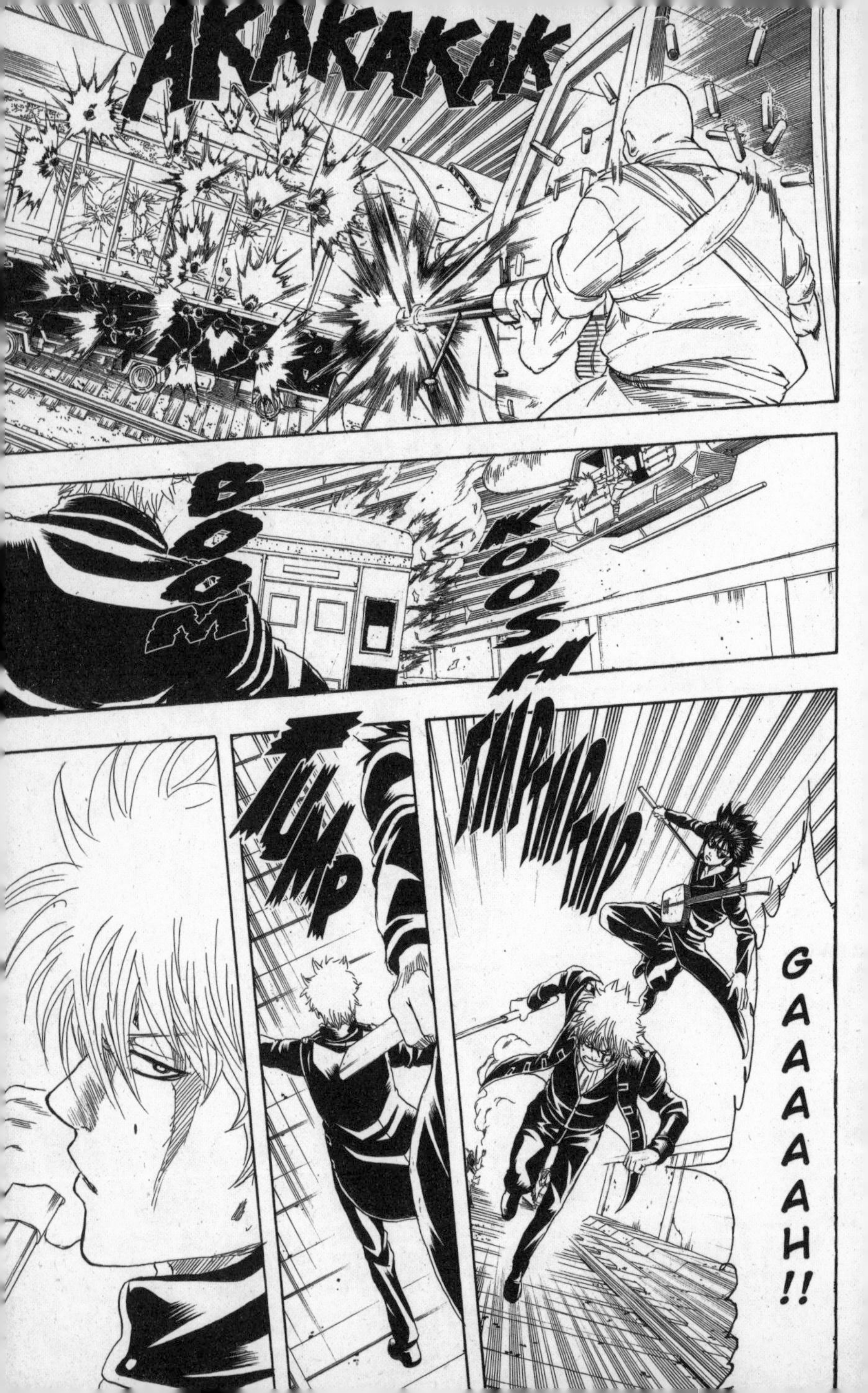
AKAKAKAK
KOOSH
BOOOM
GAAAAAAH!!
TMPTMPTMP
TUMP

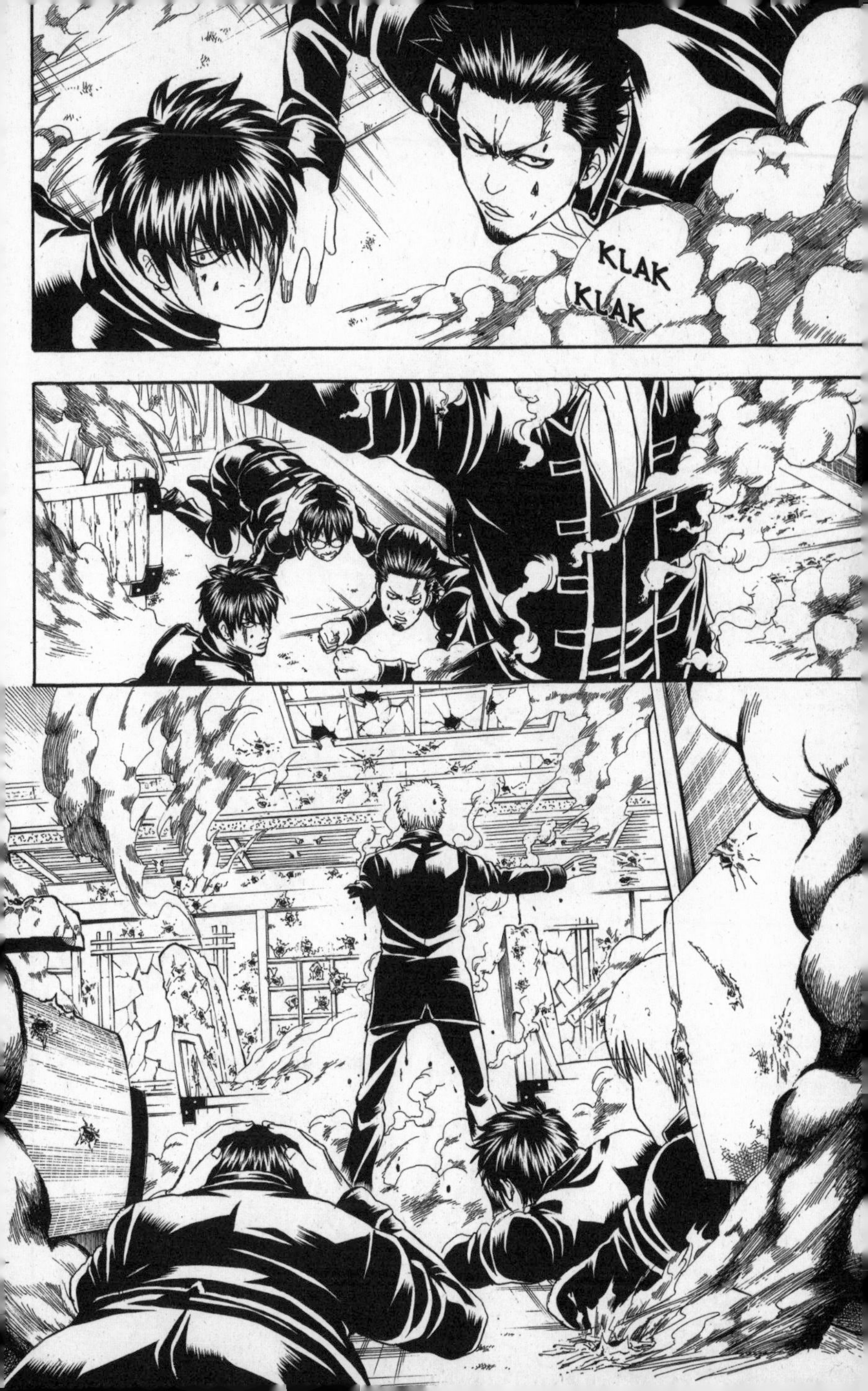
KLAK KLAK

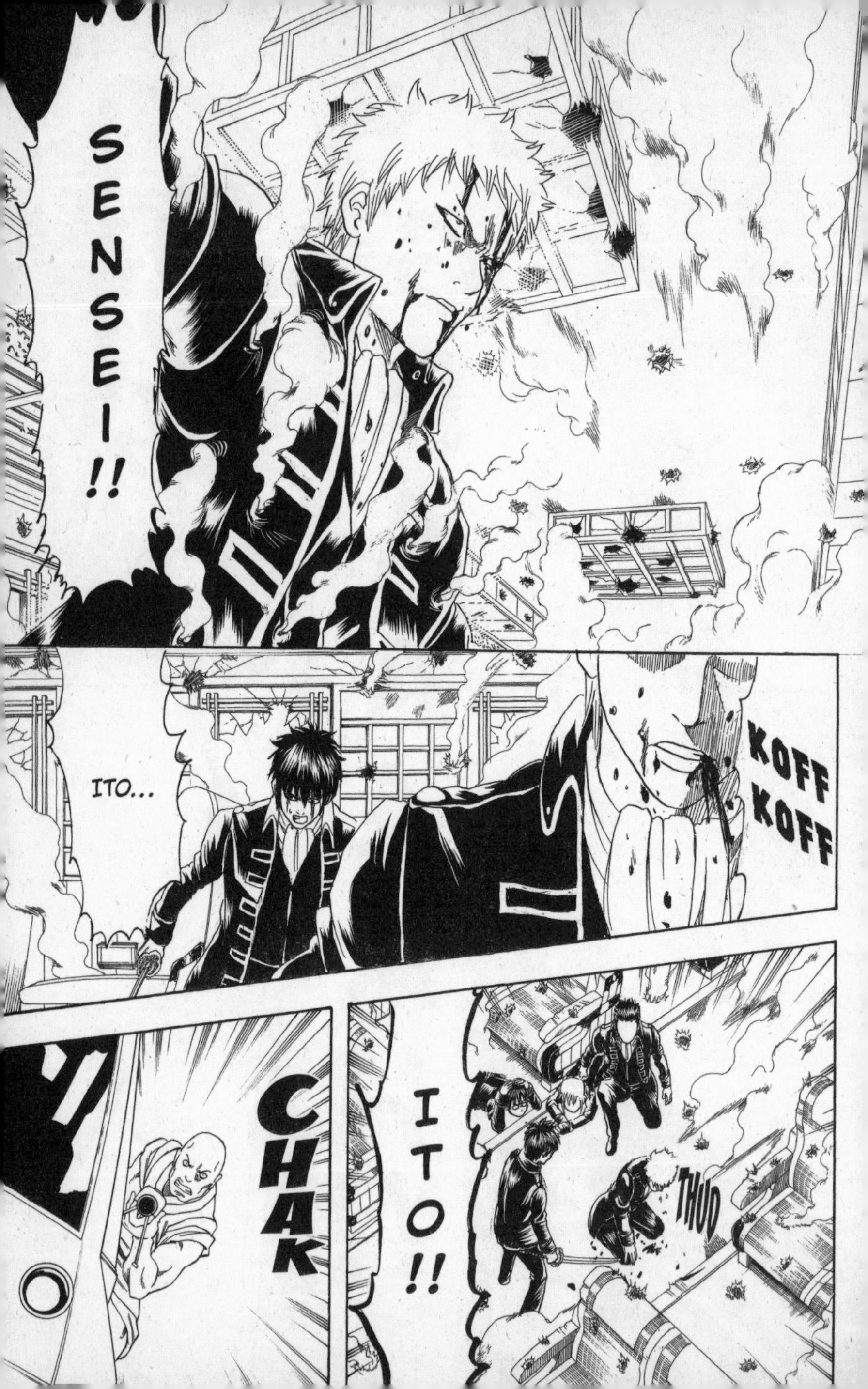
SENSEI!!
KOFF KOFF
ITO...
ITO!!
THUD
CHAK

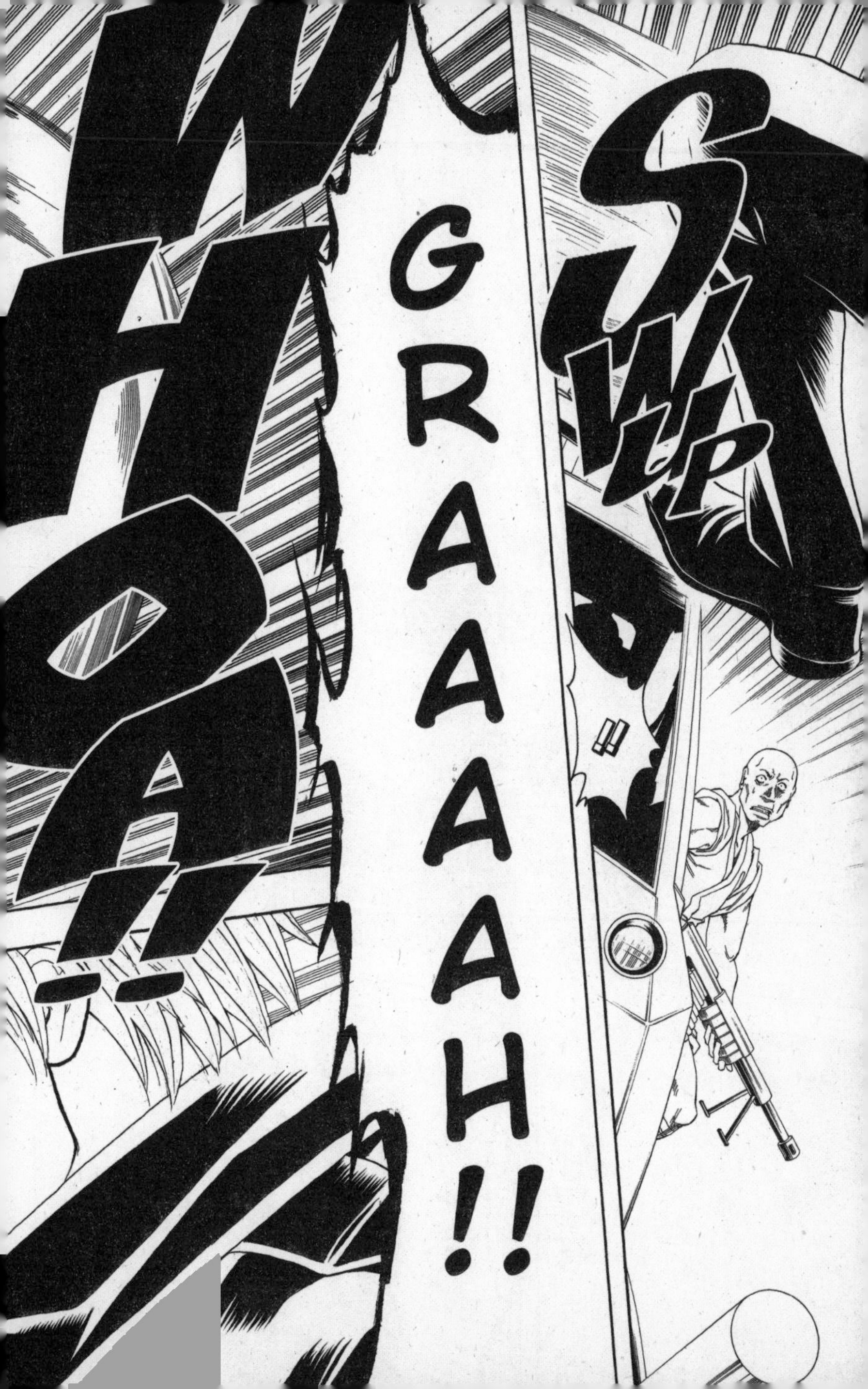
SWIP
!!
GRAAAAH!!
WHOA!!

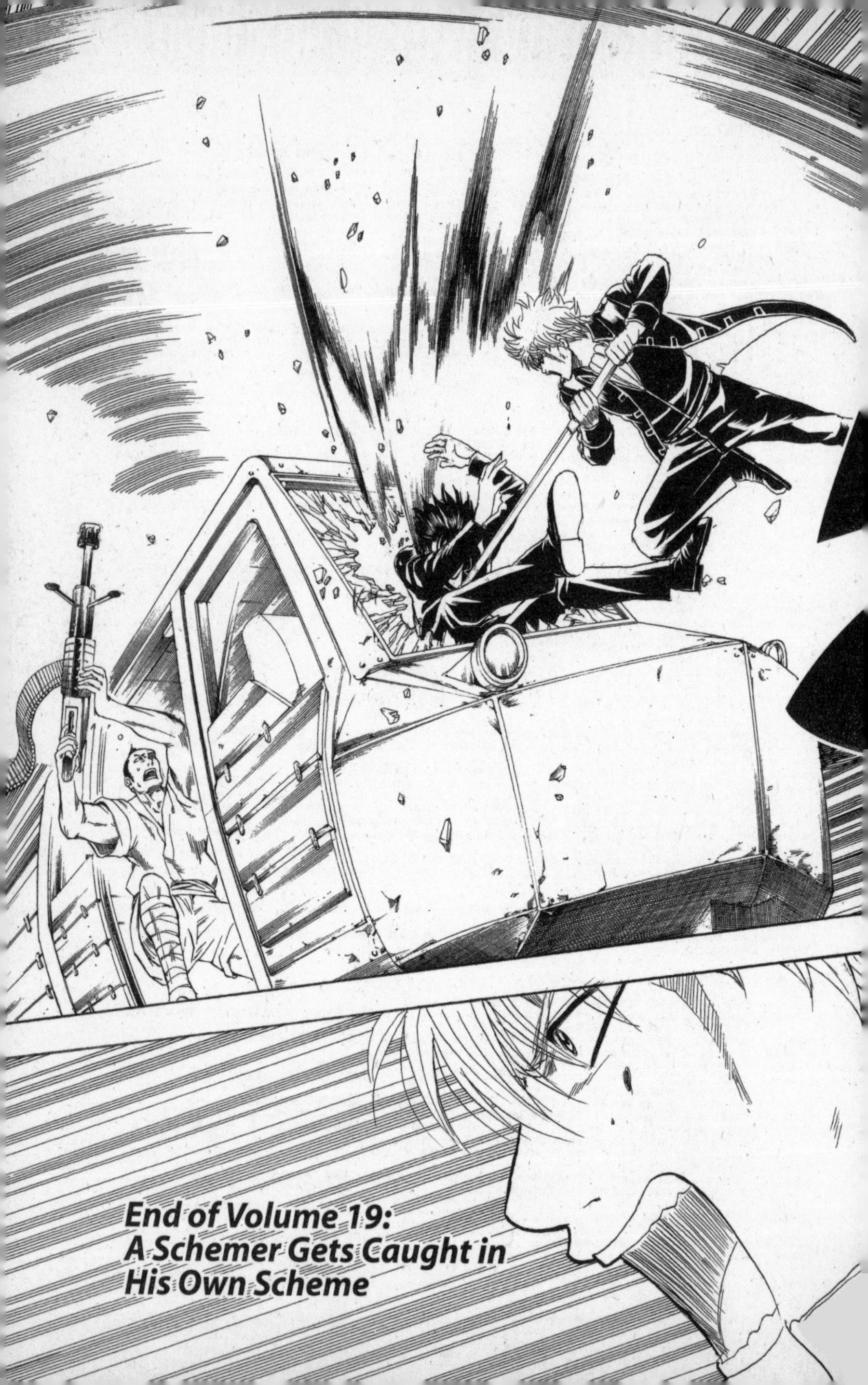
End of Volume 19:
A Schemer Gets Caught in His Own Scheme

SORACHI: I FELT LIKE I WAS ABOUT TO CRY.
ONISHI: I GUESS COMIC AUTHORS JUST CAN'T GRASP THE REALITY OF IT SOMETIMES. EDITORS CAN BECAUSE WE HAVE TO TALK TO A WHOLE BUNCH OF PEOPLE. COMIC AUTHORS DO NOTHING BUT SHUT THEMSELVES IN THEIR HOUSE AND DRAW.
SORACHI: I DIDN'T KNOW WHETHER MY COMIC WAS POPULAR OR NOT.
ONISHI: YOU SHOULD BE ABLE TO GET A ROUGH IDEA FROM THE NUMBER OF COPIES THAT WERE SOLD.
SORACHI: THOSE ARE JUST LIFELESS NUMBERS. I CAN'T TELL UNTIL I SEE IT WITH MY OWN EYES. BUT AT THE JUMP FESTA ANIME TOUR '05, I SAW THE CROWD'S REACTION AND REALIZED THAT PEOPLE ACTUALLY KNEW ABOUT GIN TAMA. I WAS SO HAPPY.
ONISHI: IS THAT HOW IT IS?
SORACHI: I SHOULDN'T CALL THESE PEOPLE LOW ACHIEVERS, BUT GIN TAMA IS REALLY ACCESSIBLE TO PEOPLE LIKE THAT. "WE'RE STRUGGLING, BUT WE STILL TRY OUR BEST TO LIVE OUR LIVES." I DON'T THINK I'M DRAWING FAILURES, BUT THAT PROBABLY MEANS I'M A FAILURE TOO.
ONISHI: BUT THAT'S WHAT MAKES IT GOOD. YOU'RE GIVING THE MESSAGE OF "NO ONE IS REALLY A FAILURE IN THE REAL SENSE OF THE WORD."
SORACHI: IT'S NOTHING FANCY LIKE THAT.
ONISHI: IT MIGHT NOT BE YOUR INTENTION, BUT IT ENDS UP THAT WAY. IN YOUNG BOYS' COMICS, IT'S TYPICAL TO HAVE THE SITUATION OF A SUPERHERO COMING OUT OF NOWHERE AND THEN DESTROYING THE ENEMIES WITH HIS SPECIAL POWERS. IN YOUR COMIC, THERE ARE LOTS OF CHARACTERS THAT VOMIT AND PICK THEIR NOSE...
SORACHI: BUT DOESN'T EVERYONE DO THAT?
ONISHI: DO WHAT?
SORACHI: BREAK DOWN THEIR CHARACTERS.
ONISHI: NOT TO THE DEGREE THAT YOU DO IT.
SORACHI: SO I GO OVERBOARD?
ONISHI: YES, YOU DO. IF LUFFY BECAME A PEEPING TOM, WOULDN'T THAT WEIRD YOU OUT?
SORACHI: BUT LUFFY DID GO PEEPING. IT WAS IN THE LAST PART OF THE ALABASTA ARC.
ONISHI: HE DID? WELL, WHEN GIN-SAN DOES, IT MAKES HIM LOOK LIKE A TRUE PERVERT. BECAUSE IT FEELS REAL AND CLOSE TO HOME.
SORACHI: (LAUGH)
ONISHI: SO HE DOESN'T SEEM LIKE A HAPPY PERV. IT'S MORE LIKE...
SORACHI: IT'S CREEPY? ONE WRONG STEP AND HE WOULD HAVE LOST ALL OF HIS FANS. THAT TYPE OF THING. WELL, THERE IS PLENTY OF WRONG STUFF IN THE COMIC ANYWAY.
ONISHI: DO YOU EVEN READ YOUR FAN LETTERS?
SORACHI: I DO! THAT'S ALL I HAVE LEFT FOR ENJOYMENT!
ONISHI: OKAY.
SORACHI: WHAT ARE YOU TALKING ABOUT? I PUT SO MUCH EFFORT INTO DRAWING IT SO I CAN GET A REACTION FROM PEOPLE! IF I DON'T GET A REACTION FROM MY FANS, IT WOULD REALLY BE DEPRESSING. I REALLY NEED THOSE FAN LETTERS.
ONISHI: DID YOU SEE ANY WEIRD LETTERS?
SORACHI: I GOT ONE THAT CAME FROM A PRISON. HE WROTE IT INSIDE HIS CELL AND IT WENT SOMETHING LIKE, "GIN TAMA REALLY SAVED ME." I FEEL HAPPY THAT I CAN HELP SOMEONE LIKE THAT.
ONISHI: YOU GET A LOT FROM OVERSEAS, TOO, RIGHT?
SORACHI: YEAH.
ONISHI: DO PEOPLE FROM OVERSEAS EVEN UNDERSTAND THE JOKES IN GIN TAMA?

"I PUT SO MUCH EFFORT INTO DRAWING IT SO I CAN GET A REACTION!" –SORACHI

SORACHI: I'M JUST SATISFIED TO KNOW THAT GIN TAMA IS PUBLISHED IN THE NORTH AMERICAN VERSION OF SHONEN JUMP. THEY HAVE SO MUCH POPULAR STUFF IN IT. RUROUNI KENSHIN IS WAY UP THERE ON THE POPULARITY CHARTS.
ONISHI: LOOKS LIKE SAMURAI AND NINJA ARE REALLY POPULAR OVER THERE.
SORACHI: BUT THE AMERICANS STILL HAVE A LOT OF MISUNDERSTANDINGS. I REMEMBER IN THE HOLLYWOOD VERSION OF GODZILLA, THERE WAS THE OPENING SCENE WHERE GODZILLA COMES OUT OF THE OCEAN. THE FISHERMAN IN THAT SCENE WAS EATING SUSHI WHILE WATCHING SUMO ON TV IN HIS SHIP. THE MOVIES STILL DEPICT A LOT OF STRANGE MISUNDERSTANDINGS ABOUT JAPAN.
ONISHI: WELL, JAPANESE PEOPLE WATCH SUMO, AND WE EAT SUSHI. JUST LOOKING AT THE INFORMATION THAT'S OUT THERE, IT'S NOT WRONG...
SORACHI: BUT WATCHING SUMO ON A FISHING BOAT WHILE EATING SUSHI?! (LAUGH) COME ON.
ONISHI: BUT THE OPPOSITE IS ALSO TRUE. THERE ARE PLENTY OF STUFF THAT JAPANESE PEOPLE MISUNDERSTAND ABOUT AMERICANS.
SORACHI: WELL, YEAH...
ONISHI: WE HAVE THE IMAGE THAT THEY ALL WATCH BASEBALL WHILE EATING POPCORN. OUTSIDE OF THAT, THEY EAT NOTHING BUT HAMBURGERS.
SORACHI: SO THE AMERICANS WILL SAY, "WE WOULDN'T BE EATING HAMBURGERS IN THAT SITUATION" TYPE OF THING?
ONISHI: PROBABLY.

[TO ALL THE FANS...]

ONISHI: GIVE ME CLOSING COMMENTS FOR YOUR FANS.
SORACHI: CAN YOU PLEASE NOT ASK ME SUCH A SERIOUS QUESTION ALL OF A SUDDEN? (LAUGH) AND CAN YOU PLEASE BE A LITTLE MORE SPECIFIC?
ONISHI: JUST SAY SOMETHING ABOUT "WATCH OUT OR LOOK FORWARD TO THIS PART" KIND OF THING.
SORACHI: WHAT DID WE ALREADY PLAN OUT? THERE WAS A NINJA ARC AND...
ONISHI: WHAT WAS THE NINJA ARC?
SORACHI: IT WAS THE PART WHERE SACCHAN AND ZENZO GET REALLY INVOLVED. OH, AND THERE'S THE KABUKI-CHO WAR ARC.
ONISHI: THAT WAS THE ONE WHERE ALL OF THE FOUR LORDS OF KABUKI-CHO COME IN, RIGHT?
SORACHI: THERE'S ALSO THE STORY WHERE WE DELVE DEEPER INTO WHO OTOSE IS. PLUS, THERE'S ALSO THE MUTSU SAKAMOTO ARC. THAT AND THE ARC WITH KAGURA'S BROTHER. BUT IT'S KIND OF DEPRESSING HOW NOBODY EVER REALLY LOOKS FORWARD TO THE SERIOUS STORY ARCS. THEY WANT ME TO KEEP DOING COMEDY, SO IT'S REALLY HARD TO WORK WITH SOMETIMES.
ONISHI: I THINK IT'S FINE.
SORACHI: HOW DO I MAKE SERIOUS STORIES MORE INTERESTING? IS IT BECAUSE OF MY DRAWINGS? BECAUSE THEY DON'T LOOK SERIOUS? THEN MY DRAWINGS ARE...
ONISHI: IT'S NOT THAT.
SORACHI: SO MOST OF THIS INTERVIEW ISN'T GOING TO BE PRINTED, RIGHT?
ONISHI: YOU THINK?
SORACHI: IS IT GOING TO BE OKAY? (LAUGH)
ONISHI: PROBABLY...

[THE END]

Well, that's it for the *Monster Hunter* Special. Sorry about the lack of bonus pages. It's not that I've been spending too much time hunting. I've been busy drawing illustrations for the new Ginpachi novel, doing some work for magazines and hunting Yian Kut Ku. Of course, I separate my work from my hunting. I'm a professional.

I'll get the bonus pages back to normal in the next volume, so whoever wants to go Yian Kut Ku hunting with me, please send me a postcard. I'll be waiting for you at the bar!

Send your letters and fan art to:
VIZ Media
Attn: Jann Jones, Editor
P.O. Box 77010
San Francisco, CA 94107

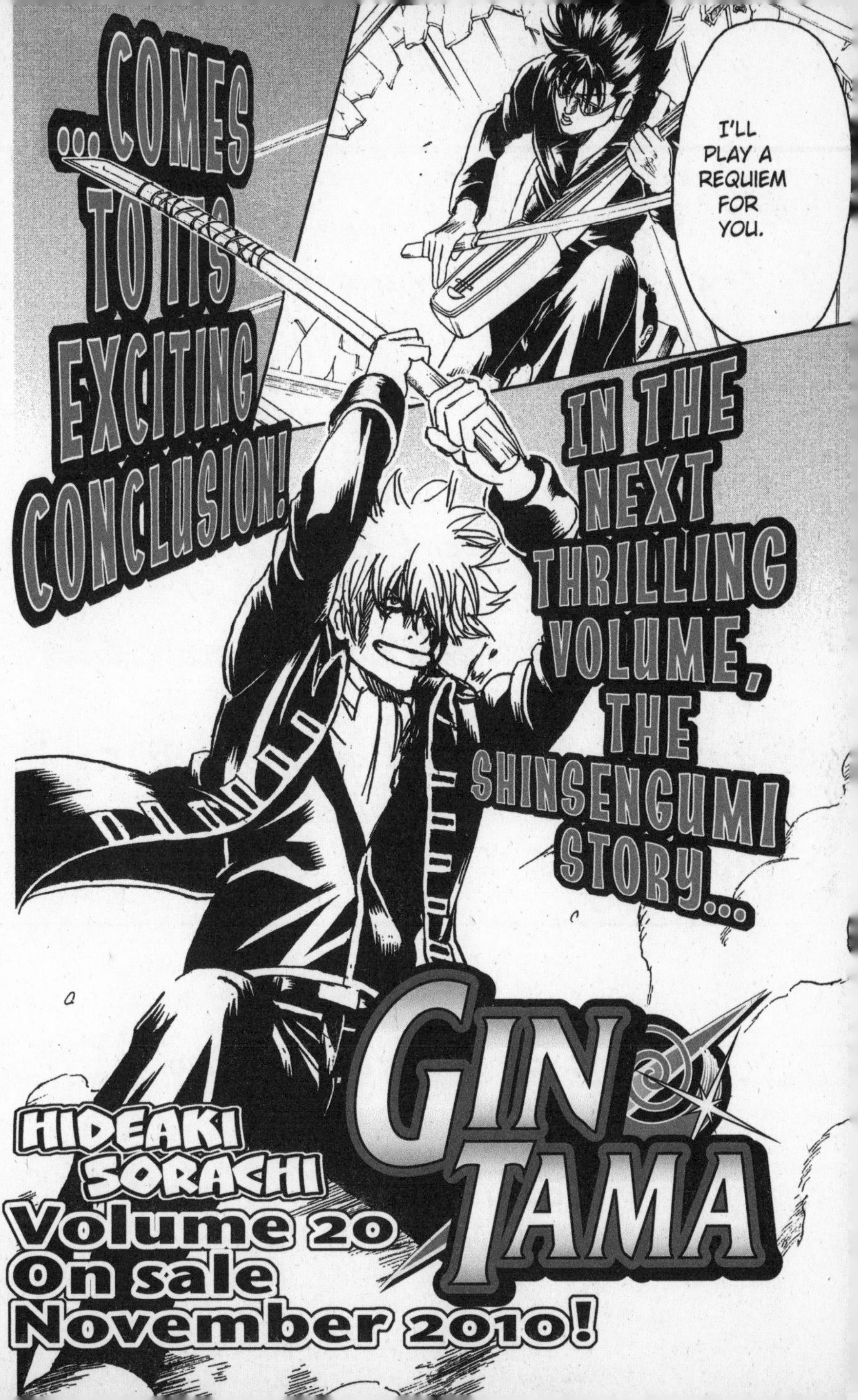
I'LL PLAY A REQUIEM FOR YOU.
IN THE NEXT THRILLING VOLUME, THE SHINSENGUMI STORY...
...COMES TO ITS EXCITING CONCLUSION!
GIN TAMA
HIDEAKI SORACHI
Volume 20
On sale
November 2010!